Interpersonal Social Work Skills for Community Practice

Donna Hardina, MSW, PhD, teaches about community practice and formal organizations in the Department of Social Work Education at California State University, Fresno. She is the author of *An Empowering Approach to Managing Social Service Organizations and Analytical Skills for Community Organization Practice*. Dr. Hardina has been an organizer and activist for over 30 years. Her career as an organizer started in the 1980s in the Chicago neighborhood of Hyde Park where, as a social work student, she served as the interim director of a neighborhood organization and later volunteered as a coordinator in a number of political campaigns for progressive candidates. In addition to teaching and writing, Dr. Hardina has continued her involvement as an advocate on behalf of a number of issues including making higher education affordable for low-income students, immigrant rights, economic justice, and civil liberties.

Interpersonal Social Work Skills for Community Practice

Donna Hardina, MSW, PhD

SPRINGER PUBLISHING COMPANY
NEW YORK

Springer Publishing Company, LLC
11 West 42nd Street
New York, NY 10036
www.springerpub.com

Acquisitions Editor: Sheri W. Sussman
Production Editor: Joseph Stubenrauch
Composition: Techset

ISBN: 978-0-8261-0811-1
E-book ISBN: 978-0-8261-0812-8

13 14 15/ 5 4 3 2

The author and the publisher of this Work have made every effort to use sources believed to be reliable to provide information that is accurate and compatible with the standards generally accepted at the time of publication. The author and publisher shall not be liable for any special, consequential, or exemplary damages resulting, in whole or in part, from the readers' use of, or reliance on, the information contained in this book. The publisher has no responsibility for the persistence or accuracy of URLs for external or third-party Internet Web sites referred to in this publication and does not guarantee that any content on such websites is, or will remain, accurate or appropriate.

Library of Congress Cataloging-in-Publication Data
Hardina, Donna.
  Interpersonal social work skills for community practice/Donna Hardina.
    p. cm.
  Includes bibliographical references and index.
  ISBN 978-0-8261-0811-1 — ISBN 978-0-8261-0812-8
1. Social skills. 2. Interpersonal relations. 3. Community-based social services. I. Title.
  HM691.H37 2012
    302'.14–dc23   2012016349

Special discounts on bulk quantities of our books are available to corporations, professional associations, pharmaceutical companies, health care organizations, and other qualifying groups.

If you are interested in a custom book, including chapters from more than one of our titles, we can provide that service as well.

For details, please contact:
Special Sales Department, Springer Publishing Company, LLC
11 West 42nd Street, 15th Floor, New York, NY 10036-8002s
Phone: 877-687-7476 or 212-431-4370; Fax: 212-941-7842
Email: sales@springerpub.com

Printed in the United States of America by Gasch Printing.

This book is dedicated to the Dream Act students who risked deportation, imprisonment, and sometimes their health and personal safety to lobby for legislation that allows them to pursue higher education, careers, and U.S. citizenship. You are my heroes! I am particularly honored to know several of the students who fought not only for their own freedom, but influenced public opinion, legislation, and at least one gubernatorial race in the course of their efforts to make the world a better place for themselves and their families.

Contents

Preface

Interpersonal skills and the ability to engage with others, are essential in both community practice and social work practice. Community organization has been considered a major component of social work practice dating back to the settlement house movement in the late 19th century. Rubin and Rubin (2008) define organizing as "working with people to help them recognize that they face shared problems and to discover that by joining together they can fight to overcome these problems" (p. 5). Such activity should logically fit with social work's focus on human relationships and the resolution of social problems. However, only a small number of social workers engage in community practice (Mendes, 2008). Many community organizers are not social workers. Some organizers have professional degrees in fields such as community studies or development, public administration, political science, public health, and urban planning (Ezell, Chernesky, & Healy, 2004, Mizrahi, n.d.). In addition, many organizers do not have professional degrees at all, but have sought organizing careers because they are committed to social justice or because they want to improve conditions in their own communities (Delgado, 1997; Szakos, 2005).

COMMUNITY PRACTICE SKILLS

As someone who spends a great deal of time interviewing, observing, and sometimes chatting with community organizers, I'm asked about educational programs at the graduate level that will help new organizers learn more about the professional skills they need for organizing careers. Many of the organizers that I've spoken to feel that once they are hired to work for community, environmental, and advocacy groups or for political campaigns, they must learn important skills "on the job." They are especially concerned about developing skills needed for working with individuals and groups. Consequently, I'm often asked if social work programs are an appropriate venue for learning how to organize. Often my response is "I don't know." Most social work programs, including the department in which I work, teach students a range of interpersonal skills in generalist social work practice classes in both undergraduate and graduate programs. However, community organization is often de-emphasized and there is little understanding of how skills such as engagement, relationship-building, and interviewing are applied in community practice (Mendes, 2008).

SOCIAL WORK AS MULTISYSTEMS PRACTICE

Knowledge and application of these community practice skills are essential for social work practice across a variety of systems levels. Multisystems and generalist practice often require that social workers engage in practice with individuals, families, and groups and use organizing methods in conjunction with other types of interventions. For example, school social work and innovative child welfare approaches such as family group conferencing and team decision making require that interpersonal "micro" practice skills be applied within a macro context. These skills are needed for recruitment and engagement with parents, facilitation of decision-making processes that include both consumers and professional staff, and collaboration with community leaders and organizations (Annie E. Casey Foundation, 2002: Harvard Family Research Project, 2003; Connolly, 2006; Pennell, n.d.).

In my graduate social work classes on macro practice, I often struggle with the notion that I will need to teach skills such as engagement and relationship-building in a macro context. Often my students have difficulty applying such skills outside an agency setting. For example, one group of students that decided to do an educational campaign on bullying in elementary schools, struggled to obtain permission to set up a literature table on the university campus, hand out flyers to disinterested students, and explain the purpose of their campaign to people passing by. Without these types of basic macro skills, a typical generalist practitioner may lack the ability to effectively intervene across systems.

THE PURPOSE OF THE BOOK

The purpose of this book is to examine how social work skills can be used to organize communities and achieve social change. Curriculum in social work programs is based on the assumption that there is one overall set of skills that can be applied by practitioners for work with individuals, groups, families, organizations, and communities. The Council of Social Work Education (CSWE) (2008) defines core practice competencies for practice across each of these systems as engagement, assessment, intervention, and evaluation. While CSWE guidelines are broad enough so that they can be applied in micro and macro settings, macro curriculum in schools of social work tends to focus on tasks such as conducting community or organization assessments, program planning, and evaluation (Johnson, 2000; Salcido, Ornelas, & Lee, 2002). Although field practicum is one place in which students should be able to acquire knowledge and competency in using interpersonal skills, field instructors often have limited expertise in providing supervision to social work students in community organizing methods (Gamble, Shaffer, & Weil, 1994; Mendes, 2008).

One of the reasons that the absence of instruction in these critical micro practice skills for macro practice is problematic, is that community organizers seldom conduct community assessments, carry out interventions, or evaluate the impact of their activities by themselves. They must recruit volunteers to engage in social action or community development. Organizers must have good interpersonal skills in order to build relationships with volunteers, community leaders, and local decision-makers, and facilitate group activities (Bayne-Smith, Mizrahi, & Garcia, 2008; Staples, 2004).

These volunteers are usually encouraged to actively engage in planning and conducting assessments, actions needed to affect social change, and evaluations of those actions. For example, these participants may assist in conducting assessments of community needs and strengths by identifying community resources and mapping where community assets (such as schools, parks, businesses, and leaders) are located or pointing out trouble spots in the neighborhood (Kretzmann & McKnight, 1993; Santos, Ferguson, & Trippel, 2010).

BOOK CONTENT: THEORETICAL, PHILOSOPHICAL, AND CURRICULUM ORIGINS

As I began work on this book, one of the early reviews by a macro practitioner of the first few chapters questioned whether micro practice content on such topics as interviewing and motivating people could or should be used in a macro practice text. Also questioned was where I found some of the community practice material for inclusion in the book. The answer to this question is that while a small portion of the content draws from traditional social work sources on generalist practice and some material is drawn from a few standard social work textbooks on community practice, much of the content comes from available literature on social movements and activism. There is a great deal of empirical literature in social psychology and the field of health promotion about how and why people participate in social change. Much of this research is consistent with the practice wisdom and skills possessed by working community practitioners including social action organizers, community developers, social planners, and those individuals using popular education approaches for organizing work. While many organizers learn their trade "on the job," training institutes such as the Midwest Academy, the Center for Community Change, and the Center for Third World Organizing also offer workshops and courses to help organizers conduct "one-on-one interviews," recruit volunteers, sustain involvement in community action, and facilitate group decision making. Some of the material in the book draws from training material and organizing manuals published by these institutes. What is notable about much of this material is that the language used to describe methods for community engagement often runs parallel to language used in introductory social work texts to describe how to conduct interviews or to work with groups!

To emphasize the community practice and micro social work linkages described in the book, I use frameworks drawn from generalist social work practice as well as core practice competencies identified in the Educational Policy Standards developed by the Council of Social Work Education. In addition, I have tried to make this book accessible to all social workers, regardless of systems focus or practice experience by focusing on a broad range of community practice models. Although my own practice experience is primarily in social action and social planning, the text also includes content on transformative/popular education and community development approaches; discussions of multicultural and feminist approaches are also included. Another feature of the book that is intended to make the book of interest to most social workers is that each chapter starts with a quotation from a community organizer about how interpersonal skills are utilized in practice.

A description of chapter content can be found in Chapter 1. My goal in writing this book is to make it accessible to both students who are interested in organizing careers and those who are likely to apply some of these skills in practice for tasks such as facilitating meetings, coalition-building, facilitating public participation, engaging in political activism, and lobbying. I also hope to make a persuasive case that community practice is no different from any other form of social work practice. Interpersonal skills are essential and critical components in building relationships, motivating people to engage in personal and societal transformation, and achieving social justice.

Acknowledgments

I would like to acknowledge three community organization colleagues. Dr. Matthew Jendian (Chair of the Department of Sociology and Director of the Nonprofit Management and Leadership Program at California State University, Fresno), Catherine Garoupa-White (MSW, Former Director, Central Valley Air Quality Coalition, Doctoral Student in Geography at University of California-Davis), and Hector Cerda (MSW, Former Central Valley Organizer for the ACLU of Northern California and a participant in the 2012 Peace and Dignity Journey, a spiritual run across North and South America by members of indigenous communities) who were my partners on a project involving interviews with community organizers. Quotations from this research are featured in this book. Several quotations are also used from a study of staff members in local agencies involved in community-building activities conducted by one of my former MSW students, Adelina Carr. The data in these two studies inspired much of the content in this book and I am in awe of the hard work and dedication of these community practitioners—both my research partners and former students who conducted many of these interviews—and the people who gave us much insight into their daily practice as community workers and change agents.

In addition, some of the practice scenarios in this book were inspired by the work of community organizers and activists in the Central Valley of California who struggle every day to make the world a better place, advocating for peace, safer streets, clean air and water, civil rights, and economic justice.

1

Introduction: The Application of Interpersonal Skills in Community Practice

What happens is that in reality, if one sole individual decides
what to do, then there is no organization.
—Interview with an immigrant rights organizer,
Hardina, Jendian, Garoupa-White, & Cerda, 2011

In this chapter, community organization as a method of practice that emphasizes both task- and process-oriented activities is examined and models of practice that include different mixtures of task and process are identified. Ethical values associated with social work and community organization practice are examined. Specific interpersonal skills that are commonly used in community practice are also described. The author constructs a framework for understanding how relationship-building and engagement are essential for accomplishing common community organization tasks such as interviewing prospective constituents, recruiting volunteers, creating group consensus, and conducting participatory needs assessment, planning, and evaluation. In the last section of this chapter, the organization of the book is described.

COMMUNITY ORGANIZING MODELS: COMBINING TASKS AND PROCESS

Successful community organizing involves a combination of process- and task-related skills (Hardcastle, Powers, & Wenocur, 2004). However, unlike other areas of social work, organizers are usually more focused on task accomplishment such as passing new legislation, electing politicians, and improving communities rather than on the process for achieving these goals (Mizrahi & Rosenthal, 1998). There are a number of models or approaches used in community practice. Each of these models requires attention to task accomplishment as well as process, although in some approaches, practitioners may give more emphasis to outcomes while in others, process is more important.

Rothman (1979) has identified three primary models of community organization: social action, social planning, and community development. Community development is a process through which a variety of community residents, groups, businesses, churches, and organizations come together to reach a consensus about community problems and work cooperatively to improve the community. The primary method used to achieve results is through consensus and cooperation among group members (Korazim-Korosy et al., 2007). The emphasis of this method is often on the process of bringing people together to work cooperatively or strengthening relationships among individuals or between individuals and community institutions rather than specific outcomes (Rubin & Rubin, 2008). Experts in the field also identify several process-oriented approaches such as consensus organizing, the assets-based approach, capacity building, and community building as subtypes of the community development model (Kretzmann & McKnight, 1993; Ohmer & DeMasi, 2009; Singh, 2003). These community development-related models are often used to improve economic conditions in a community, increase the number of jobs or businesses in a geographic area or improve community infrastructure, the supply of affordable housing, or services (Rubin & Rubin, 2008). Capacity building, engagement in activities designed to increase individual and organizational capacity to participate in community change activities, is also considered one of the main components of community development practice (Cnaan & Rothman, 2008).

In contrast to the emphasis on cooperation in community development, social action involves putting pressure on individuals or groups by lobbying government officials, running for political office, or engaging in social protest (Mondros, 2005). Social action is generally regarded as the most task- or outcome-oriented of the three models identified by Rothman (1979). Activity, especially in political and legislative campaigns, is oriented toward winning. In social protest, the desired outcome is having a law, policy, practice, or program adopted or stopped (Staples, 2004). However, these activities require an extensive amount of engagement and relationship-building with other groups. Candidates must persuade individual voters to support them and ask potential donors to make campaign contributions. Lobbyists must meet with elected officials to persuade them to support or oppose a piece of legislation. Protests are most successful when numerous people and groups participate. In addition, people who participate in protest activities must be able to reach consensus about their goals and the strategies and tactics used to achieve them. Often it is necessary to form coalitions or to cooperate with people who may have different views about the issue or who prefer to use different strategies to support the cause (Hardina & Obel-Jorgensen, 2011). Larger alliances of groups, called social movements, are also formed to support collective action to advocate for the redistribution of goods, services, civil, and political rights for, or on behalf of under representative groups or people who perceive themselves to have grievances that should be addressed by government (Pyles, 2009a). For all these activities, social workers in community practice must be able to engage with others and build sustainable relationships.

The third approach identified by Rothman (1979) is social planning. Planners apply expert knowledge to resolve social problems. They identify a problem, conduct an assessment, develop a program plan or social policy, facilitate the implementation of the plan, and evaluate the outcome. Planners often are employed by government agencies or nonprofit groups. Often these planning processes are conducted in a manner that solicits participation of the people likely to be affected or who are likely to benefit from a particular program or policy. Consequently, much of their work is conducted in consultation with or on behalf of others (Netting, O'Connor, & Fauri, 2008). Facilitation of citizen participation in planning efforts is likely to be one of the primary responsibilities of the planner (Brody, Godschalk, & Burby, 2003). According to Forester (1999), it is critical that planners have good interpersonal skills to keep participants engaged during the life of a typical community project, build consensus among a variety of people and groups about the choice of the best plan, and lobby government decision-makers for support and funding. Consequently, both the creation of the plan and the process used to create the plan are important.

Other authors have conceptualized the activities identified in these approaches as representative of other models or methods. For example, Gamble and Weil (2010) identify eight different approaches that vary in terms of social work practice roles, scope, the people served, change targets, and the intended outcomes. In addition to social planning, and social/political action, these models include neighborhood organizing, advocacy for a particular issue or a population, social/economic, and sustainable development, program development, coalition building, and social movement organizing.

Additional models identified in the literature on community organizing include transformative, multicultural, and feminist organizing methods (Hardcastle et al., 2004). The transformative model is associated with the work of Paulo Freire (1970). The goal of this approach is the personal transformation of participants through education and activism. Freire's model of "popular education" was originally intended to meet the needs of marginalized, uneducated populations in Brazil; it focuses on using the education process to study social problems so that members of marginalized communities can understand and analyze the political, economic, and social origins of oppression (Pyles, 2009a). Once members of the group develop a "critical conscious" about social problems and the social institutions that sustain these problems, they take action to change oppressive systems. Adapted for use in community organizing, the method requires strong bonds and dialogue among group members; one of the primary methods used is called "praxis," a group process involves a combination of action and reflection in order to perfect social change techniques (Castelloe, Watson, & White, 2002).

Multicultural and feminist organizing incorporate many popular education techniques methods. These models are designed to address political, economic, and social oppression affecting communities of color and women. Dobbie and Richards-Schuster (2008) describe multicultural practice as going "beyond simply accepting cultural differences to explore how they are linked to struggles over material conditions to structure everyday life" (p. 329). Techniques used by organizers to bring people together include intergroup dialogue, forming coalitions of organizations that represent marginalized populations, and recruiting leaders who can work to "bridge" differences among members of different backgrounds. Once consensus has been achieved among group members, participants engage in social change activities that may include social action, community development, or planning.

Feminist organizing is oriented toward the empowerment of women. Joseph et al. (as cited in Mizrahi, 2007) describes feminist organizing as:

> Based on women's contributions, functions, roles, and experiences and is derived from their strengths while recognizing the limitations of their socially ascribed roles and the nature of their oppression. A women's perspective affects which issues are selected and worked on, how a problem is defined, what needs will be met, what tactics and strategies are used, and how success or victory is defined. (p. 40)

According to Hyde (2005), feminist community practice can be characterized by the importance of relationship ties among members, the link between personal difficulties and social action, and using emotions and passion for the cause as a mechanism for recruitment and retention of members. In a study of feminist organizers, Mizrahi (2007) found that many of the women she interviewed regarded their practice as different from male organizers in terms of their use of interpersonal skills, the emphasis placed on outcome rather than process, and the use of collective or group decision-making techniques.

Hardcastle et al. (2004) describe similarities among the three approaches (transformative, multicultural, and feminist) including an emphasis on group dialogue, the personal transformation of individuals and group members, intellectual freedom from traditional ways of thinking, and the self-expression of group members. All three models also require a combination of task- and process-related activities including the building of group solidarity among members, achieving consensus, and engaging in social action to address social problems, including protests and confrontation with people, especially those in authority, and institutions outside the group (Hardina, 2002).

Young Laing (2009) has criticized the Rothman (1979), Gamble and Weil (2010), feminist, and multicultural models as being insufficient in incorporating cultural context and practice skills such as those identified by Lum (2007): cultural self-awareness, cultural knowledge, and the ability to use culturally appropriate practice methods. Other critics have focused on the relevance or appropriateness of consensus-style or conflict-oriented organizing approaches given changes in economic or political trends or social values (Conway, 2003; Ohmer & DeMasi, 2009).

INTEGRATING ETHICS, VALUES, AND A HUMAN RIGHTS PERSPECTIVE INTO INTERPERSONAL SKILL DEVELOPMENT

Each of the models described in the previous section of this chapter contains a theory about why specific actions should produce the desired outcome and a set of value assumptions about how the social worker and/or community organizer should act (Hardina, 2002). In any form of social work practice, it is essential that values and ethical principles be integrated into practice, especially because social work takes place within the context of interactions with other individuals, families, groups, organizations, and communities. Most of these values and principles are clearly identified in the National Association of Social Workers (NASW, 2000) *Code of Ethics*.

While the NASW (2000) *Code of Ethics* describes how social workers are to conduct themselves with clients, colleagues, and supervisors in social service organizations, most community organizing work takes place outside the confines of traditional social service organizations.

Organizers work to bring groups of people and organizations together. They also try to foster community change, using both collaboration and confrontational methods. Since community practice often involves advocacy for the reallocation or redistribution of goods, services, and political power, organizers may face ethical dilemmas with regard to the strategies and tactics used to facilitate social change. For example, tactics can include putting pressure on opponents or civil disobedience (Hardina & Obel-Jorgensen, 2011). In some instances, organizers may apply principles in the Code of Ethics in a manner that is slightly different from processes used in other types of social work practice. For example, rather than having clients sign a consent form, a social worker attempting to organize people to participate in protest will engage volunteers in detailed discussions on various organizing options so that the group chooses the method with which they are the most comfortable. If in fact, people do not actually participate in the protest, this is an indication that individual members have withdrawn consent (Hardina, 2004a). In addition, there may be some principles that form a basis for community organization work that are not identified in the Code. For example, the creation of equal partnerships between organizing staff and the volunteers who participate in community organizing efforts is one of the bedrock principles followed by most organizers (Carroll & Minkler, 2000).

Values are statements of an ideal that we try to achieve, while ethics describe actions that should be taken to uphold these values (Lowenberg & Dolgoff, 1996). In this text, at least one value assumption will be featured in each chapter. In addition, ethical principles associated with these values and practice activities that can be used to put these principles into action will be identified. The values include: social justice, self-determination and empowerment, the strengths perspective, the development of a critical consciousness, mutual learning and partnership, the use of culturally competent practice methods that incorporate an understanding of cultural and social diversity, power, and oppression, and the human rights perspective.

Social Justice

Social justice pertains to the distribution of resources such as income, food, education, health care, jobs, civil liberties, voting rights, and political power. People who do not have these things are considered to be at a disadvantage vis-à-vis other individuals and groups in society (Gil, 1998). The terms *oppression* and *marginalization* are used to describe political, economic, or social arrangements that prevent some groups of people in society from gaining access to resources or the opportunity to acquire them. Oppression is often based on demographic characteristics that differentiate these groups from the dominant society or social stigma based on social or economic status or specific attributes such as homelessness or mental illness (Reisch, 2011). The term social justice is generally used to describe efforts to make the distribution of these resources fair or equal by changing laws, policies, or social institutions (Rawls, 1971). The NASW (2000) *Code of Ethics* states that:

> Social workers should engage in social and political action that seeks to ensure that all people have equal access to the resources, employment, services, and opportunities they require to meet their basic human needs and to develop fully. Social workers should be aware of the impact of the political arena on practice and should advocate for changes in policy and legislation to improve social conditions in (Section 6.04) order to meet basic human needs and promote social justice.

Self-Determination and Empowerment

NASW Code of Ethics (2000) also states that "social workers respect and promote the right of clients to self-determination and assist clients in their efforts to identify their goals (NASW, 2000, Section 1.02)." In practice with individual clients, therapeutic groups, and families, this clause refers to the right of clients, in most circumstances to contract with social workers for the services they want or need. The second part of this section carves out an exception for circumstances in which the client could harm him or herself or others.

In organization and communities, the right of self-determination is often equated with the term "empowerment." Empowerment is a concept that, when incorporated into social work practice, pertains to efforts to increase feelings of personal self-efficacy and self-esteem (Gutierrez, Parsons, & Cox, 1998; Rose, 2000). In formal organizations and community practice, empowerment is used to refer to a set of assumptions that focus on the participation of individuals and in decision-making processes in nonprofit organizations, public institutions, and the political process. A number of studies have documented that individuals who have participated in social change-related activities have a greater sense of personal self-efficacy than nonparticipants (Checkoway & Zimmerman, 1992; Itzhaky & York, 2002; Zimmerman & Rappaport, 1988). A social worker's responsibility for ensuring that the public has an opportunity to participate in the development of social policies is also included in the NASW Code of Ethics in Section 6.2.

The Strengths Perspective

The strengths perspective is a set of assumptions used by many social workers to conduct assessments of the people they serve. Rather than look at people in terms of the resources they lack or their personal problems, social workers should identify the strengths, personal skills, and resources that people have that can be used to address personal and community problems (Saleeby, 2008). This value assumption runs counter to the medical model used by some social workers to describe client problems as weaknesses (Mackelprang & Salsgiver, 2009). In the literature on social policies, low-income communities are sometimes discussed as experiencing problems such as unemployment, substance abuse, and crime because of the moral failings of residents rather than things that occur as a consequence of poverty, a lack of opportunity, and limited political power (Segal, 2007). Consequently, perceiving residents as possessing skills and resources that can be used to empower communities is critical for successful organizing (Hardcastle et al., 2004; Kretzman & McKnight, 1993; Ohmer & DeMasi, 2009).

Development of a Critical Consciousness

In his book, *Pedagogy of the Oppressed*, Paulo Freire (1970) described the concept of critical consciousness. People who are oppressed and those individuals concerned with or engaged in social action should strive to understand how political, social, and economic institutions interact to limit access to resources, voting rights, and civil liberties for members of marginalized groups (VeneKlasen, Miller, Budlender, & Clark, 2007). According to Staples (2004), community organizers should not only increase their knowledge about how society works, but also have a responsibility to transmit this knowledge to members of the community and organization leaders. These leaders should be able to "actively reflect about their personal life experience, to recognize similar experiences shared by others, to develop a political critique of systemic oppression, and to prepare to act collectively to change the conditions of their lives" (Staples, pp. 50–51).

Mutual Learning and Partnership With Constituents

Freire's (1970) model of popular education emphasizes the creation of partnerships between educators and other professionals and members of marginalized groups. One of the primary value assumptions inherent in Freire's work is that a professional's actual status should be no better or no worse than that of the members of marginalized groups with whom the professional works (Carroll & Minkler, 2000). Hierarchy is eliminated and each party is perceived to bring valued knowledge into the relationship. One of the basic assumptions of this approach is that participants should engage in a process of mutual learning from one another (Goodkind, 2006). Mutual learning takes place within the context of dialogue among all participants in the social change process including professionals and the people who will benefit from the social change effort (VeneKlasen et al., 2007). Professionals possess formal knowledge while the other participants have knowledge that they have acquired through experience. Consequently, what each partner brings to the relationship has value and can be used to facilitate social change. In community practice, these principles are applied in the creation of relationships between the practitioner and the people the organizer recruits to participate in the organizing process (Satterwhite & Teng, 2007).

The values associated with the terms mutual learning, partnership, empowerment, and self-determination are also inherent in the term generally used to refer to volunteers or participants in the community organizing process. Rather than clients, the people who participate in or who benefit from community organizing are called "constituents." VeneKlasen et al. (2007) define constituents as "a group of people or a community who have a common concern and whose interests are advanced by organizing and engaging in advocacy to solve a problem" (p. 59).

Cultural Competency: Using Methods of Practice That Incorporate an Understanding of Cultural and Social Diversity, Power, and Oppression

The NASW (2000) *Code of Ethics* identifies respect for the dignity and worth of individuals as one of the core values of the profession and identifies actions to eliminate discrimination and oppression as one of the primary activities of social workers. The National Association of Social Workers (2007) has also developed a set of standards for culturally competent practice for members of the profession. These standards require that social workers be aware of their own beliefs and values, develop appropriate skills for cross-cultural practice, and advocate for hiring standards, education, organization procedures (such as language services), and public policies that promote diversity. Most community organizers view their work as an opportunity to empower marginalized communities, promote social equality, and to advocate for improvements in living conditions. Organizing work is conducted either in partnership with community members or on behalf of people (such as children) or entities (e.g., the environment or animals) that may not be able to speak for themselves (Alinsky, 1971; Bobo, Kendall, & Max, 2010; Homan, 2011; Rothman, 1996).

It is expected that most community organizers will engage in a set of learning activities that permit them to become culturally competent. Cultural competency is critical if the organizer is to engage in dialogue with participants and other partners to identify community problems and implement solutions. Many community practitioners work cross-culturally or within groups that contain diverse groups of people who may vary in terms of age, race, ethnicity, income, gender, immigration status, sexual orientation or identity, and physical/mental abilities (Gutierrez, Lewis, Nagda, Wernick, & Shore, 2005; Mackelprang & Salsgiver, 2009). Consequently, it is imperative that organizers be aware of their own personal biases, strive to overcome stereotypical beliefs or values that may limit their ability to work cross-culturally, and engage in a process of life-long learning about people who are different from them. Specific skills used by community organizers to engage in culturally competent practice are discussed throughout this text. Chapter 2 identifies many of these skills and describes how they may be applied by organizers for "getting to know" the community and the cultural groups they serve.

However, it should be noted that mere competency in delivering services to people who are demographically different from you is not sufficient. Organizers must also understand the power dynamics that contribute to the disempowerment of community members, the historical context of oppression and stigmatization affecting cultural, ethnic, and other oppressed groups, and work in partnership with group members to address the conditions that foster marginalization (Satterwhite & Teng, 2007).

Human Rights Perspective: Toward an Integrative Framework for Ethics and Action

In addition to the NASW (2000) *Code of Ethics* and the general principles associated with popular education with which most organizers adhere, additional sources of values and ethical standards can be found in the *Code of Ethics* of the International Association of Social Workers (2012). IFSW ethical principles include standards of professional conduct for social workers and identifies two primary principles associated with social work practice: human rights and social justice. The Code mandates that social workers recognize individual strengths, foster self-determination, and ensure the empowerment and participation of service users. Social workers are also expected to fight discrimination and unjust policies. They are also reminded that social workers often have divided loyalties among service users, colleagues, and employers as well as obligations to professional organizations and the legal system that may conflict; consequently, they should engage in ethical discussions in their agencies and with coworkers to ensure that they make appropriate decisions.

The IFSW (2012) *Code of Ethics* also mandates that all social workers advocate for their governments to implement the standards in the United Nations' *Universal Declaration of Human Rights.* This mandate also includes a number of other charters of rights adopted by the UN, including the *International Covenant on Civil and Political Rights,* the *Convention on the Elimination of all Forms of Racial Discrimination,* the *Convention on the Elimination of All Forms of Discrimination against Women,* and the *Convention on the Rights of the Child.*

In these documents, basic human rights are identified. The United Nations' (1948) *Universal Declaration of Human Rights* includes provisions that mandate freedom from discrimination, the right to work, a prohibition against inhuman treatment and torture, the right to legal protection under the law, the right to an education, the right to marry, the right to an adequate standard of health and well-being, and freedom of expression. The other charters and conventions also require that the governments that have ratified these documents enforce provisions banning discrimination and mistreatment. For example, the UN (1979) *Convention on the Elimination of All Forms of Discrimination Against Women* includes provisions requiring governments to eliminate discrimination in employment, education, and health care and take action to ensure that men and women are treated equally.

According to these documents, it is the responsibility of government to preserve these rights. The mandates in the various charters are to apply to all people, including citizens, residents, and undocumented people. However, not all governments adhere to these standards and some, including the United States have refused to ratify some of these charters. For example, the U.S. government body that under the constitution must ratify all treaties, the U.S. Senate, has only approved the *Charter of Rights,* the *International Covenant on Civil and Political Rights,* the *Convention on the Elimination of Racial Discrimination,* and the *Convention Against Torture* (Wronka, 2008). Members of the Senate have opposed ratification of the other covenants and conventions for a variety of reasons, mostly ideological. For example, the *Convention on the Rights of the Child* was opposed because it was perceived to conflict with U.S. labor laws and the legal rights of parents (Wronka, 2008). It was also opposed because of a provision that prohibits the execution of children under 18 (Clifford, 2009).

In countries in which they have been ratified, the standards do provide a framework for the distribution of resources and the enforcement of human rights (Fox & Meier, 2009). Each government that has ratified the charters or conventions is required to file an annual report to the United Nations documenting process toward meeting these goals (Wronka, 2008). In addition, advocacy groups may file complaints with the United Nation against governments that fail to live up to them. For example, women's and human rights organization in Ciudad Juárez, Mexico were able to draw attention to the murders and disappearance of over 500 women from that city between 1993 and 2003 by requesting an investigation by the United Nations (Ensalaco, 2006).

According to Lundy and Van Wormer (2007), the human rights framework helps social workers understand that social problems are simply not attributable to individual struggles, but have their origins in social and political structures. It also leads us to the recognition that social work, as a profession, should not stop at simply helping individuals acquire resources to meet their needs, but also work toward changing the social, economic, and political systems that perpetuate social inequality.

INTERPERSONAL SKILLS DEVELOPMENT AND COMMUNITY PRACTICE

In addition to values and principles, organizers must have good interpersonal skills. The ability to interact with a diverse group of people is essential. According to Staples (2004):

> The bulk of an organizer's time is spent working either with individuals—in their kitchens, on their front door stoops, and over the phone—or with small groups in an endless array of meetings for recruitment, action research, community education, leadership training, executive decisions, grassroots fundraising, strategic analysis, action planning negotiating, lobbying, and evaluating organizational actions and activities. (p. 29)

After recruiting individuals and groups, organizers also use interpersonal skills to assist people from diverse groups representing a variety of interests and opinions to identify common problems or issues that affect them (Dobbie & Richards-Schuster, 2008; Ohmer & DeMasi, 2009). The development of a consensus among group members and the establishment of alliances or coalitions among members of diverse groups are critical for the success of organizing efforts (Mulroy, Nelson, & Gour, 2005).

Korazim-Korsoty et al. (2007) identify a number of skills needed by organizers to help facilitate group consensus including an understanding of personal motivation, facilitating the development of leadership skills among group members, managing conflict, and negotiation. In addition, organizers need good communication skills to bring people together such as listening, writing, and speaking in public. The application of the community organizing principles associated with the transformative model of community practice also requires that the social worker use group work skills to foster partnerships among the participants regardless of social status, encourage mutual learning, and facilitate ongoing dialogue among participants (Pyles, 2009a).

Organizers must also work with constituents and partner organizations to plan intervention or action plans. These plans consist of a primary focus or strategy and a set of individual actions or tactics that make up a typical organizing campaign (Bobo et al., 2010). In his book on the United Farm Workers, Marshall Ganz (2009) describes the use of interpersonal skills in organizing campaigns:

> Indeed, in complex, changing environments, devising strategy requires team members to synthesize skills and information beyond the ken of any one individual, like a good jazz ensemble. And good strategy, like good jazz, is an ongoing creative process of learning to achieve a desired outcome by interacting with others to adapt to constantly changing circumstances. (Ganz, 2009, p. 10)

Organizers also work with constituent groups to carry out action plans, lobby government, and participate in the decision-making process in nonprofit organizations and government agencies. Basic group work skills are needed by organizers to coordinate activities and provide support for constituent leaders who are critical for the success of organizing campaigns and planning efforts (Brody et al., 2003; Zachary, 2000).

In addition to planning and conducting campaigns, constituents are also likely to participate in conducting community needs or assessments or to join with the organizer to evaluate the outcomes produced (Hardina, 2002). One primary model for establishing partnerships between academics and organizers and the beneficiaries of social change efforts is called participatory action research (Reason & Bradbury, 2002). In this model, constituents work with a researcher or an organizer to identify a community issue or problem, conduct an assessment, develop research methodology, conduct the study, and analyze the findings (Homan, 2011). Based on the results, constituents develop a social change-oriented campaign to resolve the problem affecting the community. In order to facilitate such a project, the organizer needs a number of interpersonal skills including engagement with participants, group facilitation, conflict management, and the ability to assist the group in developing trusting relationships and reaching a consensus around research questions, goals, methodology, and the interpretation of findings (Schmuck, 2006; Stoecker, 2005).

Many of the skills identified by community organizers and planners easily fit into a classification system developed by Rothman and Zald (2008). They identify three types of interpersonal skills commonly used in community practice including the facilitation of the process of organizing, using influence, and using interpersonal skills for interacting with people. Skills for facilitating the process include informing people, staffing committees, encouraging participation in decision-making, and developing and training new leaders. Influencing skills include advocating, bargaining, mediating, influencing powerful decision-makers, and forming coalitions with members of a variety of groups. Skills for interpersonal interaction include the personal use of self (competent practice that incorporates ethics and values), interviewing people to collect information and to persuade them about issues, and facilitating groups.

Hardina and Obel-Jorgensen (2009) have also identified a set of skills for social action organizing that can be applied to most methods of organizing and incorporates engagement and relationship skills with the various phases of the organizing process. These phases are consistent with the problem-solving model that guides social work practice with individuals, groups, families, organization and communities: problem identification, assessment, intervention, and evaluation (Kirst-Ashman & Hull, 2009).

- Self-awareness and cultural competency.
- Using verbal and written communication.
- Engagement and dialogue with constituents, key informants, and decision-makers.
- Facilitating constituent self-determination and empowerment.
- In partnership with constituents, problem identification, and assessment.
- In partnership with constituents, weighting the ethical implications of tactics and strategies.
- In partnership with constituents, planning campaigns, and taking action.
- In partnership with constituents, evaluating outcomes and processes (Hardina & Obel-Jorgensen, p. 91).

These skills can be conceptualized as occurring in sequential order. An organizer must first exhibit self-awareness and cultural competency to work effectively in communities. The organizer must also have excellent verbal and written communication skills to engage effectively and participate in dialogue in order to develop relationships with and persuade constituents, the public, and decision-makers. Organizers must also be able to facilitate empowerment and self-determination among members of constituency groups; they must also be able to work with group members to develop a consensus around problem identification, assessment, weighing the ethical implications of various strategies and tactics, developing and carrying out action campaigns, and conducting evaluations of their work (see Figure 1.1).

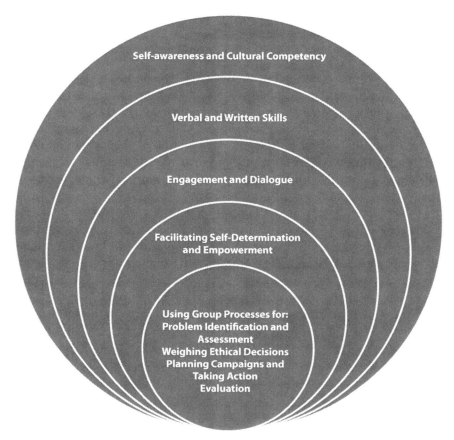

FIGURE 1.1
Progression of skills for community organization practice.

BUILDING A FRAMEWORK FOR EXAMINING THE ROLE OF INTERPERSONAL SKILLS IN COMMUNITY PRACTICE

As described earlier in this chapter, the Council on Social Work Education (2008) has identified a set of core competencies that practitioners should possess including:

* Personal awareness and professional identity.
* Engagement in ethical practice.
* The use of critical thinking.
* Life-long learning about the impact of culture and oppression.
* Advocacy for social justice and human rights.
* The ability to use research to make decisions about practice.
* The ability to apply theories and conceptual knowledge to practice.
* Engagement in policy advocacy.
* The ability to advocate for improvements in service quality and increases in consumer access to services.
* The development of practice skills for engagement, assessment, intervention, and evaluation at multiple system levels.

All these skills can be applied across all systems with which social workers typically practice. The remaining chapters of this book contain material about how to apply engagement skills and the process of dialogue in the facilitation of constituent participation in assessment intervention, and evaluation in community organizing. These skills can be used either in community organizing or as components of generalist or multisystem-oriented social work practice.

Using these components, a theoretical framework can be developed to understand how community organizing skills can be used in a manner consistent with generalist practice models that are designed for social work with individuals, families, groups, and organizations. For example, Poulin (2010) identifies components of a collaborative model of generalist practice in which the practitioner works in partnership with service users to develop a strong helping relationship that empowers the service user and is carried out in a manner that respects their needs and strengths. It consists of three phases: *pre-engagement, engagement,* and *disengagement.* In pre-engagement, the service user has not made a definite commitment to enter into a relationship with the practitioner. In the engagement phase, service users work to achieve specified goals. In the disengagement phase, gains made during the engagement phase are solidified. Tasks in this phase include evaluation and identifying next steps in the change process. Since these types of activities in community practice often involve constituents in reviewing what happened in the program and whether intended outcomes were produced, this process will be referred to as *post-engagement* in this text in order to emphasize the continuing involvement of volunteers and other participants in the change process.

Miley, O'Melia, and Dubois (2011) integrate an empowerment approach within a generalist practice model. As described by Gutierrez et al. (1998) the empowerment approach incorporates some important aspects of Freire's popular education model including the importance of mutual learning, equal partnerships between professional experts and service users, and dialogue among members of various constituency groups in social service agencies (e.g., staff, administrators, board members, and service users) and community groups. Using these principles and other aspects of the empowerment model, Miley et al. identify three essential types of skills for generalist practice that can be used across multiple systems and in different practice arenas: *dialogue, discovery,* and *development*. They describe the concept of dialogue as a process that involves developing partnerships with and understanding the experiences of service users in order to identify intervention goals. In the Miley et al. model, the term discovery pertains to the use of the helping relationship to conduct assessments and the development phase includes both intervention and evaluation.

Using these three typologies (CSWE, 2008; Miley et al., 2011; Poulin, 2010) as a framework and adding evaluation as a separate practice component, a model can be constructed to identify engagement, dialogue, and other interpersonal skills that are needed primarily for community practice. The skills inherent in this model also build upon previous work by Rothman and Zald (2008) and Hardina and Obel-Jorgensen (2009). The primary assumption of this framework is that organizing is not a skill that can be performed by one person alone. It must take place within a group context and requires interpersonal interaction or dialogue with constituents, beneficiaries, service users, agency administrators, elected officials, and other decision-makers. Therefore, to be successful, an organizer must have excellent engagement skills in order to facilitate dialogue with and among group members and sustain their involvement in conducting assessments, planning interventions, and evaluating whether and how they have achieved their goals (see Figure 1.2). This practice framework assumes that a typical practitioner must first engage with potential constituents and key informants in the community and secondly facilitate dialogue with members of the constituent group in order to conduct assessments, plan and participate in interventions, and evaluate the process and outcomes of these action plans.

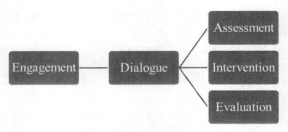

FIGURE 1.2
The relationship between engagement, dialogue, and social work practice skills
for community organizing.

The following table identifies the interpersonal skills that should be used during different phases (pre-engagement, engagement, and post-engagement) of the community organization process and also incorporates the types of activities needed during each phase. For example, during the pre-engagement phase of community organizing, dialogue-related skills focus on the recruitment of potential constituents and community leaders including the distribution of flyers, tabling, door-knocking, conducting one-on-one interviews, and using technology to reach volunteers, donors, and other supporters. During the engagement process, dialogue-related skills include using group work to facilitate problem identification, assessment, intervention planning, and the implementation of the intervention. In the post-engagement evaluation phrase, the organizer applies similar group work skills in facilitating a participatory evaluation process to assess the successes and limitations of the organizing plan. Many of the other skills discussed earlier in this chapter (e.g., interviewing, recruitment, relationship building with constituents, organizations, and decision-makers, facilitating participation in decision-making, and working with constituents to develop a consensus about strategies and tactics) can be classified based on whether assessment, intervention, or evaluation skills are used during pre-engagement, engagement, and post-engagement phases of the organizing process (see Table 1.1).

ORGANIZATION OF THIS BOOK

The next nine chapters of this text focus on one of the phases of the organizing process and the various practice components within each phase. For example, three chapters address activities typically conducted during the pre-engagement phase of the organizing process. Chapter 2 describes dialogue-related activities in the pre-engagement phase: entry into the

TABLE 1.1
Types of Interpersonal Skills Used in Organizing by Engagement Phase and Type of Activity

Phase	Purpose of Dialogue	Assessment	Activities and Skills Intervention	Evaluation
Pre-Engagement	Learn about the community and build relationships with constituents and organizations. Outreach & recruitment of volunteers, donors, supporters, constituents, and organizational partners.	Preliminary assessment of community assets and problems using the following techniques Enter and observe the community Learn about the "culture" of the community and the culture of community residents. Identify community leaders Conduct one-on-one interviews and develop relationships with community residents and leaders.	Part 1) Recruitment of constituents for participation in social change-related interventions. Part 2) Development of relationships and partnerships with organizations and groups	

(Continued)

TABLE 1.1
Types of Interpersonal Skills Used in Organizing by Engagement Phase and Type of Activity (*Continued*)

Phase	Purpose of Dialogue	Assessment	Activities and Skills	
			Intervention	Evaluation
Engagement	Form and maintain task groups. Leadership development. Dialogue with constituents to identify and prioritize community issues, conduct assessments, plan interventions, and participate in action campaigns.	Use participatory (group) methods to identify community issues and problems and to conduct: assessments, assess-mapping, and power analysis. Facilitate participant knowledge and skill building	Build and strengthen relationships with and among constituents, social networks, allies, and opponents; Facilitate participation in public and nonprofit decision-making Use group work skills to work in partnership with constituents and allied groups to: Set goals Assess ethics of plan options Choose strategies and tactics Establish evaluation criteria Implement campaigns & lobby decision-makers	Monitor and reflect on the success/failure/ process of tactics. Modify and implement tactical methods in response to what the group has learned (praxis) and situational demands. (See also Post-engagement & Assessment)
Post-engagement	Constituent participation in evaluating the organizing campaign	Group/constituent reflection on organizing successes and failures. (See also Engagement and Evaluation)	Partnership with constituents to identify evaluation questions and choose research methodology	Partnerships with constituents to conduct formal evaluations Build on successes; revise unsuccessful plans

community and "getting to know you" interviews with community members. Organizers can only be successful using these skills when they are knowledgeable about the community and culturally competent. Consequently, techniques for becoming culturally competent are discussed in this chapter. In Chapter 3, techniques for recruiting future participants in organizing efforts are identified. The recruitment methods described include the distribution of flyers, tabling, street outreach, house meetings, phone banks, using the media, and more innovative methods including text messaging and the Internet. In Chapter 4, a process for developing relationships and establishing partnerships with community groups, organizations, institutions, and key decision-makers is examined.

In the next section of the book, the process of engagement is described in detail with an emphasis on the group work skills necessary for working with multiple individuals and organizations. In Chapter 5, information is presented on forming and establishing dialogue with groups that can be used to identify community problems and issues. Chapter 6 describes group work-related methods typically used to involve volunteers and other constituents in conducting detailed community assessments. In Chapter 7, interpersonal skills used to involve constituents in the planning of organizing campaigns and facilitating public participation in planning and other types of decision-making are described. In Chapter 8, the group work skills needed to facilitate and carry out organizing campaigns are discussed.

In the third section of this book, post-engagement skills are examined. Chapter 9 describes how to use group dialogue to assess whether campaign strategies and tactics have actually worked and if they should be revised. This process of *praxis*, described earlier in this chapter involves critical reflection by constituency group members followed by taking action. Praxis-related activities can occur while campaigns are being conducted or at the conclusion of the campaign. In Chapter 10, the use of group work-related methods to involve constituents in planning and actually conducting formal evaluations of community intervention plans is described.

In the final section of the book, additional applications of interpersonal skills are examined. In Chapter 11, the importance and use of relationship and engagement skills for lobbying elected officials and other decision-makers are described. Chapter 12 provides an overview of methods used in the process of community building to develop strong bonds and solidarity among community members. Chapter 13 addresses supervisory practices that help facilitate interpersonal skill development among new organizers. Chapter 14 examines the use of the process of globalization, international social work, and interpersonal skills in organizing work outside of the United States. Chapter 15, the final chapter of the book, contains a discussion as to future directions in community organization and curriculum development for community practice.

SUMMARY

Although social work curriculum does not typically recognize the importance of interpersonal skills in community organization practice, organizers need to be able to interview community members, and recruit participants for community development initiatives, social planning, and social action. Organizers also should be able to facilitate the development of strong bonds among community members, lobby decision-makers, and work with groups of constituents to conduct assessments, plan interventions, and evaluate whether and why their actions have been successful. Excellent engagement skills are needed to establish relationships with group members and sustain involvement in campaigns and community projects. Since most community organization activities require the participation of multiple people for successful completion, engagement skills and the ability to facilitate dialogue among group members are essential if community practitioners are to carry out assessments, conduct interventions, and evaluate their work.

EXERCISES AND ASSIGNMENTS

1. Watch the movie *Invictus* (McGreary, Lorenz, Neufeld, & Eastwood, 2009) about Nelson Mandela's efforts to support South Africa's whites-only rugby team in their bid to win a world championship immediately after the dissolution of apartheid. Describe:
   (a) The interpersonal skills used by President Mandela in his interaction with supporters.
   (b) The interpersonal skills used by President Mandela in his interaction with people previously connected to the apartheid government, including government staff members.
   (c) Any similarities or differences in the way President Mandela interacted with supporters and previous opponents.
   (d) Techniques used by President Mandela to motivate members of the rugby team.
   (e) Techniques used by President Mandela to garner support for the rugby team from both white and black South Africans.
   (f) The rationale for President Mandela's efforts to rally South Africans behind the winning rugby team.

2. Observe a community outreach activity such as a health fair or informational event in which organizations set up booths or tables and distribute literature about their services or community problems. Identify:
   (a) Which of the booths seemed to be doing the most "business" in terms of the number of people coming by the booth, looking at the literature to be distributed, and chatting with organizational representatives?
   (b) What types of things draw people to the booths that are doing the most business?
   (c) Compare and contrast the behavior of the people staffing the booths that draw the most people to booths drawing the least number of people.
3. Describe how you, as a social worker engaged in community practice, would put into practice the ethical principles identified in the Code of Ethics of the International Federation of Social Workers. How do these principles compare with those in the NASW Code of Ethics? Do you think it is important to have global standards for advocacy and social justice? Explain your response.

2

Entering the Community and Using Interviewing Skills to Find Out About People

> *Creating things in a formal manner doesn't work; it is*
> *more about creating an environment that allows*
> *relationships to foster. [This happens] by*
> *going in and being real and friendly.*
> —Staff member in a community-based agency, describing the process of
> community building, Quoted in Carr, 2009, p. 43

In this chapter, the term community is defined. In addition, methods used by organizers during the pre-engagement phase of an intervention, when they first enter a new geographic community or start working with members of a group with whom they are not familiar, is discussed. One of these techniques involves observations of the community and the people who are residents of or who participate in the community. Such observations often require that practitioners gain *entry* or acceptance by community members and leaders. Techniques for gaining access and observing the community are discussed in this chapter. A second technique for getting to know the community, *one-on-one interviews* is also described. These interviews resemble casual conversations, but differ in key ways from formal interviews conducted within the context of agency-based, social work practice. Consequently, this chapter contains an overview of the skills needed for successful interviewing in community organizing and compares and contrasts these skills with techniques used in micro practice. In order to initiate relationships with potential constituents and allies, the organizer also needs to become culturally competent. In the last section of this chapter, techniques commonly used by organizers to gain knowledge about community beliefs, practices, customs, and values are examined.

DEFINING COMMUNITY

Communities can consist of neighborhoods or political districts or be composed of people with a shared culture or common characteristics, interests, or problems (Hardina, 2002). In addition, most communities consist of a group of people that are linked together through a pattern of social interactions or exchanges such as giving and receiving resources, advice, or support. The term used to describe these interpersonal trans-actions is "social networks" (Miley et al., 2011). Often organizers will use their skills to foster strong bonds among community members and to help people develop a *sense of identification with or belonging to* the com-munity (Wilson, Abram, & Anderson, 2010).

One of the requirements for defining a group of people as being part of the community is whether or not people identify themselves as commu-nity members (Longres, 2008). People may identify themselves as residents of specific neighborhoods or a group of people with common characteris-tics (e.g., age, ethnicity, income, gender, immigration status, sexual orien-tation, race, or mental and physical disabilities) or problems (e.g., parents with special needs children or homeowners at risk of foreclosure). In addition to common experiences, members of communities share common traditions, values, behaviors, language (either formal language or the use of slang), and patterns of interaction with one another (Lum, 2007). Commu-nities also can be characterized in terms of what resources are generated and distributed, the businesses, organizations, and institutions that are patronized or operated by community members, and how political, social, and economic decisions are made. Decision-making authority is often the key for identifying what people and groups have the power to determine what happens in the community (Netting, Kettner, & McMurty, 2008).

In many communities, individuals may feel isolated and discon-nected from others. It may become the organizer's task to find a way to help these individuals develop strong social bonds with one another that can be used to produce social change (Rubin & Rubin, 2008; Singh, 2003). However, the first step toward accomplishing this goal is actually finding out what people think of themselves, whether they identify themselves as part of the community, what problems they face, and what they want for themselves and their families in the future (Pyles, 2009a; Staples, 2004).

ENTRY INTO THE COMMUNITY

In his book, *Gang leader for a day,* sociologist Sudhir Venkatesh (2008), a California resident and son of Indian immigrants, describes how he was able to establish a relationship with an African-American street gang in

Chicago that allowed him to observe and even participate in some gang activities. He stumbled across members of the gang when he tried to administer a multiple choice questionnaire in a housing project that was actually vacant. Much of what Venkatesh did to gain acceptance by the gang was not standard practice among sociologists or social workers; organizers or researchers would be wise to not adopt some of his methods, for example, traveling alone and on foot to the research site, not informing anyone of his whereabouts, and bringing a six-pack of beer with him to distribute to the gang members. However, Venkatesh was able to gather valuable information for his doctoral dissertation using a number of techniques that included conveying acceptance, respect, and humility, finding common interests with members of the gang (sports and cars), sharing meals, and altering his interviewing techniques in response to suggestions from his research subjects.

An organizer seeking to gain entry into a community also needs to convey acceptance, respect, and humility. One also needs to find a way to communicate effectively, often across demographic boundaries such as race, ethnicity, age, gender, sexual orientation, or social class and differences in experiences and perspectives (Pyles, 2009a). In many ways, gaining acceptance into a new community requires skills similar to those of a qualitative researcher. Berg (2009) offers the following tips for researchers attempting to get to know a community:

- Watching, listening, and, if the community that you are studying is a geographic space, walking around. Berg also suggests smiling and greeting the people that you meet.
- Observing people, listening to conversations, and asking questions.
- Finding formal and informal groups of people in the community and identifying community leaders or people who can influence what happens in a community.

Prior to conducting an observation in the community, an organizer should find out as much as possible about the community by consulting newspaper accounts, reports, local web pages or blogs, and existing statistical information (Kirst-Ashman & Hull, 2009). The organizer should also consult with supervisors and coworkers and try to identify people who have expert knowledge or experience working in the community. Such individuals can not only provide background and historical information, but can also provide a list of key people (such as informal and formal leaders) that can give you support and refer you to additional resources as you enter the community.

One, or more, of the people that you meet in any community is likely to function as a gatekeeper, someone who is likely to control the ability of outsiders to gain access to community members or resources (Padgett, 2008). Gatekeepers give advice about what happens in the community and can help identify important decision-makers and key organizations and groups. Gatekeepers can be formal or informal. For example, you may need to ask permission to observe or interview people from administrators of a community-based organization that serves a specific population group or let public authorities know that you will be working in a specific area. Informal community leaders, often people who routinely provide assistance and support to other community members, may also serve as gatekeepers. Once the organizer has built a trusting relationship with the gatekeeper, that person should be able to link the organizer to other key individuals and groups (Staples, 2004).

There are a number of other good techniques that can be used to conduct observational research as part of your entry into the community. If you are observing a community that is based on common interests, problems, or identity, you might want to attend events, contact organizations, patronize businesses, or find other alternative methods for interacting with members of the community. For example, a flea market might be a good place to make contact with people with little income or a cultural festival may provide an opportunity to observe members of immigrant groups.

As in qualitative research, organizers should keep detailed notes about what they observe, who they meet, and what people tell them (ben Asher, 2002; Padgett, 2008). Although entry into a new community by an organizer often does not involve a formal research study, some of the things that you may want to observe are the appearance of the people in the setting, verbal and physical behavior, and how people interact with one another (Family Health International, n.d.; Neuman, 2003). The situation or context in which behaviors or actions occur is also important. In addition, you need to pay attention to the characteristics of the community such as the geographic size of specific neighborhoods, the number of people who are residents or members, the physical condition of housing and other facilities, the quality of basic city services (such as street cleaning and trash pickup), and the demographic composition of the community including factors such as racial or ethnicity diversity, age, gender, disability, and sexual orientation (Homan, 2011). Physical or socio-demographic barriers that exclude some people from participation in the community are also important to note. For example, railroad tracks or highways may separate some parts of the community;

participation in some organizations or at some events may be implicitly or explicitly restricted to some demographic groups, but not others (Hardina, 2002).

You may also want to map out some of the spatial characteristics of the community, for example, where parks, schools, or businesses are located and where people typically gather for community events (Netting et al., 2008). Some very small factors may be very significant, for example, a community without a major grocery store conveniently located may face problems obtaining healthy food, contributing to an obesity problem (Suarez-Balcazar et al., 2006). Neighborhoods without gutters and curbs may be indicative of a low-income community that has little political power with which to obtain these services from city or county governments (Saegert, Thompson, & Warren, 2005). Members of an identity community for which there may be no common meeting place (youths for example), may have few sources of social support and consequently be at risk of depression or isolation (Delgado & Staples, 2008).

An organizer also needs to think about personal safety in entering new communities, especially in terms of neighborhoods or groups that are demographically different from the organizer. Strangers may not be welcomed or they may be perceived as a threat (Clark, 2010). In such instances, organizers will find it difficult to be accepted by community residents. Until a degree of acceptance or recognition is achieved, you will need to prepare a safety plan, pairing up with another individual to walk around the community, approach people for information, or knock on doors. Also keep your supervisor aware of your schedule and plans—and make sure you carry a cell phone so that you can call or send a text for assistance.

Getting to know the community also requires interviews with members or potential participants in organizing efforts as well as relationship-building skills. In addition, it requires that the organizer become culturally competent. In the remaining sections of this chapter, these skills will be examined.

LEARNING ABOUT COMMUNITY MEMBERS: ONE-ON-ONE INTERVIEWS

In addition to entering the community, organizers use one-on-one interviews to build relationships with community members and learn more about the community. This is one of the primary interpersonal skills used in community practice. One-on-one interviews resemble conversations rather than the type of formal interviews used for survey research

(Indianapolis Neighborhood Resource Center, n.d.). These interviews have three purposes:

* They are used to obtain information about community assets, strengths, issues, and problems.
* They are used to establish relationships with people who may have information, skills, or assets that can be used for future organizing campaigns.
* They are used to recruit potential participants for organizing campaigns or organization membership (Indianapolis Neighborhood Resource Center, n.d.; PICO, n.d.; Schutz & Sandy, 2011).

Different in style and context from the typical interaction between clients and workers in social service agencies, one-on-one interviews are open ended and seldom take more than 30 min (PICO National Network, n.d.). They may be set up in advance or the organizer may find opportunities to conduct these conversations with potential constituents at community events, meetings, or when encountering people in the community. Some community organizations will provide organizers with a prepared script or format for these interviews. Alternatively, the interview may be conducted in a manner that resembles a typical conversation between two people—the content and direction of the discussion determine the questions asked by the organizer (Traynor, 2002).

Rubin and Rubin (2005) use the term "conversational partner" to describe "the uniqueness of each person with whom you talk, his or her distinct knowledge, and the different ways he or she interacts with you" (p. 14). Schutz (n.d.) describes these interviews as both "public" and "personal." The interviews are personal in that people are sharing stories about their own lives that can be very emotional, especially when people talk about personal hardships. The interviews are public in that they are being used in a strategic way to find out about community issues and connect the individual with a larger group that will advocate for social change.

Schutz (n.d.) identifies three key guidelines for conducting a one-on-one: develop a relationship with the participant, find out what motivates the participant, and ask the participant to attend an event or volunteer for an activity. In some circumstances (such as with a interviewee with severe personal problems), it may not be appropriate to make such a request, but part of the rationale for the interview is to recruit participants for community change efforts or assess whether someone can be asked to participate in the future. Another important aspect of this process is that you are trying to involve the participant in an activity that will address some type of problem or issue and make one's life better. The Center for Community Change (n.d.) emphasizes the importance of active participation in these interviews by both the interviewer and the respondent.

> It's a dance. When done well, there's a dance between two people doing relational meetings. The meeting should not be about the organizer asking probing questions and the other person responding. Along the way, the organizer should have awakened enough curiosity in the other person that they, too, are probing and sharing stories. (p. 2) (Box 2.1)

In order to gain access to a potential interviewee, the organizer must establish that one has "legitimacy," meaning someone who represents an organization or group and who can be trusted (Staples, 2004). Organizers do this by indicating the individual or individuals that might have referred the organizer to the person interviewed and identifying other people who have agreed to participate in the event or action. Organizers also should provide people with information about the organization that employs the organizer and its past activities and successes (Bobo et al., 2010). The organizer may also share personal information with the person interviewed in order to establish a bond with the interviewee. For example the organizer and the prospective recruit may have common experiences, problems, or membership in the same organization or group. Even though you are using the relationship to ask people to do something, it is important to be "genuine," honest, and truly excited or passionate about the cause or issue that you are trying to promote (Hoover, 2010).

One of the difficulties in conducting one-on-one interviews is finding interviewees. Some organizers will simply identify a particular neighborhood and knock on doors (Staples, 2004). Others will participate in community meetings or cultural and other community events and approach attendees. Gatekeepers and other community leaders and experts can provide referrals. In addition, organizers may be able to gain entry into specific community networks of people who typically know, give support, provide resources, and interact with one another. Members of such networks can generally be counted upon to refer the organizer to others with similar interests or knowledge.

In some organizing efforts, conducting one-on-one interviews is not solely the responsibility of the organizer. Volunteers may be recruited to conduct some of these interviews with their neighbors, friends, and relatives. "Block captains" might be recruited to talk to. There are a number of

BOX 2.1 SAMPLE ONE-ON-ONE INTERVIEW

Organizer: Hi, I'm Alicia Martinez, and I just started working at the West Neighborhood Organization. We're working on an air quality campaign in response to the school district's proposal to locate a new elementary school near a meat-rendering facility. I understand that people in this neighborhood have had concerns about air quality and its effects on the asthma rate for a long time. I've been talking to your neighbors about their concerns. I wonder if I can have about 10 minutes of your time?

Mrs Jackson: I don't have much time to talk, I'm baking cookies for a bake sale at my church, but yes, I have concerns about the location of the school. All of my children have asthma and I've considered moving out of this neighborhood, but we don't have the money to move.

Organizer: I'm so sorry to hear that your children are sick. My cousin has asthma too and I know how difficult things can be. How often are your children sick? Have they missed much school?

Mrs Jackson: My youngest boy, Rashid, is usually absent from school at least two days a month. I'm worried that he will need to repeat the third grade. My oldest son and my daughter have also had problems keeping up their grades because of their asthma problems. I expect that all three of my children will be transferred to the new school when it is finished. If it's located near the meat rendering plant, things will only get worse.

Organizer: We've heard that the asthma rate in this neighborhood is already very high. That's one of the reasons that we're here trying to help. We're hoping to reduce the children's exposure to polluted air by trying to put a group together to fight the school board.

Mrs Jackson: The school district doesn't seem to respond to our complaints. Mr. Brown, our neighbor, attends almost every school board meeting, trying to get them to listen to our concerns. I don't think there is much we can do. Please help yourself to a cookie.

Organizer: Sometimes complaints are more successful when many people are involved. We've talked with Mr Brown and have offered to help him make contact with the press and other people that can help him publicize the possible health effects of locating the school near the meat rendering plant. He's helping us organize a neighborhood meeting on Tuesday night. Would you be able to attend?

Mrs Jackson: Well, I can try to be there, but I'm awful busy with baking and trying to put together the fundraiser for our church.

Organizer: Your cookies are wonderful. Would you be willing to bring some to our meeting?

Mrs Jackson: I'd be happy to. Just let me know the time and the place.

advantages of using volunteers to conduct these interviews; it increases the number of interviews that can be conducted, more information is collected, and people are more likely to open up and be candid with someone they know (Homan, 2011). It also frees up some staff time and resources that can be utilized for other organizing tasks (Exley, 2008).

As in qualitative research, ethical practice in community organizing involves the concept of reciprocity—the idea that if people consent to give their time to participate in a research study, the researcher becomes obligated to give something back. According to Marshall and Rossman (2006), "reciprocity may entail giving time to help out, providing informal feedback, making coffee, being a good listener, or tutoring" (p. 81). This important principle also applies in community practice; organizers should be ready to participate in community events, provide information referrals, and emotional support, and try to address issues raised by informants as often as realistically possible. For example, providing transportation and meals to volunteers engaged in a community clean-up effort, hosting a thank-you banquet for volunteer leaders in a community change effort, or providing information about employment opportunities would be appropriate activities.

USING MICRO PRACTICE SKILLS FOR CONDUCTING ONE-ON-ONE INTERVIEWS

In addition to relationship-building, there are a number of ways in which micro practice skills can be used to conduct one-on-one interviews and community observation. For example, such techniques as engagement, using open-ended questions, exhibiting empathy, and analyzing both verbal communication patterns and body language can be used effectively in conducting interviews outside agency settings (Kirst-Ashman & Hull, 2009).

In most community organizing work, the organizer needs to establish relationships with potential constituents very quickly. As in micro practice, identifying yourself, the organization in which you are employed, and the purpose of the interview or conversation at the beginning of the meeting is critical (Cummins, Seval, & Pedrick, 2006). The organizer must also convey both interest and respect for the interviewee using verbal communication and body language. For example, the Center for Community Change (n.d.) gives new organizers the following advice for conducting a one-on-one interview.

> Relational meetings are not a cerebral exercise. You use your whole self—eye contact with the other person that doesn't

stray every time someone walks by; leaning forward or nodding the head to communicate particular interest in a story being told or point being made. (p. 1)

Poulin (2010) identifies four major activities for the social work during the pre-engagement process or phase in which the practitioner is trying to persuade the service user to commit to the relationship. These activities include:

* Studying the service user's culture and how they are affected by other systems including the economic, social, and political environment.
* Asking the service user to tell a personal story.
* Listening for emotions and feelings as well as for the meanings associated with what the service user has to say.
* Clarifying how the social worker and service user will work with one another.

All of these tasks are components of one-on-one interviews. In any macro practice encounter, it is imperative to have a good understanding of how political, social, and economic conditions may contribute to the interviewee's experiences or problems. Often, other people in the community will have experienced similar problems and interventions can be directed toward changing policies, laws, or programs that have played a role in creating the problem. For example, if multiple members of the community are experiencing depression due to long-term unemployment, interventions might be oriented toward improving economic conditions in the community. Understanding the respondent's cultural background is also important. Methods for increasing the organizer's knowledge of cultural groups are discussed in the last section of this chapter.

Although the community practitioner is not seeking information about the potential constituent's mental health or previous trauma, respondents may disclose personal hardships or distress. Therefore, it becomes important that the organizer conveys empathy and that the relationship between the organizer and the person interviewed be characterized by genuineness, and warmth. Poulin (2010) identifies several components of empathy in micro practice including conveying a nonjudgmental attitude, focused listening, reflective empathy, and validation that can also be used in macro practice. Since people in poverty or members of marginalized groups may have beliefs or engage in practices that are different from the dominant culture, it is critical that community organizers display accepting attitudes (Hardina, 2004a).

The most critical component in both micro practice and one-on-one interviews is having constituents describe situations that have meaning for them or problems that they have encountered. Essentially, such accounts are narratives or stories that are key for understanding individual or group motivation, culture, and preferences. Interviewers should use open-ended questions. Although one-on-one interviews are conversations, it is appropriate to start either with prepared scripts or checklists or simply with some ideas or assumptions that you want to test out. However, it is important that the questions be open ended. Questions that elicit "yes" or "no" answers will result in short interviews and limited contact with the interviewee. Instead, as in qualitative research, interviews should elicit as much detail as possible; longer interviews will give the interviewer more of a chance to get to know and develop a relationship with the respondent.

Nonverbal cues, such as nodding your head or making eye contact (if it is culturally appropriate), will encourage the interviewee to add detail to their remarks (Miley et al., 2011; Poulin, 2010). In addition, verbal probes requesting more information will solicit additional responses from the interviewee. Rubin and Rubin (2005) identify the following types of probes:

- *Continuation.* Encourage the respondent to keep talking about what they are saying.
- *Elaboration.* Ask for more detail.
- *Attention.* Let the respondent know you are paying attention by indicating that you understand what they are saying or conveying interest.
- *Clarification.* Ask for an explanation about what the respondent was saying.
- *Steering.* If the respondent has veered from the intended topic, remind them about the purpose of the interview and what they had said previously.

It is essential that the interviewer be actively engaged in the interview process. Focused or active listening requires that the social worker try to assess the meaning behind the service user's spoken words, nonverbal communication (such as body language), and ideas and concepts that remain unspoken (Poulin, 2010). Often the organizer must assess whether prospective constituents are really interested in the organizing effort, whether they can be persuaded to participate, whether prospective constituents are fearful of the consequences of participation, or if they are really not interested in working with the organizer. Therefore, assessment of body language and communication patterns is critical for determining whether further interaction with the participant is warranted. For example, a potential interviewee who becomes visibly angry about the presence of the organizer or the introduction of a specific topic most likely is not someone who can be recruited for participation in the organizing effort.

The organizer can determine whether one's assessment of the situation is correct by using a technique called reflective empathy or reflective responding; this involves restating the interviewee's message, including both factual and affective content (Kirst-Ashman & Hull, 2009). According to Poulin, if potential constituents feel that their feelings are understood, they have been given validation. Validation is a key component to building trust between the organizer or social worker and the potential constituent. In addition, part of the purpose of a one-on-one interview is to identifying the potential constituent's strengths. Therefore, asking respondents about their skills and interests and providing praise, interest, and support is an important part of the validation process (Miley et al., 2011).

Other micro techniques used to verify the meaning of the potential constituent's words include paraphrasing (restating what the person has said using other words), clarification (stating what you think the other party means), and summarization (restating the main points of the discussion). All of these techniques may be used in the course of a one-on-one interview, but are particularly important when interviewing someone whose primary language is different from your own or someone from a different cultural background (Kirst-Ashman & Hull, 2009).

The last phase of the pre-engagement interview process involves clarifying what you and the potential constituent will work on together (Poulin, 2010). As noted earlier in this chapter, it may be premature to ask some interviewees to participate depending on the content of the interview or your progress in developing a relationship with the interviewee. The proposed activity should be something that will benefit and empower the interviewee or the community. In addition, there should be both mutuality and reciprocity in the exchange between the worker and the prospective constituent (Miley et al., 2011). If this is not possible, you have the option of politely ending the interview. In many situations, it is appropriate to indicate that you will be back in touch or to provide contact information. In some situations, you may be able to ask the interviewee directly to participate in a follow-up meeting or a specific event or activity.

DIFFERENCES IN THE USE OF INTERVIEWING SKILLS IN COMMUNITY ORGANIZING AND MICRO PRACTICE

There are a number of differences between the type of interviews typically conducted in community organizing and the application of similar skills in micro practice. These differences include the setting in which the interviews take place, the willingness to participate or motivation of service users and/or constituents, the purpose of the interviews, the type of assessments conducted, and professional boundaries.

In micro practice, most interviews take place in agencies and are scheduled in advance. Although basic interviewing skills can be applied for other purposes inside agencies such as interaction among staff members, participants are generally willing participants. This is often not the case in community organizing. Often, people with whom the organizer will interact have no previous knowledge of the organizer and no wish to be "organized." Therefore, the application of engagement skills is critical for building relationships with potential constituents. Rubin and Rubin (2005) describe the reaction of potential interviewees:

> Once contact has been made, most people like to talk about themselves, enjoy the sociability and sense of accomplishment, and are pleased that someone is interested in what they have to say. On the other hand, they may be busy, feel incompetent, or fear exposure, in which case you may need to persuade them to participate. (p. 90)

The organizer therefore needs to find a way to find common ground with and motivate potential participants. According to Clark (2010), people are also likely to participate in interviews or organizing campaigns if it allows them to act on a political point of view, if they feel likely to benefit from participation, or out of a sense of moral or civic obligation. Even if the individual is not interested in participating in the organizing effort or may be a potential opponent, they may still be a good source of information or an ally on another issue in the future (Hardina, Jendian, & Garoupa-White, 2009). Therefore, it is the relationship that is of primary importance. The instrumental nature of the contact or interview (to recruit or encourage someone to do something) is often secondary.

The process of assessment in community organizing also differs substantially from micro practice. In both agency and community settings, individuals may request assistance with a personal problem or a referral. Both clinicians and organizers generally try to determine what the individual wants, identify personal assets and strengths that can be used to address the individual's problem, and examine how existing social networks, services, institutions, or systems contribute to the problem or can be utilized to alleviate it (Miley et al., 2011). Consequently, it may be appropriate to use eco-maps, social network mapping, or asset assessment tools when working in the community. Formal mental health or deficit-based assessments are not used in community practice. In some

circumstances, however, organizers and social workers engaged in organizing as a component of generalist practice may be called upon to make
referrals or provide assistance to people in distress or who are at risk of
harm to themselves or others.

In community organizing, assessment is most often used to determine strengths, assets, or needs of the community as a whole. This generally requires some type of formal research and is often conducted using
research methods that allow for the participation of members of the
constituency group in the assessment process (Homan, 2011). In such
circumstances, formal surveys or checklists may be used to identify individual strengths and assets and community resources (see Chapter 6).

In addition to assessment, organizers also need to pay attention to
professional boundaries, although in many situations these boundaries
might be different from those that apply in the typical relationship
between client and worker in micro practice (Reamer, 2003). Cummins
et al. (2006) identify several ways in which professional relationships in
social work practice differ from friendships. Friendships are characterized by trust, shared interests, similar values, similar levels of disclosure,
and reciprocity. Participants determine how much power is held by each
individual. Fees are not charged for participation. On the other hand, in
professional relationships between clients and workers, participants have
different interests, the values of the worker are determined by the NASW
Code of Ethics, clients are expected to disclose information, and the
relationship is not reciprocal. The worker has a position of authority
and often holds some degree of power over the client.

Using this set of criteria, the relationship between organizer and
constituent falls somewhere between a professional relationship and a
friendship. The purpose of one-on-one interviews and other recruitment
techniques are to develop relationships with individuals that are characterized by trust, reciprocity, and shared values and interests. Organizers
are not paid a fee directly by constituents, unless the organizer is an
employee of an organizations run by members of the constituency
group. The organizer also does not hold authority over the constituent.

Professional boundaries in community practice may be difficult to
set and may vary based on the specific organizing task, the role of the
constituent, and the work-related responsibilities of the organizer or
social worker. For example, giving a constituent a ride to an event or
attending a birthday party in the home of a constituent would be entirely
appropriate in community practice, but engaging in these same activities with a client for whom you are providing therapy would not.
Personal relationships between constituents and organizers may evolve
into friendships over time, but may be problematic in situations in

which the organizer is asking the constituent to participate in protests or other activities that may result in loss of employment, social stigma, or physical harm. Seek supervision or consult with peers about appropriate boundary settings in community practice (Hardina, 2004a).

VALUES IN ACTION: BECOMING CULTURALLY COMPETENT

Cultural competency in community practice entails many of the techniques for entry into the community, interviewing, and recruitment already described in this chapter. In learning the "story" of the community and about community residents, the organizer should observe, listen, and build relationships with people from all segments of the community, with special attention to the cultural norms, customs, and practices of people who are not members of the dominant culture and who may be marginalized by the larger society due to factors such as ageism, ableism, racism, classism, anti-immigrant biases, sexism, classism, and heterosexism. Skills that enhance cultural competency include self-awareness of one's own values and biases, developing knowledge about the cultural or marginalized group values, beliefs, and traditions, an understanding of historical forces and the group's status in society and how this affects their acquisition of resources, creating cross-cultural opportunities to bring diverse groups together to take action, and techniques that ensure that members of constituency groups play a primary role in community organizing efforts.

Self-Awareness

Self-awareness is an important part of cultural competency. Organizers must be aware of their own cultural identification, how this identification affects their relationships with individuals and members of other cultural and demographic groups, their knowledge about other cultural or marginalized groups, and any biases they might have about others (Miley et al., 2011). They also need to assess their own experiences and skills for working cross-culturally. Organizers should also be aware of their own status in society, for example, whether they have experienced discrimination or are relatively privileged vis-à-vis other groups in society (Pewewardy, 2004).

One component of cultural competency is the commitment on the part of social work professionals, including organizers, to advocate for the equal distribution of resources in society and against policies and practices that discriminate or disadvantage members of marginalized groups (NASW, 2007). Therefore, organizers should be aware of their own beliefs about what constitutes a just world and the degree to which they will engage in advocacy to remedy these injustices (Mondros & Wilson, 1994; Van Voorhis & Hostetter, 2006). Are all social groups deserving of equal access to jobs, education, health care, and political and civil rights?

Getting to Know the Cultural Community: Values, Beliefs, and Traditions

Many of the skills identified earlier in this chapter are those needed by culturally competent community organizers. For example, Green (1999) has identified a number of methods for "getting to know" a cultural group that are consistent with the steps described earlier in this chapter for community entry, including collecting background information about the cultural group and statistical data about the demographic composition of the community, observing members of the community, learning about leadership patterns and the way the group solves problems, and reliance on community guides. Ungar, Manual, Mealy, Thomas, and Campbell (2004) describe community guides as "a member of the group being served, whose skills and relationship in the community is valued because of his or her social position" (p. 551). The guide can be a community gatekeeper, leader, or simply someone knowledgeable about customs language, and beliefs within specific cultural groups.

Organizers also need to make an effort to learn about the community by conducting ethnographic interviews to document cultural beliefs, values, and practices (Lum, 2007). Qualitative researchers Marshall and Rossman (2006) describe ethnographic interviews, an approach originating in anthropological research as "focusing on the participant's perspective and through first-hand encounter. This approach is especially useful for eliciting participants' meanings for events and behaviors" (p. 104). Among the purposes of these interviews is that they provide a context for understanding the perspectives and opinions of individuals based on the shared experiences and values of the cultural group. They also serve as a reminder that they can be differences in language, values, beliefs, and social status among members of the same or similar cultural or ethnic groups (Lum, 2007).

According to Clark (n.d.), ethnographic interviews differ from the types of interviews typically conducted in micro practice by shifting the focus from understanding the individual to "a process of caring inquiry into the lived experiences of the other and a process of dialogically creating shared understanding of the cultural and conceptual meaning that shape that experience" (p. 9). Clark also identifies a number of principles that should be integrated into the interviewing process including the professional's role as a learner rather than an expert, a focus on the use of language and the meanings associated with it, an emphasis on understanding the context of the experience or situation described by the interviewee, and efforts to understand the interviewee's social status and self-perception of privilege or oppression.

Ethnographic interviews are open ended and make extensive use of probes and other questions used to clarify meaning of terms and concepts used by the respondent (Rubin & Rubin, 2005). Respondents might also be asked to describe situations or sequences of events and give detailed explanations of cultural practices and experiences. Interviewers may repeat key words and phrases used by the respondent to ensure that the information collected represents the interviewees own words and perceptions (Clark, n.d.).

Components of the ethnographic approach can be easily integrated into one-on-one interviews. For example, Community Tool Box (2010) provides the following guidelines for organizers interested in learning about other cultures:

- Put yourself in situations where you will meet people from other cultures.
- Examine your biases about people from other cultures.
- Ask people questions about their cultures, customs, and views.
- Listen to people tell their stories.
- Notice differences in communication styles and values; do not assume that the majority's way is the right way (Axner, 2010, p. 4).

Gaining Trust and Conveying Respect

Engagement and relationship-building are especially difficult among members of marginalized communities because members have reasons to fear public officials and social service workers. For example, Kryda and Compton (2009) conducted qualitative research with the long-term homeless to find out why they remained on the street rather than seeking shelter. Respondents indicated that they mistrusted the outreach workers who were assigned to assist them because they often stereotyped homeless people, were not empathetic, and seldom took the time to build relationships with homeless individuals in need. The homeless people interviewed indicated that they were more likely to trust outreach workers who had been previously homeless themselves because they could understand the experience of being homeless. In a similar study, Pyles and Cross (2008) examined whether civic engagement and activism among African Americans in New Orleans after Katrina was sufficient to lift members of the African-American community out of poverty. Their findings suggest that even though civic engagement increased, the success of these groups was limited because African-American participants mistrusted other community groups and institutions due to the historical context of segregation and employment discrimination in New Orleans and the slow government response to the disaster.

Organizers build trust with community members through inter-action with them and by finding out about community values and customs and conveying respect for community members. At a minimal level, one way of showing respect is for community-based organizations to incorporate culturally appropriate food and celebrations into their activities (Kahn, 1991). Organizers should also participate in customs and ceremonies if invited into the homes of community members or to cultural events. For example, if members of an Asian family remove their shoes at the door of their home, the organizer should do so as well.

If the organizer is not fluent in language, a few words of greeting in the appropriate language might help bridge cultural differences. In addition, the use of social networks and previous contacts with key people in the community can be used to establish trusting relationships with other community members (Rubin & Rubin, 2005).

Hiring Members of the Cultural Community

In order to address issues of mistrust and fear; many organizations hire organizers or recruit volunteer leaders who are from demographic or cultural groups that share a cultural identity with members of the communities or cultural groups they serve (Delgado, 1997). Some community-based organizations have developed specific models or approaches for enhancing the cultural competency of organizing cam-paigns or service delivery. For example, one technique used for con-ducting outreach and recruitment campaigns in low-income Latino communities is to use promotoras. Gonzalez, Arimendi, and Ortiz (2004) define promotoras as "natural leaders who live and work in these poor communities" (p. 26). Promotoras are usually females who volunteer or are paid to conduct door-to-door outreach, develop strong relationships with community members, and who may also be involved in organizing their neighbors to take action. Most often the focus of the promotoras' work is to engage specifically with other women in the com-munity who are often isolated, but have a critical role in preserving the health and safety of family members.

One approach for making community services culturally appropriate involves the use of cultural brokers. Montana, Rondero Hernandez, Siegel, and Jackson (2010) define cultural brokers as advocates who are able to mediate between people of different cultural groups or backgrounds to reduce conflict. Montana et al. conducted a study to examine the effectiveness of African-American brokers who served as community representatives and advocates in the team decision-making process in a child welfare agency. Team decision-making is an approach that gives a place at the table to both family members and community representatives when parental rights may be terminated (Annie E. Casey Foundation, 2002). The researchers found that the cultural broker approach increased support for the families as well as communication and trust between families and child welfare staff.

Skills for Empowering Marginalized Communities

In addition to employing organizers who are members of the same cultural or ethnic groups, organizers working with communities of color and other marginalized groups should have a specific set of skills that will allow them to obtain an understanding of the effects of social stigmatization, isolation, or the lack of economic and political power (Miley et al., 2011). According to Bankhead and Erlich (2005), organizers should seek out opportunities to obtain:

* Knowledge of customs, values, and social networks.
* Knowledge of the community's language and the use of slang.
* Historical knowledge about the community and prior organizing efforts.
* An understanding of political power and economic arrangements in the community.
* Knowledge about the groups of people who are likely to be included or excluded from decision-making in community-based organizations, social networks, and cultural groups.
* An understanding of community psychology, including the ability to assess community cohesion, the degree to which the community is hopeful that things can change, and whether there is a common problem or issue that community members can be organized to address.

This framework can be applied to any cultural, ethnic, or marginalized group. For example, applying the skills identified by Bankhead and Erlich (2005), an organizer working with the Hmong community should at minimum learn about customs and practices, learn appropriate methods to convey respect and trustworthiness to community members, take the initiative to learn about Hmong history and the development of Hmong communities outside of southeast Asia, and be knowledgeable about the role Hmong clan leaders in making decisions for community members (Moua, 2001). They should also be aware that until recently, Hmong women were largely excluded from participation in community decision-making, but that gender roles have been subject to change due to assimilation (Yoshihama & Carr, 2002). Organizers should also examine the research literature that indicates that members of the Hmong community in the United States have often been the targets of interpersonal and economic discrimination (Hein, 2000).

Cross-Cultural Organizing

Most organizers work cross-culturally or with a variety of different individuals or groups (Gutierrez et al., 2005). Some demographic groups by virtue of factors such as age, physical/mental abilities, income, gender, religion, sexual orientation, ethnicity, race, or immigration status may be relatively privileged members of society while others are disadvantaged. Therefore, it is critical that an organizer, prior to entry into a community, have some degree of insight into the relative positions of different groups in a neighborhood or how membership in a specific identity group effects community members. According to Axner (2010), these skills require active learning on the part of the organizer working cross-culturally about the community they serve, even if they make mistakes when applying cultural knowledge; organizers should also be active partners and allies with community members in social change activities.

In addition to these skills, there are a number of models of community practice that focus explicitly on cross-cultural organizing or efforts to create strong coalitions or alliances among members of diverse groups. The National Community Development Institute has developed a model for cross-cultural work that emphasizes relationship-building and engagement. They recommend that organizations recruit community leaders, coordinate leadership development programs, build strong cross-cultural relationships and social networks, and engage in participatory research to document community problems and evaluate interventions. They also focus on the importance of "telling the community's story from the residents' perspective" (Satterwhite and Teng, 2007, p. 27). Some practitioners also advocate the use of study circles and inter-group dialogue to bring diverse people together and create opportunities for mutual learning about culture, minimizing differences among groups, and engaging in social change advocacy around common issues or problems (Daley, 2007; Goodkind, 2006; Gutierrez et al., 2005).

> **BOX 2.2 APPLYING VALUES TO COMMUNITY PRACTICE:**
> **UNDERSTANDING CULTURAL AND SOCIAL DIVERSITY,**
> **POWER, AND OPPRESSION**
>
> **For Cultural Competency in Community Practice:**
>
> - Develop self-awareness about your own position in society and issues of privilege and/or marginalization vis-à-vis other individuals and groups.
> - Gain entry to the community by showing respect for diverse individuals and groups.
> - Conduct one-on-one interviews and ethnographic interviews with diverse individuals in the community.
> - Use cultural guides to get to know the community; attend events and participate in cultural activities.
> - Develop an understanding about how members of the culture or the community experience privilege or oppression.
> - Identify community leaders, gatekeepers, and networks.
> - Develop knowledge about the groups or leaders (inside the community and externally) who have the power to make decisions for the community.
> - Establish reciprocal, working relationships with community members, leaders, and organizations.
> - Involve community or cultural group members in all aspects of conducting action campaigns including problem identification, assessment, intervention planning, implementation, and evaluation.

Transparency, Partnership, and Inclusion

It should be noted that hiring staff from the cultural community served, promoting cultural understanding, and understanding the historical context of oppression in marginalized communities are important, but probably not sufficient in themselves to address social inequities. It is also critical that members of these communities have a primary role in decisions that affect their lives (Wu & Martinez, 2006). For example, Young Laing (2009) argues that community organizing in ethnic, cultural, or marginalized communities is only culturally sufficient when it is oriented toward the development of culturally specific organizing models and increasing the capacity of community members to challenge the political and economic structures that oppresses them.

The principle of inclusion makes it imperative that community organizations or agencies that hire organizers are structured in a way that promotes participation, if not control, of the decision-making process among members of the community served by the organization. According to Kahn (1991), organizations only become culturally competent when there is equity in how resources are allocated, how they are run, and how leaders are chosen. Empowering organizations also develop decision-making processes such as boards of directors and advisory boards that contain seats for community members (Hardina, Middleton, Simpson, & Montana, 2006). One of the primary assumptions of this book is that constituents in community organizations should have primary roles in running organizations, identifying community problems and assets, conducting assessments, planning organizing campaigns, taking action, and evaluating the effects of these actions (Box 2.2).

SUMMARY

In this chapter, the role of interpersonal engagement and dialogue with prospective constituents has been described. Specific techniques used by organizers to conduct preliminary assessments about what happens in the community were examined including observational studies and one-on-one interviews. The utilization of specific micro practice skills such as open-ended interviews, the use of probes, recognition and validation of strengths, and reflective empathy are critical for the development of relationships between the organizer and community members. In addition to finding out about how a community functions, the organizer also needs to find out about the cultural identification of community members and norms, traditions, and behaviors that are characteristic of and important to members of ethnic and other marginalized groups that identify themselves as members of nongeographic communities.

EXERCISES AND ASSIGNMENTS

1. Use the following scenario to answer the questions below:

   Five social work students, four males and one female, decide that they want to learn more about the homeless. During Christmas Break, they plan to spend one week living "outside" in a homeless encampment consisting of about 100 people living in tents and small huts composed of discarded lumber. Some of the homeless consist of displaced families; others seem to experience mental health and substance abuse issues.

   Questions:

   (a) Do the students have a good plan for getting to know the homeless? Why or why not?

(b) What things should they take into consideration before putting this plan into operation?

(c) What individuals or groups should they talk to before implementing their plan?

2. Review the sample one-on-one interview in this chapter. Identify the characteristics of a typical one-on-one that were evident in this interview.

   (a) What elements associated with a one-on-one interview were not included in this transcript?

   (b) What micro practice-related interviewing techniques were used in the interview?

   (c) What strengths, or assets did Mrs Jackson possess that could be used in the organizing process?

   (d) What elements of this interview made it a success?

   (e) What do you think would have happened if the respondent had not also experienced the identified problem or was not interested in becoming involved in the organizing effort?

3. Conduct a one-on-one interview with one of your classmates about an issue of concern related to the social work program or the university. [The interview does not need to include a specific request for action.] The interview should focus on the student's experience in the program or at the university. Within this context, you should be able to discuss things that the interviewer and the interviewee have in common. You should also obtain information about actions that could potentially be taken to improve or strengthen the program or university. Write a one-page paper describing the interview. Bring your written paper to class and compare your findings to those obtained by your classmates. Do students seem to share common problems? Do the findings suggest that an action is needed to address these problems?

4. Conduct a one-on-one interview using an ethnographic approach. Interview someone who is not a personal friend, relative, or business associate who is culturally different from you. Ask the respondent to describe an event or situation that has changed one's life. Be sure to probe for customs, beliefs, values, and the cultural meanings associated with their perceptions and experiences. Write a brief paper that describes what you have learned from the interview. Submit a copy of the transcript and identify those aspects of the interviewer's questions and comments that are concurrent with the characteristics of one-on-one and typical social work interviews.

3

Recruiting Potential Participants

The people then became motivated and felt that they were part of something,
and what was being demanded and remains being demanded now, was
something that would identify with their problem or situation.
We did not promise anything, we told them "Do you
want [this]? Yes? Then fight."
—Interview with an immigrant rights organizer, Hardina et al., 2011.

After a community organizer learns about and gains access to the community, one must begin to recruit participants for the community organization process. Engagement and relationship skills are essential for successful recruiting. In later stages of the organizing process, the organizer will work in partnership with participants to identify community problems and issues, conduct assessments of community problems and the strengths and resources possessed by community members, set goals, plan an organizing campaign, engage in action, and evaluate what they have accomplished. In the first section of this chapter, a general overview of the use of engagement and relationship skills for recruitment in nontraditional settings is presented. In the second section, theories related to the motivation of volunteers and community activists are identified. In the third section of the chapter, specific techniques for recruitment are addressed including, the distribution of flyers, tabling at events, phone banks, using text messaging, house meetings, street outreach, using the media, word of mouth, and using the Internet are described. One of the primary motivational techniques for involving potential constituents in action involves appeals to ethics, morality, and social justice (Mika, 2006). In the final section of this chapter, techniques for fostering individual commitments to social justice are described.

RECRUITING VOLUNTEERS AND PARTICIPANTS: APPLYING ENGAGEMENT AND RELATIONSHIP-BUILDING SKILLS IN NONTRADITIONAL SETTINGS

Recruitment of potential constituents occurs at all stages of the organizing process. However, applying the principles of self-determination and empowerment means that participants and potential beneficiaries should play a lead role in choosing the problem to be addressed and planning an intervention strategy. In order to have a group of people involved in this process, participants should be recruited during the early stages of the organizing campaign. In some instances, the community may already have identified a problem or issue to address and will invite the organizer or community organization to assist them. However, no matter who initiates the organizing process, volunteer recruitment and maintenance are ongoing challenges that need to be addressed by organizers (Staples, 2004).

In addition to one-on-one interviews, recruitment often requires that the organization plan an event or participate in an activity sponsored by another community-based organization such as a street fair, pot-luck, formal banquet, or a cultural celebration (Kahn, 1991; National Legal Council on Alcohol and Tobacco Prevention, n.d.). Events should be used to bring diverse people together and provide an opportunity for people to have fun and acquire information about the sponsoring organization and volunteer opportunities. In many instances, people can be asked to make a commitment to participate during or at the conclusion of an event. However, additional recruitment activities may be needed to encourage people to actually attend or to follow-up with anyone who may have indicated an interest in volunteering at the event (Kahn, 1991).

Brown (2006) notes the importance of using culturally appropriate methods of recruitment and relationship-building and urges the organizer to pay attention to cultural practices and interpersonal cues such as making eye contact, personal use of space vis-à-vis others, or whether it is appropriate to call someone by their first name, while interacting with individuals and groups. Sen (2003) argues that the particular outreach method used should match the target constituency group. For example, door knocking would be most appropriate when recruiting people from a particular geographic area while recruitment for prospective union members would be more likely to be effective if it took place outside the workplace.

Specific recruitment activities can include the distribution of flyers, knocking on doors, house meetings, setting up an information table at events, talking to groups, using the media, and just "hanging out" at places where people are likely to congregate (Delgado & Staples, 2008; Sen, 2003). These recruitment opportunities may provide a venue for conducting a one-on-one interview; however, as noted previously, one-on-ones may stop short of actually asking people to participate in an activity. As described in Chapter 2, the purpose of recruitment is to get people to actually do something: for example, attend a meeting, or participate in a protest. This requires specific techniques for motivating potential participants to volunteer for an activity or make a commitment to a cause (Castelloe & Prokopy, 2001).

MOTIVATING VOLUNTEERS AND CONSTITUENTS

One essential ingredient of any successful recruitment effort is finding a way to motivate potential participants. Assessment of motivation to act is therefore as important in macro practice as in micro. A basic assumption of organizing practice is that people are motivated to act out of self-interest, participating in an organizing campaign will benefit them, their families, or communities (Ohmer & DeMasi, 2009). Delgado and Staples (2008) describe self-interest in terms of several criteria identified by Saul Alinsky (1971): "the issue must be immediate enough for people to care deeply, specific enough for them to grasp, and winnable or realistic enough for them to take the time to get involved" (p. 135). One technique commonly used in community organizing to keep people motivated is to take on a small project that is easily winnable—for example, pressuring the city to clean a vacant lot. Once a victory is achieved, participants are motivated to tackle a much more difficult project (Bobo et al., 2010).

In addition, we know from the literature on more traditional types of volunteerism in civic and social service agencies that people are also motivated to participate by the opportunity to make new friends, socialize, develop new skills, and make employment-related contacts (Handy & Greenspan, 2008). Volunteering provides an opportunity for individuals to gain recognition from others, they may feel obligated to participate when asked, or they may be motivated by a sense of social responsibility or a chance to influence programs or policies (Verba, Schlozman, & Brady, 1995). Participation in community organizing or political campaigns can also be motivated by empathy with others. Appeals to morality, religious values, or a commitment to social justice also can motivate people to take action (Alinsky, 1971; Bobo et al., 2010; Haski-Leventhal & Cnaan, 2009).

Such pure or good motives are not the only reason that people want to participate in social change activities. Volunteerism can also be related to needing a sense of belonging to a group or having a personal bond with members of the group or people who intend to join it. Empirical research on why people become activists has documented the strong impact of social ties among participants in protests or broad-based social movements; people are more likely to participate if asked by someone they know well and if they have the time and resources to do so (Lim, 2010; Somma, 2009). According to Haski-Leventhal and Cnaan (2009), "carrying out pro-social volunteer tasks in the presence of one's group provides strong internal rewards and incentives for persistence" (p. 66). While relationship-building and group participation are important for many volunteers, they may be particularly salient for recruiting women who often structure work and personal lives around their friends, neighbors, and families (Ramirez-Valles, 2001; Saegert, 2006; Smock, 2004; Vaiou & Lykogianni, 2006). Women volunteers often seek out support networks in response to adversity and can often be engaged in organizing out of a desire to improve community conditions to benefit their children and people with whom they share similar circumstances.

Saegert (2006) argues that women are more likely to be motivated by group participation and building relationships with others when they consider joining a cause as an assertion that is supported by available research on social justice participation. For example, Ramirez-Valles (2001) conducted a qualitative research study that examined reasons given by female volunteers who engaged in outreach and social change activities for a family planning clinic in Mexico. Among the 15 respondents, the primary motives for participation included serving the community, helping other women, and simply getting out of the house.

People may also be motivated through identification with a particular ethnic or other marginalized group or by experiencing problems in common with others (Giguere & Lalande, 2010). The term *collective identity* refers to whether people identify themselves as members of specific communities or subgroups located outside the general population, for example as a member of the gay community, a person with a disability, or a resident of a geographic area. Collective identity also pertains to the degree to which people feel emotionally attached or committed to the community; an individual's attachment to the community often determines whether people will participate in group or collective action such as a protest or membership in a community organization (Little, 2010). One example of how a sense of collective identity affects individual commitment to a cause can be found in research conducted by Martinez (2008). She interviewed activists of Latino heritage who participated in the immigrants' rights movement that emerged in the United States in

2006. Her findings indicate that "many Latinos found themselves either directly or indirectly targeted by anti-immigrant and anti-Latino sentiments. Still others began to empathize with immigrants' plight and what they considered unnecessarily harsh attitudes, discrimination, and attacks by extremist groups" (p. 560).

A concept related to collective identity, *sense of community,* also plays a role in whether a person volunteers with a community organization. Peterson et al. (2008) define sense of community as "feelings that members have of belonging, of significance to one another and to groups, and as shared fate that members' needs will be met through their relationships" (p. 799). People who have a strong sense of community and commitment to neighbors or other groups in which they identify will be more likely to engage in community change efforts. Another factor that can determine whether people volunteer for a social change activity involves the degree to which individuals have a sense of personal self-efficacy (Little, 2010). *Efficacy* is the belief in oneself and pertains to whether individuals perceive themselves as able to perform a specific task, apply a certain skill, or influence others. Efficacy is one component of personal empowerment (Gutierrez et al., 1998). Research by Foster-Fishman, Pierce, and Van Egeren (2009) indicates that people are more likely to be involved in community change efforts when they feel that they have the ability to influence what happens in their community, have a high degree of a sense of community, are hopeful that things can change, and perceive that other members of the community will engage in the change effort.

Unlike micro practice, assessment of motivation to volunteer or engage in activism in community practice does not generally rely on standardized assessment forms or psychological indicators although researchers have sometimes utilized measures of personal control and self-efficacy when examining the effectiveness of social change activities (see, e.g., Itzhaky & York, 2002). Organizers merely assess motivation through one-on-one interviews, relationship-building with participants, experience (what works, what does not work), and feedback from constituents. Castelloe and Prokopy (2001) also offer the following guidelines for operating successful recruitment campaigns:

- Use existing helping, support, or service networks (either formal or informal) to find new members. It is often helpful to ask community leaders or gatekeepers to utilize their own networks of friends, neighbors, relatives, church, or business connections to recruit volunteers.
- Develop the organizing campaign's message so that it reflects the interests and needs of community residents and delivers the message in a

manner that is appropriate for the community. For example, in some immigrant communities it may be inappropriate to invite strangers into one's home; recruiting a community leader to contact residents or broadcasting announcements on an ethnic radio station might be more appropriate.

• Be aware that there can be both benefits and costs related to participation in an organizing campaign. For example, volunteers may need to pay for day care or transportation. The community organization that sponsors the project can seek funding to provide baby-sitting or transportation assistance or set up a system of exchanges among participants to provide these services (Parker & Betz, 1996).

ADDITIONAL TECHNIQUES FOR RECRUITMENT

There are numerous methods that can be used to recruit people for social change efforts. Recruitment involves conveying a specific message to people about why their participation is important (Pyles, 2009b). It may involve distributing information to people working with social networks and community groups, house meetings, street outreach, disseminating information using the media, word of mouth and using Internet technology, including social networking techniques such as Facebook or Twitter. While other innovative methods can also be used to recruit, one essential element of the process is that people are asked to do something or contribute to the organization or change effort (Schultz, 2003). Consequently, this engagement and relationship-building activity supplements and compliments the primary goals of a basic one-on-one interview, getting to know the community and identifying community issues.

Distributing Information: Flyers and Tabling

Some one-on-one interviews are conducted by simply knocking on doors or walking around neighborhoods. However, in addition to these methods, organizers may be called upon to use other methods to recruit. Most of these activities require some form of engagement and relationship building. They may be asked to design flyers with information about the organization, the specific issue to be addressed, a time and place in which an event will be held, and contact information (Work Group for Community Health and Development, 2010).

Posters and flyers should be put in prominent places in the community including businesses, churches, schools, and public facilities such as post offices. Distributing flyers and posters is actually an excellent "test" of engagement skills. For example, if you are asking a business or group to distribute flyers for you, you must obtain permission to leave the flyers at that location. You may need to verify who you are and your purpose before permission is granted. If you are distributing flyers at an event or on a street corner, you will want to hand the flyer to people passing by. Often individuals do not want to accept flyers from a stranger and they will quickly walk by; some people will have a legitimate fear that they will be asked to do something unpleasant or participate in a political activity that runs counter to their beliefs. Consequently, distributing a flyer requires a degree of confidence, the ability to read body language to assess if people will be willing to accept a flyer or chat for a few minutes, and the type of interpersonal skills that will permit the organizer quickly establish a relationship with people who do accept the flyer and want to know more (Kahn, 1991).

Often there will be local events that include provisions to have groups available to inform the public about what they do. Sometimes organizers will seek out these events explicitly for recruitment purposes. Most often, each group will be assigned a table or a booth that can be used to distribute information (Work Group for Community Health and Development, 2010). Organizers and members of the constituency group will "staff" the table or booth, distributing flyers and other informational materials. Most literature tables also include a sign-up sheet for potential volunteers or people who have requested more information about the organization or campaign.

The interpersonal skills "challenge" that is encountered during tabling is how to attract people to your booth. Do you just sit there? What happens if no one comes over to talk to you? There are a number of techniques used to sell your organization. Posters and banners of course help, but you also need to have things that interest people— perhaps you distribute candy or buttons and t-shirts with action campaign messages or slogans or offer people a chance to participate in a raffle. Staffing the table with local celebrities also helps (Work Group for Community Health and Development, 2010). But engagement is also the key; be prepared to answer questions, encourage people to tell their stories, and provide information and contacts. Tabling often provides an excellent opportunity to conduct one-on-one interviews.

Contacting People: Phone Calls and Texting

The same challenges apply to making contact by phone with people. Often people do not respond well to phone solicitations. Calls tend to be made during hours when people are having dinner or relaxing.

People may have had bad experiences with phone solicitors. Many for-profit organizations make obtrusive sales calls and charitable organizations and political campaigns may call repeatedly. The challenge for an organizer making a recruitment call is to establish legitimacy quickly (within a few seconds) and explain the purpose of the call.

Many organizations will develop a script for recruitment calls, but the caller is free to improvise some of the content, depending on the recipient's response (Center for Progressive Leadership, n.d.). Calls are most effective when there is actual dialogue and relationship building between both parties in the call. In addition, some calls will be made from a "phone bank," a room with a set of phones that volunteers and staff can use to make multiple calls (Organizing for America, 2008). The group nature of this process and the opportunity to socialize with other callers makes a task that some people find unpleasant, somewhat tolerable. However, increasingly, with the proliferation of cell phones, volunteers and staff may be encouraged to make these calls from their own homes.

Calls should be brief and the organizer should be ready to disengage when told that the individual does not want or is unable to talk. Unless the organizer is a real "people person," making "cold" calls to strangers is often difficult or unpleasant (Sen, 2003). Respondents may be uncommunicative, rude, or hang up on the caller. In some circumstances, volunteers may be recruited to help with these calls or asked explicitly to contact people they know with the expectation that they may have an easier time making such calls and obtaining a commitment from the prospective recruit.

Another problem associated with these calls is that organizations often fail to track who has actually received the call. If the respondent indicates that one has already received one or more calls from the organization or has already signed up to volunteer, the organizer should quickly apologize. Even with these difficulties, it is possible for an organizer to establish a relationship with a prospective volunteer and conduct a one-on-one interview on the phone. In some situations, the person contacted may simply look at the call as an opportunity to chat, share information, or have someone listen to their opinions and problems (Center for Progressive Leadership, n.d.). Often a chat, rather than reading from a script, is more likely to result in the acquisition of a volunteer.

Despite the potential for relationship building over the phone, there are some disadvantages of this recruitment method. In addition to the fact that some people will be annoyed and potentially "turned off" to the message when they receive more than one call from the same source, it also may be difficult to obtain phone numbers for potential volunteers. Some numbers may be obtained through the use of sign-up sheets at events, referrals from other volunteers, or lists from other organizations. However, privacy concerns often limit the sharing of personal information including phone numbers and email addresses among different organizations and groups. In addition, unless personal cell phones are used, operating phone banks require a create deal of time and resources. Phone lines or pre-paid cell phones are required. Skilled staff or volunteers are needed to supervise the phone bank.

Community organizations as well as political campaigns have started to send text messages to both recruit and mobilize volunteers to take action. Texting has several advantages including the fact that one text message can be sent to groups of people at a time. In addition, sending text may be a good way of reaching and motivating young people who may be more receptive to a text message than a phone call (Delgado & Staples, 2008). In addition, it is impersonal. A volunteer who may be unwilling to make a phone call to a stranger may be more than willing to send text messages to unknown persons. However, these advantages can also be disadvantages. It may take a long time to enter phone numbers into a single phone or text messaging system in order to send group messages. For sending a large number of text messages," organizations may need to hire a mobile messaging vendor to send "blasts" on a regular basis (Rock the Vote, 2008). Text messages may only gain the attention of people under 30; older people may be unfamiliar with texting or regard them as a nuisance. In addition, the impersonal nature of a text message may limit its effectiveness as a recruiting tool. Good database management systems are required to keep track of the people who have received messages or phone calls and whether these volunteers have volunteered to participate in specific activities (E-politics, 2009). The creation of these information systems is often labor intensive, requiring that volunteer contact information, including phone numbers and email addresses if available, be documented on standardized forms and that information is inputted into a computerized database system. Also, volunteers or paid staff must be able to make follow-up phone calls or send reminders about commitments to the new recruits (Rock the Vote, 2008).

In addition to phone calls and text messaging, community organizers may rely on mailed letters that either proceed or follow the phone call or text (Work Group for Community Health and Development, 2010). Letters are a common method for recruiting middle- and upper-income activists. Members of some communities (e.g., immigrants or members of socially stigmatized groups such as people living with AIDs or families receiving welfare benefits) may react negatively to "official" letters, especially if the purpose of the letter is unclear or the name of the sponsoring organization is unknown to them. Other disadvantages of mailed letters involve the cost of postage, the time and effort needed to prepare a mailing, the difficulty involved in obtaining a list of addresses, and low response rates (Rudig, 2010).

House Meetings

One of the methods for recruiting new volunteers is house meetings. House meetings are generally held in the home of a volunteer and involve a small number of people that have been identified as potential volunteers or people who may be interested in a specific issue that is affecting members of the community. The Virginia Organizing Project (n.d.) describes house meetings in the following way:

> Because house meetings are small gatherings, they provide an opportunity for people to listen to each other, ask questions, share ideas and become informed. In the process, people can discuss ways to get involved in the organization that are best suited to their personal skills and interests. A successful housing meeting will inspire guests to hold their own housing meetings and help your organization grow. (p. 2)

House meetings are often an effective way to recruit because the resident is generally the person responsible for coordinating the meeting inviting people that one knows personally to the meeting. Consequently, existing social networks or work-related contacts are used (Schultz, 2003). People can be invited to a house meeting, specifically to meet with the organizer, constituent-leader, or an expert on an issue of concern. Most of this type of recruiting operates through existing social networks. Many potential constituents are likely to be members of more than one group and can consequently serve as a linkage between groups and organizations.

House meetings are generally scheduled as part of a process in which an organizer or an interested volunteer invites people to a meeting in someone's home to learn more about an issue. They are also organized in such a manner that they provide guests with an opportunity to socialize and have fun (Delgado & Staples, 2008). House meetings often involve sharing coffee, food, or information. Participants may also be invited to watch a DVD or television program that will inform them about a particular issue (Upper Arlington Progressive Action, n.d.). In addition, they provide an opportunity to hear from a guest speaker or a political candidate and they often serve as a prelude to asking potential recruits to make a commitment to the cause that involves time, money, or resources. House meetings are essentially an opportunity to establish dialogue with a group of potential recruits, share stories and common problems, and to begin the problem-solving process (VOP, n.d.).

Street Outreach

Street outreach methods are typically used to reach people who are isolated or unattached for pre-existing social networks, or formal organizations (Hardcastle et al., 2004). Recruitment efforts may be targeted to naturally occurring groups such as pre-teens that congregate at the shopping mall or local basketball courts or people patronizing the corner grocery store, bar or beauty shop (Farrell, Johnson, Sapp, Pumphrey, & Freeman, 1995; Kahn, 1991). In many neighborhoods, businesses or open-spaces may serve as a gathering place for different demographic or cultural groups. For example, Delgado (1996) describes the importance of small grocery stores or bodegas in Puerto Rican communities in the United States in providing information, credit, and support. For recruiting members of informal or naturally occurring groups, previous contact with leaders or community guides may be the key to gaining access. If the organizer simply approaches the group, many of the interpersonal skills identified earlier in the chapter, displaying humility, finding common ground, sharing stories, having materials and other goodies to distribute (e.g., condoms are commonly distributed in efforts to reach people at risk of contracting AIDs) are key components for engagement and relationship building. As noted in Chapter 2, street outreach may be most effective when conducted by someone who is of the same identity community, speaks the same language (either formal language or slang) or who has had similar life experience as the people that the organizer is trying to reach (Kryda & Compton, 2009; National Council on Crime and Delinquency, 2009).

Outreach workers should also be able to establish strong relationships the people recruited. It is also important that street outreach methods be culturally appropriate for reaching the target population (Schultz, 2003). For example, Silvestre et al. (2006) describe outreach methods for recruiting gay men of color who have sex with men for participation in a research study. A variety of approaches were used to reach members of the community and establish trusting including the establishment of advisory boards composed of diverse members to help with the creation of the recruitment plan, creating recruitment plans specific to the geographic location of each of the study sites, locating the research clinics in places considered to be safe and confidential, and hiring culturally competent staff that included gay men of color.

It should be noted that the term "street outreach" includes three different types of activities: linking members of socially stigmatized groups with social services (National Council on Crime and Delinquency, 2009), recruiting people for participation in research studies (Clark, 2010), and identifying and recruiting potential volunteers for participation in organizing campaigns (Corrigall-Brown, Snow, Smith, & Quist, 2009). The third method, participation in an organizing effort, is the activity most often identified with community practice, primarily because of the potential for empowering constituents by involving them in community and organizational decision-making and participating in social change activities (Delgado & Staples, 2008). However, research participation and social service delivery are also potentially empowering in situations in which constituents are involved in planning or other types of decision-making for research studies or service interventions (Wang, 2006). Research studies often serve as preludes to involving people in social change activities or developing service interventions that are culturally competent and more likely to be used by the intended beneficiaries (Silvestre, Quinn, & Rinaldo, 2010). The other similarity among the three methods is that they all require that staff or volunteers have the skills necessary to create strong, trusting relationships with the people they try to recruit.

Using the Media

Media coverage of your organizing campaign also is an important tool for recruiting new members. Organizers generally work to develop a list of potential media contacts that they can use to publicize their organization (Schultz, 2003). Although it may not appear that this activity involves interpersonal skills, relationship building is critical for garnering publicity for your cause. Reporters and television and radio producers often seek out representatives of community-based organizations for comments on news items or information. They also look for good stories. Therefore, it is possible to establish exchange-oriented relationships with media sources (Hardcastle et al., 2004). It is legitimate to offer information or to even develop or frame the story from your organization's perspective. You also should be prepared to refer reporters and producers to additional contacts and information sources (Homan, 2011). Constituents who have experienced the problem or issue that your organization is addressing or who will benefit from a change in a specific law or policy should be encouraged to speak to the media.

Organizers also seek out opportunities to initiate contact with reporters when they have "breaking news" or when they are seeking pubic support for an issue (Schultz, 2003). They send out press releases to all local media outlets to inform them about and issue and list contact information for members of the organization. Community-based organizations also hold press conferences in which the media can gather to listen to the contents of a press lease or a newly issued report and ask questions of organization members (Homan, 2011). While press releases and press conferences are a good way to maximize media coverage, reporters are most likely to attend when they have an established relationship with the organizer and members of the constituency group or when they receive a follow-up call after the press release is distributed (Work Group for Community Health and Development, 2010).

Media coverage often results in television or radio interviews for the organizer and members of the constituency group. Members may also appear on talk shows to provide detailed information about issues (Hardcastle et al., 2004). While some of these invitations may be issued in response to a breaking news stories, it is also possible to use pre-existing press contacts to make it known that members of your organization are available for interviews.

There are certain hazards involved in conducting media campaigns however. Not all contacts will actually result in a story (Hardcastle et al., 2004). The story if printed may not reflect your point of view on the subject. There are alternative means of coverage, however including posting information and news stories related to your organization on Independent media sites on the web, encourage bloggers to report your organization's information, posting material on Facebook or MySpace, or creating informational videos for posting on YouTube (Goode, 2009; Sen, 2003). For many of these sources, contacting and establishing working relationships with reporters, editors, bloggers, and webmasters are also essential for obtaining coverage.

Word of Mouth

A recruitment method that is generally regarded as superior to all others is called *word of mouth,* or having information about your organization or campaign circulated by others. As discussed previously in this chapter, the purpose of contacting gatekeepers, service professionals such as doctors or teachers, organizations, and community leaders is that they can spread the word about what you are doing in the community and give you legitimacy or a "seal of approval" so that others will talk to you (Schultz, 2003). If the people you have recruited indicate that they support your organization or that the events and activities sponsored by your organization are fun, informative, or involve successful action to address a problem, other potential recruits may seek you out on their own (Rubin & Rubin, 2008). Again, as with other forms of volunteer recruitment, much of the "action" takes place within social networks: people are most likely to provide information and encourage participation among friends, relatives, and neighbors.

Using the Internet

Increasingly, Internet technology has been used for the recruitment process (Hick & McNutt, 2002). For example, it is much easier and cheaper to reach people by email than by phone. As with texting, one message can be sent to multiple people. One major disadvantage is that email messages can easily be ignored, deleted, or blocked. As with phone calls, you need to have a list of email addresses or a method for collecting email addresses from potential recruits. You also need to make follow-up phone calls, engage in some type of interpersonal interaction (often involving face-to-face contact), and make specific requests for action or volunteer activity to make sure that these new recruits are actually engaged in the organizing campaign (Citizen Works, 2004).

An attractive web page with the organization's mission and a call to action can also help with recruitment. In addition, YouTube and social networking sites/technology such as MySpace, Facebook, and Twitter have also been used successfully for recruiting volunteers for social change activities and voter registration (Dreier, 2008b). Such processes have primarily targeted people under 30 who are comfortable with the new technology and who own cell phones and use social networking sites frequently. However, with older people and those with limited access to technology, traditional methods such as face-to-face contact may prove to be superior to technological approaches (Work Group for Community Health and Development, 2010).

Stoecker (2002) has raised concerns about the efficacy of Internet-based organizing methods and argues that such methods are not as effective as traditional methods involving face-to-face contact. While conceding that the new technology is effective in providing information about organizing efforts to the global community and helping people connect with one other, Stoecker asserts that electronic media have some built-in limitations:

> But even with all this communication, what is the quality of these cyber-based relationships? Sociologists like to distinguish between "primary" relationships and "secondary" relationships also called "strong ties" and "weak ties". Strong ties or primary relationships are the "I would do anything for you kind of relationships and, for most of us, are precious few. Weak ties or secondary relationships are the "hi, how ya doin" kind of relationships. We have many more of these. How many of those chat room, e-mail, on on-line forum relationships can we really count as primary relationships? Or even secondary relationships? (pp. 147–148)

Even with the Internet and social networking applications, most researchers have found that indirect recruitment methods are not as effective as interpersonal communication (Lim, 2010). However, Brunsting and Postmes (2002) argue that although it is commonly believed that people reached through the Internet are not likely to be influenced by social cues, values, or a need for solidarity, the opposite is actually true:

> Behavior in anonymous and isolated CMC [computer-mediated communication] can even be more normative than when people are identified and proximate. Research has also shown that there can be strong social attraction to the group when its members are isolated and anonymous. (p. 528)

According to Rohlinger and Brown (2009), Internet activism is often attractive to people engaged in risky types of activism that can entail retribution or ostracism by authorities. It provides a safe venue for political expression, creates a sense of companionship and solidarity with people of similar values, and has the potential for involving people in other types of collective action including discussion groups, letters, and phone calls to public officials. There may also be opportunities for face-to-face interaction in local groups or national events or protests.

One example of using social networking technology for organizing involved a hunger strike held at the University of California, Berkeley in May, 2010 (Berton, 2010). A student group, Hunger for Justice, initiated action in order to demand university support for efforts to oppose anti-immigrant legislation adopted by the state of Arizona. The group also called for the UC Berkeley administration to drop charges against campus protestors arrested during demonstrations against student fee hikes and to rehire laid-off janitors. The action started with an email to the UC chancellor to which there was no response. To solicit additional support, the activists sent text messages and emails to students and the local media. They also opened a Facebook page and an account on Twitter. Within a week, the activists had acquired over 1,000 followers on Facebook and received a response (not entirely positive) from the university chancellor.

PUTTING VALUES IN ACTION: FOSTERING INDIVIDUAL COMMITMENT TO SOCIAL JUSTICE

Much of what organizers know about recruiting people for participation in organizing campaigns is grounded in the scholarly literature on social movements (Castelloe & Prokopy, 2001). According to Snow, Soule, and Kriesi (2007), "social movements as a form of collective action, involve joint action in pursuit of a common objective. Joint action of any kind implies some degree of coordination, and thus organization" (p. 9). Consequently, recruitment campaigns need a structure and purpose. Klandermans (2007) identifies three reasons for participation in social movements: *instrumentality*, the use of individual participation to facilitate social and political change, *ideology*, a vehicle for finding meaning in life and expressing one's personal beliefs and emotions about specific situations, and *identity*, feelings of belonging to or personal identification with a group. Consequently, for recruitment to be effective, participants need a method or "frame" that can be used to ascribe meaning to the situation at hand and the social change desired, a sense of collective identity with the group taking action or for whom the action is taken, and a belief or sense of efficacy in their ability to affect change (Little, 2010). The role of the organizer is to facilitate the development, through interaction with volunteers and potential recruits of a sense of collective identity through participation in groups and networks. The development of a sense of collective identify is facilitated through explicit efforts to overcome feelings of stigmatization and oppression among members of marginalized groups. Additional techniques to empower members and forge a group identity are efforts to integrate group and cultural values into the organizing campaign and fostering a sense of hope that the organizing effort will succeed (Box 3.1).

Developing Frames

Recruiting people for participation in social change activities requires both an appeal to self-interest and a call to action based on a sense of social justice, values, and morality. Saul Alinsky (1971) in *Rules for*

BOX 3.1   PUTTING VALUES IN ACTION: FOSTERING INDIVIDUAL COMMITMENT TO SOCIAL JUSTICE

- Create succinct messages about problems or issues that frame issues in ways that are consistent with the perspectives and experiences of people that you are trying to reach.
- Provide a rationale for why the issue must be addressed that includes factual evidence and other important information.
- Appeal to individual self-interest *and* social values, morality, and social justice.
- Help foster a sense of collective identity among potential supporters that facilitates feelings of group solidarity and empowerment.
- Use a variety of techniques including events, flyers, house meetings, street outreach, the media, one-on-one interviews, phone calls, emails, text messages, word of mouth, and the Internet and social networking technology to reach potential recruits.
- Make sure that recruitment techniques and the message associated with the organizing campaign are culturally appropriate and that frames and symbols are used to bring people together.
- Ask the potential participant to participate in a specific action.
- Use existing social networks to "expand the circle" of contacts, resources, and potential recruits.
- Make sure that participant skills are utilized and that participants are recognized and rewarded for their accomplishments.

Radicals described one of many important tactics for community organizers, "The eleventh rule of the ethics of means and ends is that goals must be phrased in general terms like 'Liberty, Equality, Fraternity,' 'Of the Common Welfare,' 'Pursuit of Happiness,' or 'Bread and Peace'" (p. 45). The use of these values in recruiting people for social activism is called framing. Frames are conceptual outlines used to describe problems or issues. According to Gillian (2008), "frames relate to people's basic beliefs and attitudes; they offer direction since they are inherently action-focused, and they allow actors [participants] to understand their own position relative to others" (p. 248). Frames are often generated through interpersonal transactions as individuals struggle to place meaning on their experiences in relation to social, political, and economic institutions and discuss these experiences with others. According to Snow (2007), the theories of social constructionism and symbolic interactionism can be applied to the study of how social movements frame issues that have salience to their members, opponents, and the general public.

Community organizers use frames to recruit people around specific causes and look for ways to portray causes in a manner that has meaning for prospective participants and that can evoke strong feelings (Pyles, 2009b). They also provide an opportunity to change public perceptions shaped by the dominant culture and create a means for looking at these issues that represent the perspectives of people who have been affected by the problem. Frames also appeal to individual's sense of morality, values, and social justice or are consistent with their past experiences, especially those that are perceived as unfair or unjust. According to Ganz (2007), a sense of morality is often critical in motivating potential participants:

> One of the key lessons of the social movements of the past—of the left and of the right—is that their power grew out of the moral energy of their people (not just their organizers), their readiness to take risk, and their resourcefulness—all of which was rooted in turn, not in "self-interest" in any obvious sense, but in the values at stake. (p. 1)

Frames are used to recruit new members, raise funds, and inform the public about a problem or issue and may involve invoking moral shocks or using visual images or symbols to illustrate potential consequences associated with social policies or practices (Harris, 2010; Mika, 2006). For example, People for the Ethical Treatment of Animals (PETA) has been effective in creating ad campaigns that illustrate the harsh or abusive treatment of animals and fostering a sense of human identification with the plight of the animals (Atkins-Sayre, 2010).

Frames also can be used strategically to gain public support for a cause and involve a variety of different groups with different perspectives in the organizing campaign, especially when the message is used to put people inside the experiences of others (Gillian, 2008). For example, in June 2010, the American Civil Liberties Union implemented a national campaign against an Arizona law that required local police to check immigration status of anyone they suspected of being "illegal" during any law enforcement related encounter. Fearful that only people of Latino ancestry would be questioned by police, ACLU affiliates organizations in a number of states issued travel "advisories," warning people that they were in danger of racial profiling and arrest if they visited Arizona. One of the purposes of the advisory was to advise the people likely to be affected of their legal rights and to inform the general public about the potential impact of these policies (Associated Press, 2010).

Facilitating the Development of Collective Identity

One factor in the decision to become a community activist is whether the individual feels as if one belongs to or is attached to the community or cause. As noted earlier in this chapter, this attribute is often referred to as collective identity or sense of community (Snow, 2001). Bandura (1990) defines individual perceptions of personal self-efficacy as:

> People's beliefs that they can exert control over their motivation and behavior and over their social environment. People's beliefs about their capabilities affect what they choose to do, how much effort they mobilize, how long they will persevere in the face of difficulties, whether they engage in self-debilitating or self-encouraging thought patterns, and the amount of stress and depression they experience in taxing situations. (p. 9)

As applied to community practice, Pecukonis and Wenocur (1994) define collective efficacy as "a shared perception, be it conscious or unspoken, that members of a collective hold about the group's ability to achieve its reform objectives in the face of opposition" (p. 13). Membership in pre-existing groups or social networks, perceptions that members of the group are oppressed or stigmatized, the use of group and cultural symbols to foster feelings of inclusion in the group, and the perception of group members that the action will be successful are factors contributing to collective efficacy among participants in social change.

Group and Network Membership

Feelings associated with collective identity can originate in membership with a specific demographic group (e.g., gender, age, ethnicity, race, sexual orientation, income, culture, or physical/mental disabilities), experiences in common with other community members (such as welfare receipt or surviving a disaster), facing a common adversary, or experiencing social stigma (Taylor & Van Dyke, 2007). For example, bad treatment from a landlord who has refused to make repairs in an apartment complex may foster a sense of collective identity among the tenants. Similarly, discrimination experienced by new immigrants may bring people of a variety of ethnic backgrounds together to develop strategies in support of immigration reform (Daley, 2007).

Membership in a social network often can be used to facilitate recruitment for social change efforts. According to Della Porta and Diani (2006), people will be more likely to participate in social change activities if they are recruited through social networks: Recruitment through networks not only expands the number of people likely to participate, but also ensures that people with similar values and perspectives are involved in the process (Polletta & Jasper, 2001). This, in turn, also contributes to feelings of belonging to the group and a sense of solidarity among members. However, one disadvantage of using this method exclusively is that it is often necessary in community practice to reach out to people with different experiences, values, and perspectives in order to garner public support for the organizing effort. People who are neutral or opposed to the social change initiative must be persuaded to change their positions, requiring that potential new networks of people must be identified and brought into the organizing process.

In order to have a sense of collective identity, group members must be able to determine group boundaries, who is in the group and what individuals or organizations remain outside the group. In many circumstances, an individual's sense of identification with a socially or politically marginalized group is imposed by members of the dominant culture who may stigmatize or isolate group members.

Reducing Feelings of Oppression and Stigma

In addition, feelings of collective identity and commitment to the cause and one another are also fostered among activists when they encounter negative public reaction to their participation or the goals of the social change effort (Van Dyke & Cress, 2006). Consequently, most organizing work and participation in activism almost always requires that efforts be made to reduce feelings of political oppression among members of socially stigmatized groups (Hunt & Benford, 2007). For example, Little (2010) describes methods used by a Center for Independent Living to facilitate the process of collective identity development and activism among people with disabilities:

> Staff members also worked to establish group boundaries between those identified as disabled and the non-disabled, or between the "challenging group" and the "dominant group." The effort included expressions of commonality among individuals with varied impairment and disability experiences. Part of the creation of "us" involved a shift in attribution for hardships experienced. Difficulties that had been ascribed to fate or tragedy were redefined as caused by social barriers and attitudes ("Constructing a Collective Identity," para 8).

As part of the identify development process, staff members also encouraged consumers to engage in self-advocacy which in turn fostered self-esteem, self-acceptance, and feelings of personal self-efficacy among constituency group members.

Adopting Group and Cultural Symbols

Another technique used to foster collective identity includes the use of cultural symbols, flyers, posters, t-shirts, or music associated with the group or that illustrate cultural values or traditions associated with the group or important principles related to the cause or situation at hand are also critical in the development of a sense of collective identity (Polletta & Jasper, 2001). One of the best-known organizing symbols is used by the United Farm Workers. In 1966, Cesar Chavez described the incorporation of cultural symbols in the UFW flag:

> I wanted desperately to get some color into the movement, to give people something they could identify with, like a flag. I was reading some books about how various leaders discovered what colors contrasted and stood out the best. The Egyptians had found out that a red field with a white circle and a black emblem in the center crashed into your eyes like nothing else. I wanted to use the Aztec eagle in the center, as on the Mexican flag. So I told my cousin Manuel, "Draw an Aztec eagle." Manuel had a little trouble with it, so we modified the eagle to make it easier for people to draw. (Chavez, 1966, p. 4)

Having values or identifiable norms and cultural practices in common with other members of the community also fosters a sense of belonging and solidarity with the group. For example, Methiratta and Smith (2001) describe the development of a sense of collective identity among members of a women's organization in India:

> Members wear Khadi (homespun cotton) to convey the organization's values of simplicity, self-reliance and anti-materialism. Khadi was popularized ruing the Indian independence movement by Gandhi, but is worn by few Indians today. Almost all SEWA members, however, wear khadi. One SEWA organizer observed that older members quickly correct new members who wear fancy silk or synthetic fabrics. (p. 2)

Fostering Perceptions of Success

In addition to cultural or group symbols, anticipation of positive outcomes is often central in the decision to join a group or take action (Corrigall-Brown et al., 2009). According to Goodwin, Jasper, and Polletta (2007), "leaders often try to arouse in participants feelings of hope or optimism, a sense that they can have a positive, transformative effect through their collective action. Optimism is associated with a heightened sense of individual and collective efficacy" (p. 421). Often, community organization recruitment efforts deliberately adopt symbols that convey either a sense of hope or explicitly references to the belief that the group can facilitate change, for example, the use of the phrase "si se puede" by the United Farm Workers or the English translation of this phrase, used by the 2008 Obama Presidential campaign, "Yes we can" (Shaw, 2008).

Collective efficacy is also fostered when the group has been effective in meeting its goals and when individuals are perceived by themselves or others as instrumental in helping the group to meet its goals (Foster-Fishman et al., 2006). Consequently, celebrating goal achievement and the recognition of individual volunteers and their contributions are critical in the development of collective efficacy (Kahn, 1991; Work Group for Community Health and Development, 2010). A number of research studies indicate that involvement in successful community change projects results in increases in feeling of personal and collective self-efficacy among participants (Itzhaky & York, 2002; Ohmer, 2008; Zimmerman & Rappaport, 1988).

SUMMARY

Organizing efforts rely on the recruitment of as many volunteers as possible. Participants increase the number of people who can share the work, tap into their own social networks for resources and additional recruits, disseminate information, and increase the power of the organization through their "strength in numbers." Organizers seek to motivate potential volunteers by appealing to personal self-interest and providing individual with opportunities to meet others, apply skills, make professional contacts, address wrongs, and improve conditions for community members. Participation can also be motivated by appeals based on morality, social values, or a sense of social justice. Recruitment methods must be culturally appropriate not only in terms of ethnicity, but also in terms of social status or income, age, gender, sexual orientation, physical/mental disability, and other demographic variables.

EXERCISES AND ASSIGNMENTS

1. Volunteer to staff a literature table or booth at a community event. What strategies did you use to attract people to your table or booth? How hard or easy was it to encourage people to take literature or sign up for a volunteer opportunity, service, or event? Why? What social work skills were you able to apply in this outreach activity?
2. Volunteer at least two hours of your time to a phone bank campaign that is designed to recruit donors, volunteers, or voters. Write a two-page analysis of your experience. What techniques did you use to persuade donors to stay on the phone or agree to provide money, time, or votes to the organization or candidate? What were some of the difficulties you encountered when you made these calls? Were all the calls successful? Why not?
3. Create a flyer, write a blog or news article, design a web page, or create a Facebook of MySpace page for a community event or recruitment effort. Make sure you provide all critical information about the event or campaign.
4. For an organization in which you are completing your social work internship or are employed or in which you volunteer, plan a recruitment campaign or event. Turn in a paper describing: the purpose of the campaign or event, your goal(s), your target population, the message that you are trying to transmit, the staff members or volunteers involved in the campaign and event and the skills and or other resources they possessed that were applied to the requirement effort, the specific recruitment method(s) used, and why the recruitment method used was appropriate for the target population. Also describe whether you were successful and any problems or barriers encountered during the recruitment process. How could your campaign or event be improved?

4

Developing Relationships and Partnerships With Formal Organizations

When you apply for grants, the efficiency of partnerships is a lot more laudable than just claiming you are doing things on your own. Everybody knows that with a staff of a few people, you are not going to be doing a thousand different things.
—Staff member in a community-based agency quoted in Carr, 2009, p. 49

In addition to recruiting individuals for participation in community organizing efforts, organizers also establish partnerships with other groups and organizations. As with individuals, existing networks of people and organizations are used for making contacts and identifying potential supporters and resources. Organizations provide access to other potential recruits and they can also provide resources such as facilities, information, staff support, and funding for the organizing drive. In this chapter, theories that explain why it may be advantageous for organizations to establish partnerships with one another and the problems often encountered when building inter-group alliances are described. Several types of structures that facilitate organizational partnerships are identified: task forces, collaboratives, coalitions, inter-faith alliances, national organizations with local affiliates, and social movements. In addition, specific interpersonal skills needed for partnership building are examined including building trust bargaining and negotiating, developing consensus, and resource- and power-sharing. In the last section of the chapter, specific steps for applying the principles of mutual learning and partnership when building alliances and partnerships are described.

THE PURPOSE OF ORGANIZATIONAL PARTNERSHIPS IN COMMUNITY PRACTICE

Most community organizations seek organizational partners for social change efforts. In community development, the organizing effort is dependent upon having wide representation from a variety of groups with different perspectives involved in the process (Ohmer & DeMasi, 2009). Social planners also seek to consult with diverse groups for plan development; some planning efforts may require collaboration among members to apply for grants or acquire the resources needed to operate a new program or organization (Forester, 1999). In social action, successful organizing requires that as many people and organizations as possible be involved in efforts to influence or pressure decision-makers to adopt a plan or pass legislation. Pressure tactics are much more successful when as many people as possible contact their legislators, attend community forums to question elected officials, or participate in protests (Staples, 2004).

Organizations can be defined as a set of pre-determined activities arranged by and carried out by two or more people (Lohmann & Lohmann, 2002). Some of the organizations with which organizers work are relatively informal groups or gatherings of individuals with similar interests and goals such as neighborhood watch groups or friends who have started a community garden. It may not be at all clear as to whether specific individuals are affiliated with or belong to these informal groups (Chaskin, 2003; Putnam, 2000). However, formal organizations have established structures, designated decision-makers, and may be legally incorporated as nonprofit or for-profit organizations or work under a government mandate, often employ paid staff and contain clear boundaries that determine who is included in the organization (Austin, 2002). Consequently, partnerships with these organizations can be subject to legal constraints (such as contractual agreements for services offered or funder requirements); financial and legal negotiations require that the organization designate a staff person or volunteer who can enter into formal agreements with collaborative partners, board members, or elected officials. Due to the number of parties involved, the establishment of formal partnerships is often a complex and time-consuming process (Gazley, 2010).

In formal organizations and groups, recruitment of organizational partners often takes place when a gatekeeper or another previously recruited participant refers to the organizer to the group. Many of the organizational techniques described in Chapter 3 can also be used in recruiting organizations; strong relationship ties are needed between the organizer and representatives of the organization (Alter, 2000). The opinions and perspectives of organization partners should be solicited to gain insight into community problems and to develop a consensus about solutions (Emshoff et al., 2007). Existing networks of organizations should be tapped to provide additional recruits and efforts should be made via meetings and planned activities to stimulate group solidarity (Staples, 2004). In addition, any recruitment drives, organizing campaigns, or service delivery partnerships should frame community problems and potential solutions for these problems in a culturally competent manner that incorporates the values of community members, the primary missions of organizational members, and beliefs about fairness and justice (Cross & Friesen, 2005; McBeath & Briggs, 2008).

MODELS OF ORGANIZATION PARTNERSHIPS

Theories and perspectives about how community-based organizations operate focus on both their internal and external functioning. Internally, organization culture can be viewed as originating in the mission, structure, and interpersonal relations among managers, staff, board members, and clientele (Netting & O'Connor, 2003). However, what happens in the organization is highly associated with what happens outside the organization in terms of funding availability, laws and social policies, and public recognition and regard for the organization. An organization's relationship, or the lack thereof, with other organizations dealing with the same issues or problems, can determine whether the organization can keep its doors open, the effectiveness of its services or advocacy efforts, and its political influence (Iglehart & Becerra, 2011). Consequently, organizations form partnerships with one another to increase their capacity to address community problems. Halseth and Ryser (2007) define partnerships as relationships among two or more organizations in which there is an explicit agreement to work together in order to benefit all members. Ideally, all members of the partnership share responsibility for making decisions, managing the activities undertaken by the group, and sharing any risks that might be encountered.

As with other aspects of the organizing effort, strong bonds are critical for the process of relationship building. Some of the elements needed for developing good relationships among partner organizations are similar to those used for entering communities and recruiting individuals for participation in community change: reciprocity, mutuality, and trust (Alter, 2000). These attributes are developed through the process of sharing resources that include, but are not limited to: constituents, skilled staff, facilities, legitimacy or positive recognition by others, money, information, board members, linkages to other organizations, and political power (Halseth & Ryser, 2007). According to Paarlberg and Varda (2009), strong organizational partnerships are also characterized by the degree to which network members are fiscally able to engage in resource exchanges and have the time and energy to do so.

Types of organizational alliances typically found in community organization practice include, but are not limited to, task forces, collaboratives, coalitions, inter-faith alliances, national organizations with local affiliates, and social movements. In many cases, an organization may participate in a number of these types of alliances. For example, the PICO National Network (formerly the Pacific Institute for Community Organizing) is a national network with local affiliates and has participated in local, state, and national coalition groups and social movements (Wood, 2007).

Task Forces

Task forces are temporary structures established to address a community issue, need, or problem that must be resolved within a short time span (Speer & Zippay, 2005). Members are generally representatives of organizations that serve a specific population group or community. However, individuals with technical expertise related to that issue or people who have experienced the problem may be included as well. Task forces may initially be informal, but if the target problem cannot be adequately addressed by existing organizations or service agencies, the task group may evolve into a collaborative effort among several organizations or an independent organization designed specifically to address the issue identified by the task group (Hardcastle et al., 2004). Task forces have some advantages that formal organizations may not. They can be flexible in structure, bringing together a diverse group of people with new ideas and a variety of skills, and may allow for the pooling of resources among different public, nonprofit, and for-profit organizations serving different populations or communities with different missions and goals. They also can be used to identify gaps in services and to address systemic problems in communities and institutions that cannot be easily addressed by one organization alone (Hooker, Cirill, & Gerahty, 2009). Task forces can engage in legislative advocacy or develop innovative programs or campaigns that will publicize issues, develop public support, and generate new resources to resolve problems. Task forces can also be used to quickly address new or emerging community problems for which there is limited knowledge, resources, and expertise available to develop solutions. For example, tasks forces were created in the early 2000s in Minnesota and California to address the sexual exploitation of teen runaways and an adolescent suicide epidemic in Hmong communities in both states. Both of these issues were related to the immigrant experience, but few service resources had been developed that were appropriate for the Hmong population (Hardina, Yamaguchi, Moua, Yang, & Moua, 2008; Saewyc, Solsvig, & Edinburgh, 2007).

Task forces, as with other types of organization partnerships can have a number of disadvantages as well. It can be difficult to reach an agreement about problem identification and goals among a diverse group of people. The time-limited nature of the task force can make this approach ineffective for addressing complex problems that require long-term changes in a variety of organizations or social policies (Saewyc et al., 2007). In addition, partners may be willing to work together, but unwilling to share their own resources, especially money and skilled staff members, on initiatives that involve risks or substantial investments of time. The issue of "protecting one's turf" rather than working collaboratively on an intractable problem often limits the success of many task force efforts, collaborations, and coalitions (Alter, 2000).

Collaboratives

Nonprofit and public organizations often establish collaborative partnerships in order to deliver services, plan programs, or engage in a specific type of joint activity (Nowell, 2009). Collaborative partnerships are often referred to as service delivery networks and involve complex systems of exchanges and resource sharing among multiple organizations. The use of the word *collaboration* implies that the various partners have developed a process of mutual exchange or sharing of resources and that these organizations can work together harmoniously in order to accomplish a task (Hardina et al., 2006). Although some community organizations do not deliver direct services to individual clients or families, they may be recruited for participation in a collaborative service partnership when the goal of the collaborative is to conduct outreach to marginalized populations, make improvement in community services, or reform existing service delivery systems (Emshoff et al., 2007).

In some cases, organizations come together because a funding source mandates such an alliance as a condition of a grant or contract (Ivery, 2008). In other cases, organization participants serving a specific community or population group establish a partnership structure out of self-interest such as acquiring new clientele constituents, obtaining funding and other resources, or cutting costs (Halseth & Ryser, 2007). The motivation for establishing collaborative partnerships can also involve correcting gaps in services or adapt to changing conditions (such as funding cuts, technical innovations, or new clients or constituents with complex needs that might require different types of services or initiatives). Collaborative members often vary in organizational affiliation (nonprofit, public, service clubs, or self-help groups), budget and staff size, and the amount of power and influence they hold in the community. Participation in partnerships and networks often helps organizations adapt to fiscal, technological, or political changes in the community or the larger political environment (Alter, 2000). For example, small organizations and organizations that have lost funding often seek to join collaboratives to survive financially (Iglehart & Becerra, 2011). Larger organizations may want to join collaboratives for similar reasons; small organizations serving hard to serve population groups or delivering unique or specialized services may have access to staffing resources or technology that the larger organizations may want to acquire (Graddy & Chen, 2006). Collaboration may also serve as a vehicle to coordinate services so that different organizations take responsibility for different tasks or to eliminate duplication of services to the same groups of clients (Gil de Gigaja, 2001).

While resource sharing and expansion and improvements in service delivery are two of the benefits of collaborative arrangements, there are also a number of limitations. Provan and Milward (2001) argue that for collaborative partnerships to work effectively, they must be able to establish strong relationships among member organizations and agencies and institutions outside the network, absorb new organizations as others drop out, and provide most essential services for the target population. Often substantial resources are necessary for these conditions to be met. Competition for funds and resources among member organizations may make it difficult for cooperation to be achieved. Also problematic is that as with task forces, members come from diverse backgrounds and often have different agendas for what they want to accomplish through membership in the collaborative. In addition, organization representatives may vary in terms of education and professional status which can result in different perspectives on problems and solutions, thus making consensus around organization goals difficult (Mizrahi, Bayne-Smith, & Garcia, 2009).

Coalitions

A coalition can be defined as groups established to take joint action to achieve a specific goal by combining resources, membership, and political influence (Roberts-DeGennaro & Mizrahi, 2005). Most coalitions that are established engage in social action to lobby government or to campaign for changes in policies or institutional structures (Rubin & Rubin, 2008). However, coalition groups can also be formed to participate in joint efforts to resolve community problems or conduct informational campaigns to encourage service utilization or health prevention. In some cases, coalitions may have multiple goals. For example, Chutuape et al. (2010) describe the efforts of health-oriented coalition to educate community members about AIDS prevention, develop additional service agencies and networks, and lobby for changes in laws and policies to support risk prevention methods (such as laws legalizing needle exchanges).

Coalitions can also be formed to bring together similar groups with similar interests, engage organizations with similar goals but varying approaches or resources with which to address the issue, or to forge relationships among diverse groups that can be persuaded to lend support to a specific cause but for different reasons (Rubin & Rubin, 2008). The primary purpose of coalitions however, is to increase "strength through numbers," the more members in a coalition, the more likely members will be able to garner political influence by pooling resources, having participants contact political representatives, gain the attention of the media and general public, and mobilize members for participation in public protests.

Unlike other types of partnership models, coalition groups generally do not establish formal, centralized structures to provide operational support and make decisions for coalition members (Wells, Ward, Feinberg, & Alexander, 2008). Membership is held by organizations rather than individuals; these groups come together to plan organizing campaigns in response to pressing issues. Decisions may be made by a steering committee or leadership council that consists of representatives of member organizations. Organizations do not give up their autonomy when they join a coalition and may drop out or refuse to participate in initiatives with which they disagree. Consequently, coalition membership is often temporary and fluid; organizations may only join forces when an issue of concern requires a quick response to a government policy, legislative initiative, or community problem. However, some coalition groups are fairly well established and take on some of the characteristics of more formal organizations in response to ongoing problems such as poverty, threats to the environment, and discrimination.

Member organizations in coalitions provide monetary and staff support for the coalition and mobilize their constituents to take action (such as lobbying government officials or engaging in protests). As a result of the loose organization structures associated with most coalitions, one of the problems often encountered is coming to an agreement among member organizations as to mission, goals, and the strategies and tactics used to address the problem or influence social change (Conway, 2003; Hardina & Obel-Jorgensen, 2011). Ideological similarities are often critical in establishing and maintaining partnerships among coalition members. However ideological "purity" may be abandoned in instances in which organization with different agendas are viewed as bringing critical resources into the partnership (Roberts-DeGennaro & Mizrahi, 2005). Cultural, gender, ethnic, and other demographic differences can also make it difficult to forge agreements among the various groups involved in the coalition (Pyles, 2009a).

Interfaith Alliances

Interfaith alliances are partnerships among organizations serving specific communities in which the lead organizations consist of church congregations, but include other neighborhood groups and institutions (Posadas, 2008). Often referred to as faith-based or church-based community organizations, these local groups and networks also can be affiliated with national organizations (Warren, 2001). For example, several national organizing groups have local congregation-based affiliates such as the PICO National Network, the Gamaliel Foundation, and the Industrial Areas Foundation (IAF). All these organizations work for social change by engaging in lobbying and social action at local, state, and national levels (Swarts, 2008).

Many of these Interfaith Alliances utilize an organizing approach pioneered by Saul Alinsky (1971) in which local churches are contacted and recruited for participation in organizing efforts (Posadas, 2008). Once churches and their leaders are involved, individual members are then recruited for participation (Rubin & Rubin, 2008). According to Swarts (2010), faith-based community organizations consist of up to 30 different congregation members and sometimes include additional organizations such as unions or schools. These organizations are typically incorporated for tax purposes as nonprofit organizations. In addition to coordinating their work with national community organizing groups, many of these local interfaith alliances are also members of local, regional, or state coalitions that are actively involved in campaigns to alleviate poverty and discrimination. For example, in 2010 priorities for organizations in the PICO National Network included health care reform and banking reform to help people affected by foreclosures (PICO National Network, 2010).

One primary rationale for the formation of faith-based organizing groups is that congregations serve as a place for contact and recruitment of large numbers of individual members. The context of what happens in these congregations is also important. In Chapter 3, the use of moral frameworks such as social justice and inclusion to recruit new members for organizing efforts was described. Given that churches focus on transmitting and maintaining good moral values, organizing campaigns often link faith-based morality to church teaching and beliefs (Cnaan, Boddie, & Yancey, 2005). They also are a low- or no-cost source of a number of resources typically employed in organizing efforts such as highly motivated volunteers, donations and membership dues, meeting space, community kitchens, recreational facilities, and office equipment (Swarts, 2008).

According to Warren (2001), characteristics of faith-based community organizations include a membership base that consists of congregations rather than individuals, using religious traditions to frame social problems and collective action to address those problems, an emphasis on relationship-building rather than simply concentrating on goals or issues, and multiculturalism and diversity. In addition, many faith-based community organizing networks provide extensive training to members, hire professional organizing staff, and engage in social action organizing and protests that often involve confrontation with public officials. One of the interpersonal skills described earlier in this book, one-on-one interviews, is used extensively in faith-based organizing to identify community problems and issues and in-depth training is offered to the volunteers that conduct these interviews (Swarts, 2008).

One limitation associated with church-based community organizations includes the difficulty inherent in forging consensus among members of individual congregations and then gaining agreement among a number of diverse congregations serving the same community (Swarts, 2010). As in other types of alliances, gender, income, ethnicity, and religious or ideological differences can make it difficult to reach agreement on problem identification, goals, and the choice of strategies and tactics. In addition, the neighborhood focus of church-based organizing may limit the power of local congregations when the issues addressed have their roots in state or national policies. One solution for this dilemma is to form coalitions with national, state, or regional organizations that are not part of faith networks and that have the resources and staff to lobby for changes in public policy (Wood, 2007).

National Organizations With Local Affiliates

Many national organizations oriented toward improving communities and fighting for social justice also work locally, working with state and local chapters to carry out an agenda developed by their board of directors. Sellsky (1998) defines federations as structures used to mobilize collective action around shared interests. Federations often address national or regional issues and can focus on single or multiple issues. The mission of federated community organizations is to increase their political influence by increasing membership and access to funding by linking with local affiliates. As with coalitions, an increase in organizational members provides access to more volunteers, individual donors, people with power and influence, and additional networks that can be used to recruit new members. According to Selsky, a structure in which there is a lead organization and affiliates or chapters has several advantages:

> They establish the ground rules and articulate the values that provide a basis for affiliates to work together. They develop an image of a shared desirable future, often with a longer-term perspective than their affiliates. Finally, they provide infrastructure support, such as administrative resources, information sharing mechanisms, and project management services. (p. 287)

One of the largest, most well-known federated community organizations was the Association for Community Organizations for Reform Now (ACORN). Started in Arkansas in 1970, ACORN focused on issues critical to the financial well-being of members of low-income communities. By the time of its demise in 2010, ACORN had affiliates in 100 cities and more than 200,000 individual members (Dreier, 2009). Agenda items included living wage campaigns, housing and mortgage reform, regulation of pay-day lenders and currency exchanges, welfare reform and voter registration. ACORN, in partnership with numerous local, state, and national coalition groups and powerful unions was able to influence policies on both local and national levels. Local members, despite being low income, were required to pay dues to the organization, helping to maintain a good financial base for the national organization. Because of its political influence and the variety of services it offered to its members (such as tax preparation and welfare case advocacy), ACORN was also able to attract state and federal and in some instances, corporate grants and contracts that helped them recruit new members and achieve their goals (Brooks, 2005; Brooks, Russell, & Fisher, 2006; Fisher, Brooks, & Russell, 2009). In addition, confrontation and other types of protest tactics as well as their ability to register and mobilize thousands of low-income African-American and Latino voters also gave ACORN a great deal of political influence. ACORN's power was also the source of its demise—both financial mismanagement and a coordinated campaign by conservatives in 2009 to paint local affiliates as staffed by corrupt employees resulted in the loss of government grants and public legitimacy (National Public Radio, 2010). This forced the national organization to shut its doors in 2010.

Most federated community organizations remain quite influential at both local and national levels. Federated organizations with local affiliates often vary in terms of to what degree agenda setting includes mechanisms for involving chapter members in decision-making. Some federations place the primary responsibility for decision-making with the local affiliates. However, for this type of federation to succeed there must be some type of process for reaching agreement among a variety of local groups that may have different priorities and agenda. Alternatively, many large federations place primary responsibility for agenda and goal setting with the national organization. One advantage of top-down centralized administrative management in national organizations is that decisions can be made quickly by the national board or executive director and do not require time-consuming negotiations within local organizations or among chapter members (Swarts, 2010).

Social Movements

As described in Chapter 3, social movements are collective efforts to achieve social change. Individuals and organizations participate in social movements through membership in broad-based coalitions and national organizations; often social movements are made of complex inter-organizational relationships among numerous organizations dedicated to the same cause (Mizrahi & Rosenthal, 2001). Social movements are effective when they have a large number of members who can pay membership fees and participate in social protests or lobbying. According to Sen (2003), "movements emerge from a specific set of conditions—rising expectations among the disenfranchised, a backlash against the status quo, or demographic shifts—in addition to explicit organizing" (p. 22).

Obtaining resources is critical for the success of social movements; Resources often include individual donors, grants funded by foundations, media connections, and links to influential people and decision-makers (Edwards & McCarthy, 2007). Although social movements have generally been viewed as a vehicle for members of marginalized or oppressed groups to improve access to resources and political or civil rights, social movements can also be formed to advocate on behalf of others or improvements in economic or environmental issues. Movements can also be formed in opposition to war or to promote ethnic solidarity or religion (Snow, 2007). In some cases, social movements advocate for the interests of affluent members of society or those who feel that their social position or income has declined as a consequence of government actions or the acquisition of rights by previously unrepresented groups (DeFilippis, Fisher, & Shragge, 2010).

While local organizations are often affiliated with social movements around specific issues, there also can be loose affiliations or networks of formal and informal groups. In addition, larger, formal coalitions of local, state-wide, or national organizations also participate in social movements and may partner with other coalitions or national advocacy groups to sustain social movements around one or a number of causes. For example, in 2010, the PICO National Network worked with large coalitions to promote health care and immigration reform as a member of larger national coalitions.

Although social movements are oriented toward promoting values or rights, activities to maintain or stabilize the movement are also essential (Smock, 2004). Not only do effective movements have designated or elected (by a vote of the membership) leaders, they must also have an ongoing source of financial support, and an organizational and decision-making structure with which to operate (Clemens & Minkhoff, 2007). A single organization does not and cannot represent an entire social movement—but multiple organizations that form partnerships with one another and join coalitions around single issues that advance the mission of the social movement organizations strengthen the movement, help generate public support, and facilitate linkages with influential public figures, politicians, and donors.

INTERPERSONAL SKILLS FOR BRIDGING DIFFERENCES AMONG ORGANIZATIONAL PARTNERS

Although the literature on the use of coalitions, alliances, and collaboratives in community practice often describes well-functioning groups, most organizers have worked in collaborative groups characterized by conflict, mistrust, few active members, ineffective leaders, and poor or no outcomes. Even when collaborative partnerships have been successful, it often requires a great deal of skill and patience to maintain an organization structure in which participants can work together to achieve their goals (Mizrahi & Rosenthal, 2001). In this section of the paper, several specific interpersonal skills that can be used by organizers to increase collaborative capacity are described including establishing relationships among partners, building trust, bargaining and negotiating effective partnerships, using group work skills to develop consensus about issues, goals, action, and evaluation criteria, and power and resource sharing.

Relationship Building

Much of the work of establishing partnerships involves building both formal and informal relationships among people and organizations. Hence, some aspects of the process are informal, developing friendships or exploring common interests, values, and experiences or formal, legal or financial agreements or contracts that require commitment and follow-through. In Chapter 2, one-on-one interviews were described as a process for building "public relationships" during the organizing process. Christens (2010) describes these relationships as "respectful and civil relationships that build trust over time through action and that work to serve converging self-interest" (p. 890). However, organizing would not succeed unless these relationships happen on a large scale and are used to link groups of people together and initiate discussions with organization representatives and political decision-makers. Christen conducted a research study that consisted of over 50 qualitative interviews with PICO volunteers in six different organizations. Respondents identified three different benefits of relational organizing: strengthening commitments to community work, developing a greater understanding of social issues and how the world works, and establishing additional networks of relationships that can be used to facilitate social change. These changes take place at both the individual and organizational level.

Relationship building is also central to maintaining collaborative and coalition decision-making structures (Carr, 2009). For example, Gil de Bigaja (2001) interviewed organization directors who coordinated collaborative efforts with other organizations. The directors viewed relationship building as a central component of their work; maintaining strong interpersonal relationships with other members in order to facilitate meetings and reach agreements about common goals.

Building Trust

The establishment of trusting relationships is critical for achieving consensus among collaborative partners. According to Lambright, Mischen, and Laramee (2010), the two primary components of trust in interorganizational partnerships are *interdependence* and risk. Organizations must rely on one another to complete tasks, unless one organization completes its work, others cannot function. Risk involves putting the organization in a vulnerable position by relying on others to follow through. Previous experience in successfully working with a member organization and frequency of interaction can both be factors in the establishment of a trusting relationship.

Nowell (2009) argues that strong interpersonal relationships among members of collaborative structures increase the likelihood that these partnerships will be effective in meeting their goals. She identifies five relationship qualities that are characteristic of strong partnerships:

* The frequency at which participants interact with one another in activities that are not related to the collaborative.
* The perception of individual members as to whether other participants are responsive to their concerns.
* The perception of individual members that other participants can be trusted to follow through on assigned tasks and responsibilities.
* The perception of individual members as to the degree to which other participants have "legitimacy," that is the ability to make a unique contribution via knowledge, point of view, or skills to the partnership.
* The degree to which individual members believe that other participants share a common philosophy about the goals of the partnership.

According to Graddy and Chen (2006), organizations seek trustworthy partners because they need a resource that they do not already have in order to exchange resources; they also want partners who have legitimacy or political power and connections. Therefore, they want partners that they already know something about through previous experience, common goals, or linkages through other partner organizations. Vangen and Huxham (2003) offer a number of strategies for establishing trust when organizations have no prior history of working relationships:

* Have clarity of purpose and objectives.
* Deal with power differences.
* Have leadership but do not allow anyone to take over.
* Allow time to build up understanding.
* Share workload fairly.
* Resolve different levels of commitment.
* Accept that partnerships evolve over time. (p. 15)

Power and Resource-Sharing

The biggest impediments to trust-building in organizational partnerships involve sharing power and resources. Members of collaborative structures often worry about the degree to which they will be able to influence how decisions are made. Most organizational partnerships occur among organizations that unequal amounts of resources and power (Sen, 2003). According to Vangen and Huxham (2003), "practitioners' perceptions suggest that unequal power relations and the need to protect individual organizations' interests by controlling collaboration agendas are inevitable difficulties pertaining to the collaborative processes" (p. 26).

Although in some types of organization, decision-making may be relatively informal, most task forces, collaboratives, coalitions, and alliances establish a formal structure for decision-making. Such structures may vary depending on available recourses, size of the membership base, ideology, and skills of the leaders. Structures may range from having one or two appointed or elected leaders making most decisions, ensuring that all decisions are made by an elected governing board, to requiring that all decisions approved by regular assemblies of all members (Checkoway, 2007). Partnerships also require some type of structure similar to those of organizations. However, the structure may be less rigid than those in formal organizations and somewhat more formal than those typically found in informal groups of friends or volunteers. According to Brown (2006), aspects of structure should include a mission statement, goals and objectives, regular meetings, and rules for making decisions. Criteria for becoming an individual or organizational member, a funding source, and an explicit leadership structure are also necessary.

The governance structure for most partnerships consists of a steering committee, often selected through a vote of member organizations, with most organizations having a representative on the committee (Rubin & Rubin, 2008). Paarlberg and Varda (2009) argue that organizational partnerships require either formal governance structures, a "honest broker" that mediate relationships among members, or an informal process for governance based upon shared values and practices among member organizations. A process is also required for sanctioning those member agencies that violate expectations or norms for member organizations. Transparency in decision-making, equal distribution of benefits and perks, and regular evaluations of the coalition's or collaborative's work may help minimize the harmful effects associated with power differentials among organizations (Sen, 2003).

While clear governance structures can minimize differences in power among members, imbalances in other resources such as political influence or connections, monetary contributions, possession of skilled staff or technology, and the size of an individual organization's membership base or constituency group can provide a source of informal power for some individuals and groups within the partnership (VeneKlasen et al., 2007). Consequently, one of the most problematic issues for coalitions, collaboratives, and other types of partnerships has to do with sharing resources, especially money. Sen (2003) argues that collaborations require an understanding among members that they all contribute a minimum amount of resources. Because self-interest is one of the reasons that organizations enter into partnerships, organizations often jockey to improve their own status, influence, and access to resources.

Consequently, at minimum, clear understanding is needed about the resources the various parties should contribute to the partnership and how much each organizational partner should benefit from the resources provided, gained, or exchanged. In many instances, organizations may enter into formal agreements or contracts with members of the partnership. Often a process of bargaining and negotiation is needed to facilitate these arrangements.

Engagement in Bargaining and Negotiation With Partner Organizations

Managing conflict among organization partners is a critical skill for maintaining collaborative arrangements and facilitating consensus around the use of resources and power-sharing. Rosenthal and Mizrahi (2004) maintain that a conflict resolution model should be used by partner organizations to reach agreement on contentious issues that includes bargaining, negotiations, and compromise. Rather than *majority rule*, decisions should be made by mutual consent. They identify a number of specific strategies for dealing with conflict and issues related to the protecting of *turf* among member agencies:

> Some remedies for managing internal conflict within collaborations include appeals to rationality, diplomacy, the use of third parties, isolating disputes, excluding controversial items from the agenda, or maintaining tacit neutrality, giving each member veto power, airing and resolving disputes, or developing caucuses to facilitate inter-group negotiations. (p. 325)

Many experts on coalition-building and partnerships advocate for the development of explicit written agreements that spell out what each of the partner organizations has agreed to contribute or do (Homan, 2011). Prospective partners can also be asked for a written letter of commitment. Staples (2004) emphasizes the need for *contracting* or specifying either explicitly or implicitly group norms or expectations for behavior such as meeting times, participant roles, use of agendas, how decisions should be made, and how people should behave in meetings. It is also important to set parameters about whether, and to what degree, conflict is handled in organizations.

Developing Consensus: Issues, Goals, Action, and Evaluation Criteria

The primary purpose of building trust is such that individuals and organizations who make up the partnership can achieve consensus about mission, goals, actions, and evaluation criteria. Mizrahi and Rosenthal (2001) identify three critical roles for coalition leaders:

1. Sustain movement toward external goals by influencing social change targets.
2. Maintaining internal relations among the core organizational representatives.
3. Developing trust with, accountability to, and contributions from, the coalition's membership base (p. 66).

Group facilitators should focus on building the capacity of members to make decisions, relying on group dialogue and mutual learning. Often, consensus can easily be developed due to the manner in which collaborative groups or coalitions are developed—relationships are established between individuals or among organization members; prospective participants share an ideology and commitment to a cause (Rubin & Rubin, 2008; Van Dyke & McCammon, 2010). As discussed in Chapter 3, member organizations also are more likely to ban together when they perceive themselves to have a common enemy or opponent (e.g., an elected official that opposes their goals or an existing law or policy that prevents a specific action or a desired outcome).

Responsibility for facilitating discussion often falls on a staff member or designated leader of the partnership, coalition, or collaborative. Many of the interpersonal skills used to achieve group consensus are related to basic group work skills commonly used in social work practice. For example, the Community Tool Box offers the following guidelines for facilitating group discussions:

- Help people feel comfortable.
- Guide the group into establishing ground rules that call for respect among participants and ensure the opportunity to participate for all group members.
- Set an agenda and have specific goals for what is to be accomplished during the meeting.
- Actively lead the discussion by asking questions of group members or suggesting a course of action.
- Make sure that everyone has a chance to speak and that one or a small group of people do not dominate the meeting.
- Summarize the important points and ask for clarification from group members.
- Wrap up the meeting by making plans for next steps and assigning tasks to specific members (Work Group for Community Health and Development, 2010).

BRIDGING DIFFERENCES THROUGH MUTUAL LEARNING AND PARTICIPATION

One of the basic principles associated with building partnerships, coalitions, and collaboratives is ensuring that membership is diverse and representative of the community. According to Checkoway (2007), in such circumstances "the challenge is to find the ties, which bind people together, that is to identify issues that have salience to diverse constituencies, enable them to realize their common cause and motivate them to take collective action" (p. 14).

Dobbie and Richards-Schuster (2008) describe a number of practice activities that can be used in partnerships with diverse members find common ground:

- Recruit leaders with multiple cultural identities and experiences who have the ability to help members of the diverse groups or constituencies "connect" with one another.
- Encourage advocacy on the part of these leaders so that the voices of people traditionally excluded (such as youth, the elderly, or persons of color) will be heard in the decision-making process.
- Provide educational activities that include discussions on the negative effects of power and privilege, the value of diversity, and inequities fostered by racism, sexism, homophobia, and other forms of discrimination.
- Provide opportunities for events and celebrations that encourage informal social interactions and dialogue among participants.

* Give priority within the partnership structure for social action activities that directly affect members regardless of their perspectives.

As noted earlier in this chapter, power and resource imbalances in collaborative structures often make partnerships ineffective. Marois (2006) argues that most conflicts in collaborative partnerships originates in power imbalances related to gender, race, and other historical or present-day inequities in terms of who holds status in the community and within the partnership. She suggests a number of strategies for minimizing conflict including shared governance, ensuring that meetings are often chaired by nonprofessionals or people who represent nondominant or marginalized groups, and using organization self-evaluation techniques to examine whether the organization is operating in an equalitarian and culturally competent manner.

PUTTING VALUES IN ACTION: SUSTAINING MUTUAL LEARNING AND PARTNERSHIP AMONG ORGANIZATIONS

Given that power and resource imbalances often make coalitions and other types of partnerships ineffective, it is critical that organization members agree to implement principles associated with mutuality and trust-building. Foster-Fishman, Berkowitz, Lounsbury, Jacobson, and Allen (2001) identify a variety of skills needed to enhance the capacity of coalitions to foster collaboration among member organizations. They identify four components of collaborative capacity:

* *Member Capacity*: the ability to recruit and support a diverse pool of members who are motivated to work and collaborate with others and possess the knowledge and skills needed to maintain the coalition. Maintenance includes the ability to fundraise and create an appropriate organizational structure.
* *Relational Capacity*: the ability to foster positive interactions among coalition members, establish group norms for participation, reach a consensus about goals, and maintain an inclusive decision-making structure. In addition, the coalition and its members should be able to build external relationships with individuals and groups and involve community members in the decision-making process.
* *Organizational Capacity*: the ability to foster leadership among members, formalize roles, assign and complete tasks, develop plans, foster communication among members, develop a committee structure, acquire funding, recruit skilled staff members, and monitor the coalition's ability to achieve outcomes.

• *Programmatic Capacity*: the ability to conduct needs assessments, solicit input from the community, and develop programs and organizing campaigns.

Lasker and Weiss (2003) incorporate many of these components into a management and leadership model designed to foster effective collaborative practice. In addition to encouraging participation from a diverse group of community members and organizations and an inclusive decision-making structure, they stress the importance of making all leaders, staff, and organizations accountable to the members and recognizing the contributions and skills of all participants. Leaders should also be responsible for fostering a productive group process that synthesizes member skills and resources. Lasker and Weiss also argue for ongoing efforts to expand the collaborative and build membership, actively connect the planning process to taking action, and provide technical assistance and other support.

Lasker and Weiss (2003) identify three outcomes that community collaborations should ideally try to achieve:

• Empower individuals by involving them in community problem-solving. Participants need to have actual rather than token influence and control of the process.
• Bring diverse people together, build trust, and develop a sense of community.
• Combine knowledge, skills, and other resources to develop creative solutions to multiple community problems.

Nowell and Foster-Fishman (2010) also identify a number of organizational outcomes associated with participation in effective community collaboratives including increases in knowledge about community systems and how they function and awareness of community issues. In addition, participation in collaboratives should increase member access to resources and improve service delivery, facilitate community change, or influence the development of policies or legislation. It should also increase the organization's ability to resolve problems. In addition, organizations increase their own power, influence, and reputations in the community by participating in collaborative efforts.

These collaborative activities and outcomes can be conceptualized in terms of a practice model that incorporates both process-oriented, interpersonal skills and concrete tasks or activities that must be accomplished to maintain the partnership and facilitate its work. In terms of process, participants and their designated leaders must recruit a diverse membership base that is representative of the demographic characteristics of the constituency served and includes people with a variety of skills and experiences. Group work skills should be used to encourage mutual learning among participants about shared experiences and community problems as well as their differences in order to build an organizational atmosphere based on trust and a sense of community or collective identity. The ability to engage with one another as equal partners is essential for the development of a consensus-oriented decision-making process. Task-oriented activities should include efforts to establish a decision-making structure for the organization, obtain resources, train and provide adequate supports for leaders and staff, and assign tasks to member organizations for goal accomplishment and organizational maintenance. Other tasks should be focused on organizational goals: planning, implementation of activities, and evaluation of outcomes.

These activities should result in both process- and task-oriented outcomes. Process-oriented outcomes include: the empowerment of individuals, creating trust and a sense of community among members, and the ability of the partners to creatively resolve problems. Concrete or task-oriented outcomes should result in an increase in knowledge about how the community works, improvement in services or increases in access to services, changes in the community, policies, and legislation, and increases in the reputation of individual member organizations and their power to affect social change (see Figure 4.1).

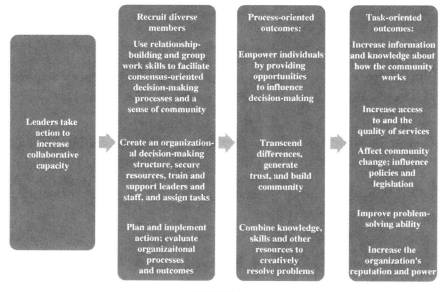

FIGURE 4.1
Conceptual model: Mutual learning and partnership among organizations.

SUMMARY

The creation of collaborative partnerships requires a combination of process- and task-related skills for creating an organizational structure to support decision-making and carrying out tasks. The interpersonal skills necessary to accomplish this include mutual learning, trust, and consensus-building. Many of the partnership structures established by alliances of social change-oriented organizations are complex, including a variety of organizations with different goals and motivations for participation. Decision-making takes place within individual organizations, within the context of the local partnership, and in the case of federations at regional, state, or national levels. Consequently, organizers coordinating organizational partnerships need to have excellent management and group work skills to facilitate such processes. In the next five chapters, the use of group work skills for facilitating consensus among group members (both individual and organization partners) for problem-solving, assessment, intervention planning, taking action, and evaluating the outcome and processes associated with these actions will be described. The theme inherent in these chapters is the incorporation of Freire's principles of mutual learning and partnership in every phase of the community organization process.

EXERCISES AND ASSIGNMENTS

1. Attend a meeting of a task group or coalition and observe the verbal and nonverbal interaction among participants, the decision-making structure, and the types of decisions made by group members. Conduct a brief interview after the meeting with at least one of the participants to find out about the respondent's perception of the meeting. Write a one to three page paper and:
   (a) Identify the participants and their organizational affiliation.
   (b) Identify the participant or participants responsible for facilitating the meeting (i.e., who is in charge? Is it one person or do multiple people seem to have responsibility for ensuring that the group runs smoothly).
   (c) Describe the decision-making structure (e.g., are decisions made by majority rule or by consensus). Were there any other rules that seemed to pertain to the decision-making process?
   (d) What decisions were made? If no decisions appear to have been made, why do you think this happened?
   (e) Were decisions made through consensus or conflict?

(f) Does it appear that members of the group were assigned specific tasks? Were the tasks completed? If not, were reasons given? What were they?

(g) Did any member of the group seem to have a specific agenda about what was to be accomplished in the meeting. Was it similar to or different from other members of the group?

2. In your internship or place of employment, facilitate a task group or committee meeting that involves staff or representatives of a number of organizations. Prior to the meeting, consult with your supervisor or other staff members and discuss the history of the group, the purpose of the group, past accomplishments, and future goals. Also make sure that you have a clear vision of what you intend to accomplish in this meeting. Prepare an agenda in advance and plan to take minutes.

For your written assignment, submit the agenda and minutes. Also submit a two-to-four-page paper that:

(a) Identifies participants and the organization that they represent.

(b) Describes group interaction during the meeting.

(c) Describes your success [or lack of success] in following the agenda.

(d) Analyzes your efforts at facilitation in terms of minimizing conflicts among members, facilitating consensus, and achieving your goal for the meeting.

3. Conduct an analysis of a coalition or collaborative group. Sources of data can include the coalition's web site, brochures, reports, newspaper, and other media accounts and interviews with members of the coalition, community members or public officials knowledgeable about or influenced by the coalition. You can also interview people who actively oppose the work of the coalition (opponents). Also observe at least board meeting or public forum sponsored by the coalition. In your analysis, describe the group's mission, membership requirements, governance structure, and funding sources. Also, assess the degree to which members make decisions through consensus or conflict and identify any procedures used to establish trust or build solidarity among members. In the final section of your paper, address whether, in your opinion, the coalition has been able to achieve any of the process- or task-oriented outcomes identified in Figure 4.1 and describe any barriers that may have prevented achievement.

5

Using Dialogue, Story-Telling, and Structured Group Work Techniques to Identify Community Problems

> *Principally, when one talks about organizing, well, we are talking about individuals, each individual has [his or her] own vision on things. Then if one wants to accomplish and if one wants to be successful in whatever action that one heads or wants to get done, the best thing is to have consensus or dialogue. [The] interchange of points of view . . . helps [us] to understand the problem in its totality.*
> —Interview with an immigrant rights organizer, Hardina et al., 2011

Problem identification is typically the first stage of the engagement process in community organizing, after the initial recruitment of individual and organizational members. In this chapter, a description of how dialogue among group members is used to identify the problems or issues to be addressed in the organizing effort is provided. A number of specific techniques used for conducting group dialogues and identifying common problems are examined including story-telling, community forums, nominal group technique, focus group interviews, and study circles. In the last section of this chapter, specific practice skills used to engage participants in the dialogue process and to facilitate the development of a critical consciousness about the origin of social problems are discussed.

THE PURPOSE OF GROUP DIALOGUE

After people and organizations are recruited for the organizing effort, they must begin to identify community problems. Since participants in the organizing effort are often a diverse group of people with different backgrounds, values, and perceptions, reaching agreement about the problem or problems to be addressed in the organizing effort is essential. Although organizers will have already conducted one-on-one interviews and interacted with numerous people who may have strong views about community issues, bringing individuals and organization representatives together to engage in dialogue about problems they face is an important "next step" in the organizing process.

These group discussions can take many forms and may include group meetings, focus groups, and community forums. They can be informal or highly structured. Although often there is a designated facilitator (most often a community organizer or community leader), the purpose of these discussions is to encourage face-to-face interaction and solicit diverse view points, hence the term used to describe this process is called "group dialogue." McCoy and Scully (2002) use two different terms to describe public discussions on social problems: dialogue and deliberation. Dialogue brings people together "to listen to and understand the other" (p. 117), while deliberation involves the use of group processes to apply critical thinking skills to problem resolution and the development of policy alternatives. Most importantly dialogue helps organizers and participants develop a collective or common understanding of an issue to be addressed in the organizing effort. It is used to find a common link among problems faced by individuals and groups and a particular "cause," institutional arrangement, policy or practice that is sustaining or making the problem worse (Hardina, 2002). For example, people living in a community in which residents have lost jobs, small businesses have closed, the suicide rate has increased and families have moved out may perceive there to be a common origin for these problems such as employee layoffs from a nearby manufacturing plant.

The process of dialogue is congruent with the preliminary phases of social work practice with individuals and families. Miley et al. (2011) identify three primary activities for the generalist practitioner during the dialogue process: building relationships with service users, validating the experiences of the service user, and identifying a preliminary purpose for the worker–service user relationship. Such problem identification helps motivate the service user to take action and guides the search for resources needed to resolve the problem. Other social work skills needed for this process include recognition of service user or constituent strengths, conveying respect for individual participants and their cultural values, recognizing and working through differences, active listening, and group work skills that are used to minimize differences among participants and develop a consensus about the problems and issues that affect them (Gutierrez et al., 2005).

USING GROUP DIALOGUE TO IDENTIFY AND SOLVE PROBLEMS

One of the primary frameworks used by social workers to make decisions is the problem-solving model. It is generally considered a component of generalist social work practice because it can be used to develop interventions across systems: individuals, groups, families, organizations, and communities (Kirst-Ashman & Hull, 2008; Poulin, 2010). This approach, also called the rational model is also used as one of the primary decision-making frameworks by organizers, planners, and policy-makers. The basic assumption inherent in this model is that experts have the time, knowledge, professional expertise, and resources to make objective decisions based on available information and logic (Netting et al., 2008). It is also assumed that the decision-maker (social worker, policy analyst, organizer, or planner) has the critical thinking skills necessary to make the best decision. Kirst-Ashman and Hull (2009) define critical thinking as "the questioning of beliefs, statements, assumptions, lines of reasoning, actions, and experiences" as well as "the creative formulation of an opinion or conclusion when presented with a question, problem, or issue" (p. 27).

The problem-solving model typically consists of five stages: problem identification, assessment, goal setting or planning, intervention or implementation, and evaluation. Some versions of this model also include a termination phase and a feedback loop that involves modification of the original plan if it has not resulted in a successful outcome (Kirst-Ashman & Hull, 2009).

The use of the rational or problem-solving model has some important limitations, however. One of the primary criticisms of this approach is that decision-makers seldom actually have the time or resources to carefully weigh all possible alternatives to a specific plan (Rothman & Zald, 2008). Many decisions are made in the political process, based on a number of criteria including who actually benefits from the decision and the amount of influence possessed by interest groups and campaign donors. Also, in many circumstances, the social values of the decision-maker have an important role in any policy or planning recommendation made. For example, should low-income people be the first to benefit from any policy or plan, should benefits be distributed equally among everyone, or should government provide minimal or no benefits to people in need? Community organizers, social policy makers, and planners often use decision-making models that make such value assumptions explicit (Forester, 1999; Larkin, 2004). Most organizers also have explicit values and ideological perspectives on how social benefits should be distributed (Mondros & Wilson, 1994). Consequently, many decisions typically made by organizers will be guided by values and will not be entirely objective or value free.

In addition to concerns about values that guide decision-making, most planners and community organizers argue that it is often not only their responsibility to make most organizing decisions (Reisch & Lowe, 2000). Colleagues, employers, board members, organization partners, beneficiaries of the action, and constituents must often be consulted or actively involved in the decision. Community organizers, planners, and policy analysts use a number of decision frameworks that guide or are used to examine how and when people are involved in making public decisions. These models include incremental (decisions are made through negotiation among political interest groups), advocacy (the planner represents the interests of one's employer), and transformative planning (Davidoff, 1973; Lindblom, 1959). The transformative approach draws heavily on the work of Paulo Freire (1970) and assumes that planning decisions should be made through dialogue and discussion between a professional or expert (planner, organizer, social worker, etc.) and constituents. In this conceptualization, the people who will benefit from the plan are actively involved in problem identification, assessment, goal setting, implementation, and evaluation (Friedmann, 1987; Kennedy, 2009). The radical planning model is also used by some community organizers, primarily to understand and critique how social and political institutions function to marginalize members of some groups and to benefit others.

In addition to these classic approaches, Netting et al. (2008) advocate the use of an alternative to the rational model, interpretive planning which is consistent with the transformative approach and allows for the incorporation of values and the perceptions and experience of individual participants in the decision-making process. These stakeholders include people who will benefit from the plan. Problem identification, assessment, data collection strategies, and goals emerge through the inclusion of constituents and other interested parties in the planning process and dialogue among participants. The decision-making process is characterized by relationship-building, compromise, and consensus and reliance on multiple sources of data. Planning is cyclical in nature; a plan may go through several phases, and can be modified during implementation based on new information about what works and what does not. Consequently, this method contains an expectation that the parties involved sustain the dialogue and engage in ongoing learning about the problem at hand and strategies used to address it.

There is one other important way in which problem-solving in community organizing differs from generalist practice. Barretti (2009) notes that the various steps in the problem-solving model used by social workers are viewed as linear (i.e., the previous step must be completed before the next step is contemplated). However, in community practice, the process is multilayered, with many of these problem-solving activities happening simultaneously or reoccurring periodically during an organizing campaign based on situational demands and group preferences:

> In organizing, the definition of the problem is a negotiated, shared process between organizers and clients that is continually in flux, and it takes substantially longer than the initial assessment phase in psychotherapy. In organizing, it is not unusual for the intervention to precede the definition of the problem, though the tenants and the organizer might initially agree on the basic concrete problematic realities that brought them together; for example, it's bitterly cold outside and they have no heat or hot water. (Barretti, 2009, p. 12)

Consequently, while there are some types of operational decisions (such as finding a location for a meeting or what individuals to recruit for participation in an organizing campaign) that may be made by a single organizer, most often decisions in community practice are made in the context of a group process. However, it is the responsibility of the organizer to help constituents define the problem and develop an understanding or "critical consciousness" about the role of social structure and power relations in the origins of the problem or barriers that must be overcome to successfully resolve the problem (Barretti, 2009). This discussion or dialogue is interactive with both the organizer and members of the constituency group or decision-makers taking part in the process. It is based on the premise, derived from social constructionism and popular education that problems affecting individuals, groups, families, and communities are socially constructed and should be identified and examined using criteria that includes the perceptions, experiences, and values of the participants.

According to McCoy and Scully (2002) there are two issues that need to be addressed before initiating a dialogue for examining problems: how to bring people into the process and how to structure the meeting or "public conversation" in which the dialogue will take place. Several techniques used to facilitate bringing people together to identify and resolve problems include story-telling, community forums, nominal group technique, focus groups, and study circles. Some of these methods are used to identify injustices that will require putting pressure on or confronting authorities; others are intended to foster cooperative methods for problem resolution, while a number of techniques can be utilized for either purpose (Hardina, 2002; Schatz, Furman, & Jenkins, 2003). Regardless of how these dialogues are structured, they are often preliminary to planned organizing campaigns; group discussions will take place at numerous points in time while action is planned, carried out, and evaluated. Initial meetings may be limited to problem identification or may include content on problem assessment and goal setting as well.

USING GROUP STORY-TELLING TO IDENTIFY PROBLEMS AND BUILD GROUP SOLIDARITY

Often when people are approached about joining a community organization or social change efforts they respond by telling a story about how they were personally affected by a social issue or problem. These stories are shared with other group members and sometimes with the media, the general public, and elected officials. Consequently, one technique that has gained national prominence through its use by the 2008 Obama Presidential campaign involves story-telling. This technique involves bringing a group of people together in a small group at the beginning of an organizing campaign to discuss their connection to the problem or issue at hand and to begin the process of "getting to know" one another, to exchange information and resources, and to initiate the development of a cohesive group or organization (Stirland, 2008).

Marshall Ganz (2001), a former organizing director for the United Farmworkers during the 1960s and 1970s, currently a Harvard professor and the chief organizing architect of the Obama campaign, views story-telling as a mechanism to inspire and motivate volunteers. According to Ganz, the process of story-telling has a number of essential components including a frame for understanding social problems, a mechanism for placing the story-telling in the context of someone who can make change happen, moral values, goals for what the story-teller hopes to achieve, a description of any barriers encountered when trying to resolve individual and social problems, and a sense of collective identity, derived from the story-teller's community, family, and culture. He also describes how story-telling is used in an organizing context:

> Arguably the most critical elements in telling a new story are the identities of storytellers and listeners. The identity of a storyteller gives credibility to the story, linking her with her listeners in a common journey. Social movements tell a new story. In this way they acquire leadership, gain adherents, and develop a capability of mobilizing needed resources to

achieve success. Social movements are not merely reconfi-
gured networks and redeployed resources. They are new
stories of who their participants hope to become. (Ganz,
2001; Conclusions section, para 1)

In addition to recruitment and motivation, story-telling can also be a
mechanism for empowering members of marginalized communities.
Rappaport (1995) describes the use of story-telling in community work
in the following way:

For many people, particularly those who lack social, political,
or economic power, the community, neighborhood, or cultural
narratives that are available are either negative, narrow,
"written" by others for them, or all of the above. People who
seek either personal or community change often find that it
is very difficult to sustain change without the support of a
collectivity that provides a new communal narrative around
which they can sustain changes in their own personal story.
Associated with such narratives are cognitive, emotional and
behavioral consequences that involve social support, role
opportunities, new identities, and possible selves. (p. 796)

According to Foster-Fishman, Nowell, Deacon, Nievar, and McCann
(2005), research on story-telling and its use in community practice is
designed to provide a vehicle for understanding the perceptions of
meaning that people have about their own lives. More specifically, story-
telling allows members of marginalized groups to describe their experiences, especially those that involve marginalization or stigmatization
by the larger society (Williams, LaBonte, & O'Brien, 2003). It also provides
an opportunity for members of these groups to challenge the way in
which the dominant culture describes or tells stories about marginalized
peoples; often these accounts are not accurate descriptions of the experiences of people from nondominant groups. Consequently, story-telling
by people who have traditionally been excluded allows them to assert
their identities and makes their perceptions and experiences known,
especially when they engage in social action to fight injustice.

Little and Froggett (2009) attribute a number of personal and community benefits involved in telling one's own story including bonding
with listeners and others who share the story or who have similar
stories and the transmission of cultural values and traditions. This in
turn drives the development of a complex narrative that contains numerous depictions (both good and bad) about the motivations and actions of

community members. Little and Froggett also describe the contents of a typical story:

> The narrative involves the protagonist engaging in a sustained period of effort which results in significant and what are often portrayed as life-changing rewards. After the period of struggle, the hero is almost unquestioningly depicted as feeling and being better. Emotional experience is, therefore, split into a before and an after. There is a teleological [purposeful] element to this narrative, an implicit sense that personal struggle will result in meaningful benefits, indeed morally just rewards. (p. 459)

The process of using story-telling for problem identification requires face-to-face dialogue guided by a skilled facilitator. Su (2009) describes the use of the story-telling process in community-based organizations as consisting of specific types of content. Typically, group members are given a series of exercises that focus on collective goals or analysis of issues. People are asked to explain how they are personally affected by an issue, but the expectation is that the exercises will not serve to exclude participants, but that all group members will be able to identify some connection to the problem or situation under discussion. Although common patterns may emerge in the stories, individual experiences may differ, making the group's common understanding of the issue or problem more complex. According to Su, disadvantages of the story-telling process are that meeting space, time, and extensive face-to-face contact is needed to facilitate these activities. In addition, while the method is often effective in producing an understanding of the perspectives of diverse community members who have actually experienced the problem, it may not result in concrete policy proposals for addressing the issue.

Story-telling also becomes a mechanism for motivating people to join the cause and take action, especially in circumstances in which resolving a problem, taking a stand, or accomplishing a goal has been achieved by an individual, group, or organization. The actual narrative of the story may be restructured or shaped in a manner that best promotes the cause or provides a moral or meaning for the general public. For example, Polletta (2006) describes how the story of Rosa Parks' refusal to move to the back of the bus in Montgomery, Alabama in 1955 is not entirely factual. Rather than making a spontaneous decision to risk arrest, Parks' action had actually been extensively planned by a group of activists in response to a previous arrest of a passenger on a segregated bus (Box 5.1).

BOX 5.1 TELLING YOUR STORY

Alicia Martinez, an organizer for the West Neighborhood Organization, has asked a former constituent, Mrs Amelia Jackson to describe the successful advocacy campaign that Mrs Jackson and her neighbors carried out to prevent the location of a new school across from a meat rending plant.

Mrs Jackson: All three of my oldest children have asthma. My youngest boy Rashid had to repeat third grade because he missed so many days of school last year due to asthma attacks. My two oldest children, Martin and Rosa also have had low grades due to their asthma. I was worried that my children would only become sicker if they were transferred to the new elementary school if it was built near the meat rendering plant.

So with Alicia's help, my neighbors and I want to the school board meeting to protest. Those school board members, they were mean. They wouldn't let us talk—said we only had two minutes to make our case. Then they adjourned the meeting without making a decision. That got us really mad. So before the next meeting we held a press conference and gave the media all our statistics about the asthma rate in our neighborhood, especially all the data about how the asthma rate was highest near the meat rendering plant. The newspaper, they wrote an editorial about the problem, said the school should be in a better location. We also had at least 100 supporters at the next school board meeting—we picketed the meeting with our signs and the TV stations came out and covered what we were doing. And you know, the school board voted that night to move the new school to a different location.

COMMUNITY FORUMS

Community forums are large meetings, typically held at the beginning of the organizing process to examine community issues and set priorities for organizing campaigns. The goal of forums is generally to identify issues facing communities and setting priorities for addressing these issues. A wide segment of the community and people with diverse viewpoints are generally invited to attend for the purpose of establishing a core group of volunteers to set the direction for the organizing process, and recruit others for participation. Forums also offer a good opportunity for organizers to conduct additional one-on-one or follow-up interviews to deepen relationships with potential volunteers, solicit information, and ask people to contribute time, money, and other resources for the organizing effort.

Generally, the forum is led by one or more facilitators or a steering committees and a previously determined structure is used to solicit input from the public. A number of issues need to be addressed in the planning process:

- What is the purpose of the event?
- What is the primary goal? What does the group hope to accomplish?
- What time and location will permit the largest number and best mix of people to attend?
- What size facility is needed and what equipment (such as seating, tables, or kitchen facilities) should it contain?
- What is the agenda for the event? How will the forum be structured?
- Who will be invited to attend and how will they be recruited or informed about the event?
- Are there any ground rules that should be set for participants? Some examples of ground rules are that participants are expected to be civil to one another, that they refrain from interrupting speakers, or that each speaker in the audience comply with a time limit for their questions and comments.
- Who has the skills, the leadership abilities, and reputation in the community to serve as a facilitator for the meeting?
- Should other speakers be invited to make presentations and what format should be used (e.g., should individuals speak or should there be a panel discussion? Should one or a variety of views of the issue be presented)?
- Is a budget needed for the event or can resources such as meeting space and printing be solicited from donors? If money is needed to pay for the event, how will these funds be obtained?
- What printed information about the topic or issue under discussion should be distributed?
- Will a sign-in or registration table be used to obtain names and contact information for participants? If not, how will organizers determine who attended?
- What other resources are needed to make sure the forum runs smoothly such as food, transportation, baby-sitting, and security?
- Will the media be contacted and asked to attend?
- Will public officials be contacted and asked to attend? If so, what type of help, assistance, or commitment should be requested from these officials?
- What type of help, assistance, or commitment should be requested from participants and how will commitment be determined or

verified? (Lukas & Hoskins, 2003; Results, 2005; Work Group for Community Health and Development, 2010).

Agreeing beforehand on a structure for the forum is essential. The purpose of the forum and what the organizing group hopes to accomplish is the most critical decision that should be made in relation to a forum (Lukas & Hoskins, 2003). Is the purpose to identify a problem or issue or does the group already know or have a general idea about the organizing campaign, community development activity, or social planning process that they want to carry out? Are there several options being considered for the organizing effort and is the intent to reach a consensus about the problem or issue to be addressed? Will a variety of groups be asked to give their input into the matter under discussion or will only people with specific views be invited to attend (Hardina, 2002). Is the intent of the forum just to consult or inform the community about the planned activity or to solicit support for a cause? (Arnstein, 1969; Sager, 2008).

Community forums are generally a good way to mobilize support for an issue, but they could also result in the presence of skeptics or opponents. If the forum results in compromise, consensus, neutralization of opposing viewpoints, or recognition or respect for people with different views, the results may be considered positive. However, forums may also be easily disrupted to the degree that speakers are repeatedly interrupted, discussion breaks down, and conflict erupts. Consequently, it is often necessary to plan forums carefully with a pre-determined structure and an agenda. Speakers may be recruited in advance and some groups may be deliberately invited or excluded. However, exclusion conflicts with the purpose of deliberative democracy and social work principles of self-determination and empowerment. Therefore, organizers need to think carefully before planning an agenda, setting a goal for the forum, and recruiting participants (Lukas & Hoskins, 2003). They also need to consult with potential participants, constituency group members, and prospective speakers in planning the event; cultural competency may be an issue in several aspects of the event such as the selection of community representatives, appropriate greetings and introductions, the venue in which the event takes place, the food served, and the language used or the translation services provided.

Another issue to be addressed during the planning stage is whether the structure of the forum should be open and free-flowing. An example of a relatively unstructured forum would be one in which a facilitator introduces a topic, but the agenda allows for unlimited participation, perhaps in the form of making an open microphone available to all audience members who wish to speak. An alternative structure might involve inviting speakers who represent diverse viewpoints on an issue who present their opinions as part of a panel discussion. Audience members are given a pre-determined amount of time to respond to these viewpoints and make suggestions. A third option might be simply to invite speakers and guests who represent a limited number of viewpoints that are consistent with the agenda or goals of the group sponsoring the forum, with the goal for the forum to be simply to mobilize supporters around a specific issue (Box 5.2).

Other options for structuring forums are to ask attendees to participate in small group discussions in order to identify issues that should be addressed and report back to the larger group or to limit individual input by restricting how people are recognized to speak, requiring that people ask to be placed on the agenda in advance, or limiting the amount of time that audience members may speak or ask questions. Typically, such restrictions are put in place to limit participation, minimize disruption, or exclude potential opponents.

In meetings in which some structure is deemed essential or preferable, but individual input is desired, the small group process is used. Group decision-making teams are established and asked to give input. In some instances, small groups may be asked to give consideration about how a specific issue or topic should be handled. In these "brainstorming" groups, participants are instructed to "think big" or come up with the best or most innovative ideas. The advantages of brainstorming is that it potentially gives all group members the chance to be involved or creative, it can be fun, and it produces a variety of ideas (Zastrow, 2009). Some of the disadvantages are that without structure or a skilled facilitator in the group, one person can dominate the discussion or group members can be without direction or specific opinions on topics that they may know little about. Alternatively, these groups can be structured in a way that provides a clear direction and goals. One such decision-making approach typically used is nominal group technique.

NOMINAL GROUP TECHNIQUE

Nominal Group Technique is a process used to engage a diverse group of people in the process of setting priorities among a variety of community issues that may affect participants. As with the other methods discussed in this chapter, it is used to obtain information on the perspectives and experiences of community members and in so doing, identify aspects

BOX 5.2 SAMPLE COMPONENTS OF A COMMUNITY FORUM

1. A community leader convenes the meeting by describing its purpose and introduces the facilitator and one's credentials for facilitating the meeting.
2. The facilitator describes the goals for the meeting and the intended outcome. A description of the agenda is provided and ground rules are identified.
3. One or more community leaders, experts, or people who have experienced the problem or issue are asked to make presentations or participate in a panel discussion about the community or a specific issue to be discussed.
4. Participants are given the opportunity to ask questions about the issues at hand.
5. Participants are assigned to or are asked to join breakout groups that will engage in brain-storming or a more structured type of dialogue about a specific issue, community problem, or community resources and assets.
6. Each group has a facilitator and/or recorder who will report back to the larger group with their recommendations about problems or issues to be addressed, resources that should be used to remedy the problem or actions that should be taken.
7. The facilitator guides the group in a discussion or structured decision-making process to choose priorities or develop a plan. If appropriate and time allows, the facilitator leads the group in an assessment of the issue, goal-setting, and planning for future action.
8. The meeting concludes. Volunteers are recruited and asked to complete a volunteer card. Dates and times are set for follow-up meetings and other activities.
9. Volunteers are asked to complete a short evaluation form to assess how they felt about the meeting, the process used to conduct the meeting, and the outcome achieved.

Note: Forum agendas vary depending on the purpose of the event and the amount of time allocated to hold the forum.

of the problem that may affect a large proportion of community residents and establish a common or joint approach for addressing the issue. The process is generally guided by a skilled facilitator. While this process is typically used in a large group setting, at least in the first stages of the process, there is limited interaction among group members (Zastrow,

2009). Instead, the facilitator poses a general question to the participants about their perceptions of their own needs, community issues, or about how programs, policies, or services could be improved. Each participant is asked to write down one to three ideas related to the topic and to give a verbal report about these items to the other participants. These items are then written down on a blackboard, a flip chart, or a large piece of butcher block paper by the facilitator or assistant.

It is anticipated that some members of the audience will list the same item; rather than writing this down again, the facilitator indicates on the board the number of people that have listed this specific item. The facilitator might choose to identify common themes among these items or suggest grouping these items together (Hardina, 2002). Three to five of the top issues chosen are identified as potential issues or problems to be addressed by the group or organization. After this first set of rankings is completed, time is allowed for discussion. If no consensus choice for a potential campaign or plan is evident, the facilitator then asks participants to assign a ranking to these top choices. For example, if three items are selected as possible priorities, each participant is asked to assign a "1" to one's first choice, a "2" to one's second choice, and so on. Based on these rankings, a mathematical calculation (averaging individual rankings of each item) is made to determine which of the final choices has the highest score. This issue is then selected as the priority for the group with the expectation that an action might be taken. The group has the option of scheduling another meeting, developing a plan to research the issue further, or to start planning some action to be taken to address the issue. As discussed earlier in this chapter, the facilitator could also lead the group in a discussion of each of the steps in the problem-solving process before the meeting concludes: a brief analysis of the issue, goal setting, and a plan for meeting the goal (Toseland & Rivas, 2008).

According to Zastrow (2009), the advantages of this method are that it is often not time consuming, the lack of interaction among members during the problem identification phase ensures that everyone generates their own ideas and that participation is not limited to people who are the most vocal. This technique also has the advantage of soliciting a variety of differing viewpoints including some new ideas or innovative proposals. Limitations of nominal group technique include that there may not be a great deal of thought or discussion on the various options presented or a clear rationale for adopting some or rejecting others; it is also possible that group members that may talk more or have more power and status than others may dominate the process (Toseland & Rivas, 2008).

FOCUS GROUPS

Focus groups are group interviews. Participants include a facilitator and generally six to 10 participants. These groups are used to obtain detailed information about a product, social phenomena, or program, gauge people's reactions, and obtain information that could not be collected through an individual survey or interviews (Zastrow, 2009). Focus groups have their origins in the world of advertisement, as a tool for businesses to test products and how they are viewed by the public (Toseland & Rivas, 2008). Focus groups are used extensively in political campaigns as candidates and office holders seek a means to test out campaign slogans, agendas, or public perceptions or support for specific policies.

Focus groups interviews may take place as stand-alone or as a component of a community forum designed to solicit community input. These group interviews have a unique structure and format. Typically, the facilitator poses a small number of open-ended questions (about six to eight) to respondents (Royse, Thyer, & Padgett, 2010). Participants answer these questions based on their own perceptions and experiences and it is expected that the group process and interaction among members will provide more detail or descriptive information about how the group perceives the issue or topic in question. Interviewers can also use probes, ask for clarification, and summarize the main points made by respondents in order to solicit more information from the participants. Designed to collect data on a common or typical view, the process works because group members not only react to the facilitator, they also react to one another, agreeing, disagreeing, or building upon comments made by other members (Berg, 2009). The process can result in identifying common needs, perceptions, or concerns about a particular issue or a clear delineation of diverse view points (Royse et al., 2010; Toseland & Rivas, 2008) (Box 5.3).

In social work, focus groups are typically used to gain information about people's perceptions about their experiences, a particular event or phenomena, or perceptions and experiences related to a specific program or policy. The data collected can be used to develop hypotheses or supplement other types of research. Focus groups are also used to understand or evaluate how specific interventions or programs work (Berg, 2009; Linhorst, 2002). Specifically, in community organizing, development, and social planning, focus groups are typically used to see how people perceive or experience life in their communities or the impact of a program or policy. In addition, focus groups can be used as a component of a community assessment to understand how people experience

BOX 5.3   SAMPLE FOCUS GROUP QUESTIONS

Please describe a typical day in your neighborhood.

Describe some of the advantages of living in your neighborhood.
Describe some of the disadvantages of living in your neighborhood.
How do you and your neighbors typically interact with one another?
Can you describe the best thing about your neighborhood?
Can you describe the worst thing about your neighborhood?
What do you think could be done to improve your neighborhood?
How can you and your neighbors work together to improve your neighborhood?

Note: Focus group questions should be open-ended. Probes and statements soliciting clarification or more details should be used to obtain detailed information from participants.

a problem and how they perceive its root causes. Focus groups can also be used to examine the cultural context of critical community issues and to generate ideas for addressing them. For example, Affonso et al. (2010) conducted focus groups with teachers, parents, school children, and community leaders to examine youth violence in rural Hawaiian communities. They found that participants attributed school violence to the lack of local resources such as social services and transportation, inadequate role modeling by adults, and a diminished connection to traditional cultural values. Respondents felt that one approach for resolving these problems should involve joint efforts by schools and the local community to integrate cultural values and practices into services for young people (Box 5.4).

Other than surveys or formal interviews with individuals, focus groups are probably the problem-identification tool that is the most consistent with formal research studies. Consequently, the use of this group interview format requires that attention be paid to the same ethical considerations as in other types of qualitative research. Respondents should be fully informed about the purpose of the study, they should also be assured that their confidentiality will be protected, and that nothing they say will affect their later participation in programs or services (Linhorst, 2002). Participants should be asked to sign a consent form and asked for permission to tape the interview. However, as Berg (2009) points out, the confidentiality agreement includes a pledge on the part of members to disclose no information discussed in the group during the interview. Invitations to participate in the interview also have ethical implications. Effort should be made to make sure that people are not put at risk by including them in a focus group that includes someone in authority (such as an employer or public official) who could retaliate against them for negative comments (Royse et al., 2010). Participants should also be assured that they can withdraw from the group at any time (Berg, 2009). As in other types of qualitative research, if responses are to be written up in a formal report, the "real" names of participants should not be used without their permission.

According to Linhorst (2002), there are several benefits of participation in focus groups including obtaining information and support about an issue or problem that other people in the group may also be experiencing and feelings of empowerment or ownership associated with being part of a social change process. Other benefits include the

BOX 5.4   SAMPLE FOCUS GROUP DIALOGUE

Facilitator: Hello, my name is Alicia and I'd like to thank you for taking the time out of your busy schedules today to tell me about your neighborhood. (Alicia explains how participant confidentiality will be protected and distributes a consent form to respondents and waits for it to be returned.) Thank you so much. I'd like to start by asking you to describe a typical day in your neighborhood.

Mrs Jackson: My day starts when I need to get up early to get my kids to school. Since they all have problems with asthma, I need to make sure that they have their inhalers as well as their lunches before they leave. Since there is a lot of crime in the neighborhood, I need to walk them to school. My oldest kids hate that.

Mr Smith: I really don't think there is a lot of crime in this neighborhood. As far as I'm concerned the police do a really good job here.

Mrs Flores: I agree that the neighborhood is safe, but I sure don't like all the pollution. It's particularly bad on days in which the meat rendering plant is in operation. The smell is so bad I don't want my kids to play outside and my mother who is in her 80's can't sit outside on the porch.

Mrs Lee: I think that's my biggest concern about the neighborhood. People aren't outside a lot. I think I would feel much better about the neighborhood if I actually saw people on the street who could keep an eye out for the kids going to and from school.

Facilitator: So is that a concern—that the air quality keeps people inside and that causes other types of problems?

low cost, the limited time needed to conduct the interview, and flexibility in how the group is conducted (Berg, 2009). It is even possible to conduct a focus group using blogs, discussion boards, and other Internet technology, although such formats eliminate the opportunity for the facilitator to observe facial expressions and body language that can help the researcher to interpret responses.

There are several negative impacts of participation. For example, there is a chance that people could receive misinformation through group participation or feel disempowered by reliving difficult or stressful circumstances (Linhorst, 2002). Toseland and Rivas (2008) also identify a number of other benefits including positive impact of group member interaction in generating creative or insightful ideas and perceptions and the collection of very detailed information that is not available from any other source.

Other disadvantages of focus groups include difficulties in identifying and recruiting a representative group of people for participation in the focus group, domination of the group process by a few members, problems regarding confidentiality if sensitive topics are discussed and the time needed to administer the interview (one to two hours) and analyze fairly detailed open-ended data (Linhorst, 2002; Toseland & Rivas, 2008).

STUDY CIRCLES

Study circles are a process of deliberative dialogue in which people agree to come together to discuss a public issue (Wilson et al., 2010). As discussed earlier in this chapter, dialogue is generally used in small groups to study issues, share diverse viewpoints, and build trust. It can ultimately lead to collective action. Deliberation, on the other hand, involves the examination of public issues by looking at different options for problem resolution and weighing the benefits and costs of each. The purpose of public deliberation is to increase the likelihood that public policy will be made through shared decision-making rather than conflict (National Center for Dialogue and Deliberation, n.d.).

Study circles typically consist of 10–15 members and generally participants consist of a diverse group of community members. Study circles take place over a number of weeks or months. In some instances, the process involves larger groups of people from a neighborhood, city, or region that break off into smaller groups for discussion. Group members are expected to examine diverse viewpoints on specific issues, find common ground, share stories about their personal connections to issues, and take action to address the social problems identified in their discussions

(Everyday Democracy, 1997; Co-Intelligence Center, n.d.). The purpose of these groups is to increase democratic participation, promote social networking and relationship-building across social differences, and increase civic participation and the ability of communities to make the complex decisions necessary to address the social issues that affect their lives (McCoy & Scully, 2002; National Center for Dialogue and Deliberation, n.d.). This method is explicitly set up with the purpose of minimizing partisan conflict and working in a collaborative manner to resolve problems; it also is intended to change individual belief systems through rational discourse, acceptance, and understanding (Schatz et al., 2003).

According to McCoy and Sully (2002), study circles emphasize both the presentation of diverse view points and the importance of really listening to others. These group discussions address some of the same issues and frame them the same way as other types of community dialogue: how are individuals and the community affected by the problem and what are the causes of the problem? The National Center for Dialogue and Deliberation (Heierbacher, n.d.) also describes the study circles as a vehicle for collective action. Participants share the findings with the general public and policy-makers and then take action to ensure that the solutions they have proposed are adopted.

Group facilitators are not professionals, but receive training in order to help members have productive discussions and work together collaboratively. Everyday Democracy (1997—formerly the Study Circle Resource Center) provides the following guidelines for facilitating study circles. The facilitator should take the following actions:

- Become familiar with the goals of the study circle and the topic under discussion.
- Prepare a set of questions to guide the discussion in advance.
- Create a relaxed and open group atmosphere.
- Assist the group in developing ground rules for participation that permit everyone to have their views heard and respected. Confidentiality should be maintained in the event that people contribute personal stories.
- Guide, but not lead the discussion. Intervention may be needed to ensure that people address one another directly and discuss, but not debate, the issues.
- Ensure that a variety of views are heard, help participants weigh alternative options, and articulate values associated with their beliefs.
- Ask open-ended questions to keep the group moving, including questions such as asking participants to clarify their main points or identify areas of disagreement.

- Help participants reach common ground, but understand that a consensus is not always achievable.
- Summarize the main points made during the discussion.
- Wrap up the meeting by asking for last comments and asking participants what they have learned. Have participants evaluate the session, either verbally or by responding to a written survey.

It is expected that the discussion in study circles will be structured in such a way that conflict will be kept to a minimum and the focus will be on ensuring the participation of all group members. One type of study circle that has gained national prominence in the last several years is called "intergroup dialogue." Dessel, Rogge, and Garlington (2006) describe the intergroup process as a community effort to provide a safe place to for people to express anger and talk about injustice. However, according to Nagda and Zuniga (2003), the purpose and outcome of these public conversations should be more clearly delineated. The dialogue process consists of "an intentional, sustained, and reciprocal processes of group interaction to examine ways in which group differences are situations in systems of oppression and privilege, and to explore ways to challenge the effects of such systems on intergroup relationships" (p. 113). Consequently, the primary purpose of these groups is to address cultural differences and other community and social issues that are divisive.

Intergroup dialogues are designed to minimize conflict, promote feelings of respect and understanding, and create strong bonds, and trusting relationships among participants. These groups are often intended to address ethnic, religious, and racial differences or conflicts. Wayne (2008) describes how intergroup dialogue is expected to work:

> Practitioners lead dialogues and encourage involvement, promising participants increased understanding of, knowledge about, and comfort with those different from themselves. They will develop better relationships, resolve conflicts, and work toward building fairer and more inclusive communities. (p. 451)

Nagda and Zuniga (2003) identify three components of the dialogue process that are similar to group dialogue techniques described earlier in this chapter:

- Participants become aware of their own biases and the role of social structure and oppression in shaping prejudice and group conflict.

* Participants share stories about their racial, ethnic, or cultural identifies, experiences related to discrimination, and their own perceptions about others. This process is intended to help participants develop empathy for one another.
* Members build relationships with one another that can be used to minimize conflict and take joint action across oppressive systems.

Wayne (2008) identifies three different types of outcomes commonly associated with intergroup dialogue: knowledge, attitudes, and behavior. Members gain knowledge about one another, change their attitudes and adopt more positive attitudes toward individuals and groups different from themselves, and decrease negative attitudes. The changes in both knowledge and attitude ultimately lead to behavioral changes as well, increasing positive interaction with members of groups that the participants perceive as "different from them."

Research studies have confirmed positive, although somewhat limited, results from intergroup dialogues. For example, Wilson et al. (2010) conducted an evaluation of a study circle that involved primarily low-income African-American women but that also included a diverse group of women from other ethnic groups and income levels with the intention of providing social support and building community. They found that participants in the study circle felt that group membership increased feelings of personal empowerment and self-efficacy and helped participants establish strong bonds with one another. Participation in the group also increased access to resources, knowledge, and policy-makers for the core group of low-income women. Wayne (2008) conducted an evaluation of an intergroup dialogue process that brought together Jewish and African-American high-school students. The program contained several components including cultural education, summer tours of important historical sites associated with both ethnic groups, and leadership development. The evaluation documented both behavioral and attitudinal changes, but researchers concluded that success was dependent upon the degree to which participants formed strong relationship bonds with other group members. In a similar evaluation of an intergroup dialogue process among a diverse group of university students, Nagda and Zuniga (2003) found an increase in racial identity among participants, but no differences were found in communication patterns among group members or relationship-building.

According to Dessel et al. (2006), one of the primary barriers to the success of these groups is unequal power relationship among participants, members of dominant groups often are eager to establish relationships with other members. However, members of marginalized populations are more likely to prefer taking action rather than talking despite the reluctance of other group members. In addition, the use of the dominant group's language or technical terms may be the prevailing method of discourse in the group and serve to alienate some members. As noted by Gutierrez et al. (2005), study circles or intergroup dialogues cannot be considered successful unless they fulfill two goals: creating strong bonds and understanding among members and taking action to achieve social change. They suggest that successful outcomes can be facilitated by using a combination of short- and long-term change strategies. Short-term strategies include encouraging study circle participants to get involved with established community groups and begin to advocate for changes in government policies. Action guides can also be developed for use by community volunteers. Long-term strategies include the formation of task groups and permanent organization structures to put group recommendations for change into action.

PUTTING VALUES IN ACTION: THE DEVELOPMENT OF CRITICAL CONSCIOUSNESS

In the context of most community organizing work, group dialogue to identify community problems is the first step in the development of a critical consciousness. In *Pedagogy of the Oppressed*, Freire (1970) describes the purpose and goal associated with this process among members of marginalized populations:

> To surmount the situation of oppression people must first critically recognize its causes, so that through transforming action they can create a new situation, one which makes possible the pursuit of a fuller humanity. But the struggle to be more fully human has already begun in the authentic struggle to transform the situation. (p. 29)

Hence, the basic premise of Freire's work is that informal knowledge is as important as formalized knowledge. However, formal knowledge is controlled by elites and the political establishment. Consequently, knowledge and knowledge acquisition are sources of power that can and should be acquired by members of marginalized groups.

Basic principles associated with Freire's (1970) conceptualization of popular education are inherent in the process of using group methods to identify social problems that contribute to the challenges faced by individuals, especially among members of marginalized communities (Spatig, Swedberg, Legrow, & Flaherty, 2010). While the process used in popular education (group dialogue, mutual learning, and maintaining equality in power and status among participants) is critical, the outcome is also important. Participants must gain an understanding of how society works and their place in the world prior to taking action. According to VeneKlasen et al. (2007), the development of a critical consciousness consists of the following components:

- Knowledge about how political and economic systems function.
- A sense of history and current events.
- A lens for analyzing why and how imbalances of power operate.
- Concern about how these things destroy human potential and dignity.
- A sense of rights, responsibilities, and solidarity with excluded groups (p. 62).

Often codes are used to illustrate the problem or issue under discussion. Codes can include stories, songs, pictures, or games (VeneKlasen et al., 2007). Sometimes organizers may involve constituents in an exercise or short play that illustrates the problem or issue. For example, labor organizing among migrant farmworkers in California often involves starting events with a play or *teatro* about how Latino farmworkers are typically mistreated by labor contractors or farmers. The portrayal of the contractors and farmers by the farmworkers themselves is used to explore issues of cultural identity, feelings of oppression, and to help participants feel empowered to discuss and take action to address hardships associated with low-wage labor and fear of deportation (El Teatro Campesino, 2010).

Freire's (1970) work provides for a three-step process: knowledge acquisition through dialogue and research, reflection on what members of the group have learned and the meaning of this knowledge, and action to produce social change. The group process, that is, a combination of knowledge, reflection, and action, or *praxis*, leads to both personal and community transformation (Pyles, 2009a). Consequently, one of the primary benefits of participatory methods includes the enhancement of participant control of how knowledge is generated and how it is used (Foster-Fishman et al., 2005).

Pilisuk, McAllister, Rothman, and Larin (2009) identify two main skills used by organizers in problem identification: active listening and posing questions. The questions posed by organizers not only help people identify common problems and develop a critical analysis of the circumstances that contribute to them, but also help the organizer learn about the individuals involved and how members of the group interact with one another and potential differences or conflicts among members.

These provide the organizer with a mechanism for helping the group work through differences and develop a consensus about the issues that affect them.

It is crucial that group members be able to communicate with one another directly. In addition to helping group members find common ground, it often is the organizer's responsibility to initiate the dialogue process. VeneKlasen et al. (2007) identify a number of steps in the dialogue process that build on Freire's original work.

1. Ask participants to introduce themselves. Also ask them to respond to an "ice-breaker" question that will allow other members of the group to get to know them. Examples of questions include "What are your hopes and fears for you and your family" or "What people in your life have inspired you"?
2. Ask participants what they see happening in the device (play, picture, story, role play) used as a code.
3. Ask why this situation is happening. Use "but why" to draw people out and to challenge misinformation or lack of knowledge about the issue.
4. Ask whether the situation discussed happens to the people present at the meeting, to people they know, or within their community.
5. Ask about the problems that the situation leads to and provide information about the problem or issue as appropriate.
6. Ask questions about the cause of the problem or group members' perceptions about situations that contribute to the problems. Essentially, this discussion should lead to a "mini-analysis" or assessment of the problem.
7. Begin to explore options for taking action. If appropriate, goals can be set and options explored. For complex issues, this stage of the meeting can be used to set up some type of a structure such as another meeting time, selection of a leader, or to obtain more information about the problem.

Code development is one of the most important components of the process. It provides an *ice breaker* that can be used to stimulate discussion and is an excellent way to assess perceptions and feelings about an issue. According to Wallerstein (2009), a code should be familiar to participants and be related to problems of concern to group members. It should also have both cultural and personal meaning that will motivate people to take action. In addition, it should be feasible to take action on both a short-term and long-term basis. Success at resolving a small part of the problem will stimulate motivation to address issues that will take longer to resolve (Foster-Fishman et al., 2006).

SUMMARY

After a community organizer becomes acquainted with a community and begins to form relationships with individuals, organizations, and groups, a particular problem or issue should be selected for a community development effort, a social planning process, or an organizing campaign. While an individual organizer or organization can make a specific problem or issue a priority, organizing is, and should be a group effort. Although problem-solving is often thought of as fact finding and data gathering, the perceptions of community residents are also critical. Group methods for problem-identification include story-telling, community forums, nominal group technique (NGT), focus groups, and study circles. In many circumstances in community work with marginalized groups, principles associated with Freire's *Pedagogy of the Oppressed* are put into action including mutual learning, and partnerships between outside experts and community members. It also can become a vehicle for learning about oneself and one's community and minimizing differences among people from different walks of life.

The second phase of the problem-solving model involves assessments of community problems, power and institutional arrangements that sustain oppression or marginalization, and strengths (such as skills and resources) that can be used for social change. In Chapter 6, participatory methods for conducting community assessments will be examined, with special emphasis on group methods that put participants in control of not only problem identification, but also the analysis of the problem or need, the assets that can be used to address it, and the distribution of power that can sustain the problem or be used for social change.

EXERCISES AND ASSIGNMENTS

1. Take a picture about something in the community that has meaning for you, or use a picture in a community publication. What story or meaning does the picture have for you? Do you think there are different meanings for different groups of people? How would you go about reconciling them if you were facilitating a constituency group meeting? Would the meaning of the code be different based on the composition of the group (i.e., demographic profile such as ethnicity, gender, age, etc.)? Would the meaning differ depending on the purpose or mission of the group, the situation at hand, or the community or cultural context? Please explain.

2. In class, take a few minutes to think about why you decided to become a social worker or community organizer. Briefly write down some

notes about how you chose your career. Share this story with your class members either in a small group or larger classroom setting. After story sharing, discuss with the larger group any themes or differences among these stories.

3. Join a group that is planning a community forum. If you cannot join a group or initiate a planning group, attend at least one forum and conduct an interview with a planner as well as an interview with a participant. Write a three- to five-page paper that addresses how the forum was conducted and the decisions made about format. In your paper address the following items:

- What was the purpose of the event?
- What individuals or groups were included in planning the event?
- How was the forum structured? What activities were included on the agenda?
- What factors did the planning committee take into consideration in planning the event?
- What resources were used to make the event successful (i.e., speakers, facilities, equipment, printed literature, etc.)? How were these items obtained?
- To what degree was the agenda controlled by the planners? Did the structure permit a high degree of participant participation? Why or why not?
- Was the purpose of the forum achieved? Please explain your answer. If successful, what components were well received? If not successful, why did this happen?

4. With a group of classmates or constituents from your field agency, conduct a focus group interview on an issue likely to have been experienced by members of this group. Ask someone to act as a recorder—you may also tape the interview with permission of the participants. (Assure participants that their confidentiality will be protected and that only you will have access to the tape.) Prepare an agenda and a consent form in advance. Write a brief summary of your findings that identifies major themes identified in the interview. With this assignment submit your consent form, interview guide, and a transcript or set of notes from the interview.

5. Attend an intergroup dialogue session or a training session for facilitators of these groups. Identify the interpersonal skills necessary to facilitate dialogue and/or deliberation among members with diverse viewpoints. What social work skills were evident in the facilitation process?

6. Use story-telling or steps in the popular education model presented in this chapter to facilitate problem identification among a group of constituents or people likely to have personal or professional knowledge about an issue of concern in the community. What problems were identified? Assess your success in facilitating this process. What problems were encountered? How would you address them in the future?

6

Engaging Participants in the Discovery, Assessment, and Documentation of Community Strengths and Problems

Decisions are made by consensus, collective leadership. [The organization]
works with a group. [The group] has a better understanding of the issue.
[The purpose] is a better life [for] the community ... Groups of
people together. Let them decide.
—Interview with an organizer for a faith-based organization,
Hardina et al., 2011

After problem identification, the next step in the engagement phase is assessment. In organizing work, assessments are generally used to discover and document community problems or needs the assets available to improve the community, or how systems, institutions, and powerful individuals function and interact with one another to facilitate or block social change. As with problem identification, many community assessments are conducted in partnership with constituents and group dialogue is often used to make some types of research and analytic decisions.

In this chapter, the purpose of community assessments is described. The process involved in conducting participatory research studies for community assessments is also examined. The rationale for focusing on community assets and resources rather than deficits is discussed. A specific approach to conducting research in which constituents serve as research partners, participatory action research is examined. In addition, methods for conducting community assessments are described including the use of data collection methods, such as asset mapping, using photography to document community assets and issues, surveys and interviews, collecting statistical data about the community, and geographic approaches for identifying and analyzing community problems, are discussed. A process for using participatory approaches for mapping

125

community power relations is also examined. The use of these methods requires team work on the part of organizers and constituents and requires that both task-oriented and interpersonal skills be used to facilitate these processes. Consequently, the last section of this chapter focuses on interpersonal skills and their use in incorporating the strengths perspective into the community assessment approach.

THE PURPOSE OF COMMUNITY ASSESSMENTS

The practice of community organization within the social work profession, dating back to Jane Addams and Hull House, has emphasized social research as a professional skill needed to scientifically document the prevalence of social problems and make a case for the adoption of sound social policies (Harkavy & Puckett, 1994). In community practice, a specific social research technique, often referred to as *needs assessment*, examines how organizations, communities, and social structures (including political, economic, and social systems) contribute to or sustain problems or issues experienced by the multiple individuals, families, groups, and organizations that comprise the community (Kirst-Ashman & Hull, 2009). Community assessments have traditionally been used to document the degree to which people are affected by specific social problems, service priorities, the geographic or spatial distribution of these problems, and gaps in the availability, accessibility, or delivery of services (Royse et al., 2010). Separate assessments are also conducted about how power is distributed in communities, how it is used, and the people or institutions that actually possess power. Power analysis is also a component of developing a critical consciousness (Harrell & Bond, 2006).

Most often, organizers have conducted formal needs assessments by distributing surveys, analyzing statistical data, or interviewing key informants among community members (Chernesky & Gutheil, 2008; Marti-Costa & Serrano-Garcia, 1995). Such studies have traditionally been considered part of the second phase of the community organizing process. Once the organizer has conducted one-on-one interviews and consulted potential constituents about issues that should be addressed, a structured process is used to document how people experience the community and the prevalence of the problems or issues that concern them. While the data collected may replicate information obtained through one-on-one interviews, it is often critical to have research evidence collected through a standardized process because it is believed to be more credible than information collected by one person, it is less likely to be biased or perceived to be biased, and it can be disseminated to a general audience (Royse et al., 2010). Often formal needs assessment data are required as part of a funding proposal by foundations and government agencies. Organizations that receive funding may also be asked to have some data on hand to establish whether a specific program or initiative worked. Therefore, having data collected prior to the start of the project helps to establish a baseline against which outcomes can be measured.

There are important differences between community assessment and other types of research; however, formal assessments often do not rely on standardized instruments; surveys constructed explicitly for the study are generally used. Random sampling and large samples may be cost prohibitive for many community-based organizations; instead assessment may focus on methods that involve short surveys or interviews with key people in the community who may have direct knowledge of the issue or problem studied (Balcazar, Garcia-Iriarte, & Suarez-Balcazar, 2009; Meenaghan, Kilty, & McNutt, 2004). Often a mixture of research or data collection methods (both qualitative and quantitative) may be used to enhance the reliability of data collection (Marti-Costa & Serrano-Garcia, 1995).

One of the primary rationales for community assessments for organizing purposes is that they are snapshots or impressions of what is going on in the community and may not always require intensive or rigorous data collection or analysis, especially when time and resources are limited. For example, the purpose of a community assessment may be simply to find out what hours of operation or services are likely to attract maximum service users (Royse et al., 2010). Consequently, qualitative methods or short surveys may be preferred data collection methods for many organizations. In addition, the need for standardization of research instruments or data collection methods over multiple sites, replication of the study, or generalization of findings is minimal; conditions in any one organization or community are different from all others due to demographic differences in the population, the manner in which community members interact with one other, values, organization or community culture and traditions, the issues affecting members, and the strengths, skills, and power possessed by individuals and groups (Fals Borda, 2002; Harrell & Bond, 2006).

Although time and money constraints often determine how community assessments are conducted, there are many situations in which findings will be subjected to rigorous review, especially when it is used to verify the legitimacy of "the cause," a lobbying campaign, or an appeal for more or new services (Royse et al., 2010). With time and resources, it is possible to conduct studies with large randomly selected samples that are representative of the community or make comparisons across geographic areas using standardized measures. Therefore, the purpose of the assessment, the preferences and goals of people who will potentially benefit from, fund, or design the study, and how the data will be used are important considerations when developing assessment methods; the methods used to conduct these studies will vary substantially by specific projects or organizations (Chernesky & Gutheil, 2008; Hancock & Minkler, 2009; Meenaghan et al., 2004).

One recent development in how community assessments are generally conducted is the focus on strengths and assets possessed by community members rather than the problems or needs experienced by people in poverty or members of marginalized groups. In addition, community practice has moved away from previous assessment models in which the organizer or outside consultant had the primary responsibility for conducting formal assessments of community needs. Constituents are involved in data collection and analysis as a means of incorporating their perspectives into the research and motivating them to take action (Hancock & Minkler, 2009). These participatory research methods that focus on assessment contain a heavy reliance on theories associated with social constructionism, feminist theory, and qualitative research methods (Fenge, 2010; Lincoln, 2002; Wallerstein & Duran, 2008).

IDENTIFYING ASSETS AND SOCIAL CAPITAL

Increasingly, community-based research has incorporated the strengths perspective in its approach to conducting assessments and other types of research to document the experiences of community members. In 1996, Kretzmann and McKnight (1993) developed an *asset-based* approach to conducting community research and facilitating community development. This model is related to the concept of social capital, the theory that interpersonal relationships and social network formation can be used to leverage resources needed to improve communities (Putnam, 2000). Putnam differentiates between bonding social capital, the development of strong relationships, trust, and shared values among friends, relatives, and neighbors and bridging capital, contained in links between diverse local groups with a variety of different interests. The concept of social capital is discussed in greater detail in Chapter 12.

Methods used to assess social capital in communities focus on examining social networks. Johnson, Honnald, and Stevens (2010) describe social network analysis as a method used to examine interpersonal relationships as a specific form of social structure that changes depending on the nature of the relationship: family, neighbor, friend, community, business, or organization. Within these relationships, specific types of exchanges take place in which tangible (e.g. food, housing, jobs) or intangible (such as emotional support) resources flow back and forth among the network's participants. Social network analysis also documents network strength or density (number of linkages that connect a specific group of people). Network analysis can tell us several important things about a community:

- The degree to which individuals perceive themselves to be connected to or trust others.
- The extent to which organizations communicate or work together on issues.
- The degree to which individuals and groups within a community are linked to organizations within and outside their community (Kay, 2006; Krishna & Shrader, 1999).

According to Theall et al. (2009), network formation can be influenced by both the social and physical environment in the community. Therefore, the amount of social capital in a community can be measured by examining the number and size of community networks as well as the characteristics of the communities in which they are located.

The asset-based approach is a process that involves residents of geographic communities in documenting resources that can be mobilized for community change including the knowledge and skills of individual residents, local institutions (such as schools, churches, and businesses), or *free space* such as parks and other places in which people gather (Kretzmann & McKnight, 1993). The basic premise is that deficit models that frame community assessments in the context of problems or needs imply that individuals that do not have access to political, economic, or social resources are responsible for the poor quality of life in some communities. This in turn minimizes the role of oppressive political and economic institutions that are responsible for marginalization and rendering communities powerless. McKnight and Kretzmann (2009) are also skeptical that the provision of services by government and non-profit agencies will actually improve low-income communities, arguing that residents see themselves as "people with special needs to be met by outsiders" (p. 159).

Instead of traditional service-related approaches, McKnight and Kretzmann (2009) advocate for the use of a community development model that relies on existing resources, the skills of community members, and monetary and other resources controlled by community members. Residents come together to identify these assets, and develop a plan to use them to improve economic conditions in the community (e.g., to create more jobs or businesses). Rather than waiting for external resources to come to them, community members can leverage assets controlled by outsiders through negotiation and relationship-building.

According to Mathie and Cunningham (2003), the common element in asset-based community development, and participatory research methods is the emphasis on personal relationships and strengthening social networks. The focus on local control of the development process and inclusive decision-making practices in the asset-based approach also corresponds to best practices in participatory research (Wallerstein & Duran, 2008). One of the key features of the asset-based approach is a process called asset mapping in which an organizer or consultant works with constituents to create an inventory of community facilities, monetary and other resources available for community improvements and the skills of community residents (Kretzmann & McKnight, 1993). This data collection technique will be discussed in greater detail in a later section of this chapter.

PARTICIPATORY RESEARCH: WORKING IN PARTNERSHIP WITH CONSTITUENTS

Participatory research is based on the premise that knowledge is often generated through personal experience and that different individuals and groups, with different experiences, perceptions, and values, will construct an understanding of social phenomena in a variety of different ways. Although at least some of the focus of participatory research is on community needs and perceptions of barriers to social change, it is also extensively used to document community assets (Balcazar et al., 2009).

One of the methods used to incorporate informal knowledge into the research process is to involve community members in identifying social problems, identifying research questions, and planning research studies (Stoecker, 2005). They may also be involved in actually collecting data, analyzing it, and making recommendations based on that data. The actual degree of participation can vary depending on the purpose of the research, the manner in which the research is funded, the preferences of members of the constituency group and the ideology or philosophy of the organization or organizers involved in the process. Involvement can range from the hiring of an external consultant by a community group who is given carte blanche to conduct the study, limited consultation with constituents by government or nonprofit organizations responsible for specific research projects, to a structured process that facilitates problem identification or setting research goals or full involvement of constituents in every phase of the study (Stoecker, 2008).

The literature on participatory action research credits three sources for the development and philosophy associated with this method (Wallerstein & Duran, 2008). Lewin (1951) views research as a process that examines how people assign meaning to everyday experiences. He developed an approach for examining social problems that specified specific steps for knowledge production: problem identification, collecting factual information, planning, taking action, evaluating outcomes, moving on to the next stage of the plan, and repeating the cycle. One of the purposes of this approach was planned change in social systems. Another critical component of Lewin's model is the idea that the involvement of nonacademics in the production of new knowledge of how society works would motivate them to work for social change (Gaventa & Cornwall, 2002). The second source of influence in the development of participatory research is Paulo Freire's popular education model in the 1960s; the notion of praxis, that knowledge is developed through a cycle of action and reflection, is the inspiration for the process of choosing research methods through dialogue among researchers and community members. A final approach that has provided a framework for participatory research was the adoption of participatory rural appraisal methods in global development projects in the 1980s. There were two rationales for the adoption of this method. The first was that traditional methods used by outsiders to conduct research in rural communities as a precursor to development were too slow and costly and failed to reflect the knowledge of local residents (Chambers, 1994). Also, researchers tended to collect data, but then take it outside the community for analysis. Consequently, while the community was often consulted about local conditions and potential projects to address them, researchers made most of the critical decisions. As a solution for this problem, participatory planning methods in which local residents made the actual development and planning decisions were developed.

According to Stoecker (2005), there are at least three ways in which participatory research differs from traditional research studies conducted by trained professionals:

- It is expected that the data will be collected and used for a specific purpose, primarily to make a change in the community.
- A number of research methods will be used. There is no one primary "right" or "wrong" approach; reliability and validity may not be as important as whether the data are useable and interpretable by research participants.

• The process involves a collaborative relationship between the researcher and members of the community and decisions are often made through group dialogue and consensus rather than simply at the expert's "recommendation."

PARTICIPATORY ACTION RESEARCH

Participatory action research is the approach most often used to fully involve constituents in community assessments. The method is also referred to as action research or community-based participatory research (Wallerstein & Duran, 2008). The basic assumption of the method is that a professional or expert will work with a community group to identify an issue that affects members of the group, conduct an assessment of the issue using a variety of formal and informal research strategies, set a goal for community change that is derived from the research, and then engage in social action to achieve that goal. PAR has also been used successfully to facilitate social planning and community development processes (Sager, 2008). However, in addition to citizen involvement, this approach is intended to explicitly facilitate the use of data to advocate for changes in programs, procedures, policy, and legislation that will improve the community. Consequently, outcomes associated with PAR focus on both the individual participants and society: personal empowerment and transformation (through skill-building, power, and action) and social justice and the transformation of oppressive institutions (Sohng, 1995).

Participatory action research is generally classified as a type of qualitative research study. However, sources of data for participatory research can range from interviews, story-telling, photography, focus groups, and art, music, spoken word performances or theater to structured or semi-structured surveys, census data or other statistical data sources, and quantitative research designs (Grodach, 2009; Hancock & Minkler, 2009; Incite: Women of Color Against Violence, (n.d.). Its classification as a qualitative study has to do with the fact that the social distance between the research and participants is minimized, that the research expert and community members have equal status and benefit equally from participation, and that informal knowledge is valued as much as formal knowledge (Lincoln, 2002; Stoecker, 2005). In addition, many participatory action researchers reject the notion that research should strive to be value-free or conducted in a manner that does not incorporate specific goals or a social change-oriented purpose (Fals Borda, 2002). The inclusion of community members in the research process renders it a method that relies on subjective knowledge collected, analyzed, and disseminated in a manner that reflects the perspectives and the standpoint (social status, power, and values) of participants (Wallerstein & Duran, 2008). Participatory research differs from other types of research in that methodological decisions are made collectively using a group process. This method has a variety of advantages and limitations when compared with other types of research.

Application of Group Methods for Conducting Participatory Research: Empowering Constituents to Take Action

The PAR research process essentially requires excellent use of interpersonal and group work skills on the part of the facilitator to arrive at a consensus about research goals and methodology. PAR projects may be facilitated by an organizer or a constituent. However, some of these projects employ outside experts such as consultants or researchers to collaborate with constituency group members. Ongoing dialogue and discussion is the primary vehicle through which decisions are made. In some cases, training in research methodology may be provided. Issues of power and trust must be dealt with by the outside expert during the early stages of the process and good working relationships must be built with all group members. Stringer (2007) describes the role of the researcher as minimizing conflict, showing respect and sensitivity toward group members, listening to what group members have to say, and encouraging people to perform research tasks and act for themselves.

For PAR to be effective, participants must be willing to learn and apply basic research methodology, motivated and vocal enough to bring their own perceptions and values into the research process (Israel et al., 2008; Sohng, 1995). One of the characteristics of PAR that differentiates it from other types of research is the emphasis on Freirian methods in which group members engage in both reflection and action. Therefore, the process requires more than mere negotiation around research questions and methods, it incorporates specific values and principles into the research process. The primary goals of participatory research are to create an atmosphere characterized by trust, equality among participants, and a sense of ownership of the process by community members (Castleden, Garvin, & Huu-ay-aht First Nation, 2008). Incite: Women of Color Against Violence (n.d.), an organization that works to prevent police violence against women and transgendered people of color has incorporated these principles in a statement that describes their use of participatory action research in their advocacy work.

- We are experts in our own experiences and have many different ways of knowing and getting information about our conditions.

- We control the gathering and use of information about our communities. We decide what information we need to make the changes we want and how to get it. We decide what questions we need to answer and how. We lead and are integrally involved in all aspects of the design and implementation of the research, and of the analysis and distribution of the information gathered.
- We gather information to inform our actions for change.
- We reflect on the information we have gathered and the way in which we are gathering it throughout the process. We also reflect on the action we have taken and decide if we need more information before taking further action.
- The people we gather information with and from are active and not passive participants in the process. We use information gathering to build community and movement, to develop leadership, and to empower ourselves to make change.
- We are not trying to "prove" an assumption or hypothesis, but we want to learn more about ourselves and our communities as a way to make change.
- We agree on principles and values that will guide our information gathering and stay accountable to them throughout the process (p. 1).

The incorporation of these principles into a group research process results in what Freire (1970) has described as praxis, the development of tacit knowledge by participants that leads to both empowerment and engagement in social change.

Often, community members have no reason to trust outside experts who have limited knowledge of the community. According to Castleden et al. (2008), trust is an essential component of power-sharing:

> Specifically, trust is established when researchers work in an open, honest, and transparent manner. Trust is also built when researchers become involved in the community's activities, listen to and address community partners' needs, and reciprocate in some way. For example, there is a growing trend towards building capacity in the community through training and employing local people in research. (p. 1395)

In addition to trust-building, the application of appropriate interpersonal skills is essential for this process. Stringer (2007) describes the components or praxis, of research, reflection, and action process as a spiral or cyclical process consisting of looking, thinking, and acting:

> As participants work though each of the major stages, they will explore the details of their activities through a constant

process of observation, reflection, and action. At the completion of each set of activities, they will review (look again), reflect (reanalyze), and re-act (modify their actions) . . . . People will find themselves working backward through the routines, repeating processes, revising procedures, rethinking interpretations, leapfrogging steps or stages, and sometimes making radical changes in direction. (p. 9) (Figure 6.1)

The personal empowerment component of PAR is a consequence of the process of dialogue between participants and the researcher/facilitator. Sohng (1995) identifies a number of critical components inherent in the interaction among the participants including:

- Recruiting people who previously may have been isolated to examine common problems and concerns.
- Validating personal experiences and making them the basis of critical analysis about the societal factors and institutions that contribute to or sustain these problems.
- Making what seems to be entirely personal into a call for political action.

As with problem identification, the dialogue process requires the facilitator to pose a series of "why," "what," "when," and "how" questions to participants about their daily experiences, the quality of their lives, and how social programs, the economy and the political system work (Stringer, 2007).

FIGURE 6.1
Cycle of action and reflection in praxis.

Advantages and Limitations of PAR

Sager (2008) describes the difference between traditional types of university or expert lead research process and PAR "as shift[ing] attitudes from stealing to sharing" or transferring power and control from researchers to community members (p. 211). A number of studies have documented that participation in PAR-related research can increase participants' feelings of personal empowerment and self-efficacy. For example, Oden, Hernandez, and Hidalgo (2010) conducted a qualitative research study to document whether persons with disabilities who are members of nondominant ethnical and racial groups felt empowered through their participation in a PAR project to increase the degree to which their community was physically accessible. Participants were interviewed about their participation in conducting accessibility assessments of local businesses. The respondents reported that the project increased their knowledge about the Americans With Disabilities Act (ADA), strategies that could be used to increase the accessibility of local businesses, and physical barriers that affect people with disabilities. They also gained a greater sense of independence in terms of dealing with the business community and increased their motivation to be advocates. In a similar study, Jennings, Parra-Medina, Hilfinger-Messias, and McLoughlin (2006) examined the impact of a PAR program for youth. The participants were paired with adult leaders knowledgeable about community research and action. Once a youth received training from a mentor, the leadership dyad of an adult and young person then trained teams of youth using a process of dialogue, reflection, and action to develop community service projects. The evaluators found that the youth participants experienced an increase in personal self-awareness and efficacy and a greater degree of engagement with the community.

Other advantages of participatory action research identified in the literature include: the development of research methods and instruments that allow for the collection of reliable, valid, or trustworthy data, increases in the number of strong social networks, improvements in neighborhood conditions or knowledge, and increases in the production of useful data easily understood by community members and disseminated to policy-makers (Lincoln, 2002; Nygreen, Kwon, & Sanchez, 2006). PAR contributes to the cultural competency of programs and services, ensures that community organizing or advocacy campaigns honor cultural or community customs and traditions, and enhances feelings of collective identity control or political power that participants feel that they have over their communities; the cultural competency of programs, policies, and services developed through the PAR process is also enhanced, increasing the likelihood that they will actually be used by community members (Collie, Liu, Podsiadlowski, & Kindon, 2010; Durst, MacDonald, & Parsons, 1999; Itzhaky & York, 2002; Reed & Cook, 2007; Silvestre et al., 2010; Yoshihama & Carr, 2002). PAR is also effective in the development of critical consciousness about social conditions and power relationships and the likelihood that participants will take action to address these conditions (Carlson, Engebretson, & Chamberlain, 2006; Goto, Pelto, Pelletier, & Tiffany, 2010).

PAR processes are flexible enough such that they can be used to facilitate a variety of different types of studies, research methods, reports and dissemination techniques; they may also be adopted for use with computer technology. For example, Flicker et al. (2008) describe the use of e-PAR methods, using the arts (photography, video production, and theater) and social media including interactive web sites, blogs, and text messaging to engage youth in problem identification, goal-setting, and social action; this approach also facilitated the development of strong social networks among the participants.

There are a number of limitations of PAR-related methods as well. For example, involving a large number of people in decision-making of any kind requires time (especially in terms of the time required in reaching consensus) and resources such as a skilled facilitator (Fenge, 2010). There may be issues of power and control inherent in the group process, with group members who have more power or status dominating the process (Fenge, 2010). Group members may have hidden agendas in terms of what they want to achieve from the group and there may be a number of different groups involved in the process that have more resources, members, or the ability to make their opinions known than others (Wallerstein & Duran, 2008). There also may be external barriers that limit goal achievement including information that it is difficult to obtain the lack of adequate funding for the research study, and political opposition to collecting information, taking action to promote social change, or making the change that the group hopes to achieve (Chernesky & Gutheil, 2008). Power and status differentials may also play themselves out in the group process, with people being fearful of having their say in front of an outside facilitator or simply distrustful of the facilitator or the process (Carlson et al., 2006). In addition, it is essential that the facilitator be respectful of the participants, culturally competent, and willing to provide information about how to conduct research and shape research questions in a nontechnical, clear manner (Stoecker, 2005).

PARTICIPATORY DATA COLLECTION METHODS

Participatory research can include a variety of data collection methods to document community problems, needs, strengths, and assets. These methods include asset mapping and the use of photography, employing a specific PAR-related method called *Photovoice*. Traditional methods for conducting community assessments such as surveys and formal interviews, the collection of statistical data about the community, and geographic mapping processes can also be used in a manner that includes community members in the actual collection and analysis of data.

Asset Mapping

The assets approach as defined by Kretzmann and McKnight (1996) requires that participants (constituents and organizers) map or take an inventory of all the assets, resources, and skills available for use in making improvements in geographic communities. The term "mapping¤ in this context refers to the creation of a conceptual model or picture that identifies broad categories of assets within and outside the community such as businesses, public institutions, individual skills, sources of income, and organizations. McKnight and Kretzmann (2009) contrast an asset-based conceptual model with a neighborhood "needs map" that simply list the types of problems experienced by residents such as poverty, unemployment, and substance abuse. However, in some circumstances, participatory community research approaches may involve using geographic maps to identify the location of major community assets such as parks, schools, or businesses.

Asset maps used for inventory community assets contain three primary components or what McKnight and Kretzmann (2008) identify as "building blocks."

- Primary building blocks or assets controlled by community members. These assets include personal income, individual skills, local businesses, community organizations, professional and business associations, local media, and religious institutions. Although not included in the McKnight and Kretzman classification system, social media such as blogs or the use of text messaging, the Internet, Facebook, or Twitter to communicate, build social or business networks or interfaces, or market products would also be included in this category.
- Secondary building blocks or community assets controlled by people or institutions that are not located in the community. These assets include institutions such as churches, hospitals, and schools, social

service agencies, and public services such as the police, fire department, libraries and parks or recreational facilities. In this category, McKnight and Kretzmann also place vacant land, unused, and uninhabited housing. Such resources can be potentially used for community improvement and economic activity, for example, converting a vacant lot into a community garden or playground or a warehouse into a community center or new enterprise.

- The third-level building blocks consist of potential assets controlled by forces outside the community. These assets include public information such as social indicators and data that can be used to document conditions in the community and generate public support for improvements, government assistance for individuals, and government expenditures for improving buildings, parks, streets, and housing. Such assets help to generate government grants and contracts, jobs, and income for community residents.

These conceptual maps or inventories are used to guide the development process and identify individuals, agencies, facilities, and businesses that are most likely to be useful in maximizing community capacity. Other steps in the asset-building process include establishing an appropriate organization and representative decision-making structure to guide development, and identifying those organizations, government agencies, and businesses from outside the community with whom productive partnerships can be built to sustain the development effort.

Using Photovoice to Document Community Assets and Issues

Photovoice is a type of participatory action research that involves community members in documenting issues and community strengths using photography and digital technology (videos and films). McDonald, Sarche, and Wang (2009) describe this process as one that adopts techniques commonly used to integrate the arts and cultural symbols into community organizing and assessment techniques. Its theoretical underpinnings include popular education, feminist theory, and social constructionism. Foster-Fishman et al. (2005) describe Photovoice as a type of participatory research that "puts cameras in the hands of individuals often excluded from decision-making processes in order to capture their voices and visions about their lives, their community, and their concerns" (p. 277). It builds on the concept of story-telling in that participants are given access to cameras and encouraged to take pictures of their community that have significance about their lives and perceptions. Once photos are taken, participants are asked to share stories about the photographs and what they mean to them, reflect on what the photos mean in terms of community context and problems experienced, barriers faced, and strengths possessed by community residents. The pictures and these constructed stories are then shared with members of the public, the media, and political decision-makers.

Photovoice was initially used in the mid-1990s by researchers interested in developing a technique to promote intergenerational dialogue about reproductive health issues in China (Wang & Pies, 2008). The technique is often designed to assist with the development culturally appropriate health promotion and social service programs and facilitate multicultural understanding. In addition, it has been used extensively as a component of the community assessment process and in some circumstances it may be the primary data collection method used.

The process is congruent with techniques used in the development of critical consciousness described in Chapter 5 (Wang, Yi, Tao, & Carovano, 1998). The photos become "codes," developed by members of the community that are used to stimulate and guide dialogue among group members. The discussion is used to generate proposed solution and mobilize members of the group to take action and ultimately is used to promote changes in policies (Catalani & Minkler, 2010).

The Photovoice process includes a number of distinct components that are similar to those used in other types of participatory action research (see Box 6.1). The dialogue process uses a set of questions that is designed to facilitate reflective dialogue from participants about the story that the picture-taker narrates about the photo, the sharing of stories among the participants, commonalities or themes identified in these pictures by participants, issues and community strengths identified, and possible solutions for community problems (Catalani & Minkler, 2010).

Photovoice typically relies on a standardized set of questions posed by a facilitator:

- What do you see here?
- What is really happening here?
- How does this relate to our lives?
- Why does this problem, concern, or strength exist?
- What can we do about it? (Wang & Pies, 2008, p. 188).

Numerous studies have examined the use of Photovoice in communities and have documented a number of positive effects. Participants have been found to experience increases in personal perceptions of self-efficacy and feelings of empowerment as well as increases in their knowledge about community processes and commitment to participate in

> ### BOX 6.1 STEPS IN THE PHOTOVOICE PROCESS
>
> Wang (2006) identifies a number of standard steps commonly used in Photovoice projects:
>
> 1. Recruit community leaders and other decision-makers to service as a target audience that can offer constructive feedback and guidance.
> 2. Recruit participants from a specific target or demographic group.
> 3. Provide training on safety, using cameras, and the ethical implications involved in picture taking.
> 4. Use established research procedures to obtain informed consent.
> 5. Provide some sample "themes" or ideas for the initial picture-taking process. In some cases, participants may generate their own ideas about the issues that they wish to address.
> 6. Distribute cameras and have participants start taking pictures.
> 7. Bring participants together to share the pictures and start to identify themes or codes.
> 8. Develop a strategy for presenting the format to decision-makers.

social change activities (see, e.g., Foster-Fishman et al., 2005; Gant et al., 2009; Wang, 2006; Wang et al., 1998). In addition, the process is also effective in helping people gain awareness of diversity—both the diverse perspectives of participants, and also diversity across cultural, social class, and race as well as the development of critical consciousness about social conditions (Carlson et al., 2006; Catalani & Minkler, 2010).

There are a number of limitations associated with Photovoice, however. Catalani and Minkler (2010) conducted a review of the academic literature on the use of Photovoice; they point out several flaws in the method as well as in the available research literature: Most of the research involves case studies and there is a great deal of variation in the actual methods used and the degree of constituent participation in Photovoice projects. Often these procedures are not well explicated in the research literature. In addition, it is often not clear as to whether action taken as a consequence of the photography and group identification of community issues actually contributed to community change.

In response to these limitations, some researchers have modified Photovoice to make it more responsive to community norms, values, and decision-making structures. For example, Castleden et al. (2008) describe a Photovoice process conducted with the Huu-ay-aht First Nation community in Canada. The tribal council initiated the study, hired a university-affiliated researcher, and established a community advisory committee to oversee the study. A cross-section of community members was recruited for participation and training was provided. Once photos were taken, each participant was interviewed about their pictures and asked to pick two for display. Updates on the project were provided to all community members by newsletter and by conducting potluck dinners in which the photos and the participants' narrative descriptions of the photos were displayed. An ongoing participatory process for analyzing the photos and interview data was established and feedback on action initiatives undertaken as part of the project was provided to the community every 6 months.

USING TRADITIONAL COMMUNITY ASSESSMENT METHODS: SURVEYS AND INTERVIEWS WITHIN A PARTICIPATORY RESEARCH FRAMEWORK

Research instruments used in most community assessments include standardized or semi-standardized questionnaires in which people are asked a series of questions about their perceptions of the community and the issues that affected them. Respondents can include community members, experts or people perceived to have academic or professional knowledge about community issues, or specific interest groups such as religious leaders or business owners. In some circumstances, respondents are asked to choose among a list of community needs or to rank order their top choices. The questionnaire may include some open-ended questions to gauge their perceptions or concerns. One criticism of this method is that the survey may incorporate technical language that is not familiar to community residents (Kissane & Gingerich, 2004; Salahu-Din, 2003). Another concern about survey research is that it may allow the researcher to pre-determine responses to individual questions or reach conclusions that do not adequately reflect what community members think or feel.

Another method used to collect data for community assessments are interviews. Interviewees may include community leaders, "average" community members, members of specific cultural or identity groups, or experts (Meenaghan et al., 2004). These interviews differ from one-on-one, conversational interviews in that they generally employ a predetermined list of questions and are administered in a fairly consistent manner among respondents. Most often, they involve open-ended questions about the individual's perceptions of the community, the services they receive or are denied, and their relationship with the power structure (Cleveland, 2010). These interviews are similar in nature to qualitative research interviews. However, structured interviews can also be conducted, especially in circumstances in which complex or technical information is required or when the researcher feels a more structured mailed survey would have a low response rate. In addition, focus group interviews can be conducted as one component of a community assessment. The use of multiple methods is one of the techniques that can be used to enhance the reliability of the data collected (Royse et al., 2010).

Participatory methods can also be used effectively to design surveys with useable data or to conduct interviews. Often this process involves building partnerships with researchers who work engage in dialogue with community members to develop community surveys or interview guides (Balcazar et al., 2009). Consequently, while the study may not necessarily involve participatory action research, there is some type of collaborative dialogue established between both parties that enhances the face validity of the research instruments. The surveys or interview guides developed through this process should reflect the lived experiences of community members. It should also increase the likelihood that the language and wording of the instrument is appropriate for potential and that people will participate in the study. Participatory methods should also increase the degree to which the study findings can be considered reliable or valid.

Training may be provided to participants on how to conduct studies or design measurement instruments. However, the process also relies on the experiences and perceptions of participants in terms of how to approach community members for participation, research design, and the choice of survey or interview questions. Essentially, it is often the role of the participants to "train" the researcher in culturally appropriate methods for engagement with and relationship-building with members of the community. For example, if a researcher is conducting a study health care utilization among members of the Hmong community knowledge of Hmong culture and language would be essential. Issues to be considered in the design of the study would be whether new immigrants, first-generation, or second-generation households should be included, the choice of language (English or Hmong), or dialect to be used, actual translation of the research instrument, and the appropriateness of the questions asked (Baker et al., 2010).

Neighborhood Data Collection: Facilitating the Development of Social Indicators of Community Needs and Assets

Another traditional method for documenting community problems is the collection of statistical data based on standardized measures about community conditions and needs. Both government and nonprofit service providers typically document the number of people with specific needs or problems as well as the number of people that receive service. Many government agencies make this information available to the public through reports and the Internet (Hardina, 2002). The advantages of using these indicators are many; this information is often accessible to the public, people generally accept that the measures reflect the need for services, legislation, or new policies, and they provide a means to make comparisons about different communities or political jurisdictions or examine trends in data patterns over time. Consequently, social indicator systems are important as a source of baseline and evaluation data about communities and can be used to persuade donors to fund local projects. However, much of the data pertain to cities, counties, states, and the country as a whole. Recently, there has been an effort to develop indicators that can be used to examine the quality of life in communities. Phillips (2003) defines community indicators as:

> Measurements that provide information about past and current trends and assist planners and community leaders in making decisions that affect future outcomes. They can incorporate citizen involvement and participation. In essence, indicators are measurements that reflect the interplay between social, environmental, and economic factors affecting a region's or community's well-being. As such, they can be extremely valuable to planners. (p. 1)

Indicators are often used for planning purposes because they are less costly or less time consuming than data collection through other sources. However, there are also a number of barriers that typically limit their use in community planning processes. For example, one primary source of data is the U.S. Census. Census data may be used to document the extent of poverty in a community, demographic composition, or home owners in a community. The advantage of this method is that the government collects these data in a standardized way and almost everyone is included (Galster, Hayes, & Johnson, 2005). A major disadvantage of census data is that some groups are likely to be excluded (e.g., homeless people or undocumented immigrants) and it is collected only every 10 years.

Other indicators complied by government agencies are also commonly used to assess health status, poverty rates, unemployment, educational attainment in public schools, and crime. However, indicators have some substantial limitations. They may under or over measure the problem, numbers may not be relevant to specific communities due to sample size, and they are often indirect or approximate measures of need (Meenaghan et al., 2004; Phillips, 2003). For example, unemployment data compiled by the Federal government excludes people who are underemployed, exhausted their unemployment benefits, or are no longer looking for work. Similar problems exist with data obtained directly from government or nonprofit organization databases; such records may be incomplete or inaccurate or fail to track data that would directly document community needs (Royse et al., 2010).

Another important disclaimer regarding social indicators is that seldom are these measures used to document neighborhood assets other than income, home ownership, or the number of businesses within a specific geographic location. In fact, the emphasis on what are perceived to be "objective" measures generally contains value assumptions about how benefits are or should be distributed. In some circumstances, to make comparisons by gender, ethnicity, or social class, such objective measures may actually serve to misrepresent the experiences or interests of some groups in the community (Driscoll Derickson, 2009; Meenaghan et al., 2004). For example, research findings that indicate a large percentage of local homeowners are having difficulty paying their mortgages may be used by government officials or members of the banking industry to argue that these residents were "bad credit risks" and should not have received mortgages in the first place, ignoring the role played by limited government regulation of the home loan industry.

In many instances, the advantages associated with the examination of social indicators may outweigh the disadvantages. However, the effective use of community-based statistical information requires that data be compiled that allows changes and trends to be tracked over time. Some types of data require additional analysis to break them down to neighborhood relevant measures. Galster et al. (2005) argue that the costs associated with maintaining such systems are prohibitive for most community groups. In some instances, universities and regional, state, and local organizations provide support to community groups for developing data management systems for obtaining and using community indicators (Hillier, Wernecke, & McKelvey, 2005). One important premise of community indicators is that they be developed and used, not simply by organizers and planners, but by the public.

Stoecker (2006) describes one effort, the National Neighborhood Indicators Partnership, to involve community residents in collecting, analyzing, and disseminating neighborhood data via the Internet. Through NNIP, the Urban Institute and organizations in local communities coordinate their work to facilitate the collect data about social conditions that affect neighborhoods. They also provide how-to manuals, conduct workshops, and disseminate a wide variety of technical information to other community groups (NNIP, n.d.). The data collected for use in these systems include census data as well as information obtained from a wide variety of government agencies and its use is intended to promote the development of assessment tools for looking at a community or a neighborhood as a whole rather than focusing on specific types of problems (Driscoll Derickson, 2009).

Although intended to give community members more control of information, NNIP data are usually housed in a university or another large organization that provides staff and technological services on a consultative basis for community members (Stoecker, 2006). However, other NNIP approaches often used either provide free neighborhood data to community groups on the Internet or provide access to larger databases from which local organizations with trained volunteers and the appropriate computers and technology may extract the data they need.

Although these data systems allow neighborhood groups access to information and consequently provide a degree of ownership and control of local planning efforts, they also require a great deal of money and technical expertise. An alternative approach for using social indicators involves the development of neighborhood level indicators of neighborhood quality and assets by community groups. This collaborative group process requires participants to identify issues of concern, examine their perceptions of the issue and its causes, and create an operational definition and a set of measures that are easy to implement. For example, in a community in which obesity is an issue, the number of walking paths or the number of parks in which it is safe for children to play may be logical indicators of the problem and reflect the perceptions of the community (Evenson et al., 2009). According to Hancock and Minkler (2009), such measures often have a high degree of face validity in that they reflect community values, are more accessible and understandable than academic or technical models, and can be used to convey a message or political point about the importance of taking action to remedy the problem. Other advantages of this method are that it increases community ownership of the research process, makes it more likely that both needs and assets will be measured, and that cultural values as well as community perceptions about quality-of-life issues will be incorporated into measurement procedures and discussions about possible solutions (Table 6.1).

Creating Geographic Maps of Community Resources or Problems

Related to the use of social indicators is the use of community mapping procedures. Community mapping processes are most often used to examine problems and assets in geographic communities and focus on

TABLE 6.1
Community Indicators for West Village Center

Type of Indicator	2008	2010	2012
Number of businesses	80	65	111
New business start-ups	5	2	10
Number of owner occupied homes	4,500	4,000	4,700
Number of rental units	5,625	5,231	5,140
Average household income	22,500	18,999	25,381
New housing permits issued	20	0	40
Number of residents	20,000	19,672	22,591
Number of parks	10	9	12
Number of civic organizations	15	12	21

spatial relationships among community problems, assets, and service providers. The type of mapping approaches used can involve maps drawn by volunteers to processes involving computer mapping and extensive databases that require access to technology and technical expertise. Consequently, these procedures range from low cost, no technology-related approaches that are accessible for community members to others that require access to funds, technology, training for volunteers, and paid consultants. Maps have a number of features that make them ideal for community organizing:

- They identify geographic patterns in the community.
- They provide a visual way to communicate these patterns to others.
- They can be used to tell a story about the community.
- They facilitate decisions about organizing initiatives, programs, policies, and legislation (PolicyLink, n.d.).

Most of the more accessible approaches to community mapping, involve having volunteers draw maps that represent how they view their community. Similar to Photovoice, the various maps produced allow for the examination of how people experience community conditions and what they identify as the strengths, assets, and deficits inherent in the community (Kirschenbaum & Russ, 2009). Maps can be compared via a group discussion process and patterns can be identified. The themes become key indicators of problems or the assets that can be used to address them. For example, these types of maps could be used to identify vacant lots in the community that need to be weeded or cleaned up. These lots that could potentially be converted to community gardens or play lots that would benefit the neighborhood. Often one type of item of interest on community maps are the physical boundaries that limit access to and from the community or that are perceived by residents to limit access such as highways, train tracks, or even gang graffiti that may mark territory as unsafe for certain individuals (Hardina, 2002).

One approach to community mapping, involves research to identify conditions in the neighborhood that are perceived to be hazardous or that affect their well-being. As with other methods of participatory research, risk mapping can take place as a group exercise with community members drawing a picture, placing labels on the drawing to identify key features of the community, marking the location of risk factors, and making a list of things that need correction (Brown, 2008).

Community mapping can also involve giving volunteers printed maps and asking them to conduct a community inventory of businesses, parks, churches, and other facilities or the overall condition of community infrastructure as a prelude to a community development effort (Community Mapping Project, n.d.). Such a process provides valuable "hard" data for the development effort and gives participants ownership of the process. This method can also be combined with photography or video technology to document community conditions (Figure 6.2).

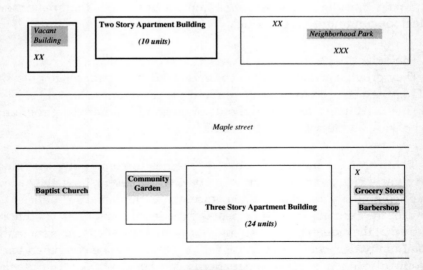

FIGURE 6.2
Constituent developed map of neighborhood assets and risks.
Key: **Community Assets**, *Potential Assets*, Incidents of Drug Dealing in the Past Month (X).

A more technical approach to mapping involves the combination of community indicators with geographic mapping technology, most often using computer technology or Geographic Information Systems (Phillips, 2003). Such systems may have several key data features in addition to street maps including the location of parks and other open space, buildings, the homes of individuals who experience certain types of problems, and the service agencies that can address these problems. As with indicator databases, GIS systems are often cost prohibitive for community groups. To use them, organizations often partner with universities, foundations, and service consortiums or employ for-profit consultants. Although the technology requires a time and resource commitment, GIS processes can be established that permit community participation in data collection and mapping (Maman et al., 2009).

For example, in post-Katrina New Orleans, a faith-based group, Churches Supporting Churches, partnered with PolicyLink and Louisiana State University to document community conditions including the location and condition of buildings in one neighborhood community (Duval-Diop, Curtis, & Clark, 2010). GIS and video technology were used to construct a web site that linked videos of individual buildings with statistical information that could be used in the redevelopment effort. Neighborhood residents collected the data and were also involved in the analysis portion of the study. This process also contributed to the identification of neighborhood gathering places such as grocery stores that could be used to facilitate social networking and also helped to identify conditions that could negatively affect the health of the community. Data were subsequently used to initiate neighborhood redevelopment efforts.

Mapping technology can be adapted for a number of different purposes and data collection methods. For example, Santos, Ferguson, and Trippel (2010) describe a community partnership in which youth from two different low-income neighborhoods in Memphis were assigned to teams to construct maps of community assets. Training was provided in photography and GIS mapping techniques; both methods were used by the participants to document community problems. In addition to training the youth in marketable jobs skills, the project also gave the researchers insight into the perceptions of the young participants about their own communities.

POWER ANALYSIS: MAPPING POWER RELATIONS IN THE COMMUNITY

The development of a critical consciousness requires that participants understand how power is distributed in their communities and how power or the lack of power affects them. Pyles (2009a) describes the purpose of *power analysis* as "to determine the winners and losers of social policies and practices, identifying how social and economic power operates in order to work to undo such retrenched power" (p. 124). Traditionally, the identification of people and groups who hold power in individual communities was a task conducted by individual organizers. Knowing who has power, why they have power, and how they use it is an essential skill in community practice (Staples, 2004). There are a number of specific methods that can be used to document power arrangements. However, it is often not sufficient for community organizers to do this work isolation. Power analysis research is often conducted in conjunction with other group assessment methods and as part of the process of praxis, working with people to develop a critical consciousness about how communities, social policies, and institutional arrangements serve to oppress and marginalize some groups of people while serving the interests of others.

Power in Communities

Questions typically addressed through power analysis are sources of power (such as money, votes, elected office, authority, information, social, economic, or professional status, or personal attributes such as demographic background or charisma). Power analysis also examines personal and business affiliations such as profession, employer, or memberships in clubs or seats on nonprofit organization boards. Often professional or social networks of the decision-maker are examined, who are their friends or relatives, with whom do they do business or socialize, and with whom did they attend school or have personal relationships? Examining relationships among businesses or corporations or nonprofit groups is also important because overlapping memberships on boards of directors can provide evidence of networks of affiliated groups, common interests, or concentrated power (Domhoff, 2009a, 2009b; Sen, 2003).

Communities tend to be of two types: elitist or pluralist (Domhoff, 2007). Elitist communities have a well-defined group of politically, economically, and/or socially influential members who are often small in number, but hold most of the decision-making authority in a community. In contrast, pluralist communities are those in which a number of different groups hold power and interact with one another in a manner that changes in response to the issue at hand, public support, and the degree to which individuals and groups benefit from or perceive themselves to be harmed by a specific issue (Conservation Partnership, 2002;

Meenaghan, Washington, & Ryan, 1982). These "interest groups" consist of members of professional, business, or advocacy organizations who have common interests and concerns (Kraft & Furlong, 2007). Interest groups typically lobby government officials to have policies and legislation adopted that reflects their values and that will benefit their own needs (vested interest) or those of an unrepresented group (such as children or animals) or the public interest (e.g., environmental causes or the negative effects of globalization). For example, a business association may be formed to represent the interests of downtown merchants who fear that the city will want to tear down their shops in order to build a sports stadium. A group of neighbors may come together to vote for a candidate for the school board who will promise to support the building of a new middle school in their area.

The degree of social stratification in communities is also important when studying power in communities. The term social stratification refers to what demographic groups are present in the community, how they interact with one another, and which of these groups actually have the power and resources to make or influence decisions (Harrell & Bond, 2006; Wolf, 2007). What groups are typically excluded or marginalized? What demographic group is most likely to hold political office or serve on corporate boards (Domhoff, 2009a).? What industry or industries are predominant in the community and what polices, practices, or legislation benefits them? In many cases, there are certainly important power differentials among members of identity communities as well that determine who holds power and who is typically excluded from decision-making. For example, in the Hmong immigrant community in the United States, male clan leaders who are often business or professional leaders make decisions for community members and settle personal disputes. (Hardina et al., 2008; Yoshihama & Carr, 2002).

Conducting Research and Documenting Power and Influence

There are a number of ways in which organizers have worked to document power arrangements. Each of these methods contains elements in common and involves the identification of community leaders, sources of power, and groups expected to support or oppose a specific decision, policy, or piece of legislation affecting the community.

* *Identifying factors that facilitate or block change.* Two related techniques force field and SWOT (Strength, Weakness, Opportunity, and Threat) analysis use a framework developed by social psychologist Kurt

Lewin in the 1940s to understand the interaction of proponents and opponents of change and factors in the social, political, and economic environment that may have positive or negative effects in social change initiatives. In force field analysis, factors that "drive" or facilitate change and those forces that resist or prevent it are identified. In SWOT analysis, participants identify similar factors affecting change in organizations, identifying strengths and weakness both inside and outside the organization.

- *Interest group analysis (positional approach)*. Analysis focuses on the relative power of the various interest groups involved in public decision-making and their ability to negotiate and compromise with one another. The groups with most power and access to resources are believed to have greater ability to affect change. However, if there are a number of issues under discussion in any community, the degree to which the same organizations line up to support or oppose specific issues can be examined. Are the same groups always allied with one another or do these alliances shift in response to different issues?

- *Analysis of campaign donations*. One way to document the power of interest groups is through examination of campaign donations. Candidates are required to report the names, employers, and profession of donors to local, state, and federal governments. This information can be used to link interest groups to individual politicians and specific pieces of legislation that may benefit or harm members of these groups. Information on campaign donations can be found in government offices or by going online. For example, the Center for Responsive Politics contains a database of donors to Federal candidates and their industry affiliations.

- *Social network analysis to identify informal neighborhood leaders*. There are two primary approaches to conducting network analysis. The first involves conducting research to identify informal community leaders or the number and strength of informal networks that provide information, social support, and assistance to friends, relatives, and neighbors. Informal assessments of networks are generally made through observations and one-on-one interviews. More formal assessments of these helping networks involve conducting interviews with community members to see with whom they give, receive, or exchange help. Leaders can generally be identified if they are repeatedly named as help givers.

- *Social network analysis to identify formal connections between individual decision-makers and organizations or among influential or powerful organizations*. Premised on Domhoff's (2009a) assertion that often there are explicit connections among powerful organizations, efforts are made to examine links among people who make decisions or their membership in organizations. This type of network analysis often involves examining membership on corporate boards, foundations, or nonprofit groups in order to document whether some of the same people sit on the same boards or whether some organizations have overlapping boards of directors and consequently influence decision-making in multiple organizations. Board membership lists are public information and can often be found online. Business or property ownership research using public records may also assist in the identification of these relationships or in documenting vested interests.

* *Newspaper and other media accounts of community activities and political decision-making.* Are the same individuals often identified as involved in community issues or do these decision-makers and activists vary from issue by issue?

* *Postings on websites, Facebook, MySpace, blogs, You Tube, and Twitter, or candidate, office holder, or corporate websites.* These sources often provide information about the schedules for public meetings, the activities of nonprofit organizations, and meeting agendas. They often list who is involved in the decision-making process and any other businesses or organizations in which participants are affiliated. In addition, social media descriptions of policies and legislation often contain important information about the values incorporated into decision-making processes, the values and perspective of the writer or person who has posted the information, policy arguments for supporting or opposing the legislation, and research evidence used to support the policy argument.

* *Personal knowledge about people with power (reputational method).* Information collected through one-on-one interviews with community residents regarding their own affiliations, their personal knowledge about who has been involved in a previous decision-making processes, the people in the community who are perceived to have power, the people to whom community members typically go to for help, and the interrelationships among people perceived to have power or influence. For example, knowing that Margarita Sanchez serves on the board of the United Way, runs the constituency office for the local state senator, and is married to City Council Member Gonzalez provides important information about how contacting or persuading her to take a specific decision can be used to influence community decision-making (Conservation Partnership, 2002; Domhoff, 2009b; Hardina, 2002, 2005; Meenaghan et al., 1982; Minkler & Coombe, 2009; Work Group for Community Health and Development, 2010) (Figure 6.3).

FIGURE 6.3
Network map: Social and political network for Margarita Sanchez.

Group Methods for Conducting Power Analysis

Group methods for conducting power analysis often involve meetings in which participants working with a designated facilitator identify people, individual groups, legislation, strength in numbers, and other driving or restraining factors that can facilitate or block change or weaknesses and opportunities inside and outside the organization or coalition group that is coordinating the change effort. Often a chart or piece of butcher block paper is used to record suggestions and comments from attendees—and it provides space to list positive and negative factors or forces that can influence the organizing effort. Sometimes conceptual or network maps can be constructed that identify driving and oppositional forces or that diagram relationships among powerful groups or people in the community (Noy, 2008) (Figure 6.4).

In addition, formal research studies can be conducted to supplement the knowledge of community members. The use of the Internet makes much of the formal research necessary to identify community power arrangements accessible on the web. If a group meeting is not sufficient for obtaining all information necessary to identify community power holders, group members can be asked to conduct web searches

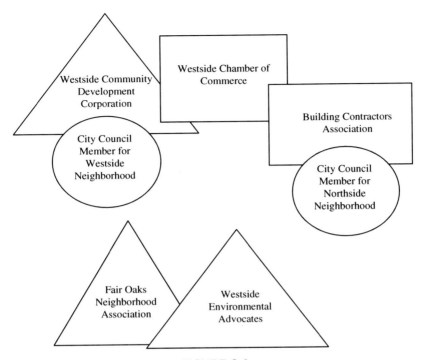

FIGURE 6.4

Conceptual map: Overlapping boards in the Westside Neighborhood. This type of map is described in Noy, D. (2008). Legend: Triangle = Community Groups, Circles = Government Decision-makers; Squares = Business Associations.

of campaign donations, board membership, or newspaper archives and social media sources. The Center for Community Engagement and Service Learning also recommends that individual group members construct a power map that illustrates their own relationships with individuals and groups in the community who can influence the decision-making process. Some of the people on these personal maps are those with whom the constituent has built relationships through one-on-one interviews (Whitcher, Coyne, McCauley, & Rauenhorst, 2009–2010).

Once the community group has a sufficient understanding of community power, the next step involves the identification of patterns or themes by participants and development of a plan for action that neutralizes the opposition or increases the power of the community group to take action and influence policy, legislation, and other public decisions. Ritas, Minkler, Ni, and Halpin (2008) identify a number of steps that can be used by group facilitators to involve participants in power mapping: Generally, these issues can be addressed by using some of the same questions and techniques used in other types of participatory research studies—focusing on who is involved and what, why, and how things happen. Participants should engage in the following activities:

- Identify the change objective.
- Identify key decision-makers and organizations.
- On a sheet of butcher block paper, list these key people and groups under one of three headings: allies, opponents, and undecided.
- Choose the three most important people and groups to influence.
- Reflect on how difficult it was to identify people or choose the most influential among a number of possibilities. Determine if group members have any relationships with these decision-makers that can be used in the social change endeavor.
- Conduct a force field analysis by listing the people you want to influence on a separate sheet of paper with three columns, Positive Factors, Negative Factors, and Strategies for Change. Identify driving or resisting forces and the relative strength of these forces.
- Begin to develop social change strategies that are appropriate for persuading or pressuring opponents, developing partnerships with potential allies, or asking potential opponents to join your coalition or engage in dialogue to seek common ground (Table 6.2).

PUTTING VALUES IN ACTION: BUILDING ON STRENGTHS

While the very nature of participatory action research seems to incorporate basic tenants associated with the strengths perspective and community empowerment, there are a number of ethical dilemmas that characterize efforts to include community members in efforts to conduct community assessments. For example, Stoecker (2008) acknowledges that the original purpose of PAR is to encourage self-sufficiency, personal and political process and control of the research process and knowledge production by members of marginalized communities. However, a PAR process that assigns oversight and most research responsibility for technical tasks or basic research design to an academic or other consultant does not necessarily fulfill this goal. Stoecker is also concerned about the prospect of the researcher fulfilling "the educator's role," in that there is potential for the imposition of an ideological perspective or predetermined methodological stance. Control of projects and goal setting can also impose contradictions and questions about power and status in circumstances in which an outside organization approaches a community for participation in a new project or initiative.

TABLE 6.2
Power Map and Force Field Analysis of Allies and Opponents
of New Environmental Regulations Affecting Businesses
in the Westside Neighborhood

Change to be Made:

Primary Allies	Opponents	Uncertain or Neutral
Westside Community Development Corporation	Westside Chamber of Commerce	Westside Council of Churches
Fair Oaks Neighborhood Association	Council of Realtors	Westside Civic Organization
Consumer Rights Association	Building Contractors Association	Members of the City Council
Westside Environmental Advocates	Individual Business Owners	
Individual Homeowners		

Groups to be Influenced	Positive or Driving Factors	Negative or Restraining Factors
Westside Chamber of Commerce	Limited power and influence	Ideology that opposes must regulations
Building Contractors Association	Actively trying to improve their image in the community	New regulations would affect building costs
Members of the City Council	Can be influenced through lobbying and the prospect of votes	Westside Council Member is also a member of the Building Contractors Association

Proposed Strategies and Tactics:

Note: Additional items that can be included in the analysis are the types of organizations involved, and the source or amount of power possessed by the various organizations or individuals identified in the chart.

Much of our knowledge about how to navigate these ethical issues comes from qualitative research. For example, Maiter, Simich, Jacobson, and Wise (2008) describe the importance of reciprocity in conducting PAR projects, the principle associated with ensuring that all research participants benefit directly from a community-based study as well as the researcher. They view reciprocity as a process that develops over time through relationship-building, using dialogue to develop consensus among all participants and to promote the exchange or resources and knowledge. Fenge (2010) also emphasizes the importance researcher solidarity with the participants, making sure that "the process of mutual trust works both ways. This involves a recognition that the term 'researcher' applies to both local actors and those people who contribute specialized skills, knowledge, and/or resources to the PAR process" (p. 886).

For Harrell and Bond (2006), the primary ethical challenge in community practice and research is functioning as a culturally competent professional in diverse community. They identify a number of practice behaviors needed to put diversity principles in action including identifying the various ethnic and other demographic groups in the community and, finding out how these groups interact with one another. Organizers should also examine community context and the historical, social, and political forces that make the community unique. They also recommend that practitioners engage in reflection about their own location in the social structure, the power and privilege they process, and any biases that may affect their ability to work with members of the community. Harrell and Bond argue that the appropriate stance for a culturally competent practitioner is one of "empowered" humility that is characterized by:

> A willingness to identify limitations, to experience feelings of vulnerability and tolerate the ambiguity of "not knowing." This vulnerability is in the services of gaining greater awareness, insight and understanding. To connect, to learn, and to understand are empowering experiences that build confidence to walk in unfamiliar terrain and meet diversity challenges head on. (p. 372)

Israel et al. (2008) identify practice activities that incorporate assumptions about the importance of mutual, reciprocal, and equal partnerships and cultural competence into the PAR research process:

- Members of the research partnership must be able to define the community that is to be studied, the people who are to be included in the study, and appropriate individuals and organization who serve as the community's representatives on the research team.

* The PAR-related research methods used in specific situations may and should differ based on the research questions, the situation addressed, and the people involved. A standard methodology used for a number of different studies may not adequately reflect the preferences of participants.

* Members of the community should set research priorities and participate in the choice of research design and methodology. Researchers should not impose the specific methods used, but engage in dialogue with team members to develop the best approach.

* Group dialogue should be used to address differences among participants in terms of culture, ethnicity, social class, gender, sexual orientation, education, and other demographic characteristics. It should be recognized and acknowledged that different members have different perspectives, goals, agenda, and knowledge, both tacit (experiential) and formal. Proactive efforts should be made to bridge these differences so that participants "speak a common language" and forge a consensus about goals, methodology, and outcomes.

* All members of the research partnership have responsibility for ensuring that the process of collaboration in undertaken in a way that facilitates equality among all participants, keeping in mind that some inequities in terms of power and status are likely to are likely to exist and affect the PAR process. Such differences should be examined and addressed.

* All members will not be involved in every activity undertaken. Many tasks will be assigned to members based on skills and interests. However, all members should be involved in interpreting the data collected.

* A formative or ongoing evaluation of the degree to which the research partnership actually reflects PAR principles should be conducted, with adjustments made in procedures and activities as necessary.

* A process should be mutually agreed upon for disseminating the findings to others, either for use by the community or publication in professional journals or presentations by the researchers.

Toward this end, the Oakland Community Based Public Health Initiative has developed a protocol that can be used to guide dialogue between researchers and other participants:

1. How will research processes and outcomes serve the community?
2. How will the community be involved in defining the objectives of the research?

3. Are researchers committed to doing the follow-up necessary to implement larger projects?
4. How will the community be involved in the analysis of the data?
5. How, when, and why should the findings be released?
6. What is the focus of the research vis-à-vis addressing long-term community needs?
7. Are the research methods sufficiently rigorous yet true to community-based principles that incorporate perspectives and beliefs of community residents? (Brown & Vega, 2008, p. 396)

SUMMARY

Community assessment is a critical step in the problem-solving process in community practice. Data help guide us to document community issues and assets, suggest changes in services, policies, and legislation that address community needs, and give us an indication of how to engage in action to address these concerns. However, some of the primary questions in community assessment practice are who determines community preferences for change, who has control of data and other information, and how, and to what degree, community residents are involved in the social change efforts. Participatory action research provides a vehicle for incorporating basic social work and community organization principles including self-determination, empowerment, the strengths perspective, respect for diverse cultures and underrepresented groups, equal partnerships, mutual learning, and partnership in the research process. Data collection methods such as Photovoice, asset mapping, participatory community mapping, social indicator partnerships, and power analysis require a commitment to these values as well as the appropriate application of appropriate interpersonal and task-related skills on the part of the researcher or organizer. In Chapter 7, the next stage of the problem-solving process, goal setting, and planning will be examined and techniques to enhance the inclusion of community members in decision-making will be described.

EXERCISES AND ASSIGNMENTS

1. In your classroom, divide members into two teams to plan and stage a debate. The topic of the Debate is the "Limitations and Advantages" of Qualitative (Impressionistic) versus Quantitative (Objective) Data in Participatory Research. You may use library and Internet research sources to inform your argument.

2. Conduct a power analysis of a geographic or identity community using at least three of the data collection methods listed in this chapter. At least one of these data collection methods should include either individual interviews with community members or consultation with constituency group members. Prepare a report that: lists primary decision-makers and their sources of power and identifies their positions on at least one issue of importance to the community. For that issue, identify driving and restraining sources and existing or potential allies and opponents. Develop a map of the power relationships (conceptual or network) that affect this community.

3. With a group of constituents or classmates, develop an asset map of a specific geographic community. This assignment may be combined with photography of community assets if cameras are available for use. With members of the group, combine the information collected into a geographic map using low-technology (such as butcher block paper) or high-technology computerized maps to identify important community assets. Write a brief report in consultation with group members that describes these community assets and why they are important to community members.

   In a second part of this assignment, describe your experience conducting this project with a group. What was your primary role as a facilitator? Was the decision-making process characterized by consensus or conflict? How were differences of opinion resolved? How easy or difficult was it for you to refrain from making all the decisions for the group?

4. Work with constituency group members to identify a research problem and an appropriate method for conducting research using at least one of the methodological approaches identified in this chapter (e.g., constructing a survey or interview guide, creating community indicators, or using Photovoice). Once a measurement tool has been identified and created, work with the group to carry out the study and analyze the findings. Work with the group to develop a report about the findings, making sure that findings are disseminated to both community members and influential decision-makers. The report does not need to be written—for example, it can be a photo exhibit, a video, a play, or a set of drawings, or an art installation. The report may also include the group's assessment of the research process.

In addition to the "report," submit an assessment of the group process that includes a reflection of your own work and how you dealt with issues regarding group maintenance and task accomplishment.

7

Facilitating Leadership Development and Group Decision Making: Encouraging Public Participation in Planning and Engaging Constituents in the Development of Action Plans

> *One is a bad leader, he who by his actions does not measure the consequences that they may have on the people, the actions by which he threatens or excites or invites them to participate.*
> —Interview with an Immigrant Rights Organizer, Hardina et al., 2011

After problem identification and assessment, during the engagement phase of community organizing, action planning must take place. This work must involve constituents, and, in many cases, be led or controlled by them. The ability of everyday people to determine what happens in their communities contributes substantially to the quality of life in neighborhoods and the well-being of individuals and families. In this chapter, the theoretical underpinnings of the philosophy associated with constituent involvement are discussed. A related concept, *leadership development* in community organizing is also described. This activity is based on the premise that engaged citizens should have the lead role in facilitating decision-making processes in community groups and neighborhood planning, but may need information, training, and support from community organizers to do so effectively. Consequently, one section in this chapter describes techniques used to recruit and train leaders while another provides an overview of techniques commonly used to facilitate and support constituents involved in public decision making and planning. In addition, this chapter also provides information on another important community organizer role, assisting constituents and community leaders with the development of action plans for community campaigns and initiatives and describes techniques for helping group members make choices about the strategies and tactics to be used in these initiatives. The use of group processes to weigh various tactical options and assess the ethical implications of these methods is also presented. In the final section of this chapter, specific practice techniques for incorporating principles of self-determination, empowerment, and cultural competency in action plans and community decision-making processes are described.

THEORETICAL PERSPECTIVES: CONSTITUENT INVOLVEMENT IN DECISION MAKING

Recently, the call for more citizen involvement in planning has gained traction due to the research by Putnam (2000) indicating that few people actually join nonprofit groups or civic organizations, volunteer, or even vote. As described in Chapter 6, Putnam argues that the quality of life in communities is enhanced by high levels of social capital: civic engagement and the strengthening of relationship ties among individuals and groups. He links current efforts to increase civic engagement to observations made by French visitor Alexis de Tocqueville in the 1830s about the role of local organizations and associations in the United States. de Tocqueville (1981) argued that he had found a high degree of participation of ordinary citizens in nongovernment organizations and associations and that such activity was a uniquely American attribute. Putnam's work on social capital has stimulated a number of government and nonprofit efforts to increase civic engagement such as service learning requirements in high schools and universities. The literature on community practice and public participation has documented the many positive effects of civic engagement on community life and public decision making. However, not everyone agrees as to the methods that should be used to increase civic engagement or even if it actually needs to be increased.

Civic Engagement in Public Decision Making: Has it Declined?

Putnam's premise has been extensively critiqued by social theorists and community organizers. Many of these critics have argued that the emphasis on social capital ignores the role of power, cultural values and norms, government, and other institutional structures in which public decision making occurs, resource inequality, and an increasingly global economic structure in determining quality of life in individual communities (Cohen, 2001; DeFilippis, 2009; Maloney, Smith, & Stoker, 2000; Saegert, 2006; Skocpol, 2004). In addition to these factors, traditional patterns of social exclusion and oppression in marginalized communities in the

United States, Europe, and developing countries may limit the degree to which strong bonds and trust can be established among community members from different economic and ethnic backgrounds (Hawkins & Maurer, 2010; Li Puma & Koelble, 2009; Pyles & Cross, 2008).

Despite these criticisms, many theorists agree that the decline in civic organizations in the United States is most likely to affect members of low-income communities or people of color. Institutional barriers to voting such as identification requirements that make it hard for people who do not drive or move frequently to register or laws that make it difficult for former felons to vote exclude large numbers of people from the voting process (Cohen, 2001; Piven & Cloward, 2000). Skocpol (2004) argues that declines in union participation and the growth of advocacy organizations that recruit participants primarily through social media have made participation less likely for people who are not affluent or well educated. Other scholars and community organizers argue that economic hardship and the availability of government funding for service provision in low-income communities has made it less likely that neighborhood organizations will engage in social action, preferring to address urgent needs of local residents (Brooks, 2005; Smith, 2010). Receipt of government funding may also make it difficult for organizations, dependent on government funding to actually advocate against government policies and legislation (Andrews, Ganz, Baggetta, Han, & Lim, 2010).

There is even some evidence that participation among low-income people may not have decreased as drastically as some scholars believe. For example, Caputo (2010) used data from the National Longitudinal Survey to compare levels of civic engagement between low-income people in the United States who received public benefits and people with higher incomes. He found no difference in the degree of community activism between the two groups. Qualitative studies conducted by Green (2005) and Hunt (2007) indicate that low-income people do participate in community organizations and other types of activism although such activity may be of lower intensity (e.g., attendance at meetings or volunteering to stuff envelopes rather serving on the board) or frequency than among people with more income. It should also be noted that some national organizations with local affiliates have reported high membership levels. For example, before its demise, ACORN reported having 200,000 families as members (Delgado, 2009). PICO (2011) estimates that it has 1,000 affiliated institutions and over 1 million member families. In addition to these formal estimates, activism can often be under reported; it may take place in informal groups or poorly funded community organizations in low-income neighborhoods (Hardina et al., 2009).

Positive Benefits Associated With Civic Engagement

As described in Chapter 3, efforts to maintain or increase levels of community engagement are critical for successful community organization. For social action practitioners or adherents of transformative approaches, membership on the boards of local organizations, involvement in social change activities and protests, engagement in lobbying for legislation, and participation in election campaigns are viewed as essential for acquiring the political power needed to improve the community's access to resources (Homan, 2011; Staples, 2004). Community developers view involvement as a mechanism for improving relationship ties among community members and developing a consensus about community goals (Ohmer & DeMasi, 2009). Social planners believe that the participation of community members in the development of programs and plans increases the likelihood that these initiatives will adequately address the needs, lived experiences, and cultural values of the people who are likely to use the goods and services produced. (Laurian & Shaw, 2009; Parker & Betz, 1996; Smith, 2010).

In addition, participation in public decision making and service on the boards of community-based organizations have been found to increase an individual's leadership skills and feelings of empowerment and self-efficacy (Ayon & Lee, 2009; Gutierrez et al., 1998; Mizrahi, Lopez Humphreys, & Torres, 2009; Plitt Donaldson, 2004; Ramirez-Valles, Fergus, Reisen, Popplen, & Zea, 2005). Some studies have also verified empirically that community inclusion on boards also improves the likelihood that community-based organizations will find the resources that they need to survive financially and that they will be accountable to the people they serve (Milam Handley & Howell-Moroney, 2010; Walker & McCarthy, 2010).

The term generally used to describe involvement in public decision making and other types of civic engagement is *citizen participation* (Hardina, 2003; Richards & Dalbey, 2006). Citizen participation can be defined as efforts by residents of low-income communities to improve the quality of neighborhood life and advocate for changes in public policies (Ohmer & Beck, 2006). The term *citizen participation* was used extensively in the 1960s to describe government-mandated efforts to provide opportunities for clients to serve on the boards of nonprofit organizations (Marris & Rein, 1982). As proposed in the United States, the government policy of *maximum feasible participation* was intended as a tool for increasing access to social services for members of low-income communities as part of the government's "War on Poverty" (Moynihan, 1969). However, the purpose of the program was often subverted when local government officials and other members of the political establishment who actually controlled the purse strings appointed their own representatives to these boards. Government officials quickly ended the program as a consequence of the few instances in which low-income participants actively engaged in protests and other efforts to increase their political power (Defilippis, 2009; Rose, 1972; Smith, 2010).

Methods Used to Increase Citizen Participation

Although citizen participation has not only been highly institutionalized in the United States today, but many government agencies and foundations that typically fund nonprofit organizations and programs also require some degree of citizen or consumer participation. Most often, this manifests itself through organizational structures that provide seats on boards of directors or advisory councils to the users of services (Hardina et al., 2006; Linhorst, Eckert, & Hamilton, 2005; Mizrahi et al., 2009). Community forums, focus groups, and surveys are also used extensively by government agencies and nonprofit organizations to solicit comments and recommendations from service users, residents, and citizens. Participants can also be hired as paraprofessional staff with special expertise and knowledge about how the community operates, its values, and norms, and connections with other potential constituents and community leaders (Smith, 2010).

Often local and state governments make explicit efforts to inform program beneficiaries and taxpayers about policy proposals, plans, legislation, or budgets. Such efforts can range from public comment sessions to membership on formal citizen planning boards. Government-mandated planning councils, with appointed or elected members, have also been used extensively by governments in a variety of countries to solicit input on service decision making, redevelopment issues, and funding priorities (Chin, 2009; Dierwechter & Coffey, 2010; Moffat, George, Lee, & McGrath, 1999). As with the War on Poverty in the United States, the stated purpose of such efforts has been to counter the harmful effects of social exclusion and marginalization and increase the likelihood that scarce government resources will be distributed equitably. However, the track record for these planning efforts is often mixed, as different groups in society have more power than others to influence the decision-making process (Bowen, 2007; Gaventa & Valderrama, 1999; Rispel, de Sousa, & Molomo, 2009).

As noted in Chapter 3, social media has increasingly played a large role in social change activities. Both government and political candidates have also begun to use such mechanisms as Facebook or MySpace,

Twitter, and YouTube, to reach large audiences of people and to make information about candidates, public policy, and government expenditures more accessible to the public. These methods have also been used to target those groups of voters who are most likely to use these information sources (Dutil, Howard, Langford, & Roy, 2007). In some cases, these techniques can be used successfully to engage people as a group in public events such as political debates or consultative processes (Kirk & Schill, 2011).

There are different opinions about and assessments of the levels and impact of citizen and client participation at the agency and community levels. Arnstein (1969) has argued that efforts to empower community residents and clients by providing opportunities for input into government decision making or seats on nonprofit organization boards or establishing advisory groups have produced varying results, running the gamut from token representation, manipulation, therapy, and co-optation to simple consultation without guarantees that such advice will actually be utilized, to community partnership and control. Numerous research studies indicate that many government-mandated citizen participation efforts have been unsuccessful in transferring power from established political elites to members of low-income groups (Buccus, Hemson, Hicks, & Piper, 2008; Claque, Dill, Seebaran, & Wharf, 1984; Dierwechter & Coffey, 2009; King, Feltey, & Susel, 1998; Marris & Rein, 1982; Silverman, 2003, 2005). Nevertheless, there are numerous examples of successful community-based, citizen participation efforts (Brody et al., 2003; Checkoway & Zimmerman, 1992; Itzhaky & York, 2002; Milam et al., 2010; Ohmer & Beck, 2006). Components of successful citizen participation efforts include ideological commitment to empowerment on the part of professional staff assigned to facilitate these efforts, appropriate organization structures that provide sufficient opportunities for community input, the provision of adequate information about decision-making roles and technical decision making, and training in leadership skills for participants. Leadership training and development is generally regarded as one of the primary roles for community organizers (Hardina & Malott, 1996; Kahn, 1991; Milam Handley & Howell-Moroney, 2010). Such training often focuses on preparing constituency group members for leadership roles in community organizations or providing information and support for participants in public decision-making processes (Ayon & Lee, 2009; Kirk & Shutte, 2004; Smock, 2004).

LEADERSHIP DEVELOPMENT AND TRAINING

Often the term "grassroots leaders" are used to describe those individuals who emerge from the community organization process to lead community organizations and organizing campaigns. Boehm and Staples (2006) define grassroots leaders as "unpaid volunteers who emerge from within the community and provide and direction and guidance in specific areas of its life" (p. 78). A leader may have a position as a board president or committee chairperson or may informally provide leadership and support to other members of the community (Rothman, 1997).

Andrews et al. (2010) argue that a special type of volunteer leader is needed for community engagement efforts. They differentiate between formal social service organizations that rely on paid staff and provide services to individual clients and civic organizations:

> Civic organizations depend upon the voluntary efforts of their members, decentralize decision making across local units, govern themselves through elected volunteer leaders, and enable their members' collective voices to be heard. They thus interact with constituents, not customers or clients. Their authority rests on moral suasion rather than economic or political coercion. Their outputs require the voluntary participation of members and supporters. (p. 1192)

The nature of these organizations makes ongoing efforts to recruit and maintain effective leaders essential. Many community organizations do more than select specific individuals for leadership roles in community organizations or organizing campaigns. They may offer leadership skills training or encourage people whom they think will be effective leaders by providing them with a series of tasks or positions that allow them to gradually develop leadership abilities. The Alliance for Justice (n.d.) describes the importance of leadership development in the following way:

> One of the key features that distinguish community organizing from other types of change efforts are its focus on developing leadership and developing constituents' sense of purpose and power. Well-crafted pathways for constituent leadership development within the organizing process (including intentional processes for consciousness raising and the development of critical analysis skills) take time, effort, and skill. Ensuring that the organizing process reinforces a healthy sense of strength among constituents is also something that requires intentional action. (p. 1)

Effective volunteer leaders need a combination of skills similar to those of community organizers: the ability to facilitate task accomplishment, manage group processes, mediate conflicts, build relationships with individuals, groups, and organizations, hold members accountable for their efforts, plan organizing campaigns, and be able to work interdependently with other group members (Andrews et al., 2010; Kahn, 1991). Leaders also need to have communication skills that allow them to articulate a vision for the organization, inspire members, and disseminate the organization's message to others (Evans & Shirley, 2008; Homan, 2011). Grassroots leaders may also derive power from a number of sources including their ability to give support and advice or other resources to community members such as jobs, referrals, contacts with influential people and organizations, the ability to raise funds or obtain resources for their organization, or the ability to mobilize community members to take action or vote. Power can also accrue from simply being about to exchange or trade off these resources with others. Boehm and Staples (2006) describe this type of power as "transactional." Power can also come via personal charisma or the ability to inspire others, articulate a vision about a just society or "right" values, and the ability to inspire others to take action to change themselves or their communities. As with the process inherent in popular education approaches, this type of power can be described as "transformational" (Boehm & Staples, 2006; VeneKlasen et al., 2007). There are also approaches to leadership that can be counterproductive. For example, ineffective or poor leaders can "take over" or lead the group without input from others, actively manipulate group members to further their own self-interests or alternatively, provide little guidance for group members or fail to establish goals for task accomplishment (Zastrow, 2009).

Leadership training courses or workshops typically include content on board membership and responsibilities, advocacy methods, public speaking, the structure and functions of government agencies, and conflict resolution (Ayon & Lee, 2009; Delgado & Staples, 2008). Such courses can also include basic techniques for facilitating groups and conducting meetings (Kahn, 1991; Zachary, 2000). Some leadership development programs also contain a fieldwork component so that participants have a chance to apply their skills within a group context and begin the process of relationship building with others (Sen, 2003). Some programs may also supplement field work with peer mentorship or supervision (Kaminski, Kaufman, Graubarth, & Robins, 2000; Smock, 2004). In addition, prospective leaders may also receive technical or legal training in relation to the issues that they may wish to address or on planning or campaign-building procedures (Evans & Shirley, 2008). Training methods, derived from popular education-related approaches may also involve workshops or institutes that provide education and information that specifically helps new leaders develop a critical consciousness about social, economic, and political forces and how they can be changed to better assist marginalized communities (Smock, 2004).

Other components of leadership training can include opportunities for support from other constituency group members who face similar issues and concerns and relationship building with other advocates and influential decision makers (Shah & Mediratta, 2008). Sen (2003) identifies four primary principles for developing and training leaders.

1. After new leaders are recruited, community organizations should actively engage in activities to help them strengthen their skills over time.
2. Community organizations should commit resources and staff time to establish formal leadership training programs.
3. Community organizers should explicitly address issues related to culture, gender, and race when developing new leaders. For example, in some organizations there may be a leadership hierarchy in which people of a particular race or gender hold most of the leadership positions, requiring that organizers take action to ensure equal access to these positions.
4. In addition to training programs, community organizations need to continuously recruit new leaders, plan for leadership transitions, and seek opportunities to prevent leadership burnout and renewal such as leadership retreats or sabbaticals.

In addition to strengthening organizations, community practitioners also view leadership training as important for bringing about personal transformation. For example, Reinelt, Foster, and Sullivan (2003) surveyed 55 community groups to examine how leadership training programs are typically evaluated. Respondents identified a number of specific outcome measures used to determine whether these programs are successful. In addition to successful advocacy or changes in public policies and institutional systems, these outcome measures also involve changes in the leaders themselves and include:

- Development of new skills and knowledge.
- Changes in attitudes, values, behavior, and perspectives.
- Increases in self-awareness and discovery.
- An increase in the degree to which new leaders are committed to leadership roles in social justice initiatives over time.
- Improvements in ability of the new leaders to deepen their relationships and bonds with other constituents and widen their own social networks and circles of influence.

Other outcomes associated with leadership development include feelings of self-empowerment and self-efficacy or confidence in one's own skills (Boehm & Staples, 2006). According to Evans and Shirley (2008), effective community leaders move beyond a focus on furthering their own self-interests, to regarding activism as a "moral imperative" that requires them to act for the good of the community.

Sen (2003) also describes leadership development as a process in which the new leader progressively takes on a progression of skills and responsibilities, ranging from recruiting new members, acting as a spokesperson, raising funds, developing a critical consciousness, chairing meetings, serving on the board, helping to hire staff, to supervising staff, and planning action campaigns. Boehm and Staples (2006) interviewed grassroots leaders in social action-related organizations about how they developed their leadership skills. The respondents describe a process through which they became involved in social action through interest and involvement in a single issue and began to take on a number of leadership tasks overtime in order to "move through the leadership ranks" and acquire more responsibility in committees and organizations. They also viewed themselves as having the ability to overcome a variety of organizing and personal challenges, learn from experience, and articulate a vision for their constituents.

FACILITATING CONSTITUENT PARTICIPATION IN PUBLIC DECISION MAKING AND PLANNING

A major component of community organization practice focuses on providing assistance to community residents or members of marginalized groups who wish to increase their power and influence in public decision making. Organizers often recruit community residents for participation on public and nonprofit boards (Gamble & Weil, 1995). They also set up organizational structures to facilitate participation on boards, advisory committees, and public planning bodies and help people who represent low-income or marginalized groups overcome barriers that limit their participation (Daley, 2002; Hardina et al., 2006). Inclusion of the public is believed to improve the quality of government planning, make it more likely that the public will support government plans, and as in the War on Poverty, provide a mechanism to reduce the negative impact of economic, social, and political marginalization among members of low-income groups (Hardina, 2003; Mizrahi et al., 2009).

Barriers to inclusion of community members in organizational and government planning include: the use of language (technical, formal, or solely the language associated with the general population rather than specific ethnic groups), distrust among participants, distrust of government, culture, socioeconomic status, the dominance of the professionals and other experts in the planning process, and demographic factors such as gender, ethnicity or race, sexual orientation, health or mental health status and disability, and age (Evans & Shirley, 2008; Hardina & Malott, 1996; Laurian & Shaw, 2009; Potter, 2010; Shah & Mediratta, 2008). Economic hardship and stigmatization may also make it difficult for members of marginalized groups to participate in government decision making as well (Green, 2005; Silverman, 2005).

Another difficulty with government-mandated citizen involvement in planning is that the decision-making structures, the limited funding provided for planning purposes, the purpose of the planning process, and restrictions on the types of decisions that can be made come from government or from the "top" down. Grassroots decision making, as defined by organizers, are efforts made by community residents and other constituency group members, to make decisions at the local level or bottom up (Mizrahi et al., 2009). Consequently, these decisions are less likely to respond to government agendas and are more likely to reflect the preferences of community members. However, it then becomes the responsibility of these participants to influence or pressure government to adopt their demands.

Social workers, organizers, and planners can play a variety of roles in the planning process. A commitment to full participation on the part of organizational leaders is often instrumental in ensuring that people who are usually excluded from decision making are heard (Bess, Prilleltensky, Perkins, & Collins, 2009). Advocacy to ensure that decision-making groups function in a manner that conveys respect and support for members of marginalized groups and that planning groups have the financial and other resources needed to support effective decision-making is essential (Silverman, 2003). Supportive services needed for planning can include translation services, training for people who have not previously participated in planning efforts, recruiting from income and demographically diverse populations, and the provision of technical information in a manner accessible to nonprofessionals, and support for low-income people such as transportation, day care, and meals is essential (Beresford & Croft, 2001; Daley, 2002; Hardina & Malott, 1996; Parker & Betz, 1996).

The creation of organizational structures to support full inclusion of participants in planning is also essential. For example, Linhorst et al., (2005) describe explicit structures established within a public mental health facility to sure client participation that included a formal client grievance policy, opportunities for clients to participate in hospital's performance review teams and assess policies related to the quality of life in the facility such as the food provided to them and access to libraries and medical records. Clients also served on a consumer council which met with the hospital director on a regular basis. Silvestre, Faber, Shankle, and Kopelman (2002) describe a structure to enhance youth participation in HIV prevention planning that incorporated basic values of equality and respect for all participants. Participants were elected to the planning body by members of smaller groups established to represent diverse viewpoints, cultures, and interests in the community, each member had the same voting rights, and explicit efforts were made to incorporate cultural competency in the planning and decision-making process.

Drawing upon data from interviews with local officials in 10 states that mandate citizen participation in development efforts, Brody et al. (2003) identify six types of strategic choices that planners typically make when designing citizen participation efforts mandated by government agencies:

1. *Resource allocation and program administration.* What staffing and other resources will be provided for the program? Will a written plan for program operation be prepared?
2. *Program objectives.* What is the purpose of the program and what degree of citizen participation will be permitted? For example, is the effort simply about complying with government requirements or is the intent to actually learn something about citizen or consumer preferences and values? Is the intent to foster actual citizen influence in the plan or to encourage the public to support government policies?
3. *Degree of citizen involvement.* When will people first be involved to participate in the planning process? Are residents and other potential beneficiaries involved in the actual development of the plan, are they asked to help evaluate alternative planning options, or are they only consulted after the plan has been completed.
4. *Invitations to participate.* What groups of people and organizations should be targeted for recruitment and participation in the planning process. For example, should participants be limited to business representatives, elected officials, or professional groups? Should people who own property that will be affected by the planning effort or neighborhood residents be included? Should specific demographic populations such as the elderly, people with disabilities, or members of marginalized groups who may be negatively affected by the plan be included in plan development?
5. *Soliciting input.* How will input from participants be obtained? For example, should input be limited to a survey, public meeting, or

community forums or should more formal and inclusive processes such as workshops, advisory committees, or planning groups be utilized?

6. *Provision of information.* How should information about the problem to be addressed or the plan be provided to the general public or targeted groups? How much information should be provided and how should it be provided? For example, is posting the information on a government website sufficient or should planners give presentations or solicit media coverage for the planning effort?

In addition, efforts to solicit the participation of the public in planning efforts, one of the challenges involved in citizen participation involves retention of the people who do participate, organizers, social planners, and other social workers can also provide staff support services to people seated on planning councils or organizational boards or advisory groups. This type of activity includes such tasks as working collaboratively with board and committee members in developing agendas, providing financial information for managing or examining budgets, conducting research, and consulting with other individuals and groups (Hardina et al., 2006). Participation in public planning is also facilitated through the provision of technical support to participants such as data analysis and other professional expertise needed to analyze plans and implement them.

Staff support also is used to facilitate dialogue among participants so that they reach a consensus as to the problem to be addressed, assessment, goals, and planning options to be explored and used in the process (Laurian & Shaw, 2009). Kirk and Shutte (2004) describe this process in the following manner:

> Practicing dialogue can lead to an agreement between parties even though they do not have the same reasons for agreeing to the direction to be followed or the action to be taken. When the environment for dialogue feels good enough, safe enough, people are better able to deal with the uncertainties and difficulties experienced, and construct appropriate responses to the realities of the word in which their organization is to find their place. (p. 140)

Forester (1989) identifies a number of interpersonal skills that can be used to guide the decision-making process in public planning. These skills include active listening to others, recognizing the cultural identities of participants and how that affects planning preferences and values, and mediating disputes among the parties involved in the planning effort, with the intent of equalizing power relations among the participants and facilitating inclusive practices. He also views staff support for planning and decision making as a set of choices that involve providing factual information, conveying respect for participants with less power, and ensuring that people who will be most affected by planning decisions actually have a voice in the process. Forester advocates "thinking rationally" and "acting politically" in the decision-making process, taking a number of precautionary steps to insure inclusion of people with limited power resources:

- Establish relationships with community groups in order to obtain and distribute information.
- Engage in active listening to determine the interests of all groups likely to be involved in the process and to identify political barriers to inclusion.
- Notify people most likely to be excluded early on in the process about any planning decision that is likely to affect them.
- Educate individuals and community groups about the planning process and the "rules of the game."
- Develop skills for managing conflict.
- Inform historically excluded community groups about the importance of political pressure and having a constituency base that can mobilize politically in order to push for their interests to be incorporated into the plan.

Information provision, mediation, and conflict management also can take place in the context of group dialogue that includes both the planner or organizer and the various groups involved in the process. In the next few sections of this paper, the process of group dialogue in creating community action plans is described.

ENGAGING CONSTITUENTS IN THE DEVELOPMENT
OF COMMUNITY ACTION PLANS

In addition to participation in public decision making, community groups influence legislation and public policy through participation in community organizations and community development and social action campaigns or social planning activities through nonprofit organizations, service networks, or task forces. Consequently, one of the roles assumed by community organizers is facilitation of constituency group decision making in the development of action plans or campaigns. Action plans specify goals and objectives to be addressed, the strategies and tactics used to achieve them, how tasks will be assigned, what resources will be used, and how the campaign will be evaluated.

The Purpose and Components of Action Plans

Action plans are essentially road maps that identify what activities will be undertaken during social action and community development campaigns or initiatives or how social planning processes will proceed. Decisions are most often made through dialogue between constituents and organizers or planners or through consultation among representatives of coalition, collaborative, or task group members. In some cases, decisions involving social planning may be made by professionals or other experts working on behalf of government agencies and community groups.

Action plans have a number of components: overall strategies, tactical methods, goals, objectives, desired outcomes, and an evaluation plan (Bobo et al., 2010). Since most action campaigns are carried out through coordinated actions by volunteers and other constituents, specific roles for individuals are also identified. Organizers often act as facilitators in this process and in some cases they may have assigned tasks that need to be completed so that constituents can take action. Often the organizer's responsibility may be described in a work plan as part of a formal supervisory process designed to hold the organizer accountable to the organization (see Chapters 9 and 13). However, there is also an expectation that the staff member will be accountable to members of the constituency group as well.

As described in Chapter 1, a strategy is a long-term plan of action. There are five primary types of strategies used in organizing campaigns. Each one of these methods involves different types of activities.

- *Collaboration.* Developing a consensus for action among a variety of different groups.
- *Campaign.* Engaging in activities designed to bring opponents to the bargaining table.
- *Contest or confrontation.* Targeting opponents in order to produce social change.
- *Problem solving.* Examining a problem and all the facts associated with it in order to identify the best approach for resolving it.
- *Population Education or Transformative Methods.* As associated with practice methods developed by Freire (1970), activities that lead to personal and societal transformation (Brager, Specht, & Torczyner, 1987; Hardcastle et al., 2004; Hardina, 2002; Ohmer & DeMasi, 2009; Pyles, 2009a; Rothman, 1979, 1996, 2008).

Choices of the type of strategy utilized are determined by a number of factors, the situation to be addressed, the degree to which adoption of a policy or issue or the lack of a decision would hurt individuals, the amount of time or resources needed to successfully address the issue, the ideology or comfort of the organizer facilitating the action, and, most importantly, the preferences and comfort level of the constituents involved in the action (Brager et al., 1987; Hardina et al., 2009; Mondros & Wilson, 1994; Mondros, 2005). Since some of these methods involve a great deal of time, and in some situations, entail risks for constituents (e.g., participation in protests can involve job loss), many organizers prefer to use low-intensity methods such as collaboration and gradually escalate their use of tactical methods if needed to bring about successful outcomes (Netting, Kettner, & McMurty 2008). Another consideration in the choice of strategies involves the people or groups that will be involved in the action, the people or systems who are the target of the action or who must be influenced to create change, and the degree of communication between the people taking action (action system) and their targets (target systems). When the same people are members of the action or target systems then collaborative approaches may be used; when members of either system do not communicate with one another or some type of action (campaigns or confrontation) is needed bring them to the

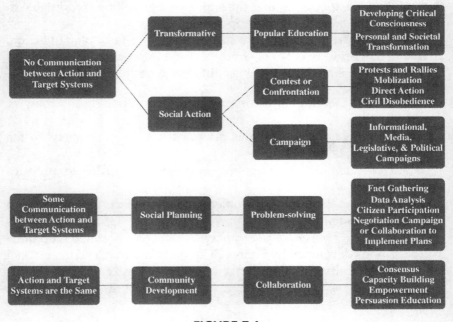

FIGURE 7.1

Choosing strategies and tactics. This conceptual model builds on models of practice identified by Rothman (1979, 1996, 2008) and strategic approaches identified in Brager et al. (1987) and Netting, Kettner, and McMurty (2008).

bargaining table (Brager et al., 1987). The group's analysis of the power resources available to them (see Chapter 6) and those held by members of the target group also enter into decisions about strategies (see Figure 7.1).

Within each of these strategic approaches a variety of short-term activities or tactics can be used within the context of a long-term campaign. Most organizers agree that tactics should be chosen by community groups through mutual dialogue between the organizer and one's constituents. Tactics should also be:

- Culturally appropriate and incorporate culturally relevant terms, activities, and symbols.
- Appropriate and relevant to the lives and experience of participants/ beneficiaries.
- Flexible in design, incorporating different methods in response to the situation at hand.
- Take into account the amount of power held by the group taking action and the power and resources of people likely to be opposed to the plan.
- Fun for participants with opportunities for social interaction with others.
- Minimize potential risks for all people likely to be involved.
- Incorporate moral principles and values that help "sell" the issue under consideration to the public or media sources (Ganz, 2009; Hardina, 2002; Homan, 2011; Kahn, 1991, 2010; Polletta, 2006; Satterwhite & Teng, 2007; Young Laing, 2009).

Tactics should also, for the most part, be consistent with the overall strategy or approach used for the organizing campaign. For example, contest or confrontation-oriented strategies employ such tactics as protests, sit-ins, strikes, or boycotts. Collaborative strategies involve consensus, individual and community capacity building, education, and persuasion. However, as noted by Rothman (2008) most campaigns take place in several phases; therefore, it may be necessary to modify tactical methods in response to situational demands or because successful outcomes often require a shift in the type of tactics used or an escalation in the type of pressure used by decision makers. For example, a community plan, developed by consensus among neighborhood residents and local organizations may represent an agreement among participants, but other efforts may be needed to persuade elected officials to support or approve the plan or to allocate funds and other resources that will assure implementation (Figure 7.2).

In addition to strategies and tactics, other components of community campaigns include the following elements:

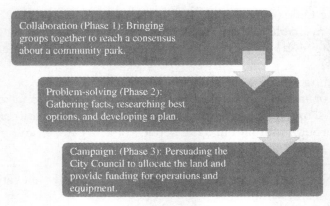

FIGURE 7.2
Mixing and phasing strategic approaches.

- Goals or broad statements about what the action plan is intended to achieve.
- Objectives or time-limited, measurable statements about the steps that will be taken to achieve the goal.
- A time-line for completing activities or objectives that places these activities in a logical sequence that will enhance their success.
- The resources needed to carry out the plan such as people, facilities, funds, media contacts, or technical support).
- Specific tasks or roles assigned to constituency group members, leaders, and paid staff that will help the group execute the plan.
- Evaluation criteria for judging the success of the action plan. Criteria can include both outcomes to be achieved as well as an assessment of the process of carrying out the plan (Bobo et al., 2010; Hardina, 2002; Hoefer, 2006; Staples, 2004) (Box 7.1).

Group processes are used to determine most of the components of the plan. In some instances, leaders, organizing staff or a small committee may be called upon to develop a plan or make specific recommendations that will be taken back to the group for approval. When the plan is developed in a group, a number of techniques are used to document decisions including note taking, formal minutes taken by one group member and reviewed for accuracy by the others, or outlining each component of the plan on butcher block paper or a blackboard. The advantage of this method is that it gives group members feelings of ownership about the development of the plan (VeneKlasen et al., 2007). It also assists group members in fitting together "pieces" of the puzzle, a time-line for goal achievement and the specific types of actions that should be taken to achieve them (Figure 7.3).

Goal: Increase Community Access to Healthy Food.

Objective 1: Recruit 60 community residents for a community garden initiative by February 1, 2013.

Objective 2: Negotiate with the city to obtain permission to purchase (at a nominal price) or lease five vacant lots that can be used for community gardens by March 2013.

Objective 3: Recruit 5 volunteer "master gardeners" to assist local residents with starting and maintaining community gardens by March 15, 2013.

Objective 4: Provide 10 "hand-on" technical workshops and demonstrations that will provide residents with the "know how" to successfully plant and maintain community gardens by March 31, 2013.

Objective 5: Start-up five community gardens by April 30, 2013.

Objective 6: Maintain the participation of a least 10 community residents in each community garden over a 5-month period by September 30, 2013.

Evaluation
Criteria: Number of volunteers and master gardeners recruited, number of workshops held, participant satisfaction survey, number of gardens established, number of gardens maintained over a 5-month period, or the amount of food harvested from the garden.

More formal methods of documentation are also used when describing plan components, especially specific goals, objectives, and evaluation criteria identified in funding proposals. Donors may also require that specific work plans be developed for the organization in which organizing activities are described in detail (Bobo et al., 2010). Written work plans can also be developed for the action campaign and distributed to members by mail or via the Internet. However, there are a number of dilemmas inherent in formalizing long-term work plans. For example, action plans are often altered in response to unanticipated events or changes in available resources. In addition, in some types of social action and transformative organizing, keeping specific tactical plans (such as protests) confidential may be critical may be essential (Considine, 2011).

It is critical that all elements of the plan fit together in some type of local manner that links problem identification, assessment, power analysis, goal setting, action planning, implementation and evaluation. However, the process is seldom so straightforward; successful campaigns

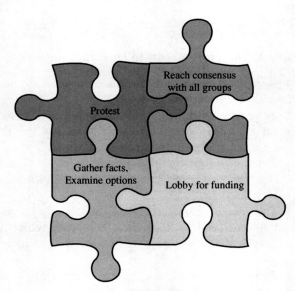

FIGURE 7.3
Putting the puzzle together: Choosing tactical methods.

require "fine-tuning," and ongoing dialogue among participants, in response to new information or when strategies and tactics prove to be ineffective. Therefore, action plans will continue to be modified throughout the course of a campaign as participants reflect on their experiences and work toward successful outcomes (Figure 7.4).

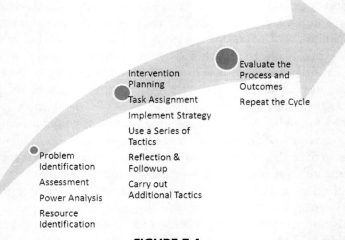

FIGURE 7.4
Campaign planning process.

Using Group Methods to Weigh Ethical Decisions and Choose Strategies and Tactics

For most organizers, the involvement of constituency group members in choosing strategies and tactics is a critical component in the social change process. Constituent involvement ensures that the methods used for action campaigns have meaning for participants, reflects their values, and increase the likelihood that constituents will actually participate in any activities needed to carry them out. Organizing campaigns are similar in nature to both coalition-building and other types of group activities. Members must depend on one another for the success of the plan; if one or more persons fail to perform an assigned task, the event or activity will fail. As mentioned previously in this text, there is strength in numbers, the more people who participate in an action the better the chance that it will be successful.

Mondros and Wilson (1994) identify four reasons that decisions on strategies and tactics should be made in the context of mutual dialogue among organizers, leaders, and constituency group members;

- Constituents are educated about the process of organizing and the various options available to them.
- Constituents develop a sense of ownership of the organizing process and begin to feel empowered to take action.
- Constituents have the primary role in determining strategies and tactics. This serves as a "safeguard" against allowing the organizer's ideology or personal biases to determine what action will be taken.
- Constituents have an opportunity to state why they would be reluctant to participate in certain actions, especially those that may involve risks to them or their families. Consequently, the planning of strategies and tactics require detailed discussions of the risks and potential benefits of any action to be carried out by the group.

The ethical implications of tactical methods and the consequences of choosing certain options are an important consideration in the organizing process (Rubin & Rubin, 2008). Saul Alinsky (1971), "the architect" of modern organizing methods, argued that in most circumstances the potential for success should outweigh the use of offensive or unethical organizing methods. Risks are often associated with tactics such as protests, direct action or confrontation with authorities, and civil disobedience (McAdam & Tarrow, 2000). Civil disobedience can be defined as "the deliberate, principled, and public breaking of a law that is perceived to be unjust" (Conway, 2003, p. 508). Direct action may include legally sanctioned activities or illegal actions, but generally involves direct confrontation with authorities (Shaw, 2001).

In some instances, there may be disagreements among coalition group members about whether direct action or potentially violent tactics should be used (Conway, 2003). Another potential risk is that in some situations, authorities may choose to arrest or engage in physical confrontation with participants (Rubin & Rubin, 2008). Consequently, it is imperative that group members thoroughly discuss the potential consequences of their actions, what they are willing to risk, the benefits of undertaking the action, and processes for minimizing or preventing these risks. Such discussions serve as an informed consent process in organizing (Hardina et al., 2009). If people find tactics inappropriate or offensive, they simply would not participate in the action. Kahn (2010) argues that it is essential that the organizer:

> Be absolutely certain that the people you work with truly understand the risks they're taking, the things that could go wrong, the losses they might suffer, before they make the decision to act, individually or together. (p. 194)

Other types of tactics may also be offensive to participants or violate basic principles such as self-determination or honesty, requiring a discussion of whether the risks outweigh the costs. For example, Hardina (2000) surveyed community organization instructors in schools of social work and asked them to identify tactics they felt were unethical. The social workers interviewed felt that harming or humiliating individuals, lying, and withholding information about the consequences of taking action were unethical practices. Hardina et al. (2009) conducted interviews with community organizers involved in social action organizing. They viewed as unethical any tactic that harmed individuals (allies as well as opponents), vandalism, lying, or deliberating misleading constituents.

In addition to issues specifically related to the practice of social action, other ethical considerations encountered in the organizing process involve the acceptance of funding from donors at odds with community preferences or values or conflicts of interests on the part of individual constituents, the organizer, or the organizer's employer. Other ethical considerations involve whether the constituency group should focus solely on long-term rather than short-term gains (e.g., advocating for improvements in the minimum wage rather than helping current constituents find employment) or whether to deliberately disseminate misinformation or discredit opponents (Forester, 1989; Hardina, 2002, 2004a; Minkler & Pies, 2009; Reisch & Lowe, 2000).

Facilitating Action Planning: The Art of Achieving Consensus

The choice of goals, strategies, and tactics require that some type of agreement or consensus is reached among members. While not everyone may be happy with the decision, there must be a degree of commitment to the plan on the part of the members if the action is to be implemented by the group members. The group process for developing and implementing action plans most resembles that of task groups. Interpersonal relationships are used explicitly to facilitate goal achievement. Task groups differ from treatment or therapeutic groups in that they are designed to foster the interdependence of members in a manner that allows for collective group decision making as well as task accomplishment. Individuals within the group must rely on task completion by others if they are to complete their assigned roles (Johnson & Johnson, 2006; Kirst-Ashman & Hull, 2009). In some ways, members of effective task groups become a team in which each member has an assigned role and expectations as to what they are to accomplish in the group in order to achieve a common purpose (VeneKlasen et al., 2007).

However, while tasks have some of the same characteristics and applications as groups of individuals engaged in social action, development or community planning efforts, there is at least one other important difference. As described by Polletta (2002), there is a dilemma inherent in the organizing process:

> The literature on organizing is rife with injunctions against leading: organizers should rather help residents articulate their own agendas and build their leadership. Yet, in the process, organizers are often expected to help identify goals, push people to question their preferences, and rally them to act. How can they do that without thereby undermining the leadership capacities of those whom they are organizing? (p. 76)

As opposed to leading a group, the organizer must merely assist the group leader in facilitating the group process, provide encouragement and information to members, set the stage for leadership by others, engage in mutual dialogue and learning with members, and suggest options that will lead to goal achievement. Organizers also must engage in group maintenance activities, continuing to build relationships with individual members and help mediate or minimize conflict among members (Homan, 2011). Another difference between the typical task group and community organizing is that the purpose and goal for the group originates with members, participants may be asked to engage in recruitment of new members, and the leader is chosen by the group.

Essentially, the organizer helps the leader to do one's job, provides technical information, research data, or helps identify policies, laws, or people that need to be taken into consideration in planning the campaign. The organizer also helps to guide the discussion on various campaign options. According to VeneKlasen et al. (2007), a nondirective approach to facilitation involves asking participants a series of questions about what they want to accomplish, how they want to achieve this, and what they perceive to be the benefits and risks of the various approaches available to them. The type of questions typically used in social work practice with both individuals and groups (reflective responding or para-phrasing, summarizing, clarification, and reframing) can be applied in this context, ensuring that all group members have a common under-standing of the issues raised, goals, activities that must be accomplished, and task assignments (Kirst-Ashman & Hull, 2009; Poulin, 2010). VeneK-lasen et al. (2007) identify some question types that may be particularly effective in this group context:

- *Questions to obtain information.* For example, who will conduct the activity, when will it happen and how?
- *Questions to obtain an explanation.* For example, what else do we need to think about and how should we do it?
- *Questions to obtain a justification.* For example, why should we do it and how do you know if this is true?
- *Questions to generate new ideas or make suggestions.* For example, is this a good idea or maybe we should think about [an alternative] as well?
- *Questions to facilitate making a choice.* For example, which of these alternatives will work the best?
- *Questions to facilitate reaching a consensus.* For example, does everyone agree that this is what we should do?

In addition to asking questions (Box 7.2), the organizer also assists the leader in developing relationships with group members, keeping the group running smoothly, and accomplishing specific tasks related to goal achievement (Schutz & Sandy, 2011).

Task groups are similar to treatment or therapeutic groups in that the stages of group development are essentially the same. For example, the Tuckman model of group development (Zastrow, 2002) can be easily applied to the type of task groups used in community organizing.

- *Forming.* Participants come together and start to think about the group's goals and start to become acquainted with one another. Members also attempt to determine their place in the group and whether there are rules that govern the operation of the group.

Organizer Alicia Martinez is assisting constituents of the West Neighborhood Organization to develop a new tactic for persuading the City Council to shut down the meat rendering plant in their neighborhood. Mrs Jackson has been elected by the group members to serve as the leader and spokesperson for the group for the next few months, Mr Smith as indicated an interest in serving as the leader in the future.

Mrs Jackson: We know that there is a proposal in the City Council to grant a new permit to the meat rendering plant. Tonight, I'd like to discuss what we can do to keep the Council from giving the plant a permit. If the permit is not approved, the plant will need to shut down. Any suggestions?

Mrs Lee: We just need to rely on our city council member to make the case against the permit.

Alicia: Do you know what Council Member Gonzalez's position is on this issue? Has anyone talked to him?

Mr Smith: He's just a bum. I've talked to him and I can't get a straight answer.

Mrs Jackson: I think the group needs to talk to him and get him to represent our interests. We voted for him and he won't be elected again without our vote.

Mr Smith: Yes, but I really think he's no good. I think we should just disrupt the City Council meeting to get our point across. That should get their attention?

Mrs Lee: I'd be afraid that we could be arrested if we disrupted a meeting.

Alicia: Could you talk to City Council Member Gonzalez first to determine his position on this issue and ask him to work with us on this issue? He seems to have a lot of influence on the other council members.

Mrs Jackson: That seems worth a try. Can anyone else suggest an alternative?

Mr Smith: I like my idea better. But I'd be willing to go along with this if we come up with a good plan to persuade Gonzalez to help us.

Mrs Jackson: Well, we have a lot of information about the asthma rates in our neighborhood and the costs involved in hospitalizing children and the number of days missed from school due to asthma-related problems.

(Continued)

> ### BOX 7.2   REACHING A CONSENSUS ON A TACTIC (*Continued*)
>
> *Mrs Lee*: I'd be glad to put that information together. We just bought my son a new computer and I could use it to put together a good looking fact sheet.
>
> *Alicia*: Do we have an agreement then?

- *Storming.* There is a certain amount of conflict among group members. Some of this may be due to perceptions of differential status among group members due to a number of factors such as race, gender, ethnicity, income, professional status, knowledge, sexual orientation, or age or based on perceptions that there are differences between newcomers and "old hands." Some members may have specific agendas, either explicit or hidden, that guide their interaction with others in the group.
- *Norming.* Members set explicit rules for behavior and decision making that are enforced in some fashion. Successful groups also develop a sense of solidarity and commitment to one another and the group as a whole.
- *Performing.* The group functions as a team to accomplish its goals. Group members also develop a sense of interdependence on one another.
- *Adjourning.* The group may end when a project is completed. What may differentiate community groups from other task groups is that the group may simply refocus its mission to achieve another goal or disband and continue in some fashion to maintain working relationships or friendships with one another.

Therefore, social workers assigned to facilitate task groups for organizing should anticipate that it is entirely normal for groups to experience some degree of distrust and conflict. The key is to move past this in order to achieve the group's goals.

Trust-building and the establishment of group norms for individual and collective group behavior are critical for achieving a sense of solidarity or belonging among group members. Group consensus rather than conflict increases the odds that the group will accomplish its goals. Also of importance is whether more than one or a small number of group members actually contribute to the success of the group (Johnson & Johnson, 2006). If only the leader performs most of the tasks, few members will maintain their participation in the group. Consequently, both group processes or maintenance and the outcomes produced are measures of the success of the group (Zastrow, 2009).

Most experts on group processes believe that often a certain amount of conflict helps to spur innovation and creativity in decision making (Rubin & Rubin, 2008). However, ongoing conflicts among group members based on personal issues or status differentials minimize chances that group goals will be achieved (Mondros & Wilson, 1994). One of the responsibilities of the organizer or social worker is to assist the leader or, in some situations, take the lead, in managing conflicts among group members.

It should be noted that task accomplishment and conflict management are not the only tasks that need to be accomplished in the community organizing process. Plitt Donaldson (2004) views the purpose and function of groups in community organization as similar to those of empowerment groups that are established to provide social support to members experiencing common problems and increase participants' sense of personal self-efficacy and power. She argues that empowerment groups have some of the same components, in a different context, as the therapeutic groups described by Yalom and Leszcz (2005). Group members bond with and build relationships with one another, share their experiences, feel good about themselves because they are helping others, acquire technical information, and develop a sense of group cohesiveness or solidarity. As described in earlier chapters of this book, all these factors should be considered elements of a well-functioning task group in community organizing. Accomplishing a group goal, establishing a group identity and values, and banding together in the face of adversity help people develop a sense of group or collective identity (Polletta, 2002; Schutz & Sandy, 2011).

PUTTING VALUES IN ACTION: SELF-DETERMINATION, EMPOWERMENT, AND CULTURAL COMPETENCY IN PLAN DEVELOPMENT

Leadership development, participation in public decision making, and community control of the organizing and development process are all commonly used methods used to apply the principles of self-determination, empowerment, and cultural competency in community practice. Constituents should have a primary role, if not complete control, in determining how social problems are addressed and be explicitly involved in actions to resolve them. Reaching this point is difficult, if not impossible, in community practice. Forester (1989) succinctly describes barriers to the inclusion of marginalized communities in this process: "Hardly an ideal form of dialogue, real public deliberation suffers from inequalities of power, poor information, inadequate representation, histories of violence brought to the table, histories that silence the voices of many parties" (p. 9).

Toomey (2009) identifies a number of roles for community practitioners and argues that while most interventions are designed to "empower" communities, some have a negative effect, particularly when they are intended to impose assistance, "rescue," or "liberate," community members or impose reforms without their consent. These roles are similar to Arnstein's (1969) description of citizen participation initiatives that are intended to provide therapy, manipulate, or "buy off" community members. According to Toomey, organizer roles that have a positive impact on community members include that of a catalyst, helping to inspire or spark a change or as facilitator by bringing people together observing the process, and providing support without imposing a specific agenda. Other roles include acting as an advocate for what the community wants or an ally, establishing relationships with community members and standing in solidarity with them.

Pilisuk et al. (2009) describe the process of being and becoming an ally as one of the primary mechanisms for engaging in mutual learning and achieving a degree of cultural competency:

> The organizer's special talent lies in a willingness to understand, and an unwillingness to collude with, such internalized oppression. ..... He or she will have to earn the people's trust and establish relationships with them in their surroundings. The organizer must also suspend the power, privilege, prestige, and protection offered by his or her own background and be willing to be less safe. (p. 99)

Hence, the culturally competent practitioner needs to engage in cultural humility, abandoning privilege and control, using one's professional status and skills for the good of the community. The organizer must be willing to listen to community members and participate in dialogue as a partner of equal status.

Quaghebeur, Masschelein, and Nguyen (2004) describe what they learned from their efforts to implement a community participation related-project in Vietnam, in which the prospective participants refused to cooperate with the professional planners' proposal for the program. They describe empowerment as a "double-bind," in which people are offered the "opportunity" by professionals or government agencies to empower themselves:

> We should pay more attention to the unexpected spaces of negotiation that go beyond the formal project. This implies

the acknowledgement that project goals and objectives can be disturbed and that these spaces, which are crucial for the participatory "success" of the project, are difficult to steer, control or evaluate within classical project cycles. But this is what "real participation might be about: the contestation, discussion, struggle and negotiation about the framework offered by the "participatory project." (p. 163)

Such challenges when using participatory methods may prove difficult for the organizer, social worker, or planner in situations in which the organizer sincerely believes the community's proposal is unsafe, unwise, or unethical, or the decision-making process itself is rife with competing goals from different groups with a variety of agendas. While conflict management skills may help in such situations, there are scenarios in which organizers may ethically be required to "take sides" or walk away from the organizing effort. For example, one ethical concern in organizing is the "Not in my Backyard" or NIMBY syndrome in which community residents oppose a group homes for mentally ill, homeless, and disabled people or affordable housing for low-income groups (Duke, 2010). Most organizers would probably support such projects as beneficial for marginalized communities and engage in dialogue or search for common ground between constituents and proponents in order to minimize the ethical dilemma involved (Piat, 2000; Stein, n.d.). Such ethical challenges need to be weighed carefully in terms of the risks and benefits to both the organizer and group members (Reisch & Lowe, 2000). It is appropriate and necessary in such situations to seek supervision from one's employer, board members, or professional colleagues (Hardina, 2004a).

To mitigate such challenges, organizers develop or seek out participatory group work models that incorporate principles related to the community-control approach to decision making. Often these programs are based on the premise that leadership in community groups should not try to replicate hierarchal decision-making processes in which one person has control and some people are excluded (Pyles, 2009a; Smock, 2004). Instead, leadership is viewed as an inclusive process involving shared decision making (Schutz & Sandy, 2011). Zachary (2000) describes a leadership training process, the City University of New York Parent Leadership Project, in which the organizer facilitates a shared leadership model among constituents. The purpose of the PLP project was to train community members to become advocates for school reform. Much of the theoretical framework used to develop these leadership training workshops was derived from principles such as mutual partnership and dialogue associated with popular education (Freire, 1970). The component parts of this model include:

- The creation of a training curriculum in which participants take an active role in the development of learning objectives through mutual dialogue with the facilitator.
- The establishment of a group culture of shared leadership and the power to make decisions that includes both participants and the facilitator.
- The development of explicit ground rules or expectations for the behavior of members by the participants themselves. This in turn created a sense of safety and trust among group members.
- The provision of opportunities for participants to share their stories and begin to develop an understanding of their shared experiences.
- The use of group-centered training techniques by the facilitator such as small group discussions and role plays to convey respect for participants and their experiences and knowledge as well as high expectations for skill attainment.
- The ability of the facilitator to use "humble facilitation" techniques. The process requires that the facilitator models appropriate interpersonal skills including the ability to make mistakes, challenges group members to improve their skills, and creates an appropriate vision for what the group should accomplish.
- Outcomes that include mutual support, trust, and respect among all participants in the training process.

According to Zachary (2000), the advantage of this model is that it transfers power from the organizer to the group as a collective entity rather than to individual leaders, limits the degree to which leadership confers special status, power, or perks, to individual members, and enhances the group's capacity to use mutual dialogue to identify problems and engage in all phases of action planning.

SUMMARY

Organizers have multiple roles in community planning and decision making. These roles include leadership development and training, facilitating citizen/constituent involvement in public planning, ensuring that constituents play leadership roles in community organizing efforts and nonprofit organizations, and facilitating the development of social action and community development campaigns or other planning efforts. Community organizers should adhere to ethical principles such as self-determination, diversity, and empowerment in assisting community leaders and constituents in efforts to improve their lives and communities. Constituents should be fully involved in the decisions that affect their lives and the choice of strategies and tactics. The use of dialogue and the inclusion of multiple voices in the planning effort help to ensure that public plans and tactical methods are ethical, safe, and serve the interests of constituents. Inclusive decision-making practices are also critical if constituents are to give their informed consent in terms of the actions or activities in which they are likely to participate. In Chapter 8, group decision-making methods for actually implementing action campaigns are discussed.

EXERCISES AND ASSIGNMENTS

1. Interview two or more community leaders using conversational interviewing techniques. Write a short paper that describes your findings. In general, your interviews should focus on how these individuals became involved in community activism, the circumstances related to how they became leaders, how they describe their leadership roles, their current leadership responsibilities, and the pluses and minuses involved in working with group members to take action.

2. Watch the movie *Boycott* (Twain, Stone, & Johnson, 2001) about the Montgomery Bus Boycott of 1955, led by Dr. Martin Luther King. With your classmates, discuss:
   - Whether you think the strategies and tactics used in the boycott were deliberately planned or arose from the situation at-hand.
   - What motivated the participants (the African-American population of Montgomery) to comply with the boycott?
   - What power resources did the African-American community possess and how did they compare with those of the white community? What resources were obtained from outside the community?
   - Were all the participants committed to nonviolent, civil disobedience at the beginning of the boycott? If not, what factors motivated the adoption of this method by Dr. King and his constituents?
   - How was informed consent for risky tactics obtained?
   - Why was the African-American community in Montgomery successful in ending the segregation of the bus system?

3. Divide the classroom into teams or pair up with a partner to debate the ethics of the following tactical methods. In the debate, describe whether you think one of the following tactical methods is ethical and in what situations should it be used:

    (a) Nonviolent civil disobedience

    (b) Direct action involving face-to-face confrontation with authorities, for example, sit-ins or disrupting events or meetings.

    (c) Mudslinging (i.e., calling one's opponent names or disclosing negative information about individuals or groups).

    (d) Deceiving constituents about the purpose or nature of a tactic, including potential risks.

    (e) Misinforming the public about the possible benefits and consequences of specific planning decisions.

    (f) Engaging in vandalism or violence or supporting organizations or groups that participate in such actions.

    (g) Inviting or soliciting participation in a planning council or advisory group in which members will have limited input into making decisions.

    (h) Offering individuals money, status, positions, or other benefits for public support of a planning decision made by others.

    (i) Placing all responsibility for decision making with the group leader, using charisma or coercion to motivate constituents to act.

4. Attend a meeting of a public agency in which the public has been invited to give input or make comments. Write a short paper that describes the purpose of the meeting, the public officials in attendance, the type of decision made, the structure of the meeting, provisions made for public comment or input, the degree to which the public was actually able to participate, and whether you think that public participation was actual effective or had the potential to influence the final decision. In addition to observation, you may use newspaper or other news or social media reports, or interviews with public officials and members of the public who were present at the meeting.

5. Examine either a redevelopment plan developed by a government agency a community group. Write a three- to-five-page paper that analyzes the contents of the plan. What are the component parts of the plan? How did the planning agency, group, or the author describe the purpose of the plan? What information did they provide to persuade the reader that the plan was feasible, cost-effective, or oriented toward improving the lives of people living in the community? Do you think this plan should or should have been adopted? Why or why not?

8

Taking Action: Group Processes
for Implementing Action Campaigns

*You know sometimes you may start out with an ideal decision,
but once you open it up and have a conversation and everybody
gets to discuss whatever that had to do with that decision or not
even about the decision, but about the material the topic or the
activity or the situation, then at the end of that you have a more real
decision to make right? You can't just make a decision off of ideals*
—Interview with an environmental justice organizer, Hardina et al., 2011.

Once constituents reach an agreement on a plan for an action campaign during the engagement phase of the organizing process, it must be implemented. Members of the community or constituency group must have a primary role in carrying out the overall strategy for the campaign. In this chapter, action campaigns are defined and components of successful campaigns are identified. Restraints that limit the group's ability to put plans into action and situational demands that require the alteration of tactical methods are also discussed. A variety of interpersonal and communication skills needed by organizers to facilitate constituent implementation of the plan are also described: group decision-making processes, handling logistics, facilitating and participating in formal meetings, public speaking, using the media, keeping notes and other documentation, and bargaining or negotiation. The process of ending campaigns is also discussed. In addition, specific techniques for incorporating social justice-related principles in the process of carrying out action plans are identified.

DEFINING ACTION CAMPAIGNS

When they are carried out, actual action campaigns are long-term efforts to implement a specific strategy. Sen (2003) describes a campaign as "a sustained intervention on a specific issue; they have clear short- and long-term goals, a timeline, creative incremental demands, targets who can meet those demands, and an organizing plan to build a constituency and build internal capacity" (p. 81). As described in the previous chapter, to be effective campaigns should be planned in advance with assigned roles for constituents, a time-line that puts various activities in a logical sequence and with logistical details addressed well before the action actually takes place (Schutz & Sandy, 2011) (Table 8.1).

Kahn (1991, 2010) describes an action plan as a road map that describes the starting point of the campaign, the resources to be used, and the route to be taken contingent upon anticipated as well as unexpected road blocks that may occur during the journey. He recommends that the road map be defined starting at the end of the map, rather than the beginning in order to assess what is needed to accomplish the goal by a specific date. This also helps in setting a time-line for complying with relevant deadlines (e.g., the last day new legislation can be proposed in the state assembly) and determining when specific campaign objectives should be achieved and tactical methods should be used.

COMPONENTS OF SUCCESSFUL CAMPAIGNS

There are a number of ways to define "success" in social action, social planning, and community development campaigns. Success will differ depending on the goals of the campaign, the perceptions of participants, situational demands, and the type of campaign conducted. As discussed in Chapter 1, organizing work involves both process- and task-related skills. If, for example, the focus of the campaign was community development, the emphasis of the campaign may be on the process of building relationships among community leaders, citizen participation, and empowerment, or the capacity of neighborhood residents to facilitate improvements in community life. If on the other hand, a social action campaign, a lobbying effort, or political campaign was carried out, with a specific purpose and intended outcome, success is most often defined as "winning" or achieving a specific outcome (Mondros, 2005). In social planning, the development of a new program, the creation of a new service delivery system, the development of a new organization, or improvements in existing services or facilities are generally considered to be successes. However, in some circumstances, given constraints such as legislative mandates, lack of public awareness or support, time, and resources, there may be circumstances in which constituency group members accept smaller gains as measures of success. According to the Alliance for Justice (2010):

TABLE 8.1

Action Plan for On-Campus Group Assisting a State-Wide Coalition With a Campaign for Higher-Education Funding

Goal	Objectives	Time-Line	Action System	Target System	Model of Practice	Strategy	Tactics	Resource Needs	Evaluation Criteria
Increase funding for higher education	Form on-campus coalition with a minimum of at least 10 student clubs and local organizations to generate support for increased educational funding	Sept. 1, 2012	Student Groups and Allied Organizations	Members of the Legislature, Governor	Social Action	Campaign Contest	Public Education; Persuasion: Mobilization	Volunteers; Press Coverage; Social Media; Funds for Travel, Posters, Printed material, Speakers	Obtain at least 10 coalition members; obtain letters of support and resource commitments from each organization.
	Recruit 20 volunteers to coordinate on-campus events and a lobbying campaign using social media techniques	Oct. 1, 2012					Public Education; Persuasion: Mobilization		Number of volunteers recruited
	Sponsor at least two educational forums or teach-ins on issues related to funding for higher education.	Feb. 1, 2013					Public Education; Persuasion: Mobilization		Number of workshops held, workshop attendance; number of signed postcards sent to legislators urging support for AB 10

(Continued)

TABLE 8.1

Action Plan for On-Campus Group Assisting a State-Wide Coalition With a Campaign for Higher-Education Funding (*Continued*)

Goal	Objectives	Time-Line	Action System	Target System	Model of Practice	Strategy	Tactics	Resource Needs	Evaluation Criteria
	Make at least 15 lobbying visits to state legislators to solicit support for AB 10 (increased funding for higher education)	March 1, 2013					Lobbying; Persuasion:		Number of visits made; number of commitments for support made by legislators
	Hold an on-campus flash mob and rally to generate media coverage and public support for AB 10	April 15, 2013					Protest; Public Education; Mild Coercion		Attendance at rally, number of signed postcards collected to send to legislators; amount of press coverage
	Assist state-wide coalition in obtaining legislative approval for AB10	June 30, 2013					Bargaining & Negotiation		Legislation is passed.

Gaining support for an issue from key neighborhood leaders or city council members can be an important stepping stone towards an eventual policy change sought. Some internal interim objectives might be "stepping stones" toward longer-term goals, and important "wins" in and of themselves, such as changes in constituent leadership and power, or changes in organizational capacity. An organization might lose a campaign but at the same time accomplish a "win" by building its power significantly. (p. 1)

Consequently, campaign goals, strategies, and tactics will change in response to barriers or unexpected restraints encountered and situational demands that arise during the course of the campaign and require a response from the action system.

Restraints on Putting Plans Into Action

In some action campaigns, it simply is not feasible to achieve everything that the constituency group wants to achieve in a short time frame or with limited resources, volunteers, or power. Therefore, constituency group members need to assess how feasible it will be to achieve their goals. One advantage of assessing power resources or conducting force field or SWOT analyses (see Chapter 6) is that this process permits constituents to determine what resources they will need to overcome opponents and the amount of power and resources that can be marshaled by the opposition. This also assists the constituency group in the development of strategies and tactics that will counterbalance these restraints (Homan, 2011). Other types of restraints on successful achievement of campaign goals include existing laws and regulations, community traditions and customs, the lack of public awareness regarding a new or emerging issue, and established vested interests (e.g., does someone with power stand to benefit or lose from the social change initiative). To some degree, a well-developed action plan takes these expected impediments into consideration. Strategies and tactics should be chosen that help the group to overcome these obstacles. In addition, a monitoring plan can be put in place in the event that these anticipated problems do occur (Homan, 2011). In such cases, the organization can be ready with *Plan B* or a number of alternative strategies or tactical methods.

Situational Demands

Unintended effects or unexpected occurrences can also affect goal attainment during campaigns. One reason for this is that the organizing team really cannot always predict what targets will do in response to specific tactical methods, how the public will react to a particular issue, and even what some of the members of the campaign team will do in the course of tacking action. As with restraints, the best course of action for the organizing campaign involves contingency planning, that is, what options do we have if specific things happen? Schutz and Sandy (2011) suggest that the best way to think about the various options for tactical implementation is using a decision tree diagram to explore the possible options associated with each tactic. For example, if we choose Plan A, these are the things that are likely to happen or that may backfire. Alternatively, if we choose Plan B, the benefits and consequences may be different. The advantage of diagrams for tactical decision making, are the same as those that apply in power mapping. It allows all participants to visually see patterns and themes in the information provided and to build on that information in ways that employ their own experiential knowledge. Consequently, it moves away from a reliance only on the expert knowledge of the organizer and places control in the hands of participants, permitting organizers to facilitate the process by providing concrete information and asking "why" questions (Figure 8.1).

In addition to consideration to the types of tactics used, organizers can work with the group to minimize risks by engaging participants in role plays, assisting leaders in writing scripts or scenarios to use when lobbying or carrying out a tactic, and make adequate preparations in the event that the action will not take place as planned (Staples, 2004). According to Sen (2003), "a good action has stages; people play roles, and everyone prepares and practices" (p. 87). Typical roles include

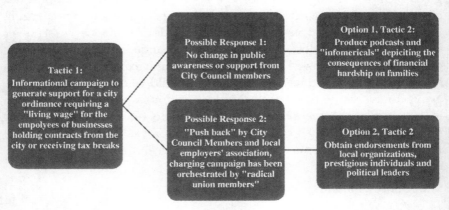

FIGURE 8.1
Developing a Plan B in response to situational demands.

handling logistics, leading the action, liaison with the media, carrying out the action, producing and distributing posters and printed material, making sure that volunteers arrive at the event or the action in a timely manner, and ensuring participant safety or providing security. Safety is often a major concern for community organizations engaged in social action activities. For example, in many events, there is a potential risk of disruption by opponents, people simply seeking attention, or allies who may agree with campaign goals, but not the tactical methods employed. There may also be disagreements with law enforcement in terms of how event permits will be enforced or the parameters associated with free speech (Risher, Schlosser, & Swain, 2010). In addition to pre-planning and training, safety measures can include establishing "rules" for participants, asking volunteers to serve as "safety monitors" to minimize conflict and enforce the rules, or asking legal observers to attend the event and advise participants and local authorities about their rights and responsibilities (Maxwell, n.d.; Hardina & Obel-Jorgensen, 2011).

CONSIDERATIONS IN ADJUSTING AND IMPLEMENTING STRATEGIES AND TACTICS IN RESPONSE TO SITUATIONAL DEMANDS

These unexpected occurrences require that many tactical methods will be developed during rather than in advance of the campaign. In addition, the success of these new activities is dependent upon the degree to which constituency group members participate in making tactical decisions and in carrying them out. Consequently, group consultation sessions are required when developing new tactical methods and in some situations. There are a number of factors that must be taken into consideration when making tactical choices including whether the tactic can easily be used to frame a specific message or demand, constituent preferences, the minimization of risk, and the likelihood that success will be achieved.

Tactical Considerations: Usability and Packaging the Message

In some situations, when new or modified tactics are under consideration, there may not be time to consult everyone and key members may not always be available. Therefore, some degree of trust is necessary for members to delegate responsibility for decision-making to leaders or a small group of leaders. The ability of the leaders to talk with or bounce ideas off the organizer in such situations is critical. Most organizers use a set of principles that can be applied when working with members to come up with new tactical methods in response to situational demands. In addition to the criteria for appropriate tactical methods presented in Chapter 7, a good tactic is:

* Is easy to put into operation.
* Incorporates or illustrates the principles and values associated with the issue campaign.
* Provides an opportunity for group members to develop a sense of solidarity with one another.
* Is *outside* or inconsistent with the experiences of members of the target group.
* Minimizes risks to all participants including members of the target group.
* Educates participants and the general public.
* Contains a specific demand or *asks* someone (a policy maker, a potential organization partner, members of the public, the target) to take a specific action (Alinsky, 1971; Bobo et al., 2010; Homan, 2011; Schutz & Sandy, 2011).

The choice of the various tactical methods always present challenges, risks, and benefits to the group, the organization's goals, and individual members. Much of the literature on action campaigns focuses on the various strategic and tactical options available in different approaches to community organization. In addition to several factors identified in previous chapters of this book, such as problem identification and assessment or power resources, other considerations include whether constituency group members are low income or marginalized thus limiting their access to decision-makers, the seriousness of the issue at hand, the amount of time available to address the issue, the amount of public awareness or empathy with the cause, the degree to which the issue matches up with the self-interest of targets and the general public, and the degree to which the tactical method is likely to generate a negative reaction from the public, likely allies, and opponents (Alinsky, 1971; Bobo et al., 2010; Kahn, 2010; Mondros, 2005; Schulz & Sandy, 2011; Sen, 2003; Netting, Kettner, & McMurty, 2008).

Constituent Preferences for Tactical Methods

Constituency group members also need to consider whether they prefer tactical methods that are indirect or involve direct interaction with targets (Rubin & Rubin, 2008). For example, filing a request for information from government agencies (public record requests) or using legal resources to send "cease and detest" letters, request an injunction, or file lawsuits to stop unjust policies and laws limit group member exposure to targets, but may also subject some individuals (such as agency employees who serve as "whistleblowers") to some forms of negative fallout or harassment (Green & Latting, 2004). Alternatively, most forms of confrontation involve some type of face-to-face or direct contact with targets. However, in most long-term campaigns, it is likely that a combination of direct and indirect methods will be used.

Risk Assessment and the Likelihood That Success Will be Achieved

There are a number of additional issues to be considered when choosing overall campaign approaches and tactical options. For example, campaign strategies oriented toward collaboration and consensus-building or problem-solving often are preferred methods of community practice, simply because they involve limited risks. Most social workers are far more comfortable with collaboration rather than more confrontational approaches (Hardina, 2000). According to Netting, Kettner, & McMurty, (2008), one important consideration in applying collaboration-related tactical methods is whether all or most of the relevant groups and decision-makers actually support the proposed change or can realistically be persuaded to do so. If more than a few friendly meetings are needed to find common ground with groups that must be persuaded to join the organizing effort, then campaign-related tactics must be considered. An additional issue with collaboration is that more effort may go into sustaining partnership agreements with diverse organizations, than actually working toward a goal (Homan, 2011). As noted earlier in this text, some organizers argue that community development or collaborative strategies are inappropriate in situations in which outside organizations impose their own agendas on community members or when such efforts are designed to limit dissent or sustain institutional arrangements or policies which result in substantial resources disparities and political repression (Brager et al., 1987; Toomey, 2009; Young Laing, 2009).

Similar issues may limit the effectiveness of problem-solving approaches, especially efforts that involve consultation with numerous organizations and the public. Difficulties reaching agreements among a variety of parties with different vested interests, having sufficient time to make joint decisions, or access to all necessary information may make the planning process cumbersome and reduce the likelihood that the outcome will please all the parties involved (Rothman & Zald, 2008). Still community involvement is believed to be a better mechanism for making public planning decisions rather than leaving the dimensions of the final plan to professionals or the political process (Heywood, 2011; Netting, Kettner, & McMurty, 2008).

While of lower intensity than confrontation-related tactics, the use of campaign-style approaches when tactics are oriented toward brining opponents to the bargaining table also can be problematic. Netting, Kettner, & McMurty (2008) argue that the success of campaign-related tactics is predicated on whether people can be persuaded to adopt the organization's position on the issue. The use of these types of tactical methods is also dependent upon how people can be persuaded to change their own position on the issue. If public pressure is needed, especially if it involves the use of a variety of tactical methods over a period of time, and the target has repeatedly refused to negotiate, then contest-related tactics must be considered. Other hazards involved in using campaign-related tactics involve the length of the effort, the time and resources required, especially if "wins" involve small incremental gains over time, and issues related to keeping all allied groups involved in the effort, especially when agendas may differ among organizations (Kerr Chandler, 2009; Sen, 2003; Swarts, 2008).

As noted in Chapter 7, contest or confrontation strategies and the types of tactical methods used in these efforts are often fraught with hazards, especially if they involve direct confrontation with authorities. One potential consequence of confrontation involves whether an unwilling target can actually be forced to do something that is counter the values and interests of that individual or organization (Netting, Kettner, & McMurty, 2008). In addition, existing laws, regulations, funding limitations, or considerations about the health or safety of others may make implementing the action system's demands less than feasible (Bobo et al., 2010; Working Group for Community Health and Development, 2010). Confrontation entails substantial risks to participants and targets, especially when it involves coming face-to-face with targets, applying pressure, and engaging in activities which could, in some circumstances result in arrest (such as sit-ins, protests in public or private places without permission or the proper permits, deliberate disruption of meetings or events, or civil disobedience). Targets may "push back," deceiving, making deliberate attempts to pit members of the action group against each other, stigmatizing participants, making negative comments or false charges in the press, taking action to terminate the employment of a participant, or physically threatening or assaulting protestors (Kahn, 2010; Staples, 2004). Other hazards with confrontation tactics are that they can be emotionally draining; participants can be easily discouraged if "wins" do not come easily or require substantial amounts of time or resource commitments (Homan, 2011). In addition, certain types of tactics (such as vandalism, threats of violence or deception) employed by some community organizations, activists groups, or allied organizations are inconsistent with the ethical principles in the NASW Code of Ethics (Hardina & Obel-Jorgensen, 2011).

Popular education approaches also entail several hazards. Efforts to establish popular education initiatives in communities involving community education and training, health promotion, or participatory action research that are initiated from outside the community may receive a hostile reaction from potential recruits. Trust building and overcoming differences created by the power imbalance between professional experts and community members may take substantial time and resources away from the organizing effort (Catalani & Minkler, 2010). Truly empowered participants, once they have developed a critical consciousness, may wish to advance this organizing method to the next stage, involvement in social action which sometimes may involve direct confrontation with authorities. This mix of in-group consensus-building and confrontation with authorities outside of the group context is used in feminist organizing and some types of multicultural practice as well (Delgado, 1997; Mizrahi, 2007). Consequently, the progression and escalation of the tactical methods require that both organizers and constituents develop different skill sets appropriate for much different situations.

USING BASIC GROUP WORK TECHNIQUES
FOR GROUP MAINTENANCE AND COHESION

Constituency group members who have planned the initial campaign should also be responsible for implementing tactics and modifying them in response to situational demands. The process of doing this should result in the development of deep bonds and feelings of solidarity among group members, especially in situations in which the planning, organizing, or development effort is complex, decision-making is difficult, the effort involves a substantial commitment of time, energy, or resources, or the use of tactical methods entail substantial risks (Conway, 2003; Polletta, 2002). According to Staples (2004), for a campaign to be successful, the organization needs to develop a group culture that consists of norms, values, and a concrete decision-making structure. He compares this process to that of an individual social worker who contracts with a client for a specific service that has clear boundaries, role expectations, and an outcome. In an action group, members contract with one another; although not stated explicitly, members come to expect that the group will operate in a specific manner, with set meeting times, a location, rules for decision-making, a leadership structure, and clear roles for participants and the organizer. Basic details such as whether food will be served, who will bring food, and whether arrangements have been made for child care or transportation are crucial for creating a sense of group solidarity and comfort with the organizing process (Bobo et al., 2010; Brown, 2006).

When discussing tactical methods in a group process, the organizer and constituency group members should examine in detail the likely responses to individual tactics and how those responses should best be addressed by the organization. For example, if the opponent retaliates against the organization, what are the possible options for the organization and its members? As with the initial action plan, the leader or leaders of the group should conduct the meeting, while the organizer provides support, resources, information, and "gentle guidance," asking "why" questions, challenging assumptions, making suggests, and assisting group members in weighing options, alternatives, and likely outcomes. One of the best criteria for determining whether a tactical method fits within the experience of group members, is culturally appropriate, and will generate enough participants and public support is whether group members are willing to make a commitment, take a risk, recruit friends, or provide resources that can be used for the action. A majority vote by group members may be sufficient for a tactic to be approved, but a lack of enthusiasm by those involved in the decision often indicates that few people will actually be available or willing to carry it out. One of the organizers interviewed by Hardina et al. (2009) described the informed consent process in the organization in which he was employed:

> There is really no formal process. Just a matter does everyone agree to it—if so does everybody agree with the tactics—what role is everyone going to play. Strategically mapping out roles and responsibilities. If it were to come down to like some kind of direct action or civil disobedience something like that. Lots of planning. It might get mundane. Reiterating why we're doing it. Reminding everybody At least in my experience, when the day comes, oh some people fall off. We have Plan B. (p. 19)

In addition to establishing informed consent, the group process is critical to the success of the organizing campaign in a number of ways. Participants, particularly constituents who have volunteered over a long period of time or organizational leaders often have practical knowledge based on experience about what tactical methods work and the potential for these approaches to backfire (Conway, 2004). According to Polletta

(2006), "as they assess different courses of action, familiar stories about what has worked or failed in the past make some options seem radical, moral, fitting, even feasible, and make others seem conservative, immoral, inappropriate, or beyond the realm of possibility" (p. 171). A number of organizers, who have written about their experiences participating in or managing large-scale campaigns, argue that the participation of people who hold a variety of view points, cultural perspectives, and experiences in group decision-making increases the creativity inherent in the decision-making process and leads to the development of tactical approaches that are more likely to respond to situational demands (Ganz, 2009; Horton, Kohl, J., & Kohl, H., 1998; Kahn, 2010).

OTHER INTERPERSONAL SKILLS NEEDED TO FACILITATE ACTION CAMPAIGNS

Despite the emphasis on leadership development in the organizing processes, there are numerous tasks that need to be undertaken by the organizer. In some circumstances, the organizer acts as a backup if volunteers are not available or need support to develop skills or carry out their responsibilities. Organizer skills include coordinating logistical support for the organizing campaign and specific events and the application of tactical methods, facilitating or participating in formal meetings, working with the media, public speaking, keeping notes and other documentation, and bargaining and negotiation with potential allies or opponents.

Handling the Logistics

Most events or activities related to the implementation of strategies and tactics require pre-planning and some type of logical support to ensure that people, equipment, posters, and printed materials are obtained, moved, used, and removed as needed (Staples, 2004). While some of these activities can be handled by volunteers or support staff (if the organization is lucky enough to have them), it often falls upon the organizer to coordinate logistics. Often the organizer must contact volunteers prior to the event to confirm participation and that those people who have been assigned specific tasks have followed through. In some situations, relationship-building and motivational skills may be used to encourage volunteers to perform certain tasks or take on additional responsibilities. In addition, the organizer must keep track of what other participants are doing, when events are expected to happen, and what people are supposed to be doing at various points of time (Bobo et al., 2010). Often what this means is that the person at the event carrying a clip board and a cell or smart phone is the community organizer. The organizer may also be responsible for making sure that equipment works, food is obtained, the room or event facility is reserved, and that participants are present, physically safe, and have their needs met in a timely manner (e.g., directions, rides, special meals, etc.).

The organizer must be ready to respond to crises or unanticipated events. What are the options if an event is rained out, volunteers fail to arrive on time, a permit for a rally is not obtained or withdrawn at the last minute, or a speaker cancels hours before an event? All of these issues require back-up planning and reliance on volunteers or organization supporters to pitch-in and help make the action or event successful. What does this have to do with interpersonal skills? The organizer should have a variety of long-standing relationships with volunteers, donors, supporters and other community residents that can be used to providing free or no cost resources for an event or that can be employed in the event of a crisis. For example, if Joe's Catering Service cannot make a delivery of food for tomorrow's community forum, is there any chance that Mrs. Jackson can bake some cookies for the event or contact other volunteers to provide the food? If the plumbing breaks down in the community center in which a volunteer training workshop will be held, what are the other options for the event? Can Helen Smith, who works as a church secretary, obtain permission for the organization to use the recreation room in the church? If Mr. Brown becomes ill just before making a presentation at a city council meeting, can another volunteer be found at the last minute? In such circumstances, it is also helpful to have leaders and other volunteers who can put in a call to friends, neighbors, colleagues, and business associates who may be willing to help mitigate a crisis or provide resources at short notice.

In addition to using previous relationships in handling logistics for specific actions and events, there are other interpersonal techniques that can be used to motivate volunteers and donors. As with other organizing situations, often volunteers are motivated based on their values, or commitment to the cause or community, opportunities to socialize with others, or having the opportunity to apply their skills and special talents. It is also important to reciprocate help received, especially when someone fills in at the last minute. If Mrs Jackson caters the entire meal at the community forum, she should receive recognition from the organization, thanks from the organizer, and be assured that if she asks the organization for assistance, she will be listened to and if feasible, her concerns will be addressed (Bobo et al., 2010).

Facilitating and Participating in Formal Meetings

Most meetings in which action planning takes place are relatively informal. Decisions may be made by consensus or general agreement or some type of vote of the group members may be required to reach an agreement. However, in many situations, the campaign may need to be approved by the organization's board of directors. Often this involves a formal process with precise rules for attendance, voting rights, and specific roles for leaders and other board members. Other types of formal meetings in which constituency group members or the organizer may take part are annual membership meetings or delegate assemblies, conferences, and coalition or other organizational partnership meetings (Rubin & Rubin, 2008). In addition, group members may attend other types of formal meeting such as government or legislative hearings, corporate board meetings, or public forums to observe, make formal presentations, lobby for legislation, or in some cases, to put pressure on decision-makers for policy changes or to make other requests or demands of elected officials and other individuals with the power to make things happen.

Formal meetings have characteristics that differentiate them from informal groups in which participants may converse freely with one another. While task or work groups use agendas developed by members, formal meetings often entail additional rules or proscriptions for how agendas are posted or disseminated, when people may speak, who may speak, and how votes are to be taken. For nonprofit and some public decision-making bodies (such as planning boards or city councils), *Robert's Rules of Order* (Robert et al., 2011), a standard, published set of rules is used to guide meetings. The meeting is called to order by a chair (usually the president of the board), formal motions must be made by one member of the board and seconded by another board member prior to calling a vote on an issue, and votes are made by majority rule. There are other rules that must be followed by organizations that interpret these procedures strictly such as requirements for postponing (tabling) votes on issues and the number of board members who must be present (a quorum) if official business is conducted.

Public decision-making processes are also guided by a set of rules that must be followed by elected officials, staff members asked to speak regarding issues of public interest, and members of the general public. Some states have legislatively established open meeting laws that specify that state and local government bodies must follow an established set of rules that allow for public input (Nadler & Schulman, 2006). For example, typical open meeting rules include requirements that agendas are made available to the public several days prior to the meeting, that most decisions be made before members of the public rather than in back rooms or the locker room of the local country club, and that the public be allowed to make comments or presentations in response to the issues raised during the meeting (California Attorney General's Office, 2003). Often public comments are limited to two or three minutes per speaker (Hoefer, 2006). Open meeting laws and rules specific to various governmental bodies also allow for public comment to be structured in a way that may minimize actual input or prevent disruption, for example, allowing public comment only at the very beginning or the end of the meeting, or requiring that people apply or register to make a presentation prior to the start of the meeting (Rubin & Rubin, 2008). Consequently, participants need to know the rules and procedures before they arrive at the meeting.

For public meetings, community organizers research the issues under discussion, obtain information about meeting agendas and rules related to public participation and voting procedures, conduct background research on decision-makers, and help prepare constituents to make presentations or for service on boards, planning councils, or commissions. Both community organizers who are working with groups that intend to lobby at public meetings and practitioners employed by public organizations must have good interpersonal skills. According to Bernhardt (n.d.):

> Meetings of one form or another are the substance behind any public participation process. They are preeminently interpersonal exercises, requiring planners not only to be approachable, personable, and professional, but also to have empathy and charisma depending on the circumstances. (Section 7.43, para 1)

It is important to note that interpersonal skills are also required for working with government officials who in most cases must make the final decision. Staff support roles for government agencies or for nonprofit board and committee meetings are somewhat similar. Staff members work in collaboration with decision-makers to set agendas, provide up-to-date information about the types of decisions to be made, maintain written records including agendas and minutes, provide technical information and data, and make recommendations as to the best course of action to be taken by those who have decision-making power (Hardina et al., 2006; Rothman, 1997).

One problem specific to staff roles in both government settings and nonprofit boards, is that the organizer or planner is not a voting member and may not be permitted to speak at board meetings unless explicitly authorized to do so. Exceptions are usually made when technical information is required. However, as noted in Chapter 7, the staff role may also require that the organizer or administrative staff member intervene in situations characterized by conflict or inaction on the part of members, asking probing or directive questions to help the chair bring the meeting back on track. In many situations, the organizer or planner may act as a "coach" or "advisor" for the chair, providing insights into the group process and providing suggestions for improving communication among members (Hardcastle et al., 2004).

Another unique aspect of the organizer's role is actually ensuring successful outcomes in advance of the meeting. Staples (2004) describes the importance using interpersonal skills to prepare for meetings in advance, talking to individuals about task assignments, what they are willing to do, and the types of decisions to be made during the meeting. Although leaders may share in some of these tasks, most of the organizer's or planner's time will be spent on this type of "prep," work; contacting respondents by phone, discussing the issues to be addressed in the meeting, following up on previous tasks, and making suggestions or offering information. In some circumstances, board members and other constituents may need support from the organizer or encouragement to volunteer for more responsibilities or provide creative solutions for some of the challenges faced by the group.

Working With News Sources and Social Media

One of the most critical things to learn in the organizing process is that local media often chooses what issues or events to cover or how report on them in ways that cannot be predicted in advance (Kirst-Ashman & Hull, 2009). Media owners are as likely to have political agendas or allegiances as anyone else and sometimes other breaking stories will have precedence over those that you would like covered (Sen, 2003). Consequently, one critical organizing task to persuade media to cover your event or provide information about an issue in a manner that supports or enhances your cause. Schutz and Sandy (2011) offer a number of suggestions increasing the likelihood that the news media will cover the event:

- Maintain personal relationships with individual reporters and keep a record of updated contact information. Developing a good working relationship with reporters requires a willingness to exchange information, assisting the reporter with additional sources of information, referrals to other people willing to be interviewed, and "quotable" quotes.

- Link the story of your campaign to other breaking news stories of interest to the media. For example, Hardina and Obel-Jorgensen (2011) describe a campaign in which members of the organizing team were able to link a story about police surveillance on a university campus to a similar story that occurred in the same city about law enforcement surveillance of an anti-war group. The previous incident received national media attention and was described by Michael Moore in the movie, *Fahrenheit 911*. Subsequent reporting on this issue noted the link between the two news stories and also mentioned the film (Marcum, 2006).
- Make the event so unique, unusual, or spectacular that the media would be foolish not to cover it. For example, using the arts (such murals, music, photography, videos) in a creative way to illustrate an issue, staging a mass assembly with hundreds or thousands of people, or arranging for the presence of a celebrity at the event are all tried and true methods for soliciting media coverage. On example of the use of this technique involved the production of a DVD for national distribution by Mayday New Orleans, an organization made up of former public housing residents in New Orleans. City government, encouraged by the U.S. Department of Housing and Urban Development, had demolished their homes after Hurricane Katrina in order to use the land for new development. The DVD, *Coming home: The dry storm*, contained the story of their efforts to lobby local and Federal governments for the "right of return," in this case, to federally subsidized housing in a new development in New Orleans (National Economic and Social Rights Initiative, 2010).
- As described in Chapter 3, other techniques often used to solicit media attention include issuing press releases just before the event with basic information (what, why, who, how) and press contact information, or holding press conferences in which your members and allied organizations can be present to show their support for the issue or event (Bobo et al., 2010). Community calendars in newspapers and on Internet sites or on local radio and television stations can be used to announce scheduled events, and local talk shows can be contacted to schedule interviews in relation to a specific event or issue.

Although group leaders should be encouraged to take on much of the media relations responsibility, organizers are often expected to assist with this type of work. They may have up-to-date information on technical issues that can be put to good use in interviews or they may need to be present to guide and provide support to constituency group members.

Often this role is similar to that of a press aide or support staff person in a political campaign. Someone needs to be responsible for scheduling interviews, ensuring that people show up on time, and helping constituents articulate a vision or message consistent with the goals of the organizing campaign. According to Sen (2003), organizers can prepare their constituents to talk to reporters by providing training for them about how to stay focused on the issue at hand and to frame the organization's message so that it is newsworthy and likely to have appeal to a general audience.

Increasingly, social media have been used successfully not only to get "get the word out" about an event, but also to document the use of tactical methods or what has happened at an event or lobbying visit. Facebook, Twitter, blogs, and even cell phone messages have been used "spread the word" about protests, rallies, and other community-organizing events. One of the advantages involved in using social media sites is that sometimes news organizations may also use these resources when researching stories or identifying events that they want to cover (Bobo et al., 2010). Sometimes participants or by-standers may simply want to share their own experiences with their friends or relatives, sending pictures from their cell phones or blogging about their participation in a campaign-related activity. However, many times posting information about successful applications of tactical methods, organizing campaigns, or events is part of a deliberately planned strategy to gain public support. A video, bog, or podcast of an event or action that is unique, provides information about an issue, or is timely, relevant, and incorporates aspects of popular culture (such as music or art) can go "viral" if posted on YouTube or other Internet site, gaining a worldwide audience (Rubin & Rubin, 2008). For example, San Francisco Pride at Work posted a video of an action that they staged with the help of the Brass Liberation Orchestra (Hogarth, 2010). The event involved a "flash mob" type gathering in which the participants sang and danced in a hotel lobby to urge the public to "boycott, don't get caught in a bad hotel" due to the owners' refusal to provide health care benefits for their employees. The musical number used during the event "borrowed" the melody from and modified the lyrics of a song by a popular entertainer known for staging her own flash mobs to promote her music.

Public Speaking

Organizers and organization leaders may also be called upon to speak at rallies, protests, legislative hearings, and formal meetings. In some cases, persuading potential allies to join the cause may involve formal presentations or speeches at board meetings or conferences. According to Homan

(2011), a good speech involves preparation and knowledge of the goals and issues of the organization that the speaker represents. Good speakers are also able to "relate" to members of the audience, make a connection between the issue discussed and the values and experiences of audience members, and respond to tough questions with factual information and confidence (Richan, 2006). Hoefer (2006) recommends that speakers practice their presentation prior to the event, focusing not only on content, but on the pacing of words and pauses, the use of gestures, the length of the speech (especially if time-limits will be imposed), and visual aids such as PowerPoint slides, videos, props, and written handouts. Effective presentations also contain personal stories about how the speaker or other individuals and groups have been affected by the issue, problem, or legislation under discussion (VeneKlasen et al., 2007). Personal stories of hardship or efforts to overcome adversity are particularly effective in situations in which constituency group members have an opportunity to speak about their own experiences.

A good speech that is part of an action campaign also persuades audience members to do something: volunteer for a cause, vote for a candidate, endorse a policy proposal or issue campaign, join a coalition, or lobby their legislator. Often at rallies, meetings, and protests, people are asked to sign petitions, asked to complete letters or postcards that can be mailed to legislators, or urged to take out their cell phones and call elected officials (Brown, 2006). Therefore, the speaker should be both informative and persuasive, urging audience members to take action (Hoefer, 2006). As with the campaign itself, a good speech contains an appeal to a moral framework and values. A good "community organization" speech also is designed to evoke emotions from people, for example, concern for people who are hurting, a commitment to work with or reach out to others, or outrage about social injustice.

Speeches also need to be tailored to the audience at the event as well as the media markets in which they may be disseminated (Richan, 2006). Bobo et al. (2010) recommend that the language used in the speech must use words and phrases likely to be known to audience members such as slang or cultural references such as books, movies, or songs. It should also go without saying that speeches should also be offered in the actual spoken language of the majority of attendees. If, for example, many of the people who attend speak Spanish, at least some of the speakers should be Spanish speaking, or if this is not possible, translation services should be provided; at minimum, some phrases in Spanish should be used to open or end the event. Flyers and other written material distributed at the event should also be language appropriate. In addition, Bobo et al. recommend gearing the speech to the life experiences, age range, social class, and geographic location of the speech and using humor in a manner that is also appropriate for the intended audience.

Keeping Notes and Other Documentation

ben Asher (2002) argues that keeping practice notes is just as important for community organizers as it is for social workers who work with individual clients. Organizers need to pay attention to details such as the names of people with whom one-on-ones are conducted, calls made, emails sent, potential recruits, potential leaders and the skills they possess or develop, and what resources are needed to implement specific activities, events, or tactical methods. They also need a method of recording what they are doing to inform their supervisors about their activities, help the organization keep track of the process of implementing interventions, and for an evaluation of the organizing effort (Bobo et al., 2010). Some organizers participate in regular accountability sessions with constituents, and reporting out what the organizer did and accomplished is an important component of these meetings (Brown, 2006). In addition, the organization will report its accomplishments to both funders and members of the community it serves or the general public. Consequently, it is important to have a written record of the tasks that are completed and the degree to which goals and objectives have been accomplished. Other records that are important to keep include action plans, newspaper, video, and audio clips of media coverage for the organization or campaign, and accounts of lobbying contacts, legislative campaigns, and other successes (or failures) related to the actions of your organization or coalition partners (Family and Community Services, New Zealand Ministry of Social Development, 2011). In addition, some of the documents maintained are useful for developing retrospective accounts of the organizing efforts. These can be published and disseminated as case studies or reports that may be helpful to organizations that are seeking to launch similar efforts; in some cases, such accounts may have historical significance and may be donated to universities or public library archives.

An additional reason for keeping records is that there should be some type of documentation of what happens in meetings. As described earlier in this chapter, *Robert's Rules of Order* is used in many organizations to guide decision-making processes. In most formal board or committee meetings, an elected or selected secretary or another volunteer take meeting minutes. These consist of a written record of who is present at the meeting, motions brought to the floor, members who have proposed the various motions, and the actual vote. In some cases, minutes may also describe issues discussed for which there was no formal vote, or statements made by attendees. However, since minutes are most likely to be drawn up by volunteers, they may be brief and consequently leave out important details. According to ben Asher (2002), it is important for the organizer to be able to describe how and why things happened and to analyze why things have occurred. This is equally as important in terms of what happens in specific meetings as during the implementation of tactical methods, community events, and overall organizing campaigns. An organizer should keep track of the individuals and groups involved, the power or ability of these participants to influence specific events or outcomes, how and why decisions were made, the impact of specific tactics or overall strategies, and outcomes produced (Hardina, 2002).

Bargaining and Negotiating With Opponents

Most organizing campaigns involve some sort of compromise among the parties involved. The techniques used in this process are called bargaining and negotiation. Hardcastle et al. (2004) define bargaining as consisting of "(a) the division or exchange of one or more specific resources or (b) the resolution of one or more intangible issues among the parties or among those whom the parties represent, or (c) both" (p. 304). Bargaining takes place in the context of a negotiation. Negotiation involves a discussion that is oriented toward finding common ground or forging an agreement among participants (Homan, 2011). In the negotiation process, the parties often agree to suspend campaigns or activities designed to suppress or react to campaigns until the talks reach their conclusion.

In some cases, such as the development of a coalition or collaborative, bargaining or negotiating tactics may be used to bring opponents or nonaligned groups into an alliance with the action system. As described in Chapter 4, the groups involved identify resources to be exchanged among participants, goals to be accomplished, rules for decision-making and specific roles and responsibilities for each group and their representatives. In social action campaigns, the last stage of the action campaign will typically involve bargaining or negotiating a resolution. When pressure tactics are used to influence people in power through public censure, humiliation, disruption of business, or other types of direct action, the purpose essentially is to force the target to come to the bargaining table. This necessitates that the people involved (both the action and target systems) actually talk to one another to develop some sort of resolution regarding the problem or issue addressed by the action campaign (Bobo et al., 2010; Homan, 2011).

Generally, in the bargaining process, there are a set of implicit or explicit rules that are used by participants to develop compromises. For example, legislative processes and union negotiations with employers must abide by existing legal frameworks or by-laws and policies developed by the institutions involved. In some cases, provisions may be made for the conflict to be mediated by a third party, with the understanding that the groups involved will abide by the decision of the arbitrator (Jansson, 2008).

One important component of negotiations to keep in mind is that most skilled negotiators have "fallback" positions. A fallback position should be consistent with at least one of the outcomes listed in the group's action plan, but the group should be ready to acknowledge that it will not receive everything it wants (Hoefer, 2006). Group members must decide to make some concessions in order to keep negotiations moving; in such situations the constituency group or organization may settle for something less than the original goal. However, this outcome should still advance the goals of the action campaign. For example, if the group is lobbying the City Council to develop a policy to ban vendors from using Styrofoam cups and plates in concession stands in city parks, it may be to the organization's advantage to simply accept an appointment to a city commission to review policies related to contracts with private food vendors in the parks.

In organizing work that emphasizes collaboration and consensus, the bargaining process focuses on producing results that will maximize benefits for all participants if concerns about resource allocation and turf can be addressed satisfactorily. However, when contest strategies are used, without some sort of bargaining process, the resolution of organizing campaigns will involve a process of accommodation or "giving in" by one party or retreat from the conflict by the other (Hardcastle et al., 2004). According to Homan (2011), there are two basic approaches to conducting negotiations during the bargaining process:

- A positional approach in which both sides stake out their positions and try to obtain as much as possible to advance their causes. This approach is sometimes counter-productive because the emphasis on "winning" may preclude reaching a compromise.
- An outcome-based approach in which the parties try to reach an agreement that will result in each one obtaining at least some of what they need or wish to achieve.

In order to achieve their goals, the constituency group needs to do some pre-planning before they enter into negotiations. Members of the negotiating team should be chosen and research should be conducted on how the opponents are likely to bargain and the composition of and power associated with their negotiating team. An accountability structure and process should also be established for reporting back to constituents about possible alternatives offered in the bargaining process and soliciting their agreement to proceed (Staples, 2004; Rubin & Rubin, 2008).

ENDING CAMPAIGNS

One of the more problematic aspects of campaigns is knowing when and how to end them. In many circumstances, a "win," is a sufficient reason to bring a campaign to an end. In other circumstances, achieving a fall-back position or winning a partial victory is sufficient. When gains have not been achieved, the group must determine if they want to give up or press on, modifying unsuccessful strategies and tactics. Sen (2003) recommends a debriefing session with participants at the con-clusion of each action. Questions for discussion during these sessions include examining whether all intended participants attended, tech-niques that should be used to sustain membership including reaching out to constituents who did not participate in the action, and determining whether and to what degree the plan was implemented as intended. Staples (2004) argues that from a strengths perspective, the first thing that the group should address is what aspects of the campaign worked as planned or were particularly effective. Problems with the campaign can be examined during later stages of the group dialogue. In addition, constituents need to analyze what happened and if the intended result was not achieved, why? The discussion process should serve as a kind of a feedback loop, a specific follow-up phrase identified in some concep-tualizations of the problem-solving model (Kirst-Ashman & Hull, 2009). It also is consistent with the reflection phase of the organizing process identified in Lewin's (1951) model of action research as well as Freire's (1970) transformative or popular education approach. Formal evalu-ations can also be conducted to guide the decision-making process.

PUTTING VALUES IN ACTION: USING ACTION CAMPAIGNS TO ACHIEVE SOCIAL JUSTICE

As noted in Chapter 5, organizing does not necessarily conform to a linear process; campaigns may involve multiple layers of activities and a variety of different phrases and processes. Participants and targets may change over time. Goals and objectives as well as tactical methods and overall strategies may be altered due to situational demands, unexpected occurrences, rising expectations, resource limitations, or the need to compromise in order to achieve results. According to Barretti (2009), many campaign activities are repeated during the organizing process in order to keep the campaign moving and to solicit new members and public support. Gilbert and Terrell (2009) conceptualize organizing campaigns as based on the problem-solving model, but incorporating activities designed to sell or "market" the campaign to others. Marketing activities include both the use of media sources and tactical methods designed to recruit and involve additional members in the action. One way to visualize the process is as a snowball that becomes larger over time, gathering more resources, support, and people "as it rolls." Campaigns in which public support drops off over time or that is limited to the work of a few staff members and volunteers can ultimately be successful in some cases, but such efforts take a personal toll (including stress, time commitment, and negative impacts on the organizer's personal life (Homan, 2011) (Figure 8.2).

Good campaigns require careful maintenance and a mix of ingredients (people, resources, media attention, and implementation of strategies and tactics to be successful). As discussed previously in this book, campaigns also incorporate values and specify goals that are acceptable to the public and incorporate ethical, legal, or moral principles. Hardina and Obel-Jorgensen (2011) describe steps that they used to wage a successful on-campus campaign to convince university administrators to

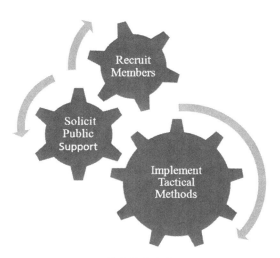

FIGURE 8.2
Component parts of campaigns.

acknowledge police surveillance of a student club and adopt policies to protect civil liberties and the free speech rights of students in the future. While the model of practice used for this campaign was social action, these steps also can be applied to other types of organizing efforts:

1. Conduct an analysis of the problem and the specific issue addressed. Make sure the issue incorporates an important moral, ethical, or legal principle.
2. Recruit allied groups that have an interest in the issue and that can contribute to the work of the coalition.
3. Conduct a power analysis that focuses both on the power held by constituents, allied groups, and the decision-makers or targets.
4. Identify resources held by constituency group members and their allies. Also, identify additional resources needed to launch a successful campaign and develop a plan to obtain them.
5. Engage in ongoing dialogue with constituents and members of allied groups. Schedule regular meetings as feasible, but also make sure to keep meeting times flexible in order to address unexpected occurrences. The dialogue process should be used to develop, modify, and assess strategies and tactics. These discussions should also be used to identify a variety of options and weigh the ethical implications, risks, and benefits of these methods.
6. Develop a group culture that facilitates an effective process to reconcile key differences among individual members and allied groups. Establish group norms and identify parameters for acceptable and unacceptable behavior among group members. Keep records of key decisions made by the group.
7. Establish good, working relationships with the media. Provide information on an ongoing basis to local reporters. Frame the campaign in a manner that is effective in illustrating key issues and principles that will peak the interest of the public. Be ready to use alternative media sources including independent Internet media sites as well as Facebook, MySpace, blogs, YouTube, and Twitter.
8. Implement the action campaign. Start by using low-impact methods such as setting emails or letters to decision-makers and holding press conferences. If these tactics are not effective, start to slowly escalate tactical methods. Remember that tactics are to be used to illustrate the legitimacy of your cause to the public and the media and to bring decision-makers to the bargaining table rather than to alienate the public or cut off dialogue with decision-makers.
9. Consult with constituents and allied organizations on a regular basis, especially when changes in tactics are under consideration. Prepare

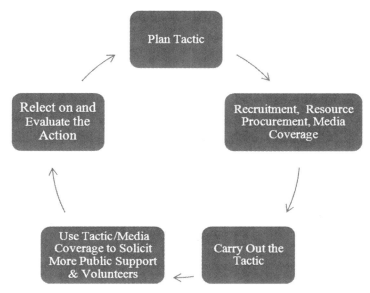

FIGURE 8.3
Campaigns as cyclical processes: Recruitment, marketing, action, and reflection.

in advance for potential risks or unexpected occurrences in order to minimize risk-taking. Make sure all participants are fully informed about potential consequences and have the opportunity to withdraw or refuse to participate.

10. Be prepared to respond to unexpected occurrences and to change tactical methods in response to situational demands.

11. Be ready to negotiate with decision-makers. Be open to compromise and ongoing dialogue, but have a specific goal and fall back positions in mind before negotiations start. Document all meetings or discussions with decision-makers.

A 12th step in campaigns, not explicitly identified in Hardina and Obel-Jorgensen's set of guidelines, is of course evaluation and termination. In Chapter 9, methods for group self-evaluation and reflection as an integral part of the campaign process are described. In Chapter 10, group approaches for formal evaluations of organizing campaigns are delineated (Figure 8.3).

SUMMARY

Carrying out an action requires strong bonds among constituency group members, careful planning, and candid dialogue among group members. The organizer essentially serves in a support role and uses interpersonal skills and the relationships built with group members to motivate participants, help them weigh tactical options and respond to situational demands, and actually carry out the action. In many situations, the organizer will employ interpersonal skills that facilitate others taking action such as providing logistical support, preparing constituents for participation in formal meetings, working with news and social media sources, giving speeches, taking notes that can be used by the organizer and group members to assess what happened, and negotiating with potential allies and targets. In circumstances in which the organizer does not perform these roles, one may be called upon to train others or to facilitate the ability of constituents to carry them out. One essential part of this process is an assessment of the tactical method used or the overall strategic direction of the campaign. In Chapter 9, the process of critical reflection or praxis on the part of the organizer and constituents is examined. In Chapter 10, the use of formal evaluation methods to assess campaign effectiveness and processes is described.

EXERCISES AND ASSIGNMENTS

1. With your classmates, watch the movie *Walkout* (Esparza, Katz, & Olmos, 2006) that depicts efforts by Latino students to advocate for reforms in the Los Angeles public schools in 1968. After watching the film, discuss with your classmates the following aspects of this organizing campaign.
   (a) What motivated these students to take action?
   (b) Were tactical methods used at the start of the campaign of low or high intensity? Why were they chosen?
   (c) What situational demands motivated students to change their tactical approaches? Did you feel that these new tactics were appropriate for the situation? Were they ethical? Why or why not?
   (d) Was the response to the protest by the police or the school board appropriate or excessive? Did it surprise you? Why or why not?
   (e) What "safety plans" were developed to minimize potential risks to the students? In what ways were these plans sufficient or insufficient to protect the students?
   (f) Did the final outcome of the campaign justify risks to the participants? Were there both short and long-term benefits and risks associated with the organizing effort? What were they?
2. With a group of your classmates, develop a "Plan B" for each of these unexpected occurrences that occur in the course of planning an on-campus rally for increased higher-education funding (Table 8.1).

Brainstorm a number of different solutions for the problem or situation and the benefits and limitations of each option.

(a) The student who is leading the effort has called to say that that he cannot prepare for or attend the rally due to a death in his family. He has left no notes about the rally, the speakers invited, arrangements with the campus administration or police, or other aspects of the rally. No one has been designated or has come forward to take his place. Should the rally be canceled, postponed, or should arrangements be made to conduct the rally as planned? Is it likely that other volunteers will have information or knowledge about plans for the rally? What other factors should be taken into consideration in determining whether the rally should go on as planned?

(b) The day before the rally, a famous celebrity who is the relative of a student has offered to attend and give a speech on behalf of higher-education funding. However, there are some conditions attached to her participation. Arrangements must be made for security and press coverage must be guaranteed. If the campus police cannot be persuaded to provide security for her, a professional bodyguard may need to be recruited as a volunteer or paid. Is the potential benefit of increased media due to a celebrity participant worth potential costs? What would be lost if the offer were simply turned down?

(c) The weather report indicates that the rally will be rained out. While postponement is an option, State Assemblywoman, Deana Jones plans to introduce legislation the day of the rally to increase the state's higher-education budget. Consequently, it is important that the rally goes on as planned. What contingency plans can be made in terms of preparing for rain or other weather-related problems?

(d) The morning of the rally, the student newspaper runs an editorial stating that the rally is a waste of time and that the organizing committee is made up of people with radical viewpoints. The editorial urges students to attend a fundraiser for a children's charity sponsored by a fraternity instead. How do you respond to this and ensure that there is a good turnout for the rally?

(e) The university President calls and asks the organizing committee to cancel the rally. He has been informed that the rally sponsors have a list of demands for the university administration, including a request that the university administration support Assemblywoman Jones' legislation. The President wishes to negotiate an agreement in private with the organizing group. Rally organizers suspect that the university is concerned about the possibility of negative press coverage. What are your options? Do you cancel the rally and negotiate or do you have alternatives?

3. In your field agency, take responsibility for staging a rally, community forum, a press conference or other tactic-related event. Write a five- to ten-page paper after the event is conducted that describes:

   (a) Background information, the purpose, and goal of the event.

   (b) How the event fits within a strategy or organizing campaign.

   (c) Resources needed for the event.

   (d) Barriers or challenges expected and actually encountered.

   (e) Any changes made in response to situational demands or resource limitations.

   (f) How you utilized interpersonal skills for at least two of the eight skill types identified in this chapter as essential for conducting campaigns (group decision-making about the use of tactical methods, logistics, participation in formal meetings, the use of news and social media, public speaking, note taking and documentation, and bargaining and negotiations).

   (g) A brief narrative of what actually happened at the event.

   (h) Your assessment of how processes and outcomes could have been improved.

4. Write a 10-minute speech suitable for delivery at a public event urging support for an issue, policy, or piece of legislation. In preparing your speech, conduct research on the issue, identify at least five facts that the public should know about the issue, and incorporate several moral or ethical principles that will garner public support. Make sure that in addition to facts, your speech appeals to emotions, incorporates a personal story (either yours or someone you know or have talked to), and contains an "ask" or call to action. Present this speech in class—your grade will be based on the content and presentation of the speech as well as to what degree your presentation is perceived to be persuasive by your classmates.

5. Design a flyer, press release, or a web or Facebook/MySpace page for a specific event or meeting that contains information that will persuade people to attend—make sure that this document contains information about the sponsor, purpose, day and time, and location.

6. Exercise on Bargaining and Negotiation.

   Using the scenario in this chapter regarding on-campus organizing for higher education, conduct an exercise with your classmates involving bargaining and negotiation. Form two groups. One group consists of university administrators and the other consists of student activists. Resolve the following problem using the bargaining and negotiation principles presented in this chapter. The circumstance or situation to be resolved involves the use of the campus "free speech zone" for the rally. The university has decided to withdraw permission for the group to hold the rally with less than 24 hours notice. The position of the two groups and the vested interest of each are:

University Administration: An alumnus who typically makes large donations to the university has asked that the free speech zone be turned over to his fraternity brothers to use for a fundraising event for the local children's hospital. The donor insists that the fundraising event can only take place the next day and has threatened to withdraw his annual donation of $25,000 unless his demands are met. He also insists that the student activists sponsoring the higher-education rally are dangerous radicals who must be stopped. The university president has offered to provide the activist group with new permit for a date after Assemblywoman Jones introduces legislation on increasing funding for higher education. The university president anticipates negative publicity regardless of any decision he makes, but wishes to minimize the fallout. However, he may hint to the students that there will be potential repercussions if they go ahead with the rally without his permission.

Student Activists: The students feel it is essential to hold their rally in the place designated on the pre-determined time and date. They also feel that their free speech rights have been violated. They have suggested some alternative venues for the charity fundraiser, but feel it is essential that they use the free speech zone. Their fallback position is that the university must provide them a venue of equal size on the planned date of the rally and provide appropriate resources (such as using the university's media contacts and posting signs) to inform students, faculty, and the public about the change in venue. However, some of the group members have hinted that they want to go ahead with the rally regardless of whether or not they have a permit.

Considerations before the negotiations start:
Make sure that you have designated a leader and a have a clear goal and fallback position.
When you've concluded the role play, come back together as a group and consider:
(a) What additional information would you need if you were actually conducting this negotiation?
(b) Did you group obtain everything they wanted, nothing, or a portion of what they needed?
(c) How easy or hard were the negotiations?

9

Working With Constituent Groups to Critically Reflect and Engage in Dialogue on the Process and Outcomes of Action Plans

> *If something is going to come from the people, your members,*
> *then you at least need to have some sort of transparent*
> *system of accountability between how decisions are made*
> *and what work staff does*
> —Interview with an environmental justice organizer from Hardina et al., 2011

In any problem-solving approach, the most important part of the process may be the feedback loop in which goal completion and the processes through which goals are achieved are examined (Kirst-Ashman & Hull, 2009). Consequently, the final or post-engagement stage of an organizing effort involves reflection about and the evaluation of the social action campaign, community development effort, or social planning process. Both these activities should take place in the context of a group process. However, reflection requires group self-analysis about how the organizing activity took place and what it achieved. It can be conducted informally based on participant perceptions and analysis while evaluation is a formal process and requires collection and analysis of "hard" quantitative data or systematically collected qualitative data from interviews, observations, or content analysis.

In this chapter, the reflection stage of the organizing process, also called praxis is described. The various uses and applications of praxis to assess the work of staff members and volunteers and the interpersonal skills needed by the organizer to facilitate this type of group dialogue are also discussed. In addition, the use of reflective practices to monitor the social change process and modify strategies and tactics in response to situational demands is explored. The use of critical reflection and dialogue in the final stages of a campaign or other community organizing, development, or planning activity to critically examine the process and outcomes associated with organizing efforts is described as well. In the last section of this chapter, the application of principles associated with the process of praxis is examined.

THE PROCESS OF PRAXIS

As described in Chapters 6 and 8, action and reflection are inherent components of any community practice effort, especially those that involve group consultation or decision-making and that rely on constituents and other volunteers to carry out the action. As noted by Miley et al. (2011), "praxis is not a linear process with a defined end point, but rather, it is a continuous looping of action-reflection-action. As the work unfolds, refection and action intertwine in praxis" (p. 98). As noted earlier in the text, although organizers tend to talk about action campaigns in terms of the problem-solving model, goal achievement, interventions and outcomes, or cause and effect, they are actually multistage, multi-layered processes that constantly evolve over time as conditions on the ground change, participants are recruited or drop out, opponents react, negotiate, or retaliate, and actions succeed or fail (Barretti, 2009; Ganz, 2008; Lee, 2001). All these occurrences produced changes in the various systems involved that affect every aspect of the process. Consequently,

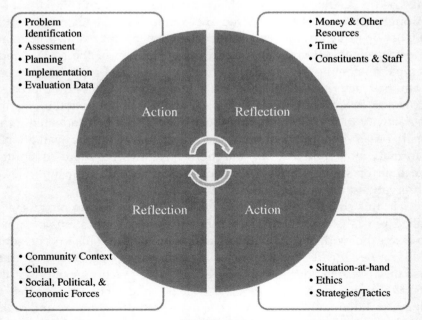

FIGURE 9.1
Action and reflection cycle and multi-stage campaigns.

the perceptions, values, and preferences, of members of the action system also change over time and require dialogue and analysis of the process (Netting et al., 2008; Payne, 2005) (Figure 9.1).

THEORETICAL FRAMEWORKS FOR USING THE PROCESS OF PRAXIS IN COMMUNITY ORGANIZING

As described by Freire (1970) and Lewin (1951), praxis or the process of action and reflection in an alternative means of constructing knowledge in which practitioners learn from past actions and use what they have learned to modify future actions. The process of action and reflection also may lead to both personal and social transformation. Social theorists such as Bourdieu (as cited in Reed-Danahay, 2005) and Foucault (as cited in Chambon, 1999) assert that knowledge is not constant or absolute, comes out of personal experience, and shifts in relation to one's position in society and the degree of political power possessed by individuals. Consequently, the experiential knowledge of members of oppressed groups differ from other individuals and groups and will often be at odds with the type of formal knowledge possessed by people with professional degrees. These authors also contend that formal knowledge often functions as a tool that serves to further oppress the powerless and that working to develop alternative sources of knowledge is the key to personal liberation. Schon (1983) argues that the recognition that knowledge varies based on experiences and social status requires that professionals working with members of marginalized groups be able to engage in reflective practice, altering practice methods in response to situational demands and client needs. However, this should be accomplished in a structured manner that requires deliberate, systematic and careful consideration of all the various factors and consequences associated with these alternative practice methods.

This collection of theories is among those considered to be postmodernist. Payne (2005) defines postmodernist as "changes in the way in which we think about our societies and the way in which we create and understand knowledge" (p. 15). The postmodernist perspective represents a paradigm shift way from "modern" or positivist approaches that rely on scientific evidence to develop knowledge about how society functions. One of the critiques of modernism is that it often represents the views or experiences of a small subset of the world's population and often excludes women, non-Caucasians, members of the LGBTQ communities, persons with disabilities, people in poverty and other marginalized groups. Alternatively, the postmodernist approach views knowledge as socially constructed and developed through personal experiences and social interaction that must be examined and understood in social and historical context, and is possessed by all members of society.

Other theoretical frameworks that guide or explain the process of reflection include social constructionism, feminist theory, critical theory and critical race theory. These postmodernist approaches have direct links to both the process of praxis and methods of community organization. For example, the theory of social constructionism pertains to how experiential knowledge is embedded in social networks and relationships and consequently is constructed in a manner that reflects multiple understandings and shared meaning. It provides a constantly changing framework for interpreting reality that is especially relevant when a practitioner is working in a group context with diverse participants (Netting, O'Connor, & Fauri, 2008). Feminist approaches to both research and community organizing practice also incorporate principles associated with social constructionism; participants in women's organizations engage in a process of consciousness-raising to examine the impact of oppressive institutions and social relations on their lives. Research studies are conducted by experts in partnership with women who have personal experiences and insight about the impact of patriarchy on their lives (Van Den Bergh & Cooper, 1995). In community practice, applying the feminist principle that "the personal is political" ensures that both personal issues and social change are addressed in the organizing process (Lee, 2001; Mizrahi, 2007).

DePoy, Hartman, and Haslett (1999) define critical theory as an approach to research that focuses on understanding what individuals actually experience in their daily lives and using this information for social change. Critical theorists view knowledge as changing over time in response to historical, social, and political forces and people's experience of their effects, especially those policies and practices that are used to marginalize and oppress some groups but not others (Fook, 2003). The production of new knowledge is viewed as a source of power and can be used to challenge existing ways of thinking associated with members of the power structure and to facilitate social change.

Some scholars and community organizers also use critical race theory in the construction of knowledge about how people of color experience everyday life and are affected by laws and social policies (Delgado, 1997; Young Laing, 2009). CRT applies morality and situational considerations to examine how the concept of race is socially constructed and used to marginalize African Americans and other communities of color (Su, 2007). One of the primary assumptions inherent in CRT is that persons of color have unique experiences and perspectives due to their status in society that are very different from cultural and social class-related perspectives associated with members of the dominant culture. As a consequence, one of the organizing tools used to develop experiential knowledge using the CRT approach is to provide a safe "space" for people to tell their own stories about what they have experienced in order to develop a counter narrative, empower the community, and create new strategies for changing policies and laws that contribute to oppression. As discussed in Chapter 5, these stories support the collection of empirical data and the development of new theories that are relevant to the lives of people in communities of color (Stovall, 2005).

PRAXIS AND KNOWLEDGE PRODUCTION

In addition to the development of "critical consciousness" or an understanding of social problems and their environmental origins, the process of praxis provides constituents with the opportunity to develop knowledge about social change and the strategies and tactics necessary to achieve social justice. Although organizers provide information and support for the preparation of action plans, constituent input and knowledge about what works is an essential part of community practice. As stated by Freire (1997):

> People have a universal right to participate in the production of knowledge which is a disciplined process of personal and social transformation. In this process, people rupture their existing attitudes of silence, accommodation and passivity, and gain confidence and abilities to alter unjust conditions and structures. This is an authentic power for liberation that ultimately destroys a passive awaiting of fate. (p. xi)

According to Conway (2004), the goal of popular education, community organizing, and participation in social movements should not only be to achieve a social change outcome. It also should produce new knowledge about how the world works and the effectiveness of various strategies used to achieve social justice. She identifies three different types of knowledge:

- Tacit knowledge or insights that come from everyday practice and are disseminated informally through personal interaction, meetings, and group activities.
- Praxis-based knowledge as described by Freire (1970), produced when practitioners and constituency group members critically reflect on and analyze what they have learned in the course of taking action.

• Empirical research reports used to persuade the public and the academic world as to the legitimacy of their interpretation of how the world functions and how social problems should be resolved.

As described in Chapter 8, these various sources of knowledge serve as a road map in the development of strategies and tactics and allow organizers and their constituents to modify their actions in response to situational demands. Some of this knowledge is used for training purposes and may be disseminated in workbooks, brochures, educational workshops, as well as in first person accounts (autobiographies) of participation in community organizing, and social movements (Somma, 2006). In addition to formal documents, information about organizing efforts and their effectiveness is transferred to others using the Internet, Facebook, Twitter, and YouTube and through popular culture in music, art, videos, television, and movies (Ganz, 2008).

Reflective practice can be used for a number of purposes and at a number of systems levels: self-assessment by individual practitioners, in the context of dialogue between the practitioner and supervisor, and for an evaluation of staff members, leaders, and other participants by members of the constituency group. It can also be used to modify ongoing campaigns in response to situational demands or to evaluate outcomes and processes of campaigns. In the next two sections of this chapter, organizer self-assessment, staff assessment by constituents, and constituent roles in assessing campaign processes and outcomes will be examined. The assessment of staff members by supervisors is examined in Chapter 13.

SELF-REFLECTION IN COMMUNITY PRACTICE

In previous chapters, one of the most critical uses of self-assessment techniques, the practice of cultural humility was described. Organizers must be knowledgeable about cultural dynamics in the community in which they work, how the social and institutional context affect community residents and intergroup relationships, and how the values and social positions of practitioners' affect their ability to interact, identify with, and form alliances with the people they serve (Harrell & Bond, 2006). In addition to this set of skills, organizers also must be able to reflect on and alter methods of practice in response to situational demands and the preferences and experiences of people they encounter, both allies and opponents. Homan (2011) refers to reflective practice as the process of learning from experiences, examining what happened, and thinking about what it means. Organizers engage in this activity in order to understand their own actions, why they acted in a particular manner, how those actions affected others, and how people perceived them. In addition, to self-examination, organizers often consult with others observers (supervisors, colleagues, constituents, board members and other key stakeholders) to improve their knowledge and community organization skills.

Organizers must be aware of their own values, their comfort level with specific types of tactics, and how their previous practice experience shape their decisions. For example, Mondros and Wilson (1994) interviewed organizers and found that they relied on ideology and a set of practice principles in choosing strategies and tactics. These practice principles were premised on a strong sense of social justice, achieving fairness for people and groups and the organizer's beliefs about how social change should be achieved. However, the respondents' preferences about strategic approaches to social change varied based on whether they believed social transformation could be achieved through politics and the legal system, through grass-roots efforts to put public pressure on decision-makers, or broad-based social movements, using mass education, moral appeals to the public, or civil disobedience. In a similar study, Mizrahi (2007) interviewed female organizers in 1989 and 2003 and examined the role of feminist theory and values in the development of strategies and tactics. She found that respondents remained committed to feminist values including women's empowerment, building consensus, and collective decision-making, but changed attitudes toward tactical decision-making over time, recognizing the role of power and the need to use it to affect social change.

According to Burghardt (2011), an organizer also needs to be aware of one's own personality type and task versus process orientation and the degree to which these factors are compatible with various organizing styles, decision-making structures, and relationship-building skills. For example, an organizer who is people oriented rather than task oriented may excel at one-on-one interviews or conducting informal meetings, but may be relatively ineffective in terms of managing an office or completing paperwork. In contrast, an organizer who does not interact well with people may focus instead on task completion and push group members too hard or too fast in order to accomplish a goal. In addition, the organizer may feel more comfortable with certain types of strategic approaches than others, preferring process-oriented methods such as consensus-building to more conflict-oriented approaches or vice versa.

Reisch and Lowe (2000) identify a number of self-assessment questions that are designed to help an organizer resolve ethical questions related to the organizing process. In addition to the assessment of ethical dilemmas that an organizer might face, they can also be used to analyze campaign activities and decision-making processes:

* What are the ethical issues that can be identified in the situation-at-hand?
* What information do I (the organizer) need to have in order to clarify the ethical principles that apply in this situation?
* What ethical criteria should be used to guide what I should do?
* If there is a conflict of interest that pertains to the decision, who should make the decision and who should benefit from it?
* Is it actually my responsibility to make the decision in this situation? If not me, then who should be involved in the decision-making process?

In addition to these questions, there are other aspects of campaigns that should be assessed by organizers. Some of these questions pertain to issues of process that were discussed earlier in this textbook and include:

* Were my goals or the organization's goals for the meeting, event, action, or campaign achieved? If not, why did this happen?
* Were there some aspects of the process or structure used during the meeting, event, action, or campaign that could be improved? If so, what should be done?
* Is there more I need to know about participants in a meeting, event, action, or campaign? Do previous relationships or rivalries among group members affect group interactions now? Do any members have hidden agendas or goals that will affect what the group decides to do?
* Could I have acted or reacted to the situation-at-hand or the people involved in a different manner? What motivated me? How can I improve my approach in problematic situations?
* Were there issues related to the interaction of two or more participants at the meeting, event, action, or campaign that could be improved? What were they? Is it up to me to address this?
* What could I do to better prepare organization leaders to manage tasks, processes, or issues related to interpersonal relationships among participants? (Burghardt, 2011; Gutierrez & Alvarez, 2000; Hardina, 2002; Homan, 2011; Kahn, 2010; Mondros & Wilson, 1994).

REFLECTION AS A GROUP PROCESS: ASSESSING THE ROLES OF PARTICIPANTS IN COMMUNITY PRACTICE

Wint and Sewpaul (2000) describe praxis in community organization as a three-part process: involving all community members in defining local problems, developing strategies and tactics to resolve them, and engaging participants in critical assessments about the process and the various roles played by the participants in the social change effort. Such assessments of participant activities can be used for evaluations of staff performance as well as to assess decisions made by group leaders, the performance of various volunteers and other constituents, and the degree to which participation has contributed to personal and community transformation.

As noted in Chapter 8, one of the chief dilemmas faced by organizers is to facilitate the leadership of others and ensure that constituents have adequate opportunities to participate in tactical decision-making. Shaw (2001) views participant and staff engagement in group dialogue for the purpose of evaluating staff performance as an appropriate method to ensure constituent control. While he concedes that community organizations should rely on staff for advice about tactics, he also believes that constituents and their leaders should be the principle decision-makers as a safe guard against staff incompetence or refusal to carry out group decisions. He views meetings with staff as the proper venue for all organization members to thoroughly discuss work performance and the success or failure of tactical methods. According to Shaw, "the process usually takes time and requires discomforting assessments of what might have been, but the staff and the organization emerge with a clearer understanding of how to achieve social change" (p. 256).

ben Asher (2010) identifies a set of criteria for constituent evaluations of staff members. One of the primary roles of staff organizers is to facilitate the development of leaders. Consequently, they help guide the personal development of those individuals who will make policies and day-to-day decisions about community organizing and the tasks to be undertaken by volunteers rather than staff. Therefore, it is the responsibility of the organizer to prepare organization leaders and other constituents to evaluate the staff member's work. Without trained leaders who can ensure the maintenance of the organization and help set the direction of future campaigns, the community group will not be able to function, volunteer capacity to take action will not be developed, and individual participants will not feel empowered to engage in social change (Burghardt, 2011; Lee, 2001). Therefore, constituents should examine the degree to which organizers have guided, trained, and prepared them to assume leadership roles in the organization.

In addition to constituent evaluations of staff, group processes are also utilized to assess the work of organization leaders and participants in social change activities and organization decision-making. According to Polletta (2002), during the evaluation process in community organizations, participants are often encouraged to challenge one another and make leaders accountable to the group for their choice of tactics and their actions. She describes this process as consultation "with a widening circle of community members, accountability, and a commitment to making leadership skills available to others" (p. 184).

As described in Chapter 8, group debriefing sessions after carrying out tactical actions help to minimize conflict among participants or diverse viewpoints while building a group consensus around tactical choices and conducting an assessment of their effectiveness (Mondros & Wilson, 1994). In addition, the various roadblocks and hazards faced when implementing a campaign often make people more determined to take additional action. Consequently, the analysis of these problems, the shared experiences of group members, the development of new knowledge, and group successes as well as failures increase both individual and organization capacity to keep working and striving toward social change.

The process of group praxis in community organizations may also be used as an opportunity for constituents to assess their own roles in the campaign, organization or community. According to Delgado and Staples (2008):

> Praxis forces the participants to tie emotions, history, and theory together in order to develop a composite picture of their own lives, as well as the life of the community in which they reside. When accomplished well, praxis represents a time for healing and for taking stock of individual and group accomplishments. (p. 142)

PRAXIS AS GROUP DIALOGUE: DECISIONS BY MANY RATHER THAN A FEW

In addition to knowledge production and assessment of participant activity, there are a number of other reasons for using group dialogue to plan and critique organizing, development, and planning efforts. According to Lee (2001), involvement in group dialogue and reflection during the community organization process ensures that "community residents must say their own words, plan their own options, and act in ways that are their own" (p. 380). As noted previously in this text, constituent involvement in tactical decision-making ensures that the methods used are culturally appropriate and have meaning and relevance for those people responsible for carrying them out (Gutierrez & Lewis, 1999; Martinez, 2008).

The inclusion of diverse voices in the dialogue also helps ensure that these tactical methods have salience for the general public the media, and policy. For example, Taylor, Kimport, Van Dyke, and Anderson (2009) describe the strategic use of cultural symbols as an effective weapon in the struggle for same-sex marriage in San Francisco in 2004. When Mayor Gavin Newsom temporarily authorized the City to issue marriage certificates to gay couples, activists used the opportunity to frame the issue in a manner that was designed to increase the gay community's identification with the same-sex marriage movement and secure public support:

> The couples who went to City Hall for the annual marriage-counter protest were among the first to marry. Media attention, however, allowed for the wedding protest to gain momentum. Soon throngs of gay man and lesbians arrived to take their place in a queue of couples sharing food, blankets, chairs, and friendship while waiting outside City Hall to obtain marriage licenses and media coverage flooded the nation with images of the couples waiting in line, and then emerging from City Hall waving marriage licenses. In an Internet-launched campaign of support known as "Flowers from the Heartland," people donated money to purchase flowers for the couples married at City Hall. (p. 871)

In addition to cultural relevance, there are a number of other practical reasons for using group dialogue to make tactical choices and assess their impact. Polletta (2002), in describing her findings from a comprehensive study of social movement organizations identifies several reasons for making strategic decisions using group dialogue and consensus:

- *Capacity building.* By talking through tactical options, group members are encouraged to state the reasons they supported one plan more than others. This in turn increases the knowledge of all group members. It also allows individual participants to hear different viewpoints, raise questions about what they have heard, and modify their own viewpoints.
- *Legitimatizing the authority of the group.* By requiring that the group members rather than individuals make important decisions, degree to which one person or a handful of people with more power than others can make decisions that affect the group as a whole is limited. This also helps increase the power, resources, and public recognition that accrue to the organization as a whole when they make recommendations on behalf of community members (Conway, 2004).

• *Ownership*. Having a say in the decision-making process will increasing commitment and participation in the group over the long haul. People who feel that their opinions are always ignored are more likely to drop out or refuse to carry out tasks with which they do not agree.

In addition to organization structure and participant knowledge, Ganz (2009) argues that it is the interaction among group members with diverse backgrounds, experiences, connections, and values that generates the energy and creativity necessary to develop innovative tactical methods. According to Hofmann-Pinilla, Olavarria, and Ospina (2005), the collective identity of group members is one of the key components that determines how they "make sense of their actions, frame issues, and handle moments of crisis" (p. 3). Collective identity also shapes relationships in the group which in turn determine how decisions are made, who makes them, and what is decided (Conway, 2004). According to Ganz (2008):

> A good campaign can be thought of as a symphony of multiple movements, each with an exposition, development, and recapitulation, but which together proceed toward a grand finale. A symphony is also constructed from the interplay of many different voices interacting in multiple ways but whose overall coordination is crucial for the success of the undertaking. (p. 13)

The ability of the constituency group to engage in collaborative dialogue is dependent not only upon the interpersonal skills of constituent leaders and staff members, but upon the structure of the organization developed to carry out the campaign. Ganz (2009), in describing the past successes of the United Farm Workers (UFW), identifies those components of organizing campaigns that contribute to a group's ability to make good tactical decisions. Strategic capacity is related to the tactical knowledge, previous experiences, and the social networks in which decision-makers are members. It can also be enhanced or impeded by the decision-making and organization structures established to carry out the campaign. The organizations should be able to find and use resources and have a means of making sure constituents and staff members are held accountable for their actions. Ganz describes the ability of participants to learn from their mistakes as critical for the adoption of successful tactical approaches. This process involves "managing the tension between generating ideas and making choices, between creative dissent and organization disunity, between change and continuity" (p. 253).

INTERPERSONAL SKILLS FOR FACILITATING PRAXIS

There are a number of interpersonal skills that can be used by organizers to guide group dialogue and analysis of organizing, development, and planning efforts in order to facilitate the process of praxis. For example, Gutierrez and Lewis (1999) describe the types of skills required for developing a consensus around tactics and managing conflicts in community practice. They argue that conflict is often a necessary by-product of organizing work, especially for white organizers working with groups consisting primarily of people of color. Group members may "test" where the organizer stands in relation to the group and one's willingness to take a stand against oppressive practices as an ally of the community.

Successfully navigating this process is often an important part of entering" into a community for organizers who are different in terms of ethnicity, social class, gender, age, physical/mental abilities, and sexual orientation from group members. Myles Horton, the founder of one of the first community organizing training centers, the Highlander School, describes the technique he used to engage with African American leaders in the south during the civil rights struggles of the 1950s and 1960s:

> You can't be accepted by people if you're trying to be what you're not. You've got to be genuinely what you are, but from what you are you've got to have empathy with and understanding of people and their situations, and you've got to relate as human beings in such a way that color isn't a factor in the relationship. (Horton et al., 1998, p. 1996)

In addition to trust-building, other skills for the organizer in situations that involve conflict include basic social work skills that include engagement, active listening, and the ability to step back from confrontation, even when it seems personal, in order to facilitate dialogue and reach consensus (Gutierrez & Lewis, 1999). The organizer must also be able to view the situation from a variety of perspectives, acquiring the ability to understand the views of others from their standpoint (such as personal histories and social status) in order to facilitate group consensus. In addition, the organizers also need to create a safe environment for people to engage in critical reflection. According to Kahn (2010):

> One of the greatest skills an organizer can have is the ability to frame and ask questions in ways that make people not only want to answer them, but also to think deeply, and in unexpected ways, about what the answers might be. (p. 194)

Gutierrez and Lewis (1999) recommend that all members of the constituency group should participate in these sessions (as feasible) and be encouraged to provide ideas, recommendations, and assessments of tactical methods during the dialogue process. Both leaders and organizers should contribute to the transparency of the group process by being explicit about the decisions that were made, who made them, and the situational factors that guided the decision. Even in these group dialogues, the organizer's role involves a dual purpose, not only facilitating a thorough discussion on tactical methods and their failures or successes, but also building up the capacity of group members to assume leadership roles, acquire tactical knowledge, develop skills, and work independently to support the organization and its actions (Zachary, 2000). One of the ethical principles incorporated into the capacity building process is the commitment to facilitating the development of leaders that can act autonomously to plan and conduct campaigns as well as the development of new organizations, controlled and operated by members of the constituency group (Gutierrez et al., 1998).

USING PRAXIS TO MONITOR THE COMMUNITY ORGANIZING PROCESS AND CHANGING COURSE

Most organizers advise that constituents, other participants and allies, and staff members should continuously engage in a process of action and reflection or active learning in order to assess the effectiveness, impact, and process involved in conducting events, the implementation of individual tactics, and the entire campaign (Chambers, 2004; Delgado & Staples, 2008; Ganz, 2009; Homan, 2011). As noted in Chapter 8, situational demands and the reactions of opponents, the general public, policymakers, and potential allies often make it necessary that tactical methods and negotiating demands be modified throughout the campaign (Barretti, 2009). According to Ganz (2008), the ability to change tactical and strategic decisions is essential because "actors do not suddenly acquire more resources or devise a new strategy, but find that resources they already have given them more leverage in achieving their goals" (p. 9).

Chambers (2004) recommends that group evaluations be conducted for every event or action that takes place in the course of a campaign because:

> Thinking and calculating go into preplanning an action, but not much thinking goes on during the action itself. We cannot think and act simultaneously. Try rubbing your belly and patting your head at the same time. Unless leaders draw

off immediately after an action and evaluate it, little or no education takes place . . . . . . The same event is evaluated two
weeks, two months, and sometimes two years later, providing
ongoing food for learning and growth. (pp. 86–87)

Group assessment of campaign activities should be pre-planned,
systematic, and tied to the organization's formal evaluation process with
specific types of information collected at each meeting or specific dates
(Ganz, 2008; Homan, 2011). Specific goals and indicators of change need
to be specified and monitored on a regular basis. The types of questions
that should be raised by leaders and thoroughly discussed by participants can pertain to specific events or tactics or the campaign as a whole:

- Are group members completing their assigned tasks? If not, what are
  the obstacles? How can task completion be improved?
- Is the group making progress toward meeting its goal? If not what is
  preventing goal attainment?
- How did people react to a specific event, tactic, or campaign and what
  does it mean?
- Has anything actually changed? How do we know this?
- What new information do we have about a specific situation? Does it
  suggest new possibilities for additional tactical methods, recruiting
  additional allies, or conducting negotiations? Are there new problems
  we should expect? (Homan, 2011).

ASSESSING WHAT AND WHY THINGS HAPPENED
AT THE END OF THE ORGANIZING CAMPAIGN

During the final stages of a campaign, group assessment is essential for
examining whether goals were achieved, why the campaign succeeded,
why it failed, or if a partial victory is acceptable to group members.
Both constituents and staff members are typically involved in these
end-of-the campaign evaluation sessions simply because participants
can view the same event differently and have diverse reactions. In some
circumstances, members of the community may also be invited to give
comments about their perceptions of the campaign and the outcomes produced (Gutierrez & Lewis, 1999). In addition to outcomes, aspects of the
campaign that are likely to be examined include the behavior of all participants, the context in which campaign activities took place, the reaction of
opponents, allies, and the general public, and what could be improved
upon the next time a similar campaign takes place (Chambers, 2004;
Staples, 2004).

In some cases, opponents or allies may weigh in with their assessment of the campaign and its effects. The end of the campaign may be preceded by successful negotiations or concessions from opponents. There may also be media coverage associated with some types of outcomes that provide an opportunity for constituents or the organizer to comment about the campaign or receive credit for its success. Media reports also provide an additional source of information that can be used to document the organization's work, obtain funding for future campaigns, and increase public awareness of the organization.

In group assessment meetings, results from formal evaluations may also be incorporated into the group assessment process (see Chapter 10). Ganz (2008) argues that outcome evaluation is an essential part of any campaign and can be structured in a manner that allows participants to both monitor campaign processes and determine how far they have come and what they still need to do. He suggests constructing charts and graphs in the campaign office that illustrate progress toward meeting group goals such as the number of volunteers recruited, the number of elected officials supporting a piece of legislation, or the number of homes repaired in neighborhood clean-up efforts.

The qualitative data obtained during these group evaluation meetings can also be used to supplement data from more formal evaluations. According to Stovall (2005), personal and group narratives about the community organizing process and the roles of participants constitute an "unspoken history" about social change efforts and consequently strengthen empirically derived evaluation data and facilitate the development of leadership skills, personal transformation, positive self-images, and feelings of empowerment among constituents.

One critical component of the group assessment process is whether the campaign has resulted in victory or defeat. According to Staples (2004), one of the questions that should be asked at the end of a campaign is "where do we go from here?" (p. 169). Members need to decide if a victory means the end of the campaign or the start of a new one. If campaigns are to be viewed as a series of reoccurring steps that permit a group to make small gains over a long period of time, then victory often leads simply to the next phase of the process. Many community organizations engage in multiple campaigns at the same time, so completion of one set of activities will just mean that resources are shifted to other initiatives.

In should be noted, however, that all tactical methods or campaigns are not successful. However, Gutierrez and Lewis (1999) point out the success of a tactic is often not as important as what people have learned from the experience and how they will use that knowledge in the future. Consequently, an unsuccessful tactic or campaign may simply be an opportunity to modify tactical methods or regroup (Ganz, 2008). In those cases in which a tactic or strategic approach was unsuccessful, it does not necessarily mean that other approaches will not work. According to Barretti (2009):

> If a chosen strategy such as a tenant's meeting with a landlord about hazardous building conditions doesn't succeed, tenants will think the game is over. The organizer's job is to get the group to see the road ahead, to reframe the dilemma as a temporary setback, simply one play in the game, and an opportunity to restrategize. By the same token, the organizer must caution tenants about battles won. Just as the game may not end when tenants lose a battle, it isn't over when the battle is won either. (p. 18)

After the group reaches a consensus about the campaign outcome, they must "wrap up": the campaign. During this last phase of the campaign, people often need a chance to let off steam, an opportunity to increase personal bonds and solidarity with other members, or say their goodbyes, and be honored for their work. Consequently, participants often come together to celebrate their success or commiserate when results are not quite what was expected. This final gathering might be a dinner, a party or picnic, or a formal rewards ceremony that honors leaders, volunteers, and allies for their hard work (Alliance for Justice, n.d.; Chambers, 2004; Kahn, 1991). In circumstances in which constituents have diverse backgrounds, these ceremonies may offer an opportunity for participants to learn about and honor the culture and traditions of their new friends and colleagues.

PUTTING VALUES IN ACTION: CRITICAL REFLECTION, THINKING, AND ACTION

Gardner (2003) describes the process of critical reflection for evaluating social change initiatives as incorporating a number of principles and practices consistent with postmodernist theories and qualitative research methods:

* Constructing new knowledge from personal histories and story-telling.
* Ensuring that diverse viewpoints are incorporated into the evaluation process, including the views of people who are seldom consulted or included in the process.

- Helping people connect personal experiences with an analysis of the impact of social structure and the process of oppression.
- Incorporating values and principles into the evaluation process.
- Fostering the ability of participants in the evaluation process to question and explore existing phenomena and to tolerate some degree of uncertainty in one's level of understanding. In many situations, data collection can consist of gathering information on individual experiences and perceptions rather than using formal knowledge to test hypotheses.
- Facilitating a sense of collective efficacy or belief among the participants in their ability to effectively engage in social change.

Successful campaigns generate good stories. Often the narrative reflects personal, organization, or community experiences, focusing on hardships and overcoming adversity through "struggle" via participation in one or more organizing campaigns, development efforts, or planning processes. Thus, these stories serve several purposes. In addition to the identification of problems and their impacts, they often contain a source of knowledge about how to organize. They also provide personal "testimonies" about an empowering experience that has changed the life of the narrator or improved the community. These stories provide a context for sharing experiences, developing common bonds, and transmitting knowledge about the organizing process (VeneKlasen et al., 2002; Williams et al., 2003). Increasingly, not only are stories and knowledge about social action campaigns, development efforts, or social planning processes simply shared with other community members, when formally or informally documented, they provide other groups with an organizing knowledge base from which to draw (Conway, 2004; Polletta, 2006). As described by Ganz (2008), a large part of the organizer's job is facilitating a process that changes the individual stories of hardship or struggles over adversity to "stories of us," how members of the group have bonded together to resolve collective problems and successfully challenged the odds to improve their own lives and their communities.

The story of campaigns often becomes one concerned not only with success or failure but also with how people interacted with one another, what happened to them after the campaign concluded, and how that experience may have contributed to additional organizing efforts. Did two participants meet and marry during the organizing campaign or development project? Did former opponents with different perspectives, positions, and values form a bond and become life-long friends? Did the idealist university student, hired as the neighborhood's housing organizer, become President of the United States? Did participants in a long-term struggle for labor rights become inspired, go back to school and become teachers, lawyers, judges, professional social workers, or community organizers (Shaw, 2008)? It is the relationships and experiences that people have and their personal transformations that become part of the "story" of the campaign and its successes.

Stories about campaigns and community projects, their failures and successes, and relationships or bonds among participants not only pertain to constituents but are also catalogued and described by organization board members and in the written campaign descriptions they disseminate and in the training material, and organizing models they develop (Conway, 2004). These models and training materials incorporate both the experiences and values of participants and change and evolve over time in response to the recruitment of new members, development of new leaders, and the implementation of campaign strategies. Hence these models become a means to illustrate how values are translated into action, cultural traditions are honored, and the "story of us" is described. Descriptions about the organization's approach to change, strategic preferences (e.g., an emphasis on consensus rather than conflict), and the degree to which constituents are consulted about, guide, or control the action are also important parts of the story about how campaigns are viewed by participants and how the story of the campaign is presented to the public.

For example, the Asian NGO Coalition for Agrarian Reform and Rural Development (n.d.), an organization based in the Philippines, but operating throughout Southeast Asia, has developed a model of community organization practice that combines traditional western methods for social action with Asian cultural practices. ANGOC's mission is to assist members of rural communities in obtaining rights to land that they have traditionally farmed, but have lost through corporate control or commercial exploitation of natural resources. The organization routinely sends organizers into rural areas in a variety of Asian countries to employ culturally appropriate tactics for social change. ANGOC describes its work as consisting of a 10-stage process:

- *Integration.* The organizer enters into the community and establishes trust through the provision of assistance with agricultural tasks, meeting with people in their homes or common areas, and attending events and ceremonies.
- *Community Study.* The organizer conducts interviews, focus groups, and group dialogues, and analyzes secondary data, and observes community life before developing a tentative organizing plan. Participatory research methods may also be used for this assessment.

- *Issue Analysis.* The felt needs of the community are determined and priorities for the campaign are set. The strategic approach used may involve only self-help efforts if people are reluctant to confront authorities.
- *Formation of the Organizing Group.* Participants and leaders are recruited for the organizing campaign.
- *Recruitment of Participants.* The organizer and members of the core organizing group use one-on-one interviews and other techniques to recruit participants and ask them to participate in a community meeting. At the meeting, campaign strategies and tactics are developed.
- *Role Plays.* The organizer prepares participants to take action by having them engage in role plays and exercises for situations that may occur in discussions, confrontation, or negotiation with members of the target group.
- *Action Phase.* The participants engage in an action or activity that they have planned. In some circumstances, this may involve a group project or cooperative endeavor rather than direct confrontation.
- *Reflection and Evaluation.* Participants examine what has been achieved and what has been unsuccessful in order to improve actions in the future. This can also involve a review of the strengths and weaknesses of the process.
- *Organization Development.* In addition to developing individual capacity through leadership development, social action, and agricultural projects, capacity development also focuses on developing a formal organization structure for carrying out further actions.
- *The Last Phase.* During the last part of the campaign, ANGOC and the organizer leave the community and transfer responsibility for the project over to local residents. Clear criteria are established for assessing whether the time is right for the transfer including whether sufficient members have been recruited, leaders have been trained, and goals for future work are established.

SUMMARY

The process of critical reflection or praxis is an essential component of social work practice. During the initial phases of the organizing process, constituency group members work together to develop a "critical consciousness" in order to understand how political, economic, and social forces have an impact on their lives and their communities. During the final stages of organizing campaigns, critical reflection is used to examine and modify strategies and tactics used in social action, community development, and social planning and other types of community interventions. Organizers engage in critical self-reflection in order to examine their own practice activities, choices, values, and reactions, and the interpersonal skills they use to facilitate group dialogue and leadership development and to identify areas in which personal performance can be improved. Constituency group members engage in critical reflection about how individual participants (leaders, other volunteers, and staff members) functioned in campaigns, the choices available to them, and how campaigns can be improved to make them more effective. They also use reflective processes to evaluate the outcomes associated with campaigns and to examine the implementation process for campaign components. Often data from these "informal" evaluations are used to supplement formal evaluations that involve systematic collection of data. In Chapter 13, methods used in community organizing to facilitate participatory evaluations will be discussed.

EXERCISES AND ASSIGNMENTS

1. Conduct a focus group interview with participants in previous campaigns or a group of long-term volunteers about their experiences in the campaign or organization. Your interview should focus on the respondents' perceptions of both processes and outcomes, specific experiences or critical events during their participation in the campaign or organization that have meaning for them, their personal contributions to the organizing effort, and how participation affected them and their relationships with others.
2. Keep a journal of your experiences and reactions in organizing a campaign, an event, a community forum, or another activity. Use the list of self-reflection questions presented in this chapter to analyze your work and identify your values, personality traits, and strengths and weaknesses associated with your performance.
3. Using the debriefing questions listed in this chapter, conduct a group dialogue with participants after an event, as part of the process of monitoring what is happening during a campaign or project, or as the "first-stage" of an evaluation at the conclusion of a campaign or project. Write a three- to five-page paper summarizing the discussion and identifying strengths and weaknesses of the methods used to facilitate the action or activities undertaken.

10

Discovering Whether and Why the Action Worked: Using Participatory Research to Conduct Formal Evaluations

> *I think you measure it [effectiveness of tactical methods] by its desired impact. Again going to that main question, "What do we want to accomplish with this?"?*
> —Interview with an Education Organizer, Hardina et al., 2011

The final, post-engagement stage of community organizing development, and planning efforts involves evaluation of what was accomplished. Many evaluations also examine the process through which the intervention achieved its goals. In some contexts, evaluation may be conducted by a single practitioner or a small group of experts. However, in community practice, evaluation takes place within the context of collaboration among constituency group members, organization staff, outside consultants, and organization or coalition partners. Consequently, it involves complex decision-making processes and procedures.

In this chapter, the purpose of formal evaluations in community practice is examined, with an emphasis on the political nature of evaluation mechanisms which often involve diverse voices and viewpoints. Also discussed are some of the challenges associated with formal evaluations of community organizing projects. In addition, the applicability of evidence-based practice approaches for evaluations of community interventions are discussed and contrasted with the use of a systematic research method, called logic modeling, to evaluate community organizing work. Specific types of community-based evaluations are described that include goal attainment assessments, quantitative research and descriptive studies, critical incident analysis and case studies, process and implementation analysis, case studies and critical incident analysis, and qualitative evaluation methods. Specific methods for conducting group or participatory evaluation studies are also discussed. In addition, the interpersonal skills that organizers and community-based researchers must possess in order to facilitate group evaluations are examined. In the last section of this chapter, ethical issues associated with participatory evaluation are considered, with an emphasis on mutual learning and partnership.

THE PURPOSE AND POLITICS OF FORMAL EVALUATIONS IN COMMUNITY PRACTICE

Formal evaluations provide information about whether an intervention, community plan, development effort or a campaign worked, why it worked, and how it worked (Homan, 2011). It can also be used to explain whether the benefits associated with goal achievement actually outweigh the costs of the intervention (McNutt, 2011). Consequently, the purpose of evaluation in community practice is consistent with social work at other systems levels and is also similar to techniques commonly used in the evaluation of social service programs to examine the effectiveness, quality, cost–benefits, and implementation of services provided by public and nonprofit organizations (Ginsberg, 2001; Hardina, 2002; Royse et al., 2010).

Evaluation in community practice is more likely to involve constituency group members in planning and conducting research studies and analyzing the results than other forms of evaluation (Stringer, 2007). As noted previously in Chapters 6 and 8, the types of knowledge produced may be formal, based on previous theories and objective forms of evidence or informal and socially constructed, derived from practice experience (tacit knowledge) as well as knowledge developed through critical reflection or praxis by individuals or groups. While many constituency group members and community practitioners will argue that tacit or praxis-based knowledge is often more accessible and relevant to the lived experiences of constituency group members, evaluations that rely on theories, systematic data collection, and evidence are also a necessary and critical component of community practice (Foster & Louie, 2010).

In addition to facilitating community participation, there are a number of good reasons for community organizations to evaluate what they are doing and determine whether an intervention or campaign worked. All organizing, development, and planning efforts focus on attaining a specific goal, regardless of whether the activity is process or task-oriented. In a political or legislative campaign, the goal is electing someone to office or achieving a legislative victory. In social action and transformative organizing approaches, the purpose is to change public opinion, policies, and laws and improve the ability of community members to obtain access to resources and political power. In community and economic development, goals include improvements in the quality of life, health, and economic resources for local residents. In social planning, improvements are made in the goods and services produced by public and nonprofit organizations; access to these programs is increased for the people who are likely to need or use them (Gjecovi, James, & Chenoweth, 2006; Ohmer & Korr, 2006). In all of these approaches to organizing, process objectives are also important: utilizing interpersonal skills to facilitate recruitment, participation, and leadership development, strengthening local networks and linkages between people and organizations, and increasing the capacity of people, agencies, and institutions to engage in activities that will increase their ability to promote social change (Delgado, 2000; Mott, 2003; National Funders Group, 2011; Pyles, 2009a; Speer, Peterson, Zippay, & Christens, 2011). Often it is how and why these activities are accomplished that ensures the success of most organizing efforts.

As noted in Chapter 9, "hard data" on goal attainment can be used to motivate participants and other community members to keep working toward their goals. Statistics and other concrete or standardized measures also allow community groups to document their success, brag about their accomplishments to others, provide a means through which to recruit people for the cause, provide persuasive evidence of hardship or deprivation and make a case that laws and policies must be changed. Unlike tacit or praxis-derived knowledge, data collected through established, formal, standardized and systematic processes, most often involving quantitative methods, is viewed by scholars as "objective" or value free. Such data provide a vehicle for communicating information about community needs and the resolution of local problems in the common "language" used by political, academic, media, professional, corporate, and other powerful decision makers who will not respond to information collected through practice experience or obtained directly from members of marginalized communities (Stoecker, 2005). Often data obtained through story-telling and other types of qualitative data approaches are labeled as "anecdotal" and are consequently easily discredited as not "generalizable" to the public at large (Maxwell, 2004; Stringer, 2007).

Another reason for conducting formal evaluations of community organizing, development, or planning efforts has to do with how such projects are typically funded. While it is possible for some community groups to engage in social change in organizations with volunteers, most organizations cannot sustain organizing efforts without a larger paid staff force. While very small efforts may be able to survive financially from individual contributions, funding a nonprofit organization and providing adequate pay for staff members requires that the organization obtain grants and contracts from foundations, government agencies, and in some cases corporations or unions. Most of these funding sources require some type of formal documentation of organization accomplishments and successes in return for funding (Delgado, 2000). In many cases, grants or contracts cannot be renewed on a year-to-year basis without evidence that campaign or project goals were achieved and that the monies received were used properly by the organization. In some instances, funders may only require simple documentation that the organization accomplished what it set out to do. In other circumstances, funders may require that a formal evaluation be conducted to fulfill the terms of the contract (Foster & Louie, 2010; Neighborhood Funders Group, 2011). Donors may differ, however, in terms of whether they provide additional funds for evaluation purposes, require that the recipient use a standardized approach predetermined by the funder to collect, analyze, and report data, or insist that an independent consultant be hired to conduct the evaluation rather than permit organization staff or constituents to do so (Mott, 2003; Stoecker, 2005).

Some funders may require that organizations provide only data from outcome evaluations, while others also want information about campaign, intervention, or development processes that describe how and why results were achieved or why the effort failed to produce the desired goals. They often want this type of evaluation in order to facilitate the dissemination of findings about *best practices* and their effects on community members, organization constituents, and social conditions to other organizations; in many instances training manuals, curriculum models, formal research reports, and Internet resources become the vehicle for distributing this information to the public (Delgado & Staples, 2008).

CHALLENGES IN CONDUCTING FORMAL COMMUNITY-BASED EVALUATIONS

There are numerous challenges in conducting credible evaluations in community practice. Mott (2003) identifies a number of problems faced by community organizations that choose to or are required to conduct evaluations by funders including:

- Limited resources including skilled staff or outside consultants to facilitate evaluation studies and the reluctance of donors to actually provide funding explicitly for the evaluations that they require.
- Donor requirements that only certain types of evaluations be conducted, limiting constituent participation in evaluation design, choice of research questions, and whether data will be produced that can actually be used to assess community needs.
- Limited time-lines given to the organizations to produce results and the frequency with which funders may change their priorities in terms of goals to be accomplished, outcomes to be produced, and measures of success.

Mott (2003) also questions whether donors actually understand that most organizing work may not consist of a linear process that progresses in a logical manner over time, but one in which the organization and its members must continually reassess, regroup, and change course in response to situational demands. According to Gjecovi et al. (2006) "outcomes for community organizing will vary based on the campaign, the socio-political context, and the skills and levels of cohesiveness that exist in the community. Therefore no single template for evaluating organizing campaigns exists" (p. 21).

Such contextual factors also limit the degree to which experimental designs or standardized measures can be used to assess campaign outcomes (Stringer, 2007). Delgado and Staples (2008) identify several additional limitations involved in formal evaluations of community practice: exclusive emphasis on outcomes rather than processes, a tendency by organizers to value the process rather than the outcome, and the tendency of organizers and donors to value only short-term achievements rather than goals that can only be achieved over time. Another methodological concern is that often the ability of donors to adequately assess the success of community change efforts is limited by the lack of adequate indicators to determine whether process objectives have been achieved, the quality and intensity of community or constituent participation, or the actual impact of the organization in facilitating social change (National Funders Group, 2011).

COMMUNITY EVALUATIONS AND EVIDENCE-BASED PRACTICE

In social work practice, the gold standard for good evaluations generally is identified as experimental designs, with experimental and control groups and randomly drawn samples that provide rigorous evidence to prove or disprove causal hypotheses (Patton, 2008; Rubin

& Babbie, 2010). This expectation is often cited as the minimum standard that a practitioner should use to make decisions about the *best* interventions to apply in professional practice; only those conducted using these rigorous standards will provide sufficient evidence that the intervention has worked. While evidence-based practice is most often applied in clinical social work practice with individuals, groups, and families, some of its advocates have also argued for the use of evidence-based practice models, in macro practice and policy (Briggs & McBeath, 2009; Gambrill, 2007; Mulroy, 2008; Roberts-DeGennaro, 2011). Most proponents of EBT agree that it involves a five-step process:

1. A practitioner identifies a research question about the best course of action.
2. The practitioner identifies available evidence from empirical research studies that employ rigorous methods to test hypotheses and collect data.
3. The practitioner examines the research studies that have been conducted and determines whether the evidence produced is reliable and valid.
4. The practitioner combines evidence from well-conducted, rigorous studies, one's clinical experience, and the unique characteristics and values of the client, to make the appropriate decision regarding what intervention method to use.
5. The practitioner implements the intervention and conducts an in-agency evaluation of the outcomes produced, generally using a single-system design to produce new empirical evidence that the intervention works (Rubin & Parish, 2007)

However, EBP definitions often vary in terms of the degree to which client preferences are factored into the choice of the intervention or whether an intervention can be used if it has not been previously established as effective through a randomized experiment rather than a quasi-experiment or single-system design (Epstein, 2011; Walker, Briggs, Koroloff, & Friesen, 2007).

Even with these slightly different interpretations and applications of EBP, the method has many critics in social work and among community-based researchers. For example, Epstein (2011) argues that instead of rigid adherence to EPB models that ignore and even stigmatizes practitioner knowledge derived from daily experiences in implementing interventions, social workers should instead strive to obtain research evidence using a mixture of research methods including document analysis, observation, and interviewing. Practitioners who have adopted participatory research and evaluation approaches in psychology, public health, community development, and social work have argued that EBP is incompatible with a research method that incorporates basic principles such as participant ownership of the research process, equal partnerships between experts and nonexperts, and reciprocity (Webb, 2001).

There is some empirical evidence that suggests that it is very difficult to incorporate EBP principles in participatory evaluations. For example, in the early 2000s in order to examine whether these community-based studies were compatible or at odds with evidence-based practice, the Agency for Healthcare Research and Quality, U.S. Department of Health and Human Services conducted a review of 60 empirical studies involving participatory research methods used in health-related, community projects. The purpose of the review was to determine whether these studies conformed to evidence-based practice guidelines (Viswanathan et al., 2004). The authors found that only 50% of the studies actually involved community-based interventions while the other 50% included assessments of community conditions; only 12 of the intervention-related studies involved completed interventions and only 4 of these projects involved randomized experimental designs. The studies also varied substantially in terms of community involvement; only a handful of studies included community participants in generating hypotheses or data interpretation. Viswanathan et al. concluded that there was little evidence that participatory methods had been utilized or that the interventions (regardless of the degree of participation) actually worked.

Another concern related to the production of rigorous research evidence has to do with the role of external consultants. Many community groups rely on university researchers for assistance with needs assessments, planning, and evaluations. Often such consulting arrangements are established as *university–community partnerships* and provide *service-learning* opportunities for students (Mulroy, 2008). There may be several types of challenges inherent in these university–community partnerships. For example, researchers often have preexpectations about what types of studies can and should be conducted in certain settings; they are required to comply with professional standards, university and government human subjects guidelines, and university and funder goals (Ibanez-Carrasco & Riano-Alcala, 2009). Often such researchers look at these projects as an opportunity to produce publishable research and as learning labs for their students (Rogge & Rocha, 2004).

Community members may have different goals and expectations for these studies. Previous experience with community-based researchers as well as concerns about the impact of the power and privilege of university faculty, students, and donors may limit the degree to which community residents will cooperate with external evaluators (Ibanez-Carrasco & Riano-Alcala, 2009; Rogge & Rocha, 2004). Alternatively, university-based researchers may experience discomfort and actual frustration when efforts to engage in inclusive practice and facilitate community control lead in unexpected directions, changing the parameters and goals of the study over time in response to community demands (Montana et al., 2010).

Comprehensive efforts involving extensive activities to engage community residents in research-related decision making also involve a heavy investment of time and resources on the part of community members, consultants, and university partners (Rosing & Hofman, 2010). In research partnerships that involve service-learning, it is often students who are responsible for engagement with community residents, facilitating community meetings, and collecting data. One limitation of this approach lies with its effectiveness as a teaching method. Engagement activities may provide a rich learning environment for students, but the time needed for community-level decision making may limit the feasibility of requiring that students complete specific assignments that involve securing community input during semester-long courses. Stoecker, Loving, Reddy, and Bolling (2010) recommend that traditional approaches to participatory research, requiring long-term commitment, community engagement, and relationship-building over time, be adapted to make it more suitable for short-term research projects conducted by students and with a management structure that ensures that community residents are in charge of the study.

SYSTEMATIC APPROACHES FOR COMMUNITY-BASED RESEARCH: USING LOGIC MODELS TO GUIDE EVALUATIONS AS AN ALTERNATIVE TO EBP

Although grant and contract administrators may recognize the complexities associated with community-based evaluations, they also must ensure that recipients of grants and contracts spend their money wisely, justifying the resources used, and establish that they have sufficient capacity to produce results. In other words, organizations and groups that receive funding must provide actual evidence that they work, although such evidence may not be consistent with EBP standards. Most government agencies and foundations require organizations to submit funding proposals that contain goals and objectives, established timelines, and a specific set of activities that are intended to produce clearly articulated outcomes. Such a plan is often referred to as a *logic model*. It contains implicit assumptions about the relationship between what the organization intends to do and what it will produce. According to Ginsberg (2001), logic models are designed:

> To show on one piece of paper, the logical connections between the conditions that contribute to the need for a program in the community, the activities aimed at addressing these conditions, and the outcomes and impacts expected to result from the activities. (p. 181)

Techniques for involving consumers of services and constituency group members in identifying the links between program goals, objectives, activities, and outcomes have their origins in a process called *evaluability assessment* or *utilization-focused evaluation* (Patton, 2008; Stoecker, 2005; Thurston & Potvin, 2003). In this approach, an outside evaluator meets with organization stakeholders to identify the program goals that they feel are the most important and the outcomes associated with them. It is important to note that these goals may not be the same ones specified in the organization's mission or preliminary campaign or project goals. Instead, the evaluator tries to determine what participants perceive to be the actual goals that currently motivate them or that they think they are trying to accomplish. This process also requires that participants come to a consensus about goals, the activities to be undertaken to reach them, and the outcomes to be produced. Consequently, evaluability assessment establishes a link between practice-based knowledge and formal, more objective approaches-based expert knowledge (Thurston & Potvin, 2003). It also allows for the development of a *theory of action* about how and why the program or plan works and the outcomes it is expected to produce or actually achieves; consequently this approach established the type of cause-and-effect relationship required for quantitative approaches to evaluation (Patton, 2008). Anderson (n.d.) identifies several primary components associated with the process of working with a group of participants to develop a theory of change:

- Developing a map of the relationship between expected outcomes and the preconditions necessary to reach the project or campaign's goals.
- Using the group process to develop measureable indicators that can be used to determine whether goals have been achieved.

- Facilitating a process in which group members identify specific interventions or actions that are needed to achieve the outcomes necessary to achieve the goal and creating a map that illustrates the linkages between each set of activities and the outcomes.
- Encouraging group members to identify the basic assumptions associated with their theory of change, essentially asking them to describe why and how these activities are expected to produce the outcomes and subsequently lead to goal achievement.

According to Patton (2008), program design should not simply describe a logical chain of events that lead to an outcome, there also needs to be an explanation or set of assumptions about why the program works in a particular manner. In other words, what do participants believe is happening in the program, project, or organizing campaign to produce a relationship between cause (process) and effect (outcome)? Another way to describe a set of assumptions about why a particular campaign or program works is in terms of the activities undertaken (specific strategies, tactics, and supportive actions such as media campaigns or efforts to facilitate citizen participation). Why do we expect such activities to have an impact? What kind of effect do we think these activities will have on opponents, allies, organizational partners, legislators, or the general public (Homan, 2011)? Essentially, what group efforts to identify a theory of action should produce is a logic model that describes how and why the program should work (Savaya & Waysman, 2005).

Logic models also conceptualize programs, projects, and organizing campaigns as consisting not only of a series of activities, but as a combination of resources, people, organization structure, policies or procedures, or inputs that create a process in which people interact with one another to produce results (Royse et al., 2010). Results are most often described as outputs (what is produced by the campaign or program) or immediate objectives. In addition, there should also be intermediate and long-term or ultimate goals as well, things or events that happen as a consequence of the outputs produced by the campaign or program (Mulroy & Lauber, 2004; Patton, 2008). These components are put together in a written framework or graph to describe a logical sequence of events: inputs, program, project or campaign activities, outputs produced, and long-term effects or outcomes.

For example, Zimmerman, Stewart, Morrel-Samuels, Franzen, and Reischl (2011) describe the theory of action they developed, using elements of empowerment and ecological theories, for an after-school violence prevention program. The theoretical assumptions associated with these theories, that increasing the skills and capabilities of youth and increasing their ability to engage with other people and organizations in social change activities would produce immediate goals such as youth participation in community change, youth attachment to positive adult role models, and the development of new community resources that could be used to sustain antiviolence efforts. The researchers also assumed that youth violence in the community would decrease and that there would be improvements in the health and well-being of these young adults. In their conceptual model about how the program should work, the researchers identified six curriculum models for the program: youth leadership, learning about the community, making community improvements, creating intergenerational partnerships, planning for community change, and reflection and action. The activities within each program component were explicated and linked to both theories and specific program goals. With such a model, program goals and activities can easily be converted into a set of measureable objectives that must be accomplished within a specific time frame. A specific theory of action also allows for additional outcome criteria to be specified prior to program implementation.

It should be noted, that the Zimmerman et al. (2011) theory of action pertains to a new program. Programs are designed using procedures and methods associated with social planning techniques. Often theories of action and logic models are based on formal theories about why specific types of social work or health-related interventions should work. In community organization practice, most theoretical assumptions are not as explicit. They are usually derived from specific models about how community practice should proceed and the outcomes it should produce. For example, putting pressure on decision makers, as described in the social action approach should facilitate goal attainment in situations in which there is competition for resources. On the other hand, the community development model contains the assumption that consensus and cooperation produce the best results; the desired outcomes are associated with improvements in community capacity to make change, strengthening social networks, improvements in the quality of community life, or economic development. Often these assumptions are implicit, rather than explicit in the logic models and list of objectives included in action plans. In some situations, theories about why these approaches should work are simply derived from everyday practice and experience about what works, and the process of praxis (Figure 10.1).

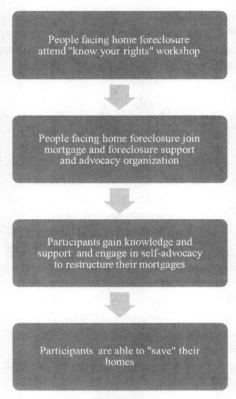

FIGURE 10.1
Theory of action for a home foreclosure prevention group.

EVALUATION METHODS FOR COMMUNITY PRACTICE

Many of the techniques used to conduct formal evaluations are consistent with methods used to collect quantitative data for community assessments: collecting data using internal or external indicators and surveys. In community assessment, methods are used that essentially fit techniques to the situation at hand or the research questions that community members or other stakeholders want to address. Consequently, most of these methods result in studies that are unique to different communities. In well-funded projects, there may be some effort to conduct systematic or standardized evaluations that allow for comparisons among different communities with different demographic characteristics and economic, social, or political challenges.

In addition, formal evaluations of community campaigns or other types of interventions involve the use of qualitative data, collected in a systematic manner as part of a formal documentation process to examine what happened during the project to make it successful or explain the lack of success. There are a number of additional reasons for using qualitative methods in community-based evaluations including the emphasis on process rather than task-related goals and the expectation that participatory methods should be used to incorporate the preferences, experiences, and values of constituents in the research process (Foster & Louie, 2010; Royse & Dignan, 2008).

Goal Attainment

The easiest, fastest, and most accessible way to conduct an evaluation study to examine campaign, program, or project-related outcomes is simply to determine when the program has achieved its goals. One of the primary reasons for including a list of measureable objectives and a time-line in any intervention plan is that they provide a mechanism through which goal accomplishment can be assessed. Measureable objectives also permit the organization to track its accomplishments over time and to modify strategies and tactics that do not appear to work. Predeveloped objectives also permit organizations to collect data prior to the start of the campaign and consequently can be employed as pretest measures. At the conclusion of the campaign, the final count of activities, events, participants and other indicators of success are essentially posttest measures. Comparison of pre- and post-test data essentially meets minimal conditions for quasi-experimental design, although one in which there a few controls for contextual and situational factors that may influence the success of failure of a community intervention.

Stoecker (2005) describes this process at a very basic level as identifying goals, identifying things to count that can be used to count the degree of goal achievement, determining how to find the things that should be counted (contained in organization records, obtained from other sources, or that will need to be collected), and deciding whether is there something is not easily countable that can be acquired if its needed to determine the degree of goal achievement. According to Patton (2008), there are a number of decisions that should be made in participatory research about the data collected to document the accomplishment of research objectives. The facilitator should ask the participants to answer the following set of questions:

- What data should be used and how can it be found?
- Who will be responsible for collecting the data?

- How often will the data be collected?
- What people, groups, organizations, or communities will be included in the sample?
- How will the data collected be used?
- How will the findings be reported to organization members, funders, and the general public? How often and in what form will it be reported?

Social Indicator Analysis and Survey Data

Some of the data used to construct indicators for measuring goal attainment will come from information that has already been collected by local organizations or government agencies. Other measures will need to be constructed by community participants or consultants. One of the simplest methods, that can easily be adapted for use by community groups are surveys of community members, organizations, and other key stakeholders in the community. As with community assessments, it is critical that constituency group members participate in constructing surveys in order to verify that questions and response categories are consistent with community cultural, local norms and traditions, and language. In addition to surveys, observational studies of community characteristics can also be conducted by research participants using some of the techniques that are used in Chapter 6. The key difference between surveys and other indicators used purely for assessment purposes is that there must be some degree of standardization in their use and interpretation that allows for pre- and posttest comparisons to be made. This may require that constituency group members be provided with training to ensure that data collection procedures are consistent among research participants and across the various time periods in which data will be collected (Minkler, 2000).

Social indicators can also be used and incorporated into a program plan, campaign, or project objectives. As described in Chapter 6, there are some disadvantages and advantages related to using social indicators. The inaccessibility of neighborhood-level data and costs involved in hiring outside experts or employing computer technology to extract data or construct geographic are two of the biggest drawbacks (Stoecker, 2006). In addition, standardized, preconstructed measures may not reflect the complexity of the problems facing the community or be adequate to measure social conditions (Hardina, 2002). Some participants may find standardized indicators irrelevant in that they may not reflect their values or culture or are inconsistent with their lived experiences or personal knowledge about what happens in their community (Fraser, Dougill, Mabee, Reed, & McAlpine, 2006). Bowers Andrews, Stone

Motes, Floyd, Crocker Flerx, and Lopez-De Fede (2005) offer an example of the reaction of an evaluation participant to a standardized indicator:

> A Latino staff member working in a program to improve relations between Latino immigrants and the police reported that he knew that the program had made a difference because community members (police and citizens) had informally told him. He viewed a survey, suggested by the grantmaker, to "capture" this change as redundant and potentially interfering with the relationships he had built. (p. 96)

However, there are also advantages associated with the use of social indicators. For example, census data and the majority of information drawn from public databases about the prevalence of social problem, public benefits, or service utilization is easily obtained online, from government agencies, or public libraries for successive time periods so that posttest outcome data can be acquired (Royse et al., 2010). These data are particularly valuable for evaluation purposes because data collection methods are standardized and can be used over multiple time periods (Hardina, 2002). In addition, supplemental indicators can be developed using administrative data from both nonprofit and public agencies can be to examine changes that occur at different intervals in population groups served, people requesting and receiving services or referrals made to other agencies (Green & Kleiner, 2011). For example, in areas with high poverty rates, there are likely to be high levels of demand for government food assistance programs and services from nonprofit food pantries and soup kitchens. Other advantages of social indicators are that there is often public consensus about what a particular measure means, such data are easy to understand and report, it can be communicated easily, disseminated to the press, and can be used as an effective tool to persuade policy makers to change their minds about a particular issue or policy (Ben-Arieh, 2008).

Quantitative Research

Often complex community change efforts involving multiple interventions, a variety of research sites, or diverse population groups; in such circumstances standardized methods are often utilized to make comparisons and test hypotheses. The research methods used may involve predeveloped surveys or standardized instruments which allow for comparisons among different demographic groups, organizations, or settings (Boothroyd, Fawcett, & Foster-Fishman, 2006). For example, Speer et al. (2011) conducted pre- and posttest study of PICO National Network affiliated church congregations that examined the degree of member participation in organizing activities, civic engagement, and feelings of psychological empowerment using standardized scales. They also used a community without a PICO-affiliated organization as a control group. Findings indicated that respondents in the community in which PICO was present had higher rates of civic engagement and personal empowerment on posttest measures than members of the comparison group.

Some of the community research studies that involve comparisons and standardization of measurement tools are "Comprehensive Community Initiatives," large, well-funded projects in which a number of interventions related to housing, infrastructure, economic development and jobs, and family well-being are conducted simultaneously, often with the help of multiple government and foundation partners (Baum, 2001; Chaskin, 2001). In such studies, funders seek to test specific interventions and determine whether results are consistent (and consequently can be generalized) across communities and different population groups regardless of the unique context in which the project is conducted (Coulton, 2005).

Experimental studies and quasi-experiments are also conducted to help researchers and government agencies and foundations determine the long-term impacts (or achievement of ultimate goals) and benefit to cost ratios of large-scale social experiments and community initiatives. Impact evaluations examine the long-term effectiveness of specific programs or components of programs over time; evaluations are generally used to test hypotheses about whether the intervention, and only the intervention has produced the intended results; consequently, its use may require random sampling, experimental and control groups, and pre- and posttests or other types of experimental or quasi-experimental designs (Boothroyd et al., 2006; Washington, 1995).

The overall impact of programs can also be determined using cost–efficiency or cost–benefit analysis. To determine cost-efficiency, program planners examine the amount of goods and services produced by a particular program option in relation to the cost. The program that produces the most for the least cost is then recommended as the preferred option (Hardina et al., 2006). Cost–benefit analyses examine whether the dollar costs of social programs exceed their potential benefits and the distributional effects of programs and policies on different population groups (Meenaghan et al., 2004). One of the difficulties inherent in this process is how to measure the economic value of social services, education, or mental health or health care on individuals and families (McNutt, 2011;

Royse et al., 2010). However, in projects designed to produce specific economic benefits or the impact of housing, transportation, or infrastructure improvements, the dollar value of the jobs or goods and services produced are fairly easy to measure. Cost–benefit and cost-effectiveness approaches also have the advantage of producing information in a fairly simple, easy-to-understand manner that can be used to persuade decision makers and the public about the value of different policy options or services, especially when options are recommended that will save taxpayers money and provide future benefits. For example, Delgado (2004) describes how cost–benefit analysis could be applied to the evaluation of a controversial program such as needle exchange for drug users despite the difficulties associated with measuring health effects:

> What value can be assigned to prevention? How does one accurately measure the number of people who do not get AIDS from contaminated needle use? We can estimate the number of IDUs [Intravenous Drug Users] in a target population and relate this to estimates that the HIV infection rate of IDUs is approximately 50%, with additional infections in their sex partners and children. The costs of drug treatment, medical care, supportive social programs, and other nondirect costs can be calculated. (p. 176)

As noted earlier in this chapter, there are disagreements among researchers as to whether randomized experiments can or should be implemented in community settings. Although acknowledging the need for empirical evidence of intervention evidence, some researchers believe that it is difficult to implement experimental and quasi-experimental designs in community settings due to time, effort, the lack of control groups and random samples, and problems associated with retaining research subjects over time (Roberts-DeGennaro, 2011; Royse & Dignan, 2008). According to Boothroyd et al. (2006), in most community-based projects, researchers also face a dilemma in terms of whether "scientific methods" that meet criteria for internal and external validity should be more or less important than the significance of the study for community members and the consistency of top-down interventions, imposed by foundations or community agencies, with local preferences and culture. Obtaining convincing evidence may result in sacrificing community control, relevance, and use of data or new intervention techniques.

However, Coulton (2005) argues that despite the difficulties inherent in applying "one size fits all" methodology in community settings, it is vital that researchers are able to document whether community interventions are effective across multiple settings and situations, requiring the use of standardized indicators, experimental and control groups, and randomized research designs. She asserts that such techniques are essential so that effective intervention plans can be replicated by others, but also notes that it is difficult to ensure that the same interventions will be implemented in the same way in all communities.

Process and Implementation Analysis

Process and implementation analysis involve the use of qualitative or a mixture of qualitative and descriptive measures to examine what happens in a program or campaign, how it happened, or why it happened (Patton, 2008). Although often times it has been difficult to examine campaign processes because of the difficulty in anticipating what happens in complex, "real time" situations involving numerous people, evaluators and community organizations have increasingly adopted specific process-oriented indicators that help participants understand how resource acquisition, the number of volunteers, the degree of participation, the number of events, workshops, or other activities, the use of Internet and other technology, media coverage, the degree of diversity in the organization or campaign, and relationship building have on the organizing process (Butterfoss, 2006; Foster & Louie, 2010). Often quantitative indicators can be developed to measure some of these factors, permitting them to be incorporated into the organization's formal list of task and process objectives (Hardina, 2002). Identification of process measures also facilitates the creation of pre- and posttest indicators or the implementation of an ongoing tracking system. In addition, qualitative types of data collection are often employed to assess campaign or project activities and decision-making processes including individual and focus group interviews with staff, participants, and other key stakeholders, observational studies by external consultants, and a review of meeting notes and other internal documents by members of the research team (Butterfoss, 2006; Royse et al., 2010). Process analysis may be employed for one of three purposes:

- To help develop a new project or campaign by observing what happens as a new set of expectations or activities are put into or how it should be modified to improve the way it works. Such assessments are generally called "formative" evaluations.
- To monitor what is happening in a project or campaign on a regular basis.

* To supplement outcome studies by finding out how and why a successful project or campaign worked and why and how unsuccessful projects and campaigns failed (Baum, 2001; Royse et al., 2010).

Another type of qualitative or mixed method evaluation involves
implementation analysis (Patton, 2008). Such evaluations focus on how
resources (including funds, staff, and volunteers) were utilized in a
program, how participants communicate with one another, how people
move in and out of a program, project, or campaign, and whether the
project was operated in the manner intended. Implementation analysis
can also be used to determine if the internal logic of the program
makes sense or is consistent with its mission or goals. It can also focus
on looking at the different parts of a project or campaign in order to determine if these components overlap, limit the effectiveness of other units or
projects, or actually complement one another (Baum, 2001). In some
instances, implementation analysis can document whether a program
exists only on paper or if it has enough resources with which to realistically obtain its goals (Patton, 2008). For example, if a new program has a
substantial budget surplus at the end of the year and there is no consistent record of project activities, an evaluator might conclude that the
program is not actually in operation. Similarly, if local community
groups are recruited to help publicize and conduct outreach for a
breast cancer awareness campaign on behalf of a local health clinic and
the number of referrals made exceed expectations and results in requests
for assistance from people outside the target population group of low-
income women, aged 40–70, evaluators would want to assess how the
campaign is functioning and how it could be modified to help people
with other health-related needs.

In projects or campaigns that take place in two or more settings,
implementation analysis can examine whether interventions, projects,
or campaigns are consistently implemented across locations or if there
are contextual (social, political, and economic differences), organizational, or demographic variations that are affecting or could affect
how the program is operating. Such an analysis may be required if monitoring data reveal serious fluctuations across sites or if local policies and
procedures differ substantially from one another (Patton, 2008).
Implementation issues may be particularly problematic in the case of
large-scale research studies or quasi-experiments that are taking place
to test the effectiveness of interventions in various locations or establishing the generalizability of findings across population groups, regions, or
countries. In such cases, implementation differences can mask or exag-
gerate findings from different locations and consequently make accurate

assessment and generalization of the findings difficult (Mowbray, Holter, Teague, & Bybee, 2003).

Case Studies and Critical Incident Analysis

One of the techniques often used to examine what happened in a community intervention is case study. Case studies can be initiated at the start of projects in order that external researchers have the opportunity to examine how community interventions are conducted or why they are successful. Researchers attend organization meetings, interview participants, study organization documents, examine archival data, review media reports, and talk to members of other organizations, stakeholders, or other people who are knowledgeable about what has happened during the course of the campaign or intervention or how they reacted to it. In some cases, researchers may actually be participant observers or active members of the organizations (Conway, 2004); in other instances they may simply be observing what happens in order to add to the formal knowledge available about community processes or participation. Members of the community group may collaborate to keep careful records of their experiences with a particular campaign, development effort, or planning process and then publish a report, facilitate media coverage, produce a video, or use social media to describe what they accomplished or how they accomplished it (Clover, 2011; Hume-Cook et al., 2010).

Case studies can also be conducted retrospectively, allowing researchers to understand what happened during a particular event, campaign, or community change process over time; examining the historical, economic, social, cultural, and political context of what happened and how it impacted on participants, the general public, public policies, or subsequent community change efforts (Delp & Quan, 2002; Vanderkooy & Nawyn, 2011). Most of formal knowledge about how community organizations and social movements recruit members, frame their message, and carry out campaigns comes from case studies (Clemens & Minkoff, 2007; Speer et al., 2011). For example, Smock (2004) conducted intensive case studies of 10 community organizations in order to identify a set of capacity building, governance, strategies, and outcomes associated with five different community organizing models: transformative, woman-centered, community building, power-based, and civic engagement-oriented approaches. Smock's analysis identified strengths and weaknesses inherent in each of the models. While some case studies are conducted while the activity is taking place, data can also be collected years after the actual activities occur, using historical documents and interviews with participants (Polletta, 2006).

One of the approaches for conducting such a retrospective study is critical incident analysis. Critical incident analysis can be used in historical context or a short time after the event has occurred to examine the perspectives and feelings of participants (Hardina et al., 2008). A critical incident is an event, behaviors, a crisis, or an opportunity associated with specific sets of circumstances that constitute a "significant contribution, either positively or negatively to an activity or phenomenon" (Gremier, 2004, p. 66). The methodology used for this approach makes it feasible for use by community groups. Constituency group members can be encouraged to keep notes or diaries to document their participation and reactions to events as they occur. At the conclusion of the event or community change activity, participants are interviewed about what they experiences and the degree to which the strategies, tactics, and other methods employed helped them to achieve their goals and how it affected them (Sitt-Gohdes, Lambrecht, & Redman, 2000). Consequently, this method helps document the type of knowledge generated through practice activities or through the process of praxis (Ross, 2010; Treleaven, 2001).

Other Qualitative Approaches

Often community-based research simply is intended to measure the perceptions of community members about their lives, the people they know and interact with, local services, organizations, and institutions, and the quality of life within their community. Consequently, a host of qualitative methods can be used to assess perceptions including focus groups, one-on-one interviews with community members, leaders, organization staff, and other stakeholders, or community forums conducted at the conclusion of an intervention (Vanderkooy & Nawyn, 2011). Observational studies or document analysis using contemporary or archival sources to tell the "story" of the organization, project, or campaign are also useful and are often employed as a component of more comprehensive case studies.

Another qualitative approach to evaluation is often referred to in the literature as emergent or constructivist evaluation (Guba & Lincoln, 2001; Lincoln, 2002; Netting et al., 2008). Patton (2008) describes this approach as consistent with the process of reflective practice. A practitioner or evaluator coordinating such efforts would ask constituent group members or agency participants to respond to a series of questions and take action:

- What is the issue or problem to be addressed?
- Can you agree to try something to resolve this problem?
- Can you observe what you and group members are doing and report back to the group about what you did and what was accomplished?

- Can you identify themes or patterns in the separate reports made by each of the participants?
- Can you decide what to try next based on these findings?

As described by Stringer (2007) the constructivist approach is based on the assumption that diverse participants have different experiences, values, and preferences and will agree about evaluation outcomes and recommendations for actions. In this process, group members engage in extensive dialogue and reflection to work out their differences in order to reexamine or restate the issue in a manner in which participants can agree. He argues that:

> The task of the community-based action researcher, therefore, is to develop a context in which individuals and groups with divergent perceptions and interpretations can formulate a construction of their situation that makes sense to them all — a joint construction . . . . new meanings emerge as divergent views are compared and contracted. (Stringer, 2007, p. 41)

PARTICIPATORY EVALUATION METHODS

One of the primary challenges in community-based evaluations is that instead of a small number of researchers making decisions about research questions, methodology, data analysis, findings, and recommendations, numerous other individuals may be involved in day-to-day planning and implementation decisions in participatory evaluations. Such demands require that researchers possess adequate group work, conflict management, and other relevant interpersonal skills to conduct evaluations (K. M. Roe, K. Roe, Goette Carpenter, & Berenstein Sibley, 2009). Stoecker (2005) identifies two traditional types of evaluation approaches in community practice: those in which external evaluators who are considered "experts" in their field are hired to assess the project or intervention or internal evaluations in which a single staff person is responsible for monitoring the progress or outcomes of a campaign or program at regular intervals. He argues that whether or not an external or internal evaluation is conducted is not as important as whether or not, and to what degree, constituency group members participate in the process. In some cases, an external evaluator may be hired who uses participatory methods to facilitate constituent involvement in the study. Whatever method is used, it can be considered participatory only if constituents are actively involved in every aspect of the study. According to Coombe (2009):

Participatory evaluation also departs from traditional evaluation by rethinking who owns and controls the process, of creating, interpreting, and applying knowledge and to what end. In the emancipatory stream of participatory evaluation, both the process and products of evaluation are used to transform power relations and promote social action and change. (p. 369)

Although the degree of participation and control can vary by organization, setting, and community preferences and needs, the literature on participatory methods typically identifies at least three different approaches: participatory action research, empowerment evaluation, and agency self-evaluation (Hardina et al., 2006; Stoecker, 2005). The term participatory evaluation is also used to describe a process nearly identical to participatory action research and used primarily for evaluative purposes, this approach may not necessarily require participation of constituents in community assessments or comprehensive social change processes. All these models contain different assumptions about the role of staff or external evaluators and the degree of constituent control of the research process.

Participatory Action Research and Participatory Evaluation Methods

As described in Chapter 6, PAR is a community-based approach to research in which organization constituents and other stakeholders work collaboratively with organization staff or external consultants to conduct research studies designed to identify community problems and develop solutions. The primary goal of such efforts is social change. As described in Chapter 6, PAR methodology is also used extensively for public health or health promotion-related projects and in that context is often referred to as community-based participatory research or CBPR. Viswanathan et al. (2004) define CBPR as "collaborative approach to research that combines methods of inquiry with community capacity building strategies to bridge the gap between knowledge produced through research and what is practiced in communities" (p. v). Consequently, one of the rationales for participatory methods is to ensure that community assessments, intervention plans, and evaluations reflect the values, perceptions, and interests of community residents.

In the assessment phase of the PAR-related studies, the focus is on developing a critical consciousness or understanding of social, economic, and political processes that impact on the community. The researcher must gain the trust of community partners, gain insight into community dynamics and culture, and find ways to apply one's research knowledge in a manner that is understandable to participants, and that permits them to have some degree of input and sense of control of the project (Clover, 2011; Stoecker, 2005). The process of research question development, data collection, analysis should produce usable data that can be utilized by constituency group members to advocate for community change.

As described in Chapter 9, it is also participatory research methods and reflection that combine formal knowledge with praxis-based knowledge in a manner that can be used as a source of constituent empowerment, group inspiration, and as a tool to acquire public recognition and legitimacy for a cause (Minkler, Breckwich Vasquez, Tajik, & Petersen, 2008). Consequently, participatory evaluation is simply one component of the PAR cycle starting with the collection of data at the start of the study that includes both praxis-related knowledge construction and formal data collection processes. Coombe (2009) describes participatory evaluation as an eight-step process that combines both research and group work skills designed to facilitate constituent control of the process:

1. Members determine that an evaluation is needed and commit to conducting the research study in the context of a group-controlled process.
2. Participants are recruited, resources are obtained, and specific member roles are assigned.
3. Goals, objectives, and measures of change are identified.
4. Research methods are selected that are useable, culturally competent, and that build community capacity.
5. Training is provided to ensure that members collect data in a systematic way; members engage in data collection activities.
6. Data are analyzed and interpreted by group members. Specific findings and recommendations are identified by group consensus.
7. Results are disseminated to organization participants, the general public, donors, and other relevant stakeholders.
8. Findings from the study are put to use to make improvements in the community or organizations or to make recommendations for changes in laws and social policies.

In some cases, the evaluation process may be more complex, with the methodology used for participatory action research intended as part of a pre- and posttest study of community conditions. Pretests consist of formal community assessments, an intervention plan is developed in response to the data collection, and a formal evaluation is conducted during the posttest phase to assess the impact of the intervention. The data are explicitly intended for use in social and personal transformation (Chatterton, Fuller, & Routledge, 2007; Freire, 1970; Lewis, 2002). Community participants and constituency group members are included, and in some cases control, all phases of the project.

Empowerment Evaluation

Another approach for involving service consumers and constituency group members in assessments of projects, programs, or campaigns is empowerment evaluation. This method has its origins in the work of David Fetterman (2001), an anthropologist who argued that involving the people who will benefit from improvements in programs and services in the evaluation incorporates the principle of reciprocity into the research process, ensures that the data collected are useable, increases personal self-efficacy, self-determination, feelings of empowerment, and skill-building among participants, and makes it more likely that programs will be more effective and meet the needs of the people who use them (Roe et al., 2009). This method primarily relies on the services of outside consultants to facilitate the research process and provide training on the use of research methods to participants (Fetterman, Kaftarian, & Wandersman, 1996). Planning and evaluation within a specific organization context is generally the focus of this method; when applied in community evaluations, organizations rather than individual community members are recruited for participation (Bowers Andrews, 2004). In addition to the researchers, participants generally include a mixture of organization stakeholders including clients, staff, board members, and other constituency group members. In addition to benefiting the organization, empowerment evaluation is also assumed to benefit individuals by increasing skills, self-confidence, and feelings of personal empowerment (Miller & Campbell, 2006).

Fetterman and associates have continued to refine the method over time, making the approach both more systematic in terms of methods and methodology, suitable for use over multiple research sites, and focused on the increasing participation and skills among members of marginalized or disadvantaged groups (Fetterman & Wandersman, 2007). Consequently, this approach emphasizes research principles associated with both PAR and more traditional, quantitative approaches such as community ownership of research studies, inclusive decision-making practices, a social change-orientation, and the production of evidence-based research.

Fetterman (2001) describes the role of the researcher in empowerment evaluation as that of a "coach," providing training in evaluation methods and motivating participants to move through and complete various stages of the evaluation process. The facilitation of empowerment evaluation studies requires that the researcher ask a series of questions of group participants that focus on their resources, goals, existing evidence, and best practices related to the type of intervention that they wish to adopt, the skills necessary for participants to start a new project and evaluate its effects, how the project will be implemented, and how the participants will find out if it worked or how well it worked (Fetterman & Wandersman, 2007).

Methods to Facilitate Participation in Large, Multisite Evaluations: Standardized Agency Self-Assessments

As described earlier in this chapter, some types of community-based research are conducted to examine the effectiveness of new intervention models or social policies in different neighborhoods, geographic regions, or demographic groups. Consequently, such evaluations are often funded by government agencies or large foundations; in order to ensure that scientifically adequate comparisons can be made, external evaluators are hired, and standardized data collection methods are used. While some of these studies fit traditional prototypes for large-scale experimental or more often, quasi-experimental designs, some funders also require that there be some degree of effort to include community members in project oversight, consultation, or participatory research activities (Coulton, 2005; Stoecker, 2005). Empowerment evaluation is just one of the approaches used to facilitate standardized evaluations that incorporate some provisions for local participation in multisite evaluations (Bowers Andrews et al., 2005; Fetterman & Wandersman, 2007).

One of the mechanisms used to facilitate agency self-evaluation involves the creation, by the grant-maker, of evaluation templates that include checklists or predeveloped evaluation tools such as surveys or databases in which specific social indicators or measures of success are to be entered (Bowers Andrews, 2004; Kubisch, Auspos, Brown, & Dewar, 2010). Specification of data points and evaluation techniques may be spelled out in formal agreements between donors and recipients of research funding or predetermined in face-to-face meetings between the various organization partners and community participants.

While this technique seems to be fairly straightforward there are some difficulties. One problem inherent in standardized, multisite approaches is the issue of implementation consistency, also called "fidelity" (Mowbray et al., 2003). Castro, Barrera, and Martinez (2004) argue that while program fidelity in comparison studies is important, it is also critical that programs be adapted for use in cultural and ethnic communities that may differ in terms of language, socioeconomic status, geographic location, and factors that place families at risk of poverty, instability, and other social problems. Hence, some national and regional programs and research efforts deliberately use program planning, implementation, and evaluation models that encourage participation of local residents and service users and that "fit" the final details of program design and evaluation criteria to local values and preferences. Such efforts also address issues related to participant mistrust of researchers due to power and status differentials.

In addition to cultural competency, community groups also may have concerns about the fact that in agency self-evaluation, the overall choice of an approach to evaluation and the research methods used are made by the grant-maker rather than the community (Quaghebuer et al., 2004). External evaluators are often hired by the funding source to facilitate onsite evaluations and consequently, may conduct evaluations in a manner consistent with donor demands rather than community wishes (Bowers Andrews, 2004). If evaluations are facilitated through existing community groups that are often "resource poor" and may not have governance structures, technical capacity, or organizational culture that provide an "easy fit" for formal evaluation studies. Sufficient funds from the donor may not "filter-down" to the local level for recruitment of participants or supports such as training or transportation or food allowances that could help sustain involvement in these projects over the long term (Maiter et al., 2008). It should be noted, however, that many local organizations often welcome such grants or contracts as a means of increasing their access to funding, even if it may not be consistent with their own goals. Consequently goal conflict can be one of the biggest barriers to the completion of evaluation projects.

INTERPERSONAL SKILLS FOR PARTICIPATORY EVALUATIONS: FOSTERING INCLUSION AND SKILL-BUILDING

Patton (2008) describes participatory evaluation as a "bottom up" process that has a number of purposes. It can be used to create ongoing organizational capacity to conduct evaluations and produce data that can be feasibly used to improve interventions and organization practices. Participation in evaluations should have a transformative effect on participants, not only facilitating the development of research-skills but enhancing individual and group problem-solving abilities. It can also increase participant commitment to the organization:

> Moreover, people who participate in creating something tend to feel more ownership of what they have created, make more use of it, and take better care of it. Active participants in evaluation, therefore, are not only more likely to feel ownership of their evaluation findings, but also of the evaluation process itself. Properly, sensitively, and authentically done, it becomes their process. (Patton, 2008, p. 173)

Despite such a glowing review of the positive impact of participatory methods, there are a number of difficulties inherent in facilitating community evaluations with a diverse group of participants. For example, Delgado (2000) identifies a number of issues that external consultants and community organizers often encounter when coordinating such efforts:

- Keeping constituents actively involved in the research process.
- Providing appropriate training and guidance to participants during the course of the evaluation.
- Making sure that data collection and analysis, if these activities are to be performed by community members, are realistic, feasible, and culturally relevant and appropriate. In addition, participants should be able to easily interpret and use the information collected to make improvements in the intervention and to communicate their achievements to others.
- Making sure that evaluation procedures and the data collected also are relevant and appropriate for the funding agency and can be easily described and disseminated to others.

Royse and Dignan (2008) note that despite often glowing reports about the quality of community participation in participatory evaluations, there is no guarantee that community residents will choose to be actively involved in these projects or that local agencies will actually have the resources or ability to share responsibility for conducting the research. They also argue that sometimes researchers do not make the best partners in some circumstances:

> And to be fair, professionals can make serious mistakes affecting data collection and interpretation when they ignore the culture of community ..., fail to make sure that their instruments are culturally sensitive, or assume that the "community" research or evaluation they want to conduct, is in fact, supported by the local residents. (p. 509)

In response to these types of problems, there are a number of approaches generally used to increase participation, facilitate participant skill building, minimize conflict, and produce useable data. For example, Stoecker (2005) identifies several preconditions that can be used to determine whether participatory research methods can be used in specific situations including the ability of constituency group members to work cooperatively with one another, the time and resources available for conducting research, and the ability of the staff member to provide support and guidance for the evaluation process. In addition, constituency group members must be able to devote a substantial amount of time for the research and deliberation process. There must also be a collective commitment by members of the organization to actually use the data to improve the organizing process, intervention, or project. Minkler et al. (2008) also identify preconditions or factors that minimize conflict among participants including the ability of all participants to engage in dialogue and critical reflection, identification of an a commitment to a shared set of values, and a process through which all research partners establish a "shared sense of community" (pp. 134–135).

There are also a range of interpersonal skills, identified earlier in this book that can be used to facilitate group processes and task accomplishment and to manage member disagreements or conflicts. Schmuck (2006) summarizes these skills by identifying the following actions that should be taken by the group facilitator:

- Foster group feelings of solidarity and trust by helping members become acquainted with one another.
- Rotate leadership responsibilities among members and make sure that everyone has an important task to accomplish.
- Reinforce the perception that all group members are part of a team, make sure everyone can speak, and establish group norms that emphasize friendliness and cooperation.
- Address differences in power and status among members by making sure everyone is treated equally and with respect.
- Work with group members to establish rules that reinforce the formal aspects of conducting a meeting such as distributing an agenda in advance, rotating responsibility for taking notes, setting meeting times and establishing rules for member behaviors.
- Make sure that all decisions are made by consensus and that all members have a chance to voice their opinions.
- Conduct a short debriefing session after each meeting to assess how members perceive group functioning and to give participants a chance to suggest improvements.

- Establish procedures for determining if each group member has completed the tasks that they were assigned between meetings. The group as whole should determine how to proceed if tasks are not accomplished.

Schmuck (2006) also encourages facilitators to use basic interviewing and group work-related communication skills such as clearly defining group goals, tasks, and the work that must be accomplished, paraphrasing the words of group members in order to establish clarity about meaning and feelings, and making summarizing statements about group decisions and what the team has accomplished.

PUTTING VALUES IN ACTION: MUTUAL LEARNING AND PARTNERSHIP IN EVALUATIONS

There are a number of ethical issues that must be taken into account in participatory evaluation. The traditional concerns about confidentiality, anonymity, informed consent, and "do no harm" must be addressed in any study (Stoecker, 2005; Stringer, 2007). In addition, there are often questions about how researchers should relate to and interact with participants, the reporting of negative findings, the integrity of the research process, and control of any data produced. Patton (2008) summarizes these concerns:

> Evaluation agreements should be in writing; rights of human subjects should be protected; evaluators should respect human dignity, assessments should be complete and fair, findings should be openly and fully disclosed; conflicts of interests should be dealt with openly and honestly, and sound fiscal procedures should be followed. (p. 545)

Patton also notes that evaluators have an ethical responsibility to refrain from altering findings or manipulating the research process in response to funder or organization demands and to ensure that the voices of members of underrepresented groups are clearly heard throughout the research process.

Stringer (2007) argues that part of the researcher's ethical responsibility is to ensure that data, especially qualitative data that may be subject to interpretation, be collected and analyzed in a manner that ensures the authenticity and trustworthiness of the data. He identifies four critical elements that characterize information collected through participatory evaluation processes that originate from a description of

Fourth Generation or constructivist research developed by Guba and Lincoln (1989, 2001).

* *Credibility.* A study is credible if the interpretation of data plausible, gathered using such qualitative research techniques such as member checking, using concepts in the study that emerge from the experiences of the people studied, using multiple research sources to establish the accuracy of findings (triangulation), prolonged engagement with the community, and participant debriefing to examine how their feelings and emotions may affect their perceptions.
* *Dependability.* A study may be considered dependable if the researchers conduct it in a systematic and rigorous manner that can be verified through an independent audit of the research process. Was there a good reason that certain methodological choices were made?
* *Confirmability.* A study may be regarded as trustworthy if it can be independently verified that intended research techniques and data analysis procedures were actually used by members of the research team. For example, did the researchers keep adequate notes or documentation and did they keep journals or maintain an audit trail or description of decisions made during the analysis of data?
* *Transferability.* Although generalizability to other people, settings, and times is highly valued in quantitative research, findings from a nonrandom sample in a qualitative study or research conducted in a unique context cannot be easily generalized. However, some of the results in qualitative research may instead be relevant to other people or settings. Transferability is enhanced when researchers offer an in-depth description of the circumstances and settings in which their study was conducted. This allows other organizations or researchers to determine if the findings are relevant to their own situations.

Some funders and evaluators have sought to develop measurement tools and procedures to increase both the trustworthiness of qualitative data and the reliability and validity of quantitative methods. For example, Foster and Louie (2010) identify a number of steps to facilitate participant involvement in making evaluation decisions, carrying them out, and using the data collected to improve organizing processes and outcomes. Community organizations should:

* Develop clear indicators of successful outcomes associated with community campaigns or projects that include not only specific victories, but also measures of processes such as improvements in organization capacity, volunteer recruitment, leadership development, and power.

- Set specific benchmarks or standards to be achieved for each of the outcome measures. Set up a monitoring system that allows for data to be collected in a variety of points during the campaign so that appropriate adjustments can be made in strategies and tactics.
- Establish measurement tools that are consistent with what the organization is doing or that can be easily used by both staff members and constituents. Incorporate debriefing procedures and other qualitative research approaches into evaluation procedures in order to have systematic data about the organizing process for monitoring purposes during the course of the campaign and retrospective analysis once the campaign or project has been concluded.
- If external evaluators are hired to facilitate the evaluation, they must actively take steps to ensure organizer and constituent trust and ownership of the evaluation process in order to maintain involvement and implement evaluation procedures.

Newman (2008) argues that evaluators should not be locked into a specific methodological approach, but employ a mixture of outcome and process measures, flexible enough to reflect the preferences of all participants and designed to focus on both the project's objectives and promote values traditionally associated with participatory research including the promotion of democratic processes and the achievement of social justice. According to Lennie (2006), the legitimacy and authenticity of qualitative data is also enhanced through the process of dialogue and critical reflection by all research participants as well as participant review of the "end products" produced by researchers including data analysis, formal reports, case studies, and publications.

The Center for Evaluation Innovation has proposed that to enhance the reliability, validity, and trustworthiness of quantitative and qualitative evaluation data, documents, produced by participants in the campaign or a by-product of the organizing effort should be integrated into the evaluation process. Such documents include notes from one-on-one interviews, group debriefings, and meetings among participants (Foster & Louie, 2010). These documents can supplement process and task-oriented indicators requested by grant makers, ensure that participant perspectives are heard, and consequently increase the usability and rigor of data collected for the evaluation. This also increases organization capacity to conduct ongoing evaluations of its activities using information consistent with daily activities of staff, board members, stakeholders, and most importantly volunteers and other people who can benefit from the organization's activities. Other indicators of organizing success can be integrated into the evaluation process that are consistent with specific

TABLE 10.1
Measurement Strategies for Evaluation of Community Organizing Campaigns and Projects

Organizing Activity or Outcome	Objectives	Measures
Recruitment and relationship building	People recruited Attendance at meetings Participation in events Social networks identified or developed	Internal tracking system that documents the number of people recruited and attendance at meetings Documenting results of one-on-one interviews (written notes and oral debriefings) Social network mapping
Leadership, skill development, and personal empowerment	Number of leaders developed New skills acquired Changes in feelings of personal empowerment and self-efficacy	Number of leaders recruited "Career development" of new leaders, i.e., increases in responsibilities and progression through the ranks both in and outside the organizations. Participation in strategy sessions, serving on the evaluation team, lobbying for legislation, or chairing an event. Standardized measures of self-efficacy, personal empowerment, and skill development Focus groups and interviews with leaders and constituents
Organization capacity	Increases in the number of staff, staff skills, and new board members Growth in financial and other organizational resources	Formal assessments of organization capacity Organizational "check-ins" or meetings with organizing staff, board members, and constituents Quantitative measures of staff hired, new board members, skills obtained,

(Continued)

TABLE 10.1
Measurement Strategies for Evaluation of Community Organizing Campaigns and Projects (*Continued*)

Organizing Activity or Outcome	Objectives	Measures
		workshops or trainings attended, and grants acquired
Power resources developed	Changes in organization influence or legitimacy	Number and quality of relationships and formal partnerships; number of meetings with decision makers and legislators
	Development of partnerships and coalitions	
	Development of relationships with powerful decision makers	Amount of media coverage; effectiveness of framing and messaging efforts
	Media contacts	Internal dialogue about organizational influence and community visibility
	Electoral participation of constituents and other community members	Critical incident analysis of organizing efforts
	Organization capacity to sponsor events, protests, meetings with public officials and other activities to facilitate social change	Impact of the organization on legislative or policy decisions
		Number of voters registered; election turn out
		Number of events, protests, meetings, and other activities; number of people that participate
Ability to reflect on strategies and tactics and modify actions in response to situational demands	Development of a critical consciousness	Organizational "check-ins" or meetings with organizing staff, board members, and constituents
	Use research data to modify interventions	Increases in participant knowledge about social processes and community conditions
		Development of new models or organizing approaches
		Production of training and curriculum materials

(Continued)

TABLE 10.1
Measurement Strategies for Evaluation of Community Organizing Campaigns and Projects (*Continued*)

Organizing Activity or Outcome	Objectives	Measures
Ability to achieve results (successful campaigns or projects)	Increasing successful events, activities, protests, campaigns, and projects	Number of events or activities
		Organization documents that describe the organizing effort and the decisions made
	Successful organizing campaigns or policy/legislative advocacy	
		Social indicator analysis that documents factors such as increases in new housing units, new businesses, poverty and unemployment rates, and the number of services provided
	Improvements in community capacity, infrastructure or housing, quality of life, or economic activities	
	Improvements in service delivery	Organization debriefings, community forums, surveys, or focus groups to examine community perceptions about the effectiveness and impact of campaigns and projects
	External funding received by community groups or invested in the community	
		The amount of money obtained

Note: The objectives and measures included in this table were derived from a number of different sources: Foster and Louie (2010), Gjecovi et al. (2006), Kay (2006), and Speer et al. (2011).

strategic organizing approaches, models of practice, the community's cultural norms, and the organization's mission (see Table 10.1). Such measures are comprehensive and flexible, responding to funder requirements for documentation and reflecting participant values, goals, and actions. They also allow participants to choose those measures that are most consistent with what they do and what they want to achieve.

SUMMARY

Formal evaluations are a critical component of community practice efforts that supplement information collected through the process of action and reflection. Data collected systematically can be used to motivate participants, assess staff performance, and monitor ongoing organizing efforts, and document the organization's capacity to reach its goals. Evaluation findings also provide hard evidence that can be used to persuade funders, prospective volunteers, and the media about the legitimacy, power, and effectiveness of the organization and its members. A variety of qualitative and quantitative research techniques can be integrated into participatory research processes that facilitate the participation of constituency group members in evaluating their own work. This process can also be used to facilitate and institutionalize knowledge production, moving it from a simple process of action and reflection to one in which knowledge is packaged in a manner that allows for it to be disseminated and used by others. For evaluation efforts to be successful, organizers must be prepared to employ research, group work, conflict management, and other interpersonal skills to enhance the capacity of constituents to engage in such efforts.

EXERCISES AND ASSIGNMENTS

1. Analyze an empirical journal article that describes a participatory evaluation of a community-based intervention. Write a three- to five-page paper that describes the following aspects of the study.
   (a) The purpose of the evaluation and the goal of the intervention, project, and campaign.
   (b) The participants and how they were recruited or selected
   (c) The overall approach used to conduct the evaluation
   (d) The methodology, including sampling, data collection, instruments, and quantitative research design and/or type of qualitative study.
   (e) Ethical considerations including human subject procedures and methods used to facilitate participation
   (f) Major findings
   (g) Major weaknesses or strengths of the study
   (h) Overall, do you think this was a good study? Why or why not?
2. Working with a group of constituents, develop a set of evaluation procedures for a project, campaign, or event in which you are involved in your field practicum. Your paper should include the following:
   (a) A set of goals and measureable objectives with a specific time-line for accomplishing objectives.
   (b) Outcome measures.
   (c) An evaluation plan that specifies who should participate, overall methodology, data collection methods, data analysis procedures,

interpretation of findings, and dissemination of a final report (written report, oral presentation, video, play, art installation, etc.).
   (d) A description of who should participate in the evaluation, carry out specific roles and tasks, and facilitate group meetings.
3. Examine a research report that describes a participatory research project. Write a critique of the report that:
   (a) Describes how constituency group members were recruited for participation in the evaluation.
   (b) The role of the facilitator or researcher.
   (c) Whether the project involved a "top-down" or "bottom up" approach to community practice. For example, who initiated the project? Was it something community members wanted or needed? How is intended to assist them?
   (d) The degree to which constituency group members were involved in the research.
   (e) Whether you think participant involvement and control was sufficient? What actions should the researchers have taken to strengthen participation?
   (f) Who do you think stands to benefit from the project? Why?
   (g) What were the end results? Were community improvements made, did individuals learn new skills, did group members "bond" with one another, were existing community networks strengthened, were individuals or organizations transformed or empowered, and were specific improvements made in the quality of life in the community? Were PAR participants able to use the results to engage in social change? Why or why not?

11

Using Interpersonal Skills to Advocate
for Legislation

Latino leaders who went to bat for [Governor] Jerry Brown in last year's
campaign are now counting on the governor to help them pass bills supporting
farmworkers and illegal immigrants. Latino census growth, the pending
redrawing of political districts and the election of a Democrat for the state's top
office create a confluence of opportunity not seen in years, activists say .... The
latest action on a Latino bill came Thursday, when the Assembly passed a
measure inspired by Pedro Ramirez, student body president at Fresno State
University, that would allow undocumented immigrants to receive a stipend,
grant or scholarship for serving in student government at a state university
or community college
—Sanders, 2011, article published in the *Sacramento Bee*, May 13, 2011.

As described in the newspaper "clipping" above, a number of factors
contribute to successful lobbying for legislation including timing and
opportunity, political influence, public or voter support, and election procedures. Interpersonal skills are also important, including the ability
build relationships with legislators and interest groups and to communicate issues in a manner that solicits popular support and puts pressure on
legislators to take action. In this chapter, the terms legislative advocacy
and lobbying are defined and the structure and context of legislative campaigns are examined. A description of the background research necessary
to effectively lobby for legislation is also provided. In addition, the interpersonal skills required for participation in successful lobbying campaigns are described including written and electronic communication,
relationship-building with decision-makers, components of successful
lobbying visits, and the provision of testimony at public hearings. The
relationship between legislative and political campaigns is also examined
in terms of the types of interpersonal skills needed for each of these social
action-related approaches and barriers (such as legal regulations) that
limit the engagement of social workers and community organizers

employed by public and nonprofit agencies in these activities. In the last section of the chapter, lobbying campaign procedures used to change laws and social policies in order to achieve social justice are described.

DEFINING LEGISLATIVE ADVOCACY AND LOBBYING

Legislative advocacy can be defined as promoting or working for a cause that can be addressed by the passage of a new law or approval of a policy or regulation (Avner, 2002). *Lobbying* is a specific form of advocacy that involves putting pressure on lawmakers or government bureaucrats to pass or block a legislative proposal, policy, or regulation (Kirst-Ashman & Hull, 2009; Richan, 2006). Lobbying can be direct, involving face-to-face meetings with legislators, members of their staffs, and other government officials. However, in most cases, lobbying involves indirect contact with others (through letter writing, phone calls, emails, faxes, or the Internet) or simply urging constituents to contact their legislators. Engagement in activities that focus on urging other individuals and groups to lobby their legislators is called indirect or *grassroots lobbying* (Bergan, 2009; Haynes & Mickelson, 2003).

Legislative advocacy is generally considered to be a form of social action due to the fact that it often involves activities related to persuading, influencing, pressuring, or some forms of mild coercion to change the minds of potential opponents (Mondros, 2005). For example, offering to give an elective official something or to withhold tangible or intangible benefits such as votes, donations, or public good will or support can be used to persuade legislators to adopt specific positions on an issue. It should be noted however, that outright bribery or instances in which elected officials vote for bills from which they will financially benefit are legally prohibited (Briffault, 2008; Savage, 2011). Therefore, most lobbying takes place in a more subtle manner, in the context of the exchange of information, legal donations and gifts (such as meals or tickets to sports or entertainment events), and political support (Kraft & Furlong, 2007; Wise, 2007). Absent access to large amounts of cash for campaign donations, community organizers involved in lobbying look for alternative means to advocate for policies and legislation that would benefit their constituents. According to Amidei (2002), it takes only about a dozen calls to a single legislator to make one take notice that the public is concerned about a particular issue or piece of legislation.

As with other types of social action, constituents often have the primary roles in legislative campaigns, meeting with public officials, providing testimony at public hearings, and organizing rallies or protests to garner public support or persuade legislators to take action.

While organizers provide support for constituents in direct lobbying-related activities, they may also be called upon to manage grassroots legislative campaigns, give expert testimony at public hearings or conduct research on public issues, the impact and content of specific pieces of legislation, or the vested interests and power associated with the various groups and individuals involved in the legislative process (Hardina, 2002; Haynes & Mickelson, 2003; Mondros, 2005). In addition, organizers often facilitate trainings and workshops on legislative procedures and lobbying skills (O'Neill, Williams, & Reznick, 2008; Szakos & Szakos, 2007).

LEGISLATIVE CAMPAIGNS

As with other forms of campaigns (as described in Chapters 7 and 8), members of the action system, develop a pre-determined approach to advocate, support, block, or request modifications in legislation that may affect them, the groups they represent, or people or issues for whom they are concerned. Legislative campaigns can differ in terms of participants, goals, and components, depending on the issue involved, the amount of power held by proponents and opponents, the salience of the issue for the public, and the structure or rules that guide the legislative process.

Participants in Legislative Campaigns

Most lobbying campaigns are conducted, not by a single organization or constituency group alone, but by coalitions of organizations. One of the most important tenants of any form of organizing is "strength" in numbers: the more people and organizations involved in an organizing effort increases the amount of power, resources, skills, information, and media attention that can be used to influence an issue (Bergan, 2009; Jackson-Elmore, 2005). Since these communications are tracked (and in many cases responded to) by legislative staff, they can be viewed as expressions of support or withdrawal of support by individual voters. Consequently, a legislator may change one's support or opposition to an issue if enough letters or phone calls are received (Haynes & Mickelson, 2003). In addition, the various groups involved in legislative coalitions have a variety of resources that can be applied in the lobbying effort—money, media contacts, previous relationships with politicians, and social networks that can be mobilized for the lobbying effort (Mosley, 2010). They can also shape legislation by negotiating the parameters of the laws and policies that they wish to see passed with members of the coalition or other allied groups.

Many of the organizations participating in legislative campaigns are interest groups. Interest groups can be defined as groups composed of people with some shared values and policy objectives who are active in the political process (Hrebenar, 1997): As in social movements, sometimes interest groups are formed to represent the interests of the voiceless (e.g., children) or to advocate for the group's vision for the public good (e.g., reducing the public debt, environmental protection, or ending homelessness).

Often, interest groups have multiple goals that they wish to achieve for their members. For example, social work lobbying is conducted through local and state chapters of the National Association of Social Workers Social Workers. NASW typically advocates for legislation that improves work conditions for social workers, (e.g., wages, benefits, or social work licensing requirements), funding for the agencies in which they are employed, and to increase access to services or the well-being of the people they serve. Other professional, trade, and business groups also form associations to fight for their own interests in the legislative process. Other powerful interest groups include the Sierra Club, the National Association of Manufacturers, the National Rifle Association, and the American Association of Retired Persons. The groups actually involved in lobbying on behalf of a specific issue will vary, based on the vested interest of the organization and the amount of power they have to influence the decision-making process. According to Jansson (2008), legislative coalitions are often necessary to mitigate the influence of powerful interest groups, most often associated with businesses or corporations, with many members, financial resources, and long-term relationships with elected officials. Such alliances are believed to have substantial influence on the development of legislation, the awarding of government contracts, and the outcomes of election campaigns.

Since membership in coalitions supporting various pieces of legislation can shift in response to the issue at hand or the vested interest of participant organizations, today's ally can be tomorrow's opponent, requiring that good relationships be maintained with both prospective allies and opponents (Richan, 2006). These relationships can be employed later on in the legislative process when negotiations take place among politicians and the interest groups with which they are allied and opposition forces. The ability to compromise or reach common ground on new legislation helps to ensure "win-win" situations in which many of the groups and elected representatives involved achieve at least a portion of their goals in the final draft of the legislation (Kraft & Furlong, 2007).

Goals in Legislative Campaigns

Goals in legislative campaigns generally focus on alleviating a specific problem or addressing a social issue. For example, a legislative goal may be to increase the amount of healthy food available to school children. Adopting new legislation or changing current legislation may simply be one of many methods for achieving the goal (Avner, 2002). While passing a specific bill is often the primary focus of legislative campaigns, there can also be other reasons for lobbying for legislation. An organization or coalition group may wish to:

- Campaign for a specific package of interrelated measures designed to address a specific long-term goal. For example, child welfare advocates may submit several bills designed to increase funding for and services provided by Independent Living programs for foster children during a single legislative session.
- Campaign for increases (or in some cases decreases) in funding allocations to be set in annual budgets or changes in tax policy. Most often, community groups will request increases in funds to benefit low-income individuals, community-based organizations, or communities.
- Defeat or delay a piece of legislation viewed as harmful to individuals, organizations, or communities.
- Amend legislation that is viewed as likely to pass or that the organization may wish to support, deleting provisions viewed to be harmful or otherwise counterproductive (Amidei, 2002; Gelack, 2008; Kingdon, 2003; Richan, 2006).

Things to be considered in deciding whether to engage in legislative campaign are the issue or problem to be addressed, whether there have been other attempts to address the problem legislatively, and what options exist for addressing the problem through legislation (Gelack, 2008; Jansson, 2008). In addition, the types of provisions that should be contained in proposed legislation, positive benefits or negative consequences associated with the prospective legislation, potential opponents and allies, and those decision-makers or targets who will need to be persuaded to sponsor or vote for the legislation should be examined. In legislative advocacy, targets are almost always individuals, for example, a specific elected official, government bureaucrat, or a member of a specific committee or legislative body that will need to make a decision on the legislation (Richan, 2006).

In some cases, targets can include members of the press, influential people, and the public (Kraft & Furlong, 2007). For example, the coalition or lobbying team may engage in activities to persuade an influential newspaper columnist, TV commentator, or a newspaper editorial board to publicize or take a stand on an issue or present information that can be used to persuade to the public and elected officials that legislation should be adopted or defeated. Influential citizens (business people, church leaders, union officials, or members of specific professional groups) can be asked to sign letters or have their names listed in the press as supporters of a proposed piece of legislation. Often a good way of obtaining press coverage of an issue is asking a prominent person or a celebrity to give interviews about the issue, staging a rally, testifying at a public hearing, or sending out information about the legislation via email, Facebook, or Twitter (Marlantes, Bradley, & Burns, 2006; Schultz, 2003).

The greater the press coverage, public awareness, and support for the issue from voters, the more likely decision-makers can be influenced. Since many legislative campaigns have multiple components and may involve a lengthy time commitment, organizations are likely to have long-term, intermediate, and short-term goals. As with other types of campaigns, outcomes may be considered "wins" or partial "wins" if the legislative campaign educates the public about an issue or a bill that has been defeated or contributes to the likelihood that the bill is amended or passed in the next legislation due to increased legislative support or public awareness. In addition, legislative campaigns also include fallback positions if it seems unlikely that goals will be achieved (Richan, 2006).

Components of Legislative Campaigns

Typical roles for social workers or community organizers in legislative campaigns include advocating for changes in local, state, and federal policies, proposing legislation, lobbying for or in opposition to legislation, protesting unjust laws and policies, and using the media to inform the public about these problems or policies (Jansson, 2008). The component parts of campaigns are similar to those of action campaigns and may involve a specific strategic approach or a multistage process (Avner, 2002; Gelack, 2008). For example, if an organization is seeking to improve safety standards for playground equipment in their community, they may first need to advocate for state legislation that establishes such standards or for a funding stream that provides financial assistance so that city and county governments can afford to purchase this special equipment.

As in other types of campaigns, is critical that the action system develop a strategic approach with goals and objectives and identify specific targets to be utilized at different phases of the campaign. Tactical methods used in legislative campaigns can include a variety of activities:

- Conducting research on an issue and providing elected officials, the public, and the media with facts and figures that provide a rationale for the adoption or defeat of a particular bill; releasing a "fact-finding" report on the issue or the likely impact of proposed legislation.
- Drafting a legislative proposal that reflects the constituency group's or coalition's interests.
- Finding a sponsor for a piece of legislation or working collaboratively with an elected official to draft a piece of legislation. Bills can have multiple sponsors or can be supported by a political party. However, bi-partisan support that crosses party lines makes it more likely that a piece of legislation will have sufficient support to pass.
- Conducting news and social media campaigns to present the coalition's position on the issue and to persuade the public to support it. Media campaigns can also be used to put pressure on lawmakers to change their positions on the issue or to ensure that others continue their commitment to your cause.
- Scheduling individual and group meetings with legislators.
- Making phone calls or sending letters, faxes, or emails in order to advocate a specific position on an issue. These communications are addressed to specific individuals in the legislative process, most often the individual's own elected representative. This tactical method requires that people outside the "lobbying team" be motivated and mobilized to take action.
- Presenting testimony at legislative hearings.
- Persuading legislators to introduce, support, or oppose specific amendments to a piece of pending legislation or to identify compromises that can be made in order to obtain approval of the final bill (Avner, 2002; Haynes & Mickelson, 2003; Jansson, 2008; Mondros, 2005; Richan, 2006).

Most campaigns use multiple methods to ensure success. Often lobbying efforts require that the action system continually monitor the legislative process and be able to respond to situational demands and unique opportunities that can be used to persuade elected officials and the public to support their goals (Jansson, 2008; Kingdon, 2003). For example, in 2011, after an earthquake and tsunami struck Japan and destroyed several nuclear plants, antinuclear groups worldwide stepped up efforts to persuade government to substitute green energy for nuclear power (Betigeri, 2011; Cowell, 2011). In addition to the situation-at-hand, factors affecting tactical choices are similar to those in other types of social action and include:

- The extent of policy change desired.
- Specific objectives for the legislative campaign.
- Whether the action system is supporting or blocking the change.
- The time frame involved.
- The current positions of decision-makers on the issue.
- The power of the decision-makers, the amount of influence possessed by opponents, and the amount of power held by the group taking action.
- The importance of the issue to decision-makers and the public (Avner, 2002; Baumgartner, Berry, Hojnacki, Kimball, & Leech; 2009; Jansson, 2008).

According to Mondros (2005), the choice of strategy often depends on the degree of access that members of the action system have to decision-makers. She identifies two primary ways to plan strategy: the insider approach, working through the system and approaching decision-makers directly, and the outsider approach. The outsider approach requires that the action system put pressure on decision-makers using protest-related tactics and in some situations, legal action, including lawsuits, public records requests, and injunctions or restraining orders. Mondros argues that most lobbying groups want to have influence comparable to other insiders; consequently, collaboration, compromise, and consensus are often preferred tactical methods. As in other approaches to community practice, legislative advocates often start out using collaboration and then escalate tactical methods over time. Other things to think about when developing a strategy are similar to those considerations taken into account in other types of action campaigns:

- Adapt a strategy that is appropriate for the setting and the policy actors involved. For example, using the same strategy to lobby a city council and the state assembly would not produce the same results. Keep in mind that the interests of elected officials as well as decision-making rules are not the same in different venues.
- Constituents (people involved in the change effort or those who will benefit) should also have a leadership role in developing the strategy.
- The people who carry out the strategy should be comfortable with the style and intensity of tactics chosen.
- Frame the issue in a manner that will solicit the most support from decision-makers and the public.
- The choice of strategies and tactics are situational and often must be changed as conditions "on the ground" change (Jansson, 2008; Kingdon, 2003; McGrath, 2007).

BACKGROUND RESEARCH FOR LEGISLATIVE CAMPAIGNS

Successful lobbying relies upon both interpersonal relationships with elected officials and background research. Often the role of the community organizer is to use Internet research, newspaper accounts, literature and policy reviews, and personal interviews to obtain information about the, the content of proposed legislation, and knowledge about the legislative process, including how decisions are made and who will make them. The lobbying team also needs to identify the vested interests and power resources associated with individual decision-makers and the interest groups involved in influencing the policy debate on the legislation.

Content of the Legislation

Advocates and policy analysts examine the content of a new policy to determine policy goals, the individuals or groups who will be affected by a policy, who will benefit or lose from it, how it will be funded, what it is expected to do, and anticipate what will actually happen as a consequence of a policy (Chambers & Wedel, 2005; Gilbert & Terrell, 2009). They also examine how the policy will be put into operation or implemented. If there are specific alternatives to a policy, the potential benefits, costs, and impacts of each alternative can be compared (Dobelstein, 2003; Kraft & Furlong, 2007). After a policy is adopted, they assess the impact of the policy, the degree to which it has benefited or harmed members of the general public, specific demographic groups, or members of marginalized communities, whether it has been implemented in the manner intended, and whether policy goals have been achieved (Davis & Bent-Goodley, 2004; Meenaghan et al., 2004; Weaver, 2010).

Often policy analysis is a matter of conducting research on the effects or anticipated effects of a policy. Since most public programs publish information about the number of people who receive benefits from a policy and the amount of funds allocated or spent in associated with the policy, much of this information is accessible to the public. As with needs assessment, statistical information about community conditions is often obtainable using Internet and other public sources (Meenaghan et al., 2004). While constituency groups can do some of this research, interest groups and advocacy organizations often conduct policy research and make their data available to the public, disseminating reports, putting data on the Internet, and giving press conferences and media interviews (Jackson-Elmore, 2005). The availability of data in reference to a specific piece of legislation often increases as the bill advances through the legislative process (Gelack, 2008). Stories about how individuals and groups are affected by a specific piece of legislation or how new legislation may affect them also can be used in the legislative process, included in letters to legislators, media stories, and in public testimony presented by constituency group members, or formal reports.

Often, one of the ways in which a persuasive argument is built for or against a policy is by articulating a frame, similar to those used in other types of organizing that includes specific values important to the public such as equality, efficiency, equity, self-determination, adequacy of the benefits provided, and justice (McGrath, 2007; Stone, 2002). Policy analysis is often a matter of examining whether the policy is expected to uphold these values—based on the available facts, the amount of funding to implement the policy, the people it is expected to serve, how benefits will be distributed, and how it is expected to operate (Chambers & Wedel, 2005; Kraft & Furlong, 2007).

A third type of information needed for content analysis is an examination of policy alternatives. This requires a review of other pending policy or legislative proposals. Have alternative bills been introduced and how does the bill differ from the one that you propose? It is also helpful to determine if similar bills have actually been proposed, passed, or implemented in other jurisdictions or countries or if alternative measures have been taken to address the problem. Often this information can be found in the professional or research literature on a topic, in newspaper and other media accounts, or through Internet searches. Such reports generally include valuable information on the benefits and costs of these policy alternatives, whether policies can feasibly be implemented, and any side effects or consequences associated with them (Glover Blackwell, Minkler, & Thompson, 2009; Kraft & Furlong, 2007).

For community groups with few resources, obtaining basic facts about the social problem to be addressed, the new policy, or proposed legislation or finding out how people have been affected by the policy may be sufficient to launch a policy campaign. It is it also very feasible to rely on coalition partners, legislative allies, or national organizations for fact sheets, policy briefs, and pre-prepared campaign material. If constituency group members initiate a campaign, basic steps in the content analysis process include:

- Identifying problems or issues of concern.
- Finding out how individuals and the community have been affected by the problem. Obtaining data from other advocacy groups, government

agencies, or elected officials or document how people in the community have been affected by the problem or previous legislation.
- Identifying a set of value criteria for viewing the contents of legislation and weighing alternative approaches in terms of these criteria as well as the costs, benefits, feasibility, and consequences associated with each option.
- Determining the outcome to be achieved and any fallback positions.
- Determining if the specific approach constituency group members have chosen is feasible, given funding and other restraints.
- If supporting a specific bill, finding out the bill number, who has introduced the bill, potential allies and opponents, and how the bill will move through the legislative process.
- Asking one or more constituency group members if they would be available to send a letter to their elected representatives speak on how they or people they know have been affected by the problem (Avner, 2002; Glover Blackwell et al., 2009; Haynes and Mickelson, 2003).

Legislative Processes

In order to lobby successfully, organizers and their constituents must understand the legislative process. It is necessary to be able to identify the key decision-makers, the types of decisions that can be made, and how the decision-making process is structured, and specific steps required for a bill to become a law. Essentially advocates must determine the "rules of the game" and assess where and when they can have the most influence. For example, it may not be sufficient to have a majority of votes to achieve a legislative victory. In understanding how the U.S. Senate works, a successful lobbyist must be aware that 60 (out of 100 votes) are needed to bring a piece of legislation to the floor for debate (Davis, 2007).

In the U.S. the Federal and state governments have similar structures with bicameral (two house) legislatures, a chief executive (President or governor), and an independent judicial systems. In this type of system, there are a number of points in the legislative process at which members of constituency groups can influence legislative decision-making:

- Proposing bills and amendments.
- When bills are introduced in both legislative and budget committees.
- When bills are advanced to the floor of the house/assembly or senate.
- During the budgeting process when funds for specific policies and programs are allocated.

- When bills are finalized by conference committees that reconcile differences between bills approved by bicameral (two-house) legislatures.
- When the governor, president, or other chief executive is considering whether to sign a new bill (Amidei, 2002; Gelack, 2008).

As noted, in Chapter 8, advocates can also appeal to the courts in some cases to block unjust legislation or to take other legal action when people are harmed by a policy (Chambers & Wedel, 2005). Lobbyists need to have good working knowledge about how the legislative process works, the procedures available to introduce or amend legislation, technical aspects of the budgeting process, and how to contact elected officials and their staff members in order to influence the process.

For example, most legislative bodies establish standing committees that handle specific types of issues: budgets, public services, taxation issues, health care, transportation, etc. (Haynes & Mickelson, 2003). Legislative advocates need to know how this structure operates, the membership composition of the committees, and who is responsible for chairing or staffing them. Often it is in these committees that members of the public will be able to provide public testimony about the bill. According to Amidei (2002), discussions in committees and on the floor of the legislative body are oriented toward addressing whether the bill is based on a good idea, if it makes appropriate use of government funds, and whether the public can support it. Consequently, committee hearings provide legislative advocates with a good opportunity to influence the contents of proposed legislation or to block it from proceeding to a vote on the floor of the legislative body.

Power Analysis: Decision-Makers and Interest Groups

An important step in the lobbying process is assessing the power of individual decision-makers and groups. This type of power analysis is similar to the background research on potential allies and opponents discussed in Chapter 6. Members of the constituency group should be able to identify sources of power that they can use to lobby for legislation, the power resources held by individual legislators, potential allies and opponents, and the degree to which the various groups involved have the power to influence the legislative process.

Some of the critical things to know in terms of a specific policy or piece of legislation are the legislative positions, values, political agendas, and vested interests of individual decision-makers. While ethics rules prohibit politicians from benefiting financially from legislation, they may have other reasons for supporting the issue (Savage, 2011). For example, a social worker elected to political office can probably be expected to support legislation that benefits the profession, people who receive social services, or organizations that provide services. Similarly, if a piece of legislation that makes it easier for couples to adopt a child is under consideration, legislators that are adoptive parents or who were themselves adopted are probably likely supporters. It should be noted, however, that sometimes loyalty to political parties or campaign donors may supersede personal consideration. In addition, friendships, family relationships, and business, religious, or professional affiliations may also influence a lawmaker's support for an issue (Haynes & Mickelson, 2003). Therefore, it is important to know as much about legislators' positions on issues before approaching them about supporting or opposing a specific bill (DeVance Taliaferro & Ruggiano, 2010).

In addition, legislative advocates generally look at the following types of information to assess the degree to which lawmakers are likely to be influenced by lobbyists and degree of power they possess in the legislative process: Critical information includes the elected official's political party affiliation and the degree to which members of that party can control the legislative process (by virtue of a majority of votes or chairmanship of committees), the elected official's voting record on the issue and the names and professional or industry affiliations of campaign donors (Hardina, 2005). Voting record information is generally available online from websites maintained by the legislative body in question and by various advocacy organizations that trace voting histories and issue legislative "report cards" that rank legislators in terms of how they have voted on issues important to them.

The composition of the electoral district that the official represents is also important (Haynes & Mickelson, 2003). Members of some demographic groups may have similar voting patterns. Hence, the question of whether the district has a large number of African American or Latino voters or the number of people in the district who are wealthy may affect such factors as party affiliation, voter turnout, and those individuals who are likely to be elected in that district. In addition to potential votes and campaign donations, politicians often base support for an issue on what they perceive their constituents to need or want (Hoefer, 2006).

It is also important to know about citizens and interest groups who are likely to support or oppose legislation and to identify those people and organizations that could be persuaded to join your lobbying coalition. Linkages among interest groups and other organizations can be critical in determining whether a bill has enough public support to pass. Therefore, as with other types of organizing work, part of the background research process should focus on determining the power resources held by members of the interest group, their positions on the issue or bill, and their likely allies or opponents in the process (Jansson, 2008). As noted in Chapter 6, one of the best sources of information for documenting political power and identifying the vested interests of lobbying groups and individual politicians are campaign donations (Hardina, 2005). Information about Federal donations can be found in the online database constructed by the Center for Responsive Politics (http://www.opensecrets.org/). State and local governments in the U.S. also require that candidates for public office file regular reports on campaign donations. Much of this information can also be obtained online.

THE ROLE OF INTERPERSONAL SKILLS IN LOBBYING FOR LEGISLATION

There are a number of specific components involved in lobbying specific legislators and other public officials. Lobbying activities include disseminating written or electronic materials containing information about an issue, establishing relationships with politicians and other government decision-makers, making lobbying visits or meeting with officials, and providing public testimony at hearings. Each of these tasks requires a specific set of skills similar to those used by social workers to engage with clients and professional colleagues.

Written, Phone, and Electronic Communication

Typical types of written and electronic communications with public officials include typed or handwritten letters, postcards, faxes, or messages transmitted via email, Facebook, web pages, or in some cases, even Twitter accounts. In addition, many organizations encourage their constituents to phone legislative offices, especially in instances in which there is a short time frame prior to the scheduling of a vote on an issue. Although legislative staff are expected to both track and respond to all correspondence, letters and phone calls are considered the most effective means of soliciting attention for an issue (Gelack, 2008). Phone calls should be short, accurate, and quickly reference the issue under consideration and the bill number if the call is in reference to pending legislation (Hoefer, 2006). The staff member likely will ask for the caller's contact information in order to assess constituent support or opposition to specific legislation (Haynes & Mickelson, 2003).

In addition to phone calls, elected officials and their staff prefer to receive letters written by the constituent rather than pre-printed letters, post-cards, or web-based forms or petitions that just require the respondents name and contact information. Letters require an actual time commitment from the writer and often contain personal stories about how a person is affected by an issue. Consequently, anyone who has taken the time to complete a letter is viewed as genuinely concerned about the issue and likely to take additional action (voting, making donations, or participating in an election campaign) in relation to the issue (Gelack, 2008; Haynes & Mickelson, 2003).

Lobbying communications, written, electronic, or phone, should be short and accurate and contain the following information:

- The elected official's name and address—rather than a form letter in which this information is not specified.
- Identification of the issue of concern.
- A specific request from the writer (e.g., support or opposition for a piece of legislation or an amendment). If the letter is in reference to a pending bill, the number and title of the bill should be included.
- A description of why the letter writer is concerned about the issue, including facts, personal connections to the issue, personal experiences, stories about how others are affected by the issue, and references to common values and beliefs that should be considered in reference to the bill or issue at hand (e.g., fairness, equity, or efficiency).
- A clear statement about the letter writer's opinion on the issue.
- A reference to the legislator's personal interest or past voting history on the issue.
- Contact information for the writer (e.g., name, address, phone number or email address). In many instances, the writer should receive a follow-up letter from the legislative office, acknowledging receipt of the letter and describing the lawmaker's position on the issue) (Haynes & Mickelson, 2003; Hoefer, 2006) (Box 11.1).

BOX 11.1   LETTER—LOBBYING FOR AN ISSUE

City Council Member
Roberto Gonzalez
City Hall
123 Main Street
Milltown, California 12345

Dear Council Member Gonzalez:

> ## BOX 11.1   LETTER—LOBBYING FOR AN ISSUE (*Continued*)
>
> I'm writing for asking your support for a bill to shut down the local meat rendering plant. As you know, people in your district are adversely affected by the poor air quality and the smell from the plant. My children cannot play outside on days in which the plant is in operation. My youngest daughter, Laura, age 9, has just been diagnosed with asthma. In addition, my son's high school baseball team has been adversely affected by the poor air quality as well. Due to warnings from the local air quality district about ozone levels, the school district has been forced to cancel baseball practice at least six times this year and games have been cancelled twice. This is a problem because the opportunity to play sports is extremely important for a growing adolescent's health and well-being.
>
> In addition, I'm concerned about how the unregulated meat rendering plant and other sources of pollution in my neighborhood adversely affect the health and quality of life for members of our community. The U.S. Department of Environmental Protection reports that one of the key triggers of asthma for most children is air pollution. In addition, African-American communities are more likely to be adversely affected by asthma. According to the EPA, 13% of all African-American children have asthma compared to 8% of white children, 8% of Latino children, and 12% of Native American children. They are also more likely to be hospitalized or die from asthma than other children. In our community, based on hospital records and a state health survey, asthma rates among children are estimated at 10%, with the rate for African-American children at 14%, higher than the national average.
>
> I urge you to support our efforts to introduce legislation in the Mytown City Council to rescind the condition use permit for the meat rendering plant and shut it down as a first step in improving the health of children in the Westside Community.
>
> Sincerely,
Emma Lee
Westside Neighborhood
Organization
>
> *Note*: The source of asthma statistics cited in the letter is the United States Environmental Protection Agency (n.d.), *Children's Environmental health disparities: Black and African American children and asthma*. Retrieved from http://yosemite.epa.gov/ochp/ochpweb.nsf/content/HD_AA_Asthma.htm/$File/HD_AA_Asthma.pdf

Building Relationships With Public Officials

Relationship building with legislators and members of their staff is often the key to successful lobbying (Jackson-Elmore, 2005). Wise (2007) conducted a qualitative study with professional lobbyists working at the Federal level to represent the health care industry to examine the importance of relationship-building in their work. Respondents felt building business and personal relationships with members of Congress was critical for successful lobbying. Elements of good relationships described in the interviews included honesty, presenting both sides of an issue when lobbying, developing trust, and exchanging information with the elected officials and staff members. These actions were viewed as key to increasing the lobbyists' access to decision-makers and information they needed about the legislative process in order to do their jobs. While these lobbyists viewed all forms of communication, emails, letters, phone calls, and faxes as important tools, emails were viewed as the most efficient way to lobby and exchange information while face-to-face interaction was considered to be the most effective method. DeVance Taliaferro and Ruggiano (2010) conducted a similar study with employees of nonprofit organizations. Their respondents also emphasized the importance of building personal relationships with public officials, describing the process as "developing goodwill through communications or activities" or "just talking to one another" (p. 5).

It should be noted that developing a relationship with lawmakers themselves may not be as critical as "getting to know" legislative aides. These gatekeepers control access to public officials and their appointment calendars. In addition, staff members are often the people that will directly interact with constituents and other lobbyists to obtain information, schedule public testimony, or look for media opportunities to disseminate the lawmaker's position on the legislation. In many circumstances, the lawmaker will not be available to meet with lobbyists; instead meetings will be arranged with senior staff members.

One of the first things to assess when developing a lobbying team with constituency group and coalition members is if any participant has an existing relationship with legislative staff and even with the family members of elected officials (DeVance Taliaferro & Ruggiano, 2010). These individuals can relay the information and the requests they receive from constituents and in some cases, assist them in trying to persuade the lawmaker. They may also have positions of their own that differ from that of the lawmaker or can actively be looking for additional information to provide the decision-maker.

Components of Successful Lobbying Visits

Lobbying often occurs during individual or group visits to the office of elected officials or government bureaucrats. Successful lobbying visits require scheduling appointments in advance, careful research on the issue involved, the status of the legislation, and the decision-maker's position on the issue (Richan, 2006). Making appointments is easier if a member of the lobbying team has a previous relationship with the public official or legislative aide. Richan suggests that once an appointment is scheduled, a letter should be sent by a team member to the official's office conveying a note of thanks for the opportunity to schedule the appointment. This also has the advantage of confirming the time and date of the lobbying visit.

Another preparatory measure is to plan the meeting and an informal presentation to be given during the meeting (Hoefer, 2006). The presentation should include the same type of information to be given in a lobbying letter, factual information about the issue and the potential impact of the legislation, bill number and status of any pending legislation, and personal stories about how individuals will be impacted by the legislation. The group should also be prepared to make a specific request in reference to the legislation. The Autism Research Institute (2007) advises their members to prepare carefully for lobbying visits:

* Make sure that you have a least one ASK per lobbying visits and be able to communicate why it is important, using three key points. Limiting the message to three key points helps ensure that the members of the lobbying team stay focused on the issue.
* Decide in advance on which of the members of the lobbying team will share a personal story about the issue. The story is important for making a persuasive case for the lobbying team's position on the issue, but should not dominate the time allotted for the visit.
* Practice the presentation including the personal story and the "ASK" prior to the visit.
* Bring printed material with information about the issue or proposed legislation with you to the visit.
* Document the visit. Delegate at least one member of the team to take notes that can be shared with other members of the organization or coalition. Also take pictures of the visit. Documentation can be shared with the press and the public. This also serves as a recruiting tool to inform prospective members or volunteers about the activities of the organization or coalition group.

Richan (2006) recommends two additional steps after the visit. The first involves group reflection. As with other types of reflection, things to consider are whether members of the lobbying team feel that the visit was successful, if the official actually made a commitment to the group or indicated how one would vote on the issue, and what aspects of the presentation and the overall visit were particularly effective (Avner, 2002). The second step should be to send a thank you letter to the official.

Such a letter should be sent regardless of the success of the visit; it opens up a pathway for establishing an ongoing relationship with the decision-maker.

One other thing to be aware of in advance of the meetings includes the fact that lobbying visits are intended to be reciprocal. Lobbying visits are most successful when they provide public officials with information about an issue, particularly facts and figures that can be used during committee hearings, media interviews, and floor debates (Richan, 2006). However, as with public speaking and media relations, facts are only one component of building a persuasive argument. Respondents in the DeVance Taliaferro and Ruggiano (2010) study emphasized the importance of including agency clientele or people directly affected by an issue in lobbying visits. In addition to presentation of factual information, in order to make a "persuasive case" to the lawmaker, it is critical that people directly affected by an issue be able to describe their experiences and how the proposed legislation may help or harm them. These personal stories can also be shared by the lawmaker when justifying support or opposition to a particular issue and combine facts with emotion in order to frame issues in a manner that connect with the public. In addition to providing information during the visit, contact information should be provided and the lobbying organization should be responsive to further requests for information, public testimony, meetings, or other reasonable legislation-related requests from the lawmaker. Even when the outcome of the visit does not result in influencing the official's position on the issue, it may provide an opportunity to develop a relationship that can be used in the future for lobbying or in facilitating legislative compromises.

Public Testimony

One type of important opportunity to engage in lobbying is providing public testimony on a piece of legislation or a policy. Generally, in state legislatures and the U.S. Congress, opportunities to provide testimony take place during legislative committee hearings. Invitations to present testimony are most often extended by committee chairs, committee members, or legislative staff (Avner, 2002). As noted by Richan (2006), committee chairs and staff often have an agenda of their own when setting up a hearing. They may want to hear from people with a variety of viewpoints or simply want testimony that validates their own viewpoints. In addition, hearings may be held on controversial issues simply to give opponents the opportunity to state their views even though it may be unlikely that the final decision on the issue or legislation can be changed. Consequently, previous lobbying relationships often play a role in determining the individuals and groups that will be permitted to testify. Therefore, providing public testimony is not only an opportunity to give input on an issue, it also is one of the primary techniques used to establish "exchange" relationships with public officials.

The provision of testimony, as in other forms of lobbying, requires careful preparation. As described earlier in this chapter, background research on the issue, the decision-making process, and vested interests, values, voting records, and backgrounds of the decision-makers should be examined prior to the hearing (Avner, 2002). A written copy of the testimony should be prepared in advance as well as any fact sheets that can be distributed to the decision-makers and members of the audience. There also may be an opportunity to present the committee with a more detailed policy brief that describes policy alternatives, states the facts, and makes, recommendations for action (Jansson, 2008). Powerpoint presentations may also be used if permitted by the legislative body (Hoefer, 2006). The oral presentation should be practiced in advance. Testimony length is generally short, 10 minutes or less, unless otherwise specified (Jansson, 2008).

The lobbying team should choose an individual in advance to give the testimony, a constituency group member, an expert allied with the group, or the organizer may be called upon to give the testimony. However, the most persuasive type of testimony is presented by people who have actually experienced the problem, who are negatively affected by the previous policy, or who will benefit from new legislation (Haynes & Mickelson, 2003).

Public testimony generally includes the type of information provided in a written lobbying communication (such as a letter) or office visit: a brief analysis of the content and impact of the legislation that includes facts, figures, and a story about how the speaker or people one represents will be affected by the legislation. The Community Tool Box offers the following suggestions for the content of public testimony:

- Open the presentation by giving your name and background information (such as your job, where you live, or why you should be considered to have expert knowledge or important information about the issue).
- Describe how the situation under discussion or the issue affects you or people you know or represent.
- Describe how the policy or legislation under discussion will positively or negatively affect you as well as the people whose interests you represent. Give examples.

- Ask a value question about the impact of the policy or legislation. Is it good or bad? Who will be positively or negatively affected by it? Who benefits? Who loses?
- Close by thanking the decision-makers for the opportunity to speak to them (Work Group for Community Health and Development, 2010).

Most importantly, the testimony should contain a specific "ask" or request for the legislative body to take specific action on the legislation (Avner, 2002). The testimony should also be focused on making a persuasive case or argument that supports your request. If you cannot actively persuade the decision-makers, good testimony can also result in positive media coverage and additional public support (Baumgartner et al., 2009; Richan, 2006).

In addition, the person providing the testimony should be prepared to answer questions from elected officials. In some cases, the testimony can be expected to be friendly (from lawmakers who are allies or prospective allies) or adversarial (from opponents). To some extent, potential questions can be identified in advance and responses prepared (Richan, 2006). Often it is helpful to have additional facts and figures ready that support your position.

Other Communication Techniques for Wrapping up Support for Legislation

Successful votes to move legislation out of committee is only one stage of the process. Typically, bills are debated on the floor of the legislative house or other public decision-making body and there is a pre-defined process for voting. The final vote often requires a final push by the lobbying team. Avner (2002) recommends the following actions:

- Send a final reminder to legislators about your group's position on the issue. Emails or other communications with factual information are important. Last-minute phone calls can also be made.
- Try to obtain media support for the issue, with publication or broadcast just before the vote.
- Have members of your lobbying team with "expert" or personal knowledge of the issue on hand to advise legislative supporters during negotiations or prior to the vote.
- Mobilize supporters to be present in the legislative body on the day of the vote with matching t-shirts, buttons, or other forms of group identification and membership so that the legislators know you have "strength in numbers."

• Consider sending emails or "tweets" to supporters or potential supporters just before the vote—you can simply ask for support or set up a brief, last-minute meeting. Many legislators have access to computers in legislative chambers or carry smartphones with them.

THE RELATIONSHIP BETWEEN LEGISLATIVE AND POLITICAL CAMPAIGNS

Both legislative advocacy and political campaigning have been defined as components of "political social work" (Rocha, Poe, & Thomas, 2010). In actual practice, both these activities are interrelated. In order to obtain legislation that meets certain needs or goals, office holders must be elected that will support specific legislative priorities. Involvement in political campaigns is one of the many ways to build a relationship with elected officials. Hence, relationship-building is one of the primary ways in which these two types of social action, lobbying and political campaigns are linked (Hoefer, 2001). However, there are a number of barriers that limit the involvement of organizers and social workers who are paid employees of public and nonprofit organizations in political campaigns.

Using Political Campaigns to Build Relationships With Legislators

Many of the techniques used in community organizing are similar to those used in political campaigns. Candidates and their campaign staff must "get to know" the community, build relationships with individuals and organizations, recruit volunteers and donors, often through tapping into existing social networks, and identify community problems and solutions for alleviating them (Lane, 2011). However, political campaigns differ from other forms of organizing in terms of the almost exclusive emphasis on outcomes rather than process. Also timelines for task accomplishment are shorter. There also is a greater need to develop resources, especially money and a reliance on recruiting and retaining volunteers for many of the basic tasks associated with campaigns: raising funds, contacting and scheduling volunteers, canvassing neighborhoods to identify potential voters and confirmed supporters, and monitoring electoral processes. Consequently, relationship-building is central to successful campaign work. Often candidates and people seeking to influence the legislative process build up relationships over time that are used to recruit volunteers, voters, and donors for political campaigns (Kraft & Furlong, 2007; Schultz, 2003).

Building relationships is also a pragmatic approach for counteracting the often negative influence of campaign donations (DeVance Taliaferro & Ruggiano, 2010). Professional lobbyists often work for employers who make substantial campaign donations to candidates that can be expected to support their legislative priorities. Without monetary resources, organizers look for other opportunities to influence elected officials. Votes or the expectations that organization or community members will support one candidate over another are often influential in efforts to persuade public officials to take a stand on an issue. Sometimes it takes more than the expectation of votes to gain access to decision-makers—it may require actual fundraising or donations to the candidate or engagement in campaign activities on the part of community members and organizers. Some organizers engage in both community and election work to achieve social change, serving as volunteers on election campaigns or moving between paid positions as community workers or campaign staff. Organizers may also seek election to political office. In addition to President Barack Obama, prominent former organizers who moved on to election work include U.S. Senator Barbara Mikulski (D-MD, former civil rights movement leader, U.S. Representative John Lewis (D-GA) and the late U.S. Senator Paul Wellstone (Dreier, 2008a; Wellstone, 2001).

Barriers to Legislative Advocacy and Political Involvement

Social workers are often encouraged to become involved in the political process. The NASW Code of Ethics is very explicit about a social worker's responsibility to engage in politics:

> Social workers should engage in social and political action that seeks to ensure that all people have equal access to the resources, employment, services, and opportunities they require to meet their basic human needs and to develop fully. Social workers should be aware of the impact of the political arena on practice and should advocate for changes in policy and legislation to improve social conditions in order to meet basic human needs and promote social justice. (NASW, 2000, Section 6.04a)

Despite this mandate, there are a number of impediments to the involvement of social workers and community organizers in campaigns as volunteers. Social workers may not receive sufficient education on legislative advocacy or potential roles for social workers in political campaigns. In addition, there are legal restrictions on these activities for employees of public and nonprofit organizations (Rocha et al., 2010).

In terms of legislative advocacy, nonprofit organizations incorporated under 501 (c)(3) of the Internal Revenue Code may only spend 20% of the first $500,000 of their annual budgets on all lobbying activities and smaller percentages of additional amounts of their annual budgets (up to $1,000,000 per year) for direct lobbying and 25% of the total funding spent on direct lobbying for grass-roots lobbying activities (Internal Revenue Service, 2010). Within these restrictions are some exempt activities such as lobbying to protect the funding that the agency receives from government sources, providing nonpartisan information about policy issues, responding to a legislative request for information, or providing public testimony. Other nonprofit organizations incorporated as advocacy organizations under 501 (c)(4) of the IRS Code face no such restrictions (Kerlin & Reid, 2010). It should be noted that the difference between these two types of nonprofits is that contributors to 501 (c)(3) organizations can receive tax deductions. Most 501 (c)(3) organizations provide services although some may combine service delivery with advocacy activities consistent with the Federal expenditure limits. However, donations to nonprofits incorporated as advocacy organizations are not tax deductable. In some cases, nonprofits may set up companion organizations that operate under the two different IRS designations, allowing them to undertake both types of activities (Rocha et al., 2010).

There are similar IRS restrictions on political activities. Nonprofit organizations incorporated under 501 (c)(3) of the tax code may not be directly involved in political campaigns nor can employees of such organizations participate in election activities as part of their paid employment. In general, these organizations may not make campaign contributions (Internal Revenue Service, 2007). In addition to restrictions on organizations, the Federal Hatch Act prohibits government employees from engaging in political activities on the job, interfering with political campaigns, or soliciting donations from other government employees (U.S. Office of Special Council, 2011). This federal legislation also covers state and local government employees whose positions are paid using Federal grants. State and local governments also have similar laws prohibiting political activities by their employees (Knapp & Diehm, 2009).

Opportunities for Legislative Work and Political Involvement

In addition to conducting legislative campaigns or lobbying on individual issues, social workers and community organizers may work for advocacy organizations or interest groups in which work responsibilities can include both lobbying and policy analysis. Social workers with organizing skills may also find employment as legislative aides, working directly with politicians in the development of legislation and serving as staff members in local constituency offices. This type of employment involves casework on behalf of individuals seeking help in obtaining government services (Ortiz, Wirz, Semion, & Rodriguez, 2004).

There are a number of opportunities for organizers and other social workers to be involved in political campaigns "off the job." In the United States, nonprofit organization may conduct nonpartisan voter registration drives, provide voter information and education, or sponsor community forums (Internal Revenue Service, 2007; Jansson, 2008). In addition, social workers and organizers can make campaign donations or volunteer several hours per week on a campaign. Volunteer work on campaigns can range from stuffing envelopes and conducting one-on-one interviews, organizing house parties, or making phone calls to recruiting volunteers, voters, or donors to coordinating media opportunities, developing policy briefs or serving on the campaign's steering committee (Hardina, 2004b; Haynes & Mickelson, 2003). Volunteers can also serve as poll watchers (monitoring the election process) or election judges. Often involvement of social workers in electoral politics is essential for obtaining policies and services for low-income people. When people from a particularly demographic group are likely to vote, they have a better chance to influence legislation. However, there are numerous reasons why poor people do not vote to the same degree as other citizens including voter ID requirements and restrictive legislation making it difficult for former felons to register to vote. Consequently, ongoing advocacy efforts are needed to preserve and strengthen voting rights for the people typically served by members of the social work profession (Siegel, 2011).

Federal law permits interest groups to set up separate organizations called political action committees to make donations (Kerlin & Reid, 2010). PACs solicit donations from their members and give these donations to candidates (Haynes & Mickelson, 2003). Multiple donations from individuals give the PACs that transfer these funds to candidates a certain degree of influence and increases the likelihood that they will have access to these decision-makers if they are elected to office. The National Association of Social Workers has a political action committee, Political Action for Candidate Election (PACE). It raises money from social workers and endorses candidates that are assessed to be likely to support the profession of social work and issues of interest to social workers and the people they serve (NASW, n.d.).

In addition to campaign donations and endorsements, social workers can also manage political campaigns or run for political office (Jansson,

2008). In 2011, seven members of Congress were social workers: Senators Barbara Mikulski (D-Maryland) and Debbie Stabenow (D-Michigan) and Representatives Susan Davis (D-California), Luis Gutierrez (D-IL), Barbara Lee (D-California), Allyson Schwaryz (D-Pennsylvania), and Edolphus Towns (D-New York) (NASW, 2011). Social workers also are state and local office holders legislatures (Lane, 2011).

PUTTING VALUES IN ACTION: CHANGING LAWS AND POLICIES TO ACHIEVE SOCIAL JUSTICE

As noted in Chapter 1, social workers and community organizers have an ethical obligation to fight for social justice (Reisch, 2011). While community organization's primary goal is assisting marginalized communities to obtain resources, respect, and basic human rights, community work in itself is often insufficient or inadequate to achieve social change goals. Consequently, changes in laws and policy must be made. In fact, much of community organization practice involves asking government decision-makers to enforce existing laws or develop new ones in response to documentation of need or harm to individuals and families. For example, tenants' rights organizers often put pressure on city governments to enforce building codes when they find that people are living in rented dwellings that are unheated, without water, or unsafe. Organizers that document that little in the way of affordable housing is available for low-income people may seek a legislative solution when they find out that state governments can pass legislation and take action to make sure that Federal funds for affordable housing can be allocated for use in their community.

Such conditions require both legislative advocacy and political skills for effective community practice. As in other types of organizing, action plans must be developed and constituency group members included in designing the plan and carrying it out (Avner, 2002). Chu, Tsui, and Yan (2009) emphasize that more than simply a commitment on the part of social workers is necessary to achieve social change:

> Important as social justice is to the core purposes of social work, its pursuit would be incomplete without a concomitant commitment to the enhancement of people's well-being and problem-solving capacities. The quest for social justice must be undertaken hand in hand with the quest for individual well-being, societal harmony and mutual respect. (p. 288)

Consequently, constituency group members must be fully involved in the preparation of legislative campaigns. Steps in campaign-related action plans that integrate group dialogue and reflection techniques can be summarized in the following way:

- Organize a lobbying team consisting of constituency group members, people with experiential or expert knowledge about the issue, and individuals and groups who have contacts or relationships with lawmakers or their staff members.
- Join or form a coalition to increase the lobbying group's strength in numbers.
- Find a "window of opportunity" to introduce legislation, connecting your goal to an issue in the news or proposal from another organization or group.
- Establish policy goals. If drafting a policy proposal, incorporate both policy goals and values into the title of the proposed legislation. Make sure that you understand alternative options for addressing the issue and know the pros and cons of these approaches.
- Specify a legislative proposal's content and find legislative sponsors.
- Conduct an assessment of your coalition's power resources and sources of influence possessed by likely allies and opponents. Be ready to counter the power and influence of opposition groups.
- Use group processes to engage constituency group members in the development of a strategy for the campaign and tactical methods.
- Assign tasks to constituency group members. Identify people who can provide public testimony or who can recruit others for partici- pation in grassroots lobbying. Provide training or coaching sessions as needed.
- Implement the campaign, using tactics in a logical order consistent with the timing and requirements of the legislative process.
- Provide information to the media and use press contacts to disseminate your message and relevant facts about the legislation that you propose.
- Urge the public to take action (call, write, email, or meet with legislators).
- Set up a mechanism for group dialogue and reflection in order to make situational adjustments in the campaign and evaluate the outcome.
- Work for goal attainment, but be ready to compromise on the final version of the legislation. Always have a fallback position or a Plan B.
- Be ready to try again if the desired outcome does not work. Consider using the political process to influence legislative decision-making, endorsing a candidate, making donations, conducting voter regis- tration drives, or working on an election campaign (Hardina, 2002; Haynes & Mickelson, 2003; Jansson, 2008; Richan, 2006; Schultz, 2003) (Box 11.2).

BOX 11.2   LEGISLATIVE CAMPAIGN: THE CASE OF THE MEAT
RENDERING PLANT

Alicia Martinez and members of the Westside Organization plan their legislative campaign to shut down the meat rendering plant. They identified a number of components of their campaign

Goal: Shut down the meat rendering plant.

Background Research: Alicia describes the process for decision-making in the City Council. To submit legislation, a city council person must agree to sponsor it. It also helps if the sponsor can solicit support among the other six members of the council. Currently, only three members seem to be concerned about environmental issues, three consider themselves to be pro-development, and at least one member is considered to be a swing voter. It is also important to have the city council member from the district most affected by the legislation be the sponsor. In this case, it is Council Member Gonzalez. Two members of the constituency group know Council Member Gonzalez personally. Mr. Brown worked on his campaign and Mrs Lee's son is on the same high-school baseball team as Council Member Gonzalez's son Mateo. Other key information about council members is that at least one member of the council, Council Member Jones, is a business associate of the owner of the meat rendering plant. For additional information about their legal rights, the group meets with s a local attorney who suggests contacting the Environmental Protection Agency to report pollution if city council action fails or suing the city. Alicia also informs the group that she has received calls from other local and state-wide coalition groups that are willing to lend support to the cause.

Strategy: Social Action

Tactics: Establishing a coalition of organizations to lobby City Hall. Soliciting support from Councilman Gonzalez; Scheduling lobbying visits with other City Council members (both potential allies and opponents), asking coalition members to send letters and make calls to members of the City Council, taking local reporters on a pollution "tour" of the neighborhood near the meat rending plant, preparing fact sheets about environmental racism and the effects of asthma on children, and staging a press conference and rally on the day of the city council vote. Group members also plan to "pack" the council chamber with supporters in matching "Shut it Down" T-shirts on the day of the City Council vote.

Plan B: Legal action or making a formal complaint to the EPA.

An example of a national campaign that applied most of these techniques involved efforts, sponsored by a variety of immigration, student, community, and religious groups was the Dream Act campaign of 2010. The Dream Act offers a path to citizenship for undocumented children of immigrants if they complete military service or college (United States Student Association, 2009). Supporters formed a broad-based coalition and recruited supporters via the news media, YouTube, and the Internet. They further publicized the issue through rallies, media interviews, marches and acts of civil disobedience such as hunger strikes and sit-ins (Brumback, 2011; Hoggard, 2010). Media attention was also brought to the issue when numerous participants in the campaign came out or were exposed by others as undocumented (Marcum, 2010). The campaign also involved a broad-based grassroots lobbying effort and visits to members of Congress. A *Dream Act Lobbying Kit* that included sample letters to elected officials and flyers were made available to supporters via the Internet (USSA, 2009). While the 2010 Dream Act campaign was not successful, supporters and their allies in Congress did not give up. A comprehensive immigration reform bill that included provisions included in the 2010 Dream Act bill was reintroduced in Congress in June, 2011 (Foley, 2011).

SUMMARY

Legislative campaigns are similar to other types of action plans, but they focus on lobbying government officials to take specific types of action. Lobbying may be carried out as part of a larger campaign to achieve a goal for which there must be a change in legislation. Alternatively, a legislative campaign can simply focus on the passage of a bill, amending proposed legislation, or blocking a bill. In order to effectively carry out a legislative campaign, advocates must be knowledgeable about the content of legislation, the structure of the legislative decision-making process, and the vested interests and backgrounds of the government officials that must be influenced to make the decisions. In addition to research, members of the lobby team must use a variety of interpersonal skills to influence lawmakers. Lobbyists send letters, make phone calls, use electronic communications to influence decision-makers. They also meet with public officials and provide testimony at public hearings. The organizer's role in the process includes the provision of information and training to constituency group members and relationship building with public officials and their staff that can be used to facilitate the lobbying process. In some cases, both constituents and organizers may participate in election campaigns in order to elect potential allies to office and build working relationships with them. In both legislative and political campaign work, building strong relationships with participants and decision-makers is essential. In Chapter 12, another intervention method that requires strong interpersonal skills, community development, is described.

EXERCISES AND ASSIGNMENTS

1. Engage in at least two of the following activities and present an oral report to your classmates on your experiences.
   (a) Write a letter or send a fax or email to a legislator about an issue of concern to you.
   (b) Participate in a lobbying visit with a group. Observe the process and participate in the presentation or dialogue with the legislator or legislative staff.
   (c) Attend a legislative hearing and observe the process: the role of the chair, the roles of additional committee members, and the types of questions asked of the people providing testimony, the content of and the values expressed in the testimony, and the positions or groups represented in the presentation of oral testimony.
   (d) Observe a strategy session of a political campaign, attend a poll worker training session, or volunteer for a campaign activity such as precinct walking or making phone calls to prospective voters.
2. Write and present testimony on an issue of concern to you in class. The testimony should contain facts, a personal story, and an "ask." Make sure that the content of the testimony is accessible to your audience (your classmates). Your grade will be based in part on the degree to which you can present a persuasive argument.
3. Interview an elected official or a legislative staff member. Focus the interview on the official's perception of the effectiveness of various lobbying methods and the degree to which decision-makers can be influenced by these various approaches.
4. With constituency group members, design a legislative campaign that focuses on a specific issue, contains a goal, identifies specific values that should be incorporated into the legislation, and outlines a specific strategic approach and tactical options. Use the action plan chart in Chapter 8 to plan your campaign.

5. Conduct background research on a legislator to identify one's vested interest and likely position on a specific issue. Use public records, Internet databases, and personal interviews to document this information.

6. With your classmates, debate the following questions about the legislative action plan presented in Box 11.2:

   (a) Is a lobbying campaign an appropriate mechanism for addressing this problem?

   (b) Should other methods be used prior to using this method? What are they? What factors should determine the use of a specific strategic approach?

   (c) What power resources are held by the members of the lobbying team?

   (d) What power resources are likely to be held by opponents?

   (e) Should background research be primarily focused on Council Member Gonzalez? What other information is needed about power resources and vested interests of likely opponents? Is information that indicates that Councilman Jones is a business associate of the owner of the meat rendering plan sufficient to identify a possible conflict of interest? Why or why not?

   (f) In what circumstances, if any, is it appropriate to use the threat of legal remedies in the lobbying process?

12

Interpersonal Skills for Community Building

I think one of our successes is just being [in] a place that
welcomes all types of people. All races and all classes
can come together and work together and find value
in that. That is definitely a success — being a
bridge-builder between classes.
— Agency administrator quoted in Carr, 2009, p. 54

One of the traditional goals of organizing work has been to build a sense of community or belonging among people living in the same location or individuals experiencing similar problems or issues. Recently, *community building* has been given heavy emphasis in community practice, in part due to efforts to increase social capital, civic engagement, and improve neighborhood capacity to create healthy communities. In this chapter, theoretical perspectives on community building, social capital development, and capacity building are examined. While some of these concepts have been previously discussed in this textbook, this chapter will define community and economic development and examine models of that can be used to increase community connections: community building, asset development, the social capital approach, capacity building, and consensus organizing. Specific types of interpersonal skills used for the community building process are also described: building strong relationships among people, strengthening social networks, strengthening relationships between people and organizations, and strengthening participant or stakeholder engagement and commitment to community building efforts. In the last section of this chapter, the application of these techniques to principles associated with the strengths perspective in social work practice is examined.

THEORETICAL PERSPECTIVES ON COMMUNITY DEVELOPMENT: COMMUNITY BUILDING, SOCIAL CAPITAL DEVELOPMENT, ASSET BUILDING, AND CAPACITY DEVELOPMENT

Biddle and Biddle (1979) describe community development as a process of social change that is based on the premise that all people have good intentions and will act collectively to make their communities better, acting not merely based on self-interest but also for the common good. As with other types of community practice, this method also contains a combination of process and task goals. Vidal and Keating (2004) describe community development as "a place-based approach; it concentrates on creating assets that benefit people in poor neighborhoods, largely by building and tapping links to external resources" (p. 126). Essentially, community development, in its current context, is viewed as using collaboration and consensus-oriented methods to improve the collective well-being of community residents. However, what is often debated is the best process for accomplishing this (Stoecker, 2004).

In addition to asset development, the concept of building community is often explicitly used as a rationale for community development practice. It is based on a belief, most recently articulated in the social capital literature, that people (primarily in urban areas) have few connections with one another and, as a result, are limited in their ability to address neighborhood conditions such as crime, substance abuse, poor housing quality, and lack of access to nutritious food (Fraser & Kick, 2005; James, Schulz, & van Olphen, 2001; Theall et al. 2008). Consequently, neighborhood residents without sufficient social support may also experience poor health, hunger, homelessness, be unprepared for jobs that pay more than the minimum wage, and be less likely to have completed high school (Fertig & Reingold, 2008; Ohmer, 2010; Petersen, 2002; Small & Newman, 2001). This lack of personal relationships is also viewed as interrelated with the concept of sense of community and feelings of personal and political empowerment (Peterson et al., 2008; Hughey, Peterson, Lowe, & Oprescu, 2008). As noted earlier in this book, in addition to identification with a specific community, other aspects of sense of community include perceptions of emotional safety or security, feeling as if one has a personal stake in what happens within the community, and the recognition by community members of markers or indicators that tell others who belongs in the community such as common traditions or values, the use of formal or informal language, clothing, or geographic boundaries (Cnaan & Rothman, 2008). Sharing an emotional connection to the community with others, feelings that the individual can influence what happens in the community or that collective action is possible, and that individual needs can be met are also indicators of a sense of community (Nowell & Boyd, 2010). The degree of individual participation in community decision-making is often used to determine whether people feel a sense of belonging, commitment, or responsibility to the community or their neighbors. As noted previously in this text, strong empirical evidence suggests that sense of community and citizen participation increase feelings of personal and collective self-efficacy (Itzhaky & York, 2002; Ohmer, 2010).

Given the recent attention to Putnam's (2000) research on civic engagement and other empirical literature (Figueira-McDonough, 1991; Sampson, Morenoff, & Gannon-Rowley, 2002; Small, 2007; Wilson, 1996) that seems to indicate that low-income communities are characterized by feelings of alienation and low levels of participation in social networks, community development has focused on community building and increasing the capacity of community residents to improve conditions in their neighborhoods (Kay, 2006). Chaskin (2001) defines community capacity as the:

> Interaction of human, organizational, and social capital existing within a given community that can be leveraged to solve collective problems and improve or maintain the well-being of a given community. It may operate through informal social processes and/or organized effort. (p. 295)

Cnaan and Rothman (2008) describe capacity building as a method of community development that encourages neighborhood self-help efforts, responsible leadership, and a commitment to civic engagement. Other goals they identify include promoting social change with a minimum of conflict and simulating economic growth. Inclusion of local residents in the development process through consensus-oriented decision-making is also an important goal of this process. According to Saegert (2006), other activities associated with this approach include increasing the organizational skills of participants, assisting residents in identifying common goals and taking action, sustaining resident involvement in change efforts, and increasing the ability of local organization to engage in social change. Often these activities are facilitated through intermediary organizations that provide resources, training, and technical assistance and link community groups to institutions and government organizations outside of the neighborhood (Vidal & Keating, 2004).

Delgado (2000) has developed a neighborhood-initiated approach to capacity building that focuses on the resources and talents of neighborhood residents. He calls this approach *capacity enhancement* rather than capacity development because:

> It fundamentally implies that there is a resource-asset in place and that all one needs to do is foster its growth. To use the metaphor of a seed, after a seed is planted, all it needs is water and sunshine. With development, the assumption is that there is no resource and, as a consequence, the practitioner must create it through some form of active intervention. (pp. 9–10)

Delgado argues that a focus on capacity enhancement is critical because little in the way of community practice models address community building from a strengths perspective rather than a deficit model, especially when applied to communities of color.

A focus on building on neighborhood strengths is also evident in Kretzmann and McKnight's (1993) work on the asset-based approach. Asset building as a community organizing model was developed in part due to John McKnight's strong belief, as expressed in his book, *the Careless Society* (1995), that the provision of social services often fosters the dependence of low-income people on service provision and actually harms individuals rather than helps them. He argues that instead of services, community change should focus on the right of individuals to have jobs, live in good neighborhoods, and be free of racism and other oppressive practices. Community development should "increase interdependence in community life through a focus on the gifts and capabilities of people who have been excluded" (McKnight, 1995, p. 132).

According to Oliver (2001), asset and social capital approaches are preferable to deficit-based approaches that view low-income people as captive to social and economic forces and incapable of taking action to improve their communities. He argues that communities already contain assets that can be used for community improvements and defines an asset as:

> A special kind of resource that an individual, organization or entire community can use to reduce or prevent poverty and injustice. An a asset is usually a "stock" that can be drawn upon, built upon, or developed, as well as a resource that can be shared or transferred across generations. (p. xii)

Asset building has an explicit link to the philosophy associated with social capital development. As noted in Chapter 6, Putnam (2000) described two types of social capital. *Bonding social capital* consists of relationships among individuals that originate within social networks and are characterized by reciprocity and trust. Members of these networks have similar values. Consequently, a strong network may facilitate social control by bringing order and stability to a community. *Bridging social capital* consists of relationships that are developed among members of different networks and demographic groups. To this typology, Woolcock (1998) added a third type, *linking social capital*, which involves relationships between local networks and institutions, including organizations located outside the community. Social capital theory in community development is based on the assumption that local networks can use these linkages to effectively leverage assets from outside the community.

The community development perspective on social capital often draws upon the sociology literature on this topic that predates Putnam's *Bowling Alone* (Aguilar & Sen, 2009; Frisch & Servon, 2006; Kay, 2006; Saegert, 2006; Theall et al., 2008). Bourdieu (1986) and Coleman (1990) both used the term social capital to describe how communities function. Bourdieu (1986) described social capital as consisting of actual or potential resources held collectively by groups or social networks that are generated through exchange-related relationships that could be material or symbolic, such as feelings of obligation. Such networks can be used to develop connections with others to advance an individual's or group's interests and political power. He viewed social capital as something that could be exchanged with or used to generate other forms of capital, including cultural, physical, and economic resources. By cultural resources, he meant expectations about how people should act in society rather than the values associated with specific sub-cultures or ethnic groups. Coleman (1990) focused on the individual's role in developing resources that can be used to for individual and community improvement. He argued that social capital is produced when individuals use their skills and capabilities to exchange resources with others. Both social capital and building trust among social network or community members are essential for accomplishing collective goals, disseminating information and obtaining resources from outside the community.

Warren, Thompson, and Saegert (2001) define assets as a type of social capital found in collaborative relationships and through trust-building among individuals and groups. Drawing on Kretzmann and McKnight's (1993) definition of asset building, they argue that the purpose of social capital development in low-income communities is to obtain investments, from sources outside the community, in education and training in order to improve the financial condition of families. As noted by Putnam (2000), social capital is only one form of capital available to community residents. Other types of community capital include *human capital* (jobs and job training), physical capital (housing and infra-structure), *financial capital* (money and the availability of loans and credit), *environmental capital* (land use), and *cultural capital* (Green & Haines, 2002; Light, 2004). However, as noted by Delgado (2000) cultural capital is often more broadly defined, especially when applied to communities of color, focusing on the strengths, values, and traditions of ethnic or other historically excluded demographic groups. Silverman (2004) argues that in addition to these forms of capital, community residents also need decision-making and political power in order to effectively use these resources.

In all these approaches, community building, capacity building, asset development, and social capital formation in community develop-ment common threads include three primary approaches for bringing people together: increasing the strength of community networks, especially in terms of resource exchange and interpersonal relationship development, forming or increasing membership in local community organizations and associations, and increasing linkages between local groups and external organizations (Kay, 2006; McKnight, 1995; Schnei-der, 2007). Such linkages are to be used to increase neighborhood access to capital and technical assistance that can be used for community improvements. These assumptions are based on a belief that neighbor-hood residents are not only alienated from one another, but are also rela-tively isolated from the greater society and have difficulty obtaining financial capital.

The literature on these interrelated theories that guide community development also identifies both advantages and disadvantages of each approach. Warren et al. (2001) argue that while political oppression and social exclusion are legitimate concerns that contribute to the lack of social connection in many communities, the difference between this approach and deficit models is that it is based on the belief that through the collective action of community residents, partnerships can be forged with government agencies and other investors that can be used effectively for community improvement. However, Fraser and Kick (2005) identify a dilemma in the use of this approach: in an era of reduced funding for urban reinvestment and programs to assist low-income people, this model places responsibility for community improve-ments on individuals and families who historically have been excluded from the political process and the market system. Their review of case studies related to community building indicates that often such efforts are either initiated or dominated by government agencies and private enterprises, but can be successful if governance systems are established that ensures a balance of power as well as shared responsibility among participants.

According to James et al. (2001), viewing communities purely in terms of their social capital can be problematic. Communities may contain strong networks that lack some characteristics other than bonds among members such as political power. In addition, some groups of people in these communities may be, due to tradition or social stigma, excluded from these networks. We also know very little about how people view their participation in networks and what membership actual means to them. For example, DeFilippis (2001a) argues that while low-income people lack economic capital, they are not necessarily lacking in the social capital as defined by Putnam (2000): interpersonal relationships, social networks, and trust; they merely lack the ability, in some circumstances, to leverage social capital to obtain financial rewards. Stoecker (2004) expresses concern that aspects of asset-based and social capital approaches focus on self-reliance and place the blame squarely on the backs of disadvantaged groups if they fail to generate the assets needed to improve their communities or find jobs.

COMMUNITY AND ECONOMIC DEVELOPMENT APPROACHES

Community and economic development efforts often focus on a few specific activities designed to improve community relations, the financial well-being of community residents, improvements in housing stocks and affordable housing, job creation and training, strengthening community business and industries, and increasing the availability of credit, mortgages, and investment opportunities (Gittell & Thompson, 2001; Krumholz, Keating, Star, & Chupp, 2006; Littrell & Brooks, 2010). Development and reinvestment programs may be state or federally funded, distributed by state and local governments, and operated through local governments or community organizations. Intermediary organizations such the Local Initiative Support Corporation and the National Reinvestment Corporation are often established in some cities and regions to link local community development organizations with a variety of partner organizations, funding sources and private investors (Garkovich, 2011; Gittell & Vidal, 1998). These nonprofit organizations also provide technical and administrative assistance to local development projects. As noted in Chapter 10, inspired by the research literature that links poor family outcomes to specific neighborhoods, there are also specific foundation or government-funded community change initiatives (CCIs) that focus on improving the quality of life of families and communities in specific "place-based" areas (Coulton, Chan, & Mikelbank, 2011; Petersen, 2002).

Community development efforts may also focus on smaller-scale changes such as initiating health promotion and prevention activities, engaging residents in physical activity, improving recreational facilities, increasing access to nutritious food, encouraging families to accumulate savings; building worker cooperatives, providing financial counseling to families, increasing educational attainment or opportunities, or negotiating community benefit agreements with developers in return for tangible benefits such as jobs or housing (Birkenmaier & Curley, 2009; Majee & Hoyt, 2009; Ohmer, Meadowcraft, Freed, & Lewis, 2009; Parks & Warren, 2009; Shobe & Boyd, 2005; Subban, 2007).

Recently, community development efforts have also included initiatives designed to include principles related to sustainability in development efforts (Portney, 2005). Sustainability is a concept that incorporates a set of principles about how communities should utilize available resources in planning and development efforts. These principles are based on the recognition that many natural resources such as oil and coal or clean air and water may soon be depleted and that concrete steps should be taken to limit their use or to develop new technologies as alternatives to their use. According to Hembd and Silberstein (2011), sustainability practice focuses on what communities explicitly need rather than want. Current needs are to be met in a manner that does not compromise the use of these resources by future generations. Sustainability practice places priority on distributing scarce resources to members of low-income and marginalized communities as well as residents of developing counties. It also recognizes the interconnections between the health, well-being, skills, and capabilities of individuals and the natural environment, physical capital such as housing, roads, public transportation, buildings, and the global economy. Sustainable development practices often incorporate environmental concerns, green technology, and characteristics designed to promote healthy living such as bicycle paths and programs intended to the use of pesticides and other pollutants (Portney, 2005).

Although much community development work is facilitated through government agencies, resident-controlled community development corporations also play a role. Many of these organizations coordinate their efforts with Federal programs, state and local redevelopment agencies, and other community-based organizations (Frisch & Servon, 2006). However, researchers such as Silverman (2003, 2009), have examined decision-making in CDCs and found that legal, jurisdictional, and cooperative relationships with local and state governments often limit the power of local residents to make decisions for their own communities. In addition, the composition of CDC boards often is not representative of community residents in terms of race, gender, and class. Research indicates that participants in community development efforts often have difficulty agreeing on goals due to different perceptions of self-interest influenced by racial identity, ethnicity, and social class; women, people of color, and members of other marginalized groups may also encounter barriers to asset acquisition related to sexism, racism, and classism, when trying to acquire resources from government agencies, banks and other private investors, and foundations (Gittell & Thompson 2001; K. Moore, 2005).

Consequently, concerns about the degree to which CDC and other community development organization boards represent the interests of community members have resulted in increased effort by organization directors and funders to increase community participation (Dorius, 2009). According to Midgley (2005):

> Effective community development involves the creation of an authentic partnership between government and local people and the judicious use of the market to promote sustainable growth. Too often, traditional community development has involved a prescriptive, bureaucratic "top down" process that has stifled local initiative. Community development must institutionalize pluralism and recognize the right of local people to manage their own affairs. (p. 164)

Several specific models of community development practice have been developed to facilitate equal partnerships between community members, government agencies, business interests, and private investors. These models include practice modules consistent with consensus organizing, asset building, social capital formation, capacity development or enhancement, and community building approaches. Saegert (2006) argues that these approaches and traditional types of social action organizing have similar goals: problem resolution, developing common social change objectives, leadership development, and fostering participant commitment to the change effort. However, she differentiates between both types of community organization models. While social action organizing focuses on power and resource differentials, community builders "seek to nurture a broad range of overlapping social networks within which different combinations of individuals and organizations can reach a consensus about the achievement of particular goals" (p. 279).

COMMUNITY DEVELOPMENT MODELS THAT STRENGTHEN
CONNECTIONS AMONG PEOPLE

Community development approaches focus on bringing people in communities together often from diverse ethnic, cultural, and income groups with a variety of interests and needs. Each of these models requires practitioners to identify community issues and needs as well as existing assets and resources. Community groups set goals, develop action plans, implement interventions, and evaluate what they have done (Green & Haines, 2002; Ohmer & DeMasi, 2009). While some community developers may not exclusively use one model or another, there are a number of distinctive approaches identified in the research, training, and practice literature. These approaches roughly correspond to the major concepts identified earlier in this chapter, the asset building approach, social capital development, capacity development, consensus organizing, and community building.

Community Building

The term community building is often used generically to refer to efforts to improve relationships among diverse groups that can be used to facilitate community improvements through consensus and cooperation. Community building may be oriented exclusively for developing a sense of commitment to a community or collective efficacy with a focus on individuals, families, and groups that are typically marginalized or isolated by society such as youth, people with disabilities, or members of the LGBTQ communities (Walter, 2009). Communities can also be established online in chat rooms or live blogs as people exchange ideas and resources (Leung, Lam, Yao, & Chu, 2010). However, building a sense of community is often a necessary first-step in efforts to engage in other activities to improve neighborhood life. As described by Neighborhood Works (2011):

> Community building is a people-focused process that increases the collective capacity of neighborhoods to improve the quality of life for the individuals who live and work in that community. These processes must occur through sustained collaborative efforts involving and engaging stakeholders and be led by the integral participation of residents and the affected constituency. Community building includes incremental and measurable projects, programs, and activities that lead to positive long-term, systemic

change. Successful community building enhances opportunities for the effective and efficient investment of human capital as well as financial resources. (p. 1)

Community building efforts can be used for a wide variety of efforts including neighborhood revitalization, economic development, increasing affordable housing or improving existing homes or apartment buildings, health promotion or prevention activities, or improving access to healthy foods (Messinger, 2004; Petersen, 2002; Singh, 2003). One of the main goals of this approach is to increase connections among community members and decrease feelings of isolation among individuals and families as a means of increasing the health and well-being of community members. In many conceptualizations of the word community building, the term self-help is used. It can be applied to locally initiated improvement projects or well-funded initiatives promoted by government agencies or foundations to "help the community help itself." According to Labonte (2009), external funding often is needed for neighborhood development in marginalized communities. Hence the purpose of such efforts should be not to foster self-help, but community self-reliance, the ability of local residents to negotiate development initiatives, goals, and implementation procedures with external funders and organizations and have a significant amount of decision-making control of each project.

There are more extensive, broad-based approaches to community building as well. Community building as a form of community development practice is often associated with Comprehensive Community Initiative approaches. CCIs focus on asset-enhancement and social capital development and often combine the provision of social services, economic development, and individual, organizational, and capacity enhancement activities to improve social and economic conditions for children and families in low-income communities (Brisson & Roll, 2008; Mulroy & Lauber, 2002). Lisbeth Schorr (1997) describes the rationale for this approach:

It endorses the idea that the multiple and interrelated problems of poor neighborhoods require multiple and interrelated solutions. The new synthesizers are determined to reverse "the economic, social, and political marginalization that has turned the urban poor into an "underclass" and their neighborhoods into "battle zones.". . . . . They insist on combining physical and economic development with service and education reform, and all of these with a commitment to building community institutions and networks. (p. 318)

CCIs typically operate through national intermediary organizations such as and the Annie E. Casey Foundation, the Ford Foundation, and the Local Initiative Support Corporation and partner with CDCs, other local development agencies, and community groups (Brisson & Roll, 2008; Chaskin, 2001; Gittell & Vidal, 1998). They typically receive funding from national foundations as well as local, state, and federally funded redevelopment programs. Both funding and development activities are concentrated on a single neighborhood (Coulton et al., 2011) reducing fragmentation of services and the design of programs to meet local needs). Citizen participation in development consensus-oriented, collaborative decision-making is an essential part of the development process and helps reduce the likelihood that development planning and implementation will solely be the responsibility of outside organizations or funders (Brisson & Roll, 2008; Messinger, 2004). Increasing resident sense of belonging and commitment to the community, strengthening social networks, forming new community organizations, and enhancing the capacity of individuals and local organizations to engage in development activities are also important components of this approach (Gittell & Vidal, 1998; Good Neighbors Initiative, 2007).

Asset Building

Most community building efforts are designed to put the principles associated with the Kretzmann and McKnight (1993) asset building approach into action (Lafferty & Mahoney, 2003). As described in Chapter 6, the assets approach incorporates the principles of self-determination and empowerment as well the strength perspective or the assumption that everyone has a special skill, resource, support network, or is resilient in the face of adversity, and can take proactive steps to make their own lives and their communities better. Hence, this is an approach that focuses on tapping and strengthening the existing capacities of community members to take collective action to improve their neighborhoods (McKnight & Kretzmann, 2009).

Instead of dependency on funds provided by outside agencies and private investors, community members take action to leverage the external resources they feel are needed for neighborhood improvements. In such circumstances, these partnerships are characterized by mutuality and reciprocity rather than dependency on the donor. For example, if the community lacks a full service grocery it can choose a location, find local investors and entrepreneurs, and conduct research to document the potential market value of an untapped customer base. These resources can be used to persuade a national chain to establish a store in the community. In addition to improving the assets of individual residents, McKnight and Block (2010) describe the formation of new organizations or "associations" as one of the most important building blocks that should be used to bring people together for community change. It is through these associations of neighbors that residents come together to plan community development activities, obtain funds from outside the community, and take control of neighborhood improvement efforts.

One asset building approach, not associated with the Kretzmann and McKnight (1993) model, focuses on increasing resident access to credit and financial institutions. Research indicates that low-income people have difficulty obtaining home loans, obtaining credit to start businesses, or even using basic banking services due to check cashing or bank fees or limited information about how such services work (Sherraden, Schreiner, & Beverly, n.d.). One type of financial asset building program, Individual Development Account (IDA), focuses on helping people accumulate personal assets or wealth that can be used to purchase homes, enroll their children in college, or start small businesses. IDA programs are designed to increase access to banking services and the amount of money saved by low-income families as a mechanism for increasing human capital and providing a vehicle that may assist families to move out of poverty (Grinstein-Weiss, Curley, & Charles, 2007). Participants receive financial education and matching funds through government programs when they make a deposit in a savings account. In some IDA programs, access to banking services is increased by locating them in community agencies.

Community development can also include working with banks and even starting new banks or credit unions to ensure they make home loans to community residents or help families complete credit or loan applications (Green & Haines, 2002). In addition, some programs focus on microenterprise projects which are oriented to giving small start-up loans to low-income people who wish to start their own businesses (Schreiner & Woller, 2003). This approach has an obvious link to other forms of asset-based community development in terms of its emphasis on encouraging individuals to identify and develop their own hidden talents and skills that can be applied toward both personal and community transformation.

Social Capital Approaches

This model of social capital development is oriented toward increasing the size and strength of social networks and establishing or strengthening nonprofit organizations and associations that can be used to leverage external resources, develop the capacity to deliver social services, or stimulate community or economic development efforts (Kay, 2006). Therefore, it is often integral part of community building and asset-development endeavors (Mathie & Cunningham, 2003). According to Kubisch et al. (2010):

> Community change efforts seek to build social capital in dis-tressed communities for affective reasons—to ameliorate the corrosive effect that extreme poverty can have on interperso-nal bonds and supports—and for instrumental reasons—to build the civic, economic, and political power of residents for collective action and community improvement. (p. 36)

Generally, social capital approaches can be categorized in terms of whether efforts focus on bonding, bridging, or linking social capital. According to Petersen (2002), bonding social capital among neighbor-hood residents can be categorized as consisting of two types of concrete behaviors as well as a set of attitudes that make it likely that they will engage in these activities:

- *Informal.* The extent to which people talk to or communicate with or provide social support and other types of help to one another.
- *Formal.* Attending meetings or rallies, participating in neighborhood watches, or organizing other types of activities in response to neighborhood needs.

People will not engage in these types of activities unless they have a sense of belonging to or commitment to the neighborhood and are able to trust their neighbors (Green, 2011). Therefore, development efforts may be oriented toward activities that encourage communi-cation, resource exchange, and trust among local residents, strengthen-ing local networks of people and help them to exchange resources such as information, support, material goods, or skills (such as care repair or child care) that increase neighborhood resources and enhance personal feelings of self-worth (Kirst-Ashman & Hull, 2009; Stack, 1974). In addition, local governments can encourage the pro-duction of social capital by designing new housing or commercial developments that contain features such as parks, cul-de-sacs, or other forms of open or semi-public space that encourage social inter-action (Kay, 2006).

    Bridging social capital efforts often entail some of the community dialogue activities described in Chapter 6. According to Green (2011), one role for community developers or organizations facilitating local planning efforts is to ensure that a diverse cross-section of community members is recruited to participate in the process and that meetings are structured in a manner that unite people across common interests and concerns. Bridging social capital can also be created when existing social networks are expanded to include diverse members or people who typically may be excluded in their communities (Gilchrist, 2009). Lopez and Stack (2001) argue that one important task for social network approaches is to provide opportunities for cultural bridging, a process designed to assist "members of a marginalized community [to] overcome social-cultural obstacles" (p. 47).

As described by McKnight and Block (2010), social capital efforts may also focus on the development of formal associations among individuals and social networks, formalizing bridging relationships and permitting participants to establish service delivery structures that can qualify for external funding, but permitting the community to control the decision-making process. Individuals having multiple affiliations with voluntary associations in their communities also help establish bridging relationships that increase the likelihood that these organizations will engage in collaborative efforts (Wollebaek & Selle, 2002). In some instances, social capital formation efforts may involve the provision of resources such as stimulating the growth of new organizations by providing technical assistance with funding proposals, the process of formalizing (called incorporation) of nonprofit organizations for tax purposes, or recruitment and training of new board members.

Linking social capital efforts can involve establishing new intervening organizations or strengthening institutions that focus on linking community residents and existing networks to external organizations, government agencies, or the political process. In addition, intervening or intermediary organizations can act to create collaborative networks that can be used for social service or health care delivery or community development efforts (Cohen, 2001).

Capacity Building

This approach to development focuses on increasing the skills, capabilities, and assets at a number of different systems levels: individuals, families, social networks, local organizations, communities, and intermediary organizations as well as policies and institutional structures that limit the ability of low-income neighborhoods to provide support, care, jobs, education, income, and other opportunities and services for their residents (Kubisch et al., 2002; Saegert, 2006).

According to Chaskin (2001), both a sense of community and commitment to change must be present for communities to engage in capacity building. Social networks and organizational structures are also necessary if people and resources are to be engaged in the process. He identifies four basic strategic approaches associated with increasing community capacity:

- The development of relationships and social networks.
- Leadership development.
- A process in which citizen participation is facilitated.
- Resources that help increase the skills of individuals, the strength of organizations, and the amount of financial capital that can be used for community or economic development.

Specific capacity development activities identified in the community development literature include: job training for community residents, leadership training and development for neighborhood volunteers and other constituents, and technical assistance for local organizations related to board development, fundraising, evaluation, and staff development and training (Kubisch et al., 2002; Sobeck, 2008). Eisinger (2002) defines organizational capacity as characteristics related to whether organizations are able to meet their goals, use external resources and networks effectively, provide services in response to client demand, hire staff with specialized skills, and respond to changes in the external environment such as new technology or funder requirements. Capacity building efforts may also be designed to increase the skills of organization managers and program accountability (Austin, Regan, Samples, Schwartz, & Carnochan, 2011).

According to Kubisch et al. (2010), local organizations must also be able to collect community indicators and engage in social planning if these organizations are to effectively engage in the development process. In addition, Saegert (2006) argues that capacity development should also include increasing the capacity of community residents to engage in community organizing and lobbying public officials in order to increase political power and their ability to obtain funding and make improvements in their communities.

Goals associated with successful capacity building efforts include stronger community networks and organizations, an increase in the ability of neighborhood residents and organizations to problem solve, an increase in the jobs-related and leadership skills of community residents, and the achievement of specific community improvement related outcomes such as the number of housing starts, a reduction in crime, or

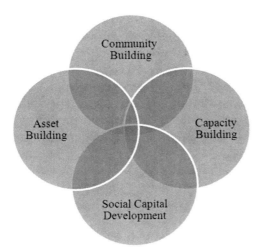

FIGURE 12.1
Interrelationships among community development concepts and theories.

improvements in the health of neighborhood residents (Chaskin, 2001; Lafferty & Mahoney, 2003; Petersen, 2002) (see Figure 12.1).

Delgado's (2000) model of capacity enhancement focuses on fostering the growth of culturally appropriate assets in urban areas and increases in the skills, self-confidence, and empowerment of community residents. Examples of the type of assets produced include community gardens, playgrounds, and art installations such as community sculptures and murals created by community members in response to the preferences and cultural values of residents. He links this model to ecological theory which he describes as the process of identifying interconnected factors that affect human interaction. Specific components of the capacity-enhancement model include:

1. Conduct an asset assessment to identify local resources. The assessment must incorporate local norms and traditions. Residents must be involved in both the assessment and project design phases of the process. However, external resources must also be used to develop the project.
2. Assessment and planning should take place within the context of extensive face-to-face engagement, meetings, and negotiation between the project beneficiaries and the community practitioner assigned to the project.
3. The intervention must correspond to the interests and common needs of project beneficiaries. The people who will benefit from the project

must be involved in providing technical advice and access to many of the resources needed to develop the project. They must also be responsible for carrying it out. For example, if the group is developing a new playground, members could clean the land used, design the playground, contract with local government for the land and equipment, construct the playground, and develop a work plan for maintaining it. The organization that facilitates the project would also play a role, providing supervision, advice, and other resources needed to develop the project.

4. Participants should use a combination of internal (participant) and external (outside evaluator) methods to assess the project. The evaluator should facilitate dialogue among the residents and other participants in order to develop appropriate research questions and methods. However, it is essential that a formal evaluation process be used to examine program impact, process, and outcomes. Data from the project can be used to make decisions about future development efforts and disseminated to other community groups.

Consensus Organizing

This approach to community development has strong links to theories about how social capital is produced, focusing on methods to build both bonding and bridging capital (Beck & Eichler, 2000; Ohmer & DeMasi, 2009). It emphasizes collaborative approaches to community change including instances in which participants have strong views about community improvements and status, income, and ethnic differences that influence their preferences among development options. Consensus organizing first gained prominence when it was used to facilitate resident participation a national community development demonstration project in the 1990s coordinated by an intermediary organization, the Local Initiatives Support Corporation (Gittell & Vidal, 1998). According to Beck and Eischler (2000), there are four basic assumptions inherent in this model:

1. When given reasonable choices, people can act rationally.
2. It is not necessary for power to be redistributed among people with different interests or social status. Instead it can simply be increased.
3. People can make collective decisions based on mutual self-interest.
4. Coalitions and alliances can be developed that consist of people of diverse backgrounds and interests.

According to Ohmer and DeMasi (2009), consensus organizers use collaboration and dialogue to build strong relationships among community residents, business owners, and members of the external power structure that influence what happens in the community. They describe the role of the community developer as a bridge between residents and external resources. Eichler (1998) describes the basic approach used in the consensus organizing process:

> Today's organizer must be seen as a skilled practitioner, a potential asset to everyone in the community wishing to be involved in civic action. Our lines of communication need to be open, and our desire to listen to everyone must be evidenced. This openness will allow us to sort through all the possibilities of partnerships and help create opportunities for future collaboration. In addition, the organizer must build cohesion and trust among all constituents. And, when allegiances are impossible, we should depersonalize our differences, so we can maximize chances for future alliances. (p. 1)

Many of the skills used in consensus organizing are similar to or the same as those used in other types of community practice: conducting assessments, engaging participants through one-on-one interviews, building relationships with potential community partners, facilitating group dialogues that bring people with different interests together, planning and conducting interventions, and evaluating outcomes (Ohmer & DeMasi, 2009). As with the capacity-enhancement model, community members work collectively to complete small projects, building skills and confidence. The central difference between this approach and social action lies in its central premise that power holders should be regarded as allies of members of marginalized groups and that all the parties involved should be able to identify mutual interests and engage in cooperative strategies for community improvements.

INTERPERSONAL SKILLS FOR STRENGTHENING COMMUNITY CONNECTIONS

Many of the models described above tend to correspond with top-down approaches to development. However, community development often is conducted in the context of people simply coming together to improve their communities. Regardless of the approach, interpersonal skills are critical for creating strong bonds among community residents and between local groups and external organizations. Although some of these methods have been described in Chapters 3 through 6 such as community dialogue, coalition-building, conflict resolution techniques, participatory action research, and Photovoice projects, community development practitioners describe additional techniques for building social capital in community development projects. These activities include interpersonal skills for fostering strong relationships among neighborhood residents, strengthening social networks and community participation in decision-making, and building linkages between individuals and organizations.

Building Strong Relationship Bonds Among Individuals

One of the basic premises of community development work prior to the relatively recent emphasis on asset and social capital development is simply that in some communities people simply do not know one another, do not have opportunities to meet one another or to act collectively, are not aware of services, policies, or their rights under the law, or believe that social and economic conditions can be changed for the better. In many cases, community members do not trust one another, or people they do not know (Pyles & Cross, 2008). Rubin (2000) describes the purpose of community development as empowering people and creating a sense that individuals who experience hardship are not alone and that with collective action there is hope that things can change for the better. Therefore, at a basic level, community development work can be oriented toward creating opportunities for people to get to know one another. This can include introducing people to others with similar interests, providing or developing free "space" such as a room in a recreation center or a church that can be used for neighborhood activities, sponsoring events such as street fairs or cultural nights, or making efforts to develop neighborhood parks and playgrounds (Delgado, 2000; Gilchrist, 2009). Another technique that can be used to facilitate resident-controlled community development is by sponsoring or providing support to neighborhood self-help or mutual aid groups, providing a time, location, supportive resources (such as food or child care), and information about a specific issue that makes it feasible for community members to engage in group organization and self-help advocacy to address a local issue that affects them all (Green, 2011; Gutierrez et al., 1998; Miley et al., 2011).

McKnight and Block (2010) describe an approach to facilitate connections among individuals that relies on community volunteers that have a gift for bringing people together and identifying individual capabilities that can be used for the organizing process. Characteristics of "connectors" include:

- They are not leaders, but rather function as hosts, issuing invitations to others to participate.
- They are trusted members of the community.
- They have numerous connections to other people and organizations in the community.
- They are able to identify gifts and skills possessed by others and link people to specific activities or roles in which they can use these skills.
- They are capable of reaching out to people or groups that are often isolated or excluded from community life.

The social work profession often refers to these connectors as natural helpers, assisting people in their communities who need information and support (Miley et al., 2011).

Strengthening Social Networks and Community Participation in Decision-Making

According to Brisson and Roll (2008), community development practice is based on the assumption that resident participation in neighborhood development can be used to increase community capacity for change and to develop additional activities to bring people together. This in turn leads to improved outcomes for individuals and the neighborhoods in which they live. Consequently, both strengthening social networks and facilitating participation in decision-making are essential components of the development process.

Gilchrist (2009) describes professional community development practice as a process that involves assisting individuals "in making strategic and opportune connections that create and maintain collective forms of organization" (p. 137). People can be encouraged to participate in ongoing activities in which their time, resources, and talents can be used for community improvement work such as community-wide clean-up days, neighborhood watches, or participation in child care cooperatives. Often these efforts recruit from or build upon existing networks. In addition, community leadership structures, especially in ethnic communities may contain opportunities for community developers to reach out to people who are already tied in to numerous networks such as clan leaders in Southeast Asian communities or church leaders in African-American neighborhoods (Grigg-Saito, Och, Liang, Toof, & Silka, 2008; Wallace, 2004). Generally, as in other types of organizing participation in successful efforts, especially in situations that require hard work over time or that encounter many obstacles, group solidarity, collective identity, and commitment are developed. People also learn to trust one another. Dialogue as well as resource and information sharing occur in the context of network building, establishing common bonds and trusting relationships (Gilchrist, 2009).

In addition to developing networks, high levels of participation is critical for ensuring that residents have a voice in development efforts is not subservient to agendas set by funders, government agencies, or private investors who are also likely to benefit and profit from the development effort (Rubin, 2000). As in other types of participatory efforts, there are a range of decision-making structures that facilitate participation ranging from local meetings of development groups, planning workshops, and formal positions on the boards of local organizations, local development oversight committees, or intermediary institutions. In addition, many development efforts are purely locally controlled and facilitated such as local business councils, churches, or neighbors who come together to clean up their block or organize to improve local educational opportunities for their children. Green and Haines (2002) suggest that initiating resident input in development efforts can be as simple as facilitating a workshop in which participants are asked to respond to three simple questions:

1. What do people want to preserve in the community?
2. What do people want to create in the community?
3. What do people want to change in the community? (p. 47)

However, beyond general guidelines about how to facilitate participant engagement in development, the practice literature on "doing community building" or "strengthening community networks" is very limited. A number of research studies have documented the observations of community development specialists about what they do. For example, Dorius (2009) interviewed directors of CDCs to find out how they approached their work. A number of common themes related to activities carried out in these organizations were identified:

- The directors perceived their primary role as bringing people together.
- The approach they used to do this was communicating with constituents and facilitating decision-making processes in a manner that conveyed dignity and respect.
- They used educational approaches to help individuals to overcome self-perceptions of failure and institutional barriers to success and develop self-confidence and skills.
- They helped constituency group members to develop common goals and create a vision for community change.

* They engaged in activities that helped individuals, families, and the community as a whole gain economic self-sufficiency.

A similar study conducted by Carr (2009) included interviews with administrators of seven organizations involved in community development work in a small city. None of these organizations were CDCs, five were faith-based. These respondents viewed community development efforts undertaken by their organizations as oriented toward strengthening relationships among community residents and organizations, creating a sense of community among participants and developing working partnerships with other organizations that increased their ability to provide concrete services to individuals and families. They assisted residents in the development of leadership and other skills and educated both local residents and the general public about social conditions and their impact on the community. These administrators also engaged in efforts to inform more affluent citizens and organizations about poverty and its effects and solicited their assistance in developing intervention for improving the neighborhoods served by the community development organization.

Strengthening Relationships Between People and Organizations

Most community development efforts rely on decision-making processes that are collaborative and consensus oriented. However, as noted by Chaskin (2001):

> Communities are not uniform collectivities. They contain people, organizations, relationships, and interests that may or may not converge around a given issue at a given time . . . . the problem of creating and acting on community consensus is often made more difficult by the breadth of the agenda, the ambiguity of roles and expectations among various actors, and the tension that arises from the conflict between the cost and the incentives for participating in the proposed action. (p. 316)

This analysis suggests a number of consensus-building strategies including limiting the initial scope of community development efforts, building on small successes overtime, negotiating specific roles and responsibilities within the group context, allowing for flexibility and change as the process evolves. As with other types of organizing and planning efforts, low-income residents need supportive services to sustain participation including meals, transportation, and child care.

The number and length of meetings should be regulated to permit involvement by people with busy and complicated lives. Meetings, events, and other practices and policies associated with the development effort should respect and incorporate cultural practices and provide mechanisms for translation during meetings or issuing documents in languages other than English. In addition, resident concerns about what individuals and groups should and do represent the community should be addressed by making the process as inclusive as possible and setting up resident councils or other participatory structures (Gittell & Vidal, 1998; Hunt, 2007).

In addition, community residents should have roles that move beyond passive participation in meetings. According to Gilchrist (2009), community volunteers who serve as "connectors" or who excel at linking people up across systems can also function in this capacity to link community residents to organizations both in and outside the community. Such connections create a community that is resilient enough to engage in community improvement activities and to adapt to changes in the external environment including economic downturns, resident mobility, and changes in laws and social policies. Community control over the process of development and at minimum, a place at the bargaining table for community members in talks with government agencies or private developers, is generally regarded by most community development specialists as essential for ensuring that community revitalization projects reflect community interests and prevent negative impacts such as the displacement of low-income residents and communities of color and higher housing prices (Kubisch et al., 2002; Saegert, 2006; Silverman, 2004; Stoecker, 2004; Wyly & Hammel, 2004).

Labonte (2009) offers some guidelines for creating equal partnerships between community residents and outside development groups:

- All groups that participate in the development process should have their own sources of community legitimacy and power.
- Each community group should have constituents in the neighborhood to which they are accountable. Constituency group members should be able to provide a source of power and support that can be used advocate for neighborhood preferences.
- All partner groups should have clearly defined mission statements and goals.
- All partner groups should commit to at least one primary goal that they all share. This may require a commitment to a long process for developing a shared agenda.

- External partners should be committed to working cooperatively with community groups.
- The various organizations and groups involved should identify common objectives and roles for the members of the partnership and community workers. Community development workers should not be expected to simply push the agendas of external organizations.
- There should be a written partnership agreement and an evaluation mechanism.
- All partners should be committed to the principles of diversity and respect for all participants.

In addition to these principles, capacity, asset, and social capital building approaches should make efforts to integrate cultural values and traditions into community building efforts (Satterwhite & Teng, 2007). According to Chino and DeBruyn (2006), culturally competent practice models "work from the 'ground up,' reversing the top-down application of Western science to classic [community development] that too often results in programs that are 'outside-in' and 'community placed' rather than community based" (p. 12).

PUTTING VALUES IN ACTION: BUILDING ON STRENGTHS

One small-scale approach to community development has gained a great deal of attention for its potential to create strong bonds among community members and contribute to improved nutrition and health among community residents (Delgado, 2000). Community gardens are suitable for multisystems interventions that increase the residents' sense of community and community capacity, assets, and social capital (Draper & Freedman, 2010). In this section of the chapter, the use of community gardens for community development will be examined using the community capacity framework in Figure 12.2. This intervention model is also consistent with the strengths perspective, an approach to social work and community practice that is intended to increase a constituent's "sense of competence, hope for the future, and motivation for change" (Miley et al., 2011, p. 211). In the community context, feelings of self-competency and empowerment are essential for the development of collective self-efficacy, the belief that adverse situations can be reversed if people, bonding and working together, take action (Rubin & Rubin, 2008).

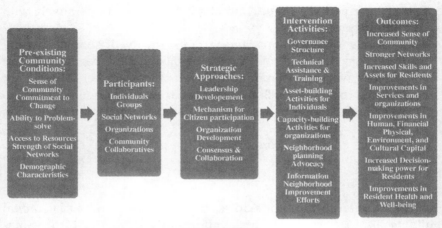

FIGURE 12.2
Theoretical assumptions about capacity building approaches.

Pre-existing Community Conditions

Community gardens are publically owned and operated, provide access to community residents, and involve some type of democratic decision-making process that is inclusive of neighborhood residents (Draper & Freedman, 2010). They have been identified in the public health and community organizing literature as an appropriate intervention for dealing with four primary issues:

- Poor health outcomes among community members, including high rates of obesity and diabetes among poor children and families.
- Limited community resources or capacity that can be used to provide healthy and nutritious food for low-income families. Many neighborhoods in marginalized communities do not have full service grocery stores. Fruits and vegetables are often expensive and seldom organic. For some ethnic populations, food resources may be available. However, these choices may not be culturally appropriate (e.g., local food pantries may not be able to distribute such products as rice or corn meal to Southeast Asian and Latino families (Armstrong, 2000; aldivar-Tanaka & Krasny; 2003: Twiss, Duma, Kleinman, Paulsen, & Rivera, 2003).
- The lack of bonding social capital, including social networks, local clubs or associations, or nonprofit organizations that can be counted on to bring people together to address social problems. The use of small-scale projects to bring neighbors together has traditionally

been used as a community intervention to reduce feelings of alienation and improve psychological well-being (Armstrong, 2000).

- Community gardens provide a vehicle for applying the principle of sustainability, minimizing resident use of assets (such as pesticides or food purchased from national chains and originating in factory farms) that may harm the environment. The use of sustainable methods may be useful as a recruiting tool to foster participation among young people or more affluent residents committed to environmental activism and consequently creating bridging social capital (Holland, 2004; Twiss et al., 2003).

Participants

The community garden approach is a method that can be implemented by a group of neighbors, facilitated by neighborhood organizations and churches, or coordinated with assistance from local government, foundation grants, or regional or national technical assistance organizations. Often community gardens are established as collaborative partnerships among a number of public agencies, nonprofit organizations, and local groups (Twiss et al., 2003; Ohmer et al., 2009). The intervention can be developed with minimal resources other than land, water, equipment and seeds, but small grants and in-kind donations from individuals and businesses may be solicited in order to obtain these resources. However, obtaining a source of water or having an analysis of soil quality conducted may require negotiations with city agencies or working with an intermediary organization. External organizations may provide staff members to coordinate the project or offer technical assistance workshops (Armstrong, 2000).

Strategic Approaches

The primary goals of most community gardens is to improve the health and well-being of community residents by providing a source of healthy, nutritious food and increasing feelings of empowerment of community residents through self-help activities. Gardens incorporate basic community development principles such as leadership development, citizen participation, and consensus and collaboration within the group and external agency partners (Draper & Freedman, 2010; Ohmer et al., 2009; Saldivar-Tanaka & Krasny, 2004). Although "outside" resources may be used, community gardens are essentially a "bottom up" approach to community development in which local residents act together to utilize available resources (such as land or "expert" gardeners) to improve their lives and the community (Holland, 2004). Gardens can also provide an opportunity to turn a community problem (such as vacant lots in which garbage and other debris are dumped or in which gang members conduct drug deals) into a community asset (Holland, 2004; Saldivar-Tanaka & Krasny, 2004). According to Schukoske (2000), up to 20% of all land in urban areas is vacant, posing a serious threat to the health and safety of residents, and reducing social capital by limiting interaction of local residents in open, public spaces in their communities. Another reason that a community garden may be an appropriate intervention method in ethnic communities is that it provides an opportunity for immigrants who formerly made a living from agriculture to carry out family and cultural traditions and obtain food that is familiar, healthy, and culturally appropriate (Twiss et al., 2003).

Intervention Activities

In addition to planting a community garden, other actions are required to conduct the intervention, which in turn lead to outcomes other than simply starting a garden or harvesting healthy food. For example, planning the garden, soliciting volunteers and resources, and performing basic gardening activities (planting, maintaining, and harvesting) require forming an organization, assigning roles and responsibilities, and motivating volunteers to complete their work. Therefore, it also increases individual capacity, including the acquisition of leadership skills, the ability to train and mentor volunteers, and the development of culturally appropriate communication and dissemination tools such as newsletters and web pages. Participants also engage in other basic community organizing tasks such as group dialogue, project implementation, media and public relations, and evaluation (Twiss et al., 2003).

Community gardens face several types of obstacles or outright barriers to success including vandalism or difficulties obtaining access to land (such as vacant lots), or city zoning requirements that require members of the group to take collective action to preserve the garden (Armstrong, 2000; Draper & Freedman, 2010). In some cases, land used without authorization or for a minimal city fee, may be subject to confiscation by the city for redevelopment purposes (Schukoske, 2000). The need for a group response to such outside threats can serve as a vehicle for capacity development (such as the use of group advocacy or organizing techniques, lobbying, research, and media relations), and the development of solidarity and stronger bonds among volunteers and their supporters.

Outcomes

Community gardens have the potential to produce numerous outcomes on multiple system levels. In addition to supplying residents with healthy food at no or low cost, and increasing physical activity, they help to create or strengthen community networks and improve individual skills as well as organization, and community capacity (Draper & Freedman, 2010). Gardens can also improve the appearance of the community, increase the likelihood that neighbors will maintain the surrounding area and engage in other beautification efforts, and provide residents with a place to meet and visit with one another. The garden is also a setting in which cultural events can occur, creating bridging social capital. Consequently, they also provide an open space in which social networks and resource or information exchanges can be facilitated and future organizing efforts can occur (Armstrong, 2000; Saldivar-Tanaka & Krasny, 2004). Some research studies on community gardens report that residents perceive the gardens to have reduced crime in the neighborhood, contributing to improvements in their sense of personal safety (Draper & Freedman, 2010). In addition, gardens have been found to contribute to the development of individual and collective feelings of a sense of community, trust among participants, and feelings of personal empowerment (Holland, 2004; Ohmer et al., 2009).

SUMMARY

Community development efforts focus on building a sense of community, connectedness, and trust among community members. While this approach is considered as one of the first steps in community practice, it is also necessary if explicit efforts are to be made to make material improvements in community conditions. Community development practice since the 1990s has been guided by theories about sense of community, capacity building, and asset and social capital development. Practice models which are derived from these theories incorporate strategies and tactical methods that require consensus-building and collaboration among different groups of community stakeholders, both the powerful and powerless. In addition to the consensus organizing approach, community development practice is oriented toward building strong relationships among individuals and groups and improving individual, network, and organizational capacity to develop assets, skills, and acquire financial capital. It also focuses on improving the community's access to jobs as well as human, physical, environmental, and cultural capital. Social workers and community organizations can use collaborative methods to link people, networks, groups, and organizations via group dialogue in order to facilitate community development initiatives. As in other types of social work and community practice, organizers often need the support of supervisors in carrying out assessments, interventions, and evaluations. In Chapter 13, supervision processes for organizers are described.

1. In class, divide the class into two teams in order to debate a community development-related issue. Conduct research on this topic prior to the day the debate is scheduled: The debate question is: Should community or economic development efforts originate inside or outside of the community? What are the pros and cons of each approach?
2. Observe and participate in a local community volunteer effort oriented toward neighborhood improvement, for example, a neighborhood clean-up, park maintenance, planting or maintaining a community garden, setting up a fundraising event, painting a mural, or neighborhood beautification. If you have the opportunity to do so, interview two or three volunteers and at least one of the project coordinators. Write a three-page paper that describes the project in terms of the problem to be addressed, goals, project activities, volunteer roles, and accomplishments. Were goals obtained? What motivated people to participate? How effective was the effort in terms of volunteer recruitment, volunteer engagement in activities necessary for goal achievement, and the sense of community or commitment displayed by the volunteers?
3. Recruit at least 5–10 volunteers for a specific community project and conduct the activity. Make sure that volunteers have a primary role in planning and conducting the event. Write a five-page paper that evaluates the process and outcome of this activity using the concepts presented in this chapter such as sense of community, capacity building, asset-development, and social capital enhancement.
4. Conduct informal interviews to identify members of at least one community network. The network should either link community residents, residents to organizations, or foster connections and joint projects in the community. Determine network membership, the number of people or organizations in the network, the type of help or assets exchanged, and the capacity of the network to encourage specific community improvements or resource attainment.

5. Conduct research on at least one community or economic development project in your neighborhood funded with grants or contracts from community agencies, institutions, private investors, or external grants and contracts. Use a combination of sources to write a historical account of the project: observation, interviews, newspaper and other media accounts, reports, and any other publically accessible documents that you can obtain. Describe the problem or issue addressed, goals, participants, intervention activities, and how the project was evaluated. In your judgment, was the project a success? What groups benefited from the project? Did some groups benefit more than others? Why? How did the various groups perceive the outcome?

13

Supervision

As an organizer it [the consequences of a bad decision] makes you look bad . . . .
It makes that organization look bad. It kind of puts you and the organization in
a bad light. And it kind of hinders that relationship or that trust that lead up to
that tactic or decision
—Interview with an education organizer, Hardina et al., 2011

In this chapter, staff supervision is defined and models of supervision for community practice in field internships, organizations, and campaigns are examined that include the development of work plans for organizing staff and the use of the supervisory process to analyze the worker's performance as well as organizational and community dynamics. Specific supervisory skills for community practice are described including the development of self-awareness and cultural competency, verbal and written communication, engagement and dialogue skills, and the ability to facilitate constituent self-determination and empowerment. In addition, supervisory skills for helping interns or staff members develop group work skills for problem identification and assessment, making ethical decisions, planning campaigns and taking action, and evaluation are described. In the final section of this chapter, supervision as a parallel process in which supervisors serve as role models and help organizers develop the skills needed to empower constituents and, in turn, are empowered themselves, is discussed.

DEFINING STAFF SUPERVISION

Supervision for community organizers is often a neglected component of macro practice. Often when social workers discuss supervision, the context involves the provision of micro or clinical interventions in which the worker and supervisor discuss the worker's options for engagement, assessment, intervention, and evaluation of practice with individuals, a family, or a group of clients as well as psychological factors (either the client's or the worker's) that may enhance or block change or affect the social worker's ability to engage with the client (McTighe, 2011). However, in most organization settings supervision also refers to monitoring, controlling, and evaluating the employee's work performance and taking appropriate actions to hire, train, sanction, reward, or terminate individual staff members (Hardina et al., 2006; Kadushin, 2002; Kirst-Ashman & Hull, 2009). It also refers to the process of professional development in which the worker's strengths, skills, and knowledge, are enhanced in order to strengthen the organization's resources and the worker's own abilities and career options (Tsui, 2005). Kramer Tebes et al. (2011) provide a definition of social work supervision that incorporates activities associated with clinical supervision and the more generic set of skills necessary to ensure accountability to the organization. Supervision is: "a supportive professional relationship in which one individual has responsibility for and authority over the work and work life of another" (p. 190). However, this description of supervision as a manifestation of power and authority may be at odds with basic social work and community organization principles that focus on establishing mutual partnerships and respectful relationships among organization participants (English, 2005; Kadushin, 2002).

Not much is known about how organizers obtain supervisory positions (Bobo et al., 2010). In some instances, community organizations may simply assign their most experienced staff member to a supervisory position and hope that the individual they appoint has the practice wisdom, patience, and background to provide guidance to others. According to Traynor (2002), organization investment in staff supervision and training is critical for two reasons: (1) turnover among organizers is often high due to burnout and feelings of isolation in the organization, (2) organizing tasks completed improperly such as constituent recruitment or forming alliances with other organizations may require hours of valuable staff time to repair. Consequently, money spent on creating staff supervisory structures or training staff is often money well spent.

New organizers may have the good fortune obtaining appropriate support from their peers or colleagues or benefit from structured training and workshops available through training academies or consortiums. However, such resources are not always available, making skill acquisition sporadic and random. According to Bobo et al. (2010), good supervision is essential because:

> It is the best kind of training that is available to organizers, helping them be strategic and thoughtful about their work

on a regular basis, forcing them to prioritize, to evaluate and learn from their mistakes, to see how their work fits into the bigger picture of the organization (p. 308).

MODELS OF SUPERVISION FOR COMMUNITY PRACTICE

For supervision to be effective it should be incorporated into an organization's administrative decision-making structure and be part of the ongoing plan to develop staff resources (Kadushin, 2002). While social work supervision focuses on integration of skills, values, and knowledge, supervision of community practice employees also focuses on verifying accountability to the organization, donors, and constituents. While there are some similarities in how interns and employees are trained, there are also differences in terms of how work performance is monitored and assessed. While social work education examines student acquisition of skills and competencies, community organizations often create explicit work plans that identify specific day-to-day activities that must be accomplished. In both approaches, ongoing dialogue takes place between the supervisor and worker to help the new organizer engage in self-reflection to analyze work performance and examine community and organizational processes.

Differences in Supervision by Settings: Comparing and Contrasting Field Instruction, Organization Settings, and Campaigns

Supervision and social work instruction in schools of social work for community practice can range from structured learning experiences in the classroom, service learning opportunities, which are connected to course or curriculum requirements, and field internships that either incorporate specific macro assignments or that focus on the students' acquisition of advanced skills required for a specific practice concentration (Gamble, 2011; Johnson, 2000; Plitt Donaldson & Daughtery, 2011; Salcido, Ornelas, & Lee, 2002). In some cases, the acquisition of community practice knowledge involves explicit research or advocacy assignments that provide opportunities for experiential learning (Danis, 2007; Heidmann, Fertig, Jansson, & Kim, 2011; Timm, Birkenmaier, & Tebb, 2011). While much of the literature on the use of experiential methods indicates that they are often successful in helping students acquire macro skills, not much is known about the consistent implementation of these methods, the skills students typically develop, or how they actually acquire these skills (Wilson, 2011).

Changes in Council on Social Work Education curriculum policies, implemented in 2008, require that programs assess whether students have developed specific social work related skills or competencies. CSWE defines competencies as specific outcomes that should be produced as a consequence of students gaining knowledge, skills, and values in field internships and the classroom (Wayne, Bogo, & Raskin, 2010). However, the CSWE Education Policy and Education Standards (2008) designated the field practicum as the best setting in which this integration should occur. CSWE describes competency-based field instruction as the *signature pedagogy* for social work programs, a unique method through which members of the profession gain instruction about practice norms and roles (Wayne et al., 2010). As part of the accreditation process, schools of social work collect evaluation data that verify if students have actually acquired these competencies. Typically, the student's performance in field practicum is evaluated using a standard list of skills or competencies that the student is expected to acquire in the internship. Field instructors are responsible for assigning these competency ratings and in some circumstances ratings may be developed through ongoing dialogue with the intern and representatives (field liaisons) from the social work program.

In contrast to social work field instruction, supervisory procedures for new organizers provide training, but are also likely to focus on ensuring that employees perform daily tasks that are essential to the organization's mission or ongoing campaigns or projects. Many of those who engage in organizing careers are not social workers; they may be graduates of other types of professional programs with content on community organizing, planning, or development (e.g., public health or urban planning) or former activists who must be trained when they enter the profession (Staples, 2009). Consequently, some community organizations and stand-alone training programs have developed explicit standards and expectations for core skills that they expect to see in new organizers (Bobo et al., 2010). The types of skills often taught in these programs include: interviewing, relationship-building, recruitment, coalition-building, and working with groups to identify common problems, assess what is happening in the community, examine power dynamics, plan campaigns, take action, and evaluate them (Alliance for Justice, 2010; Marin Institute, n.d.; Schutz & Sandy, 2011; Sen, 2003; Whitcher et al., 2009–2010).

The Midwest Academy is one of the few organizing training academies in the United States that actually offers curriculum and training manuals on supervision. They offer guidance on supervising staff that is fairly consistent with other types of nonprofit sector employment, but note that organizing work has some distinct differences from other types of employment (Bobo et al., 2010). For example, ideology and values are often more important in motivating staff than money and other employment-related benefits. In addition, the work environment changes constantly, requiring that organizers be flexible, creative, and able to respond to situational demands (Schutz & Sandy, 2011). Bobo et al. (2010) identify three primary supervisory concerns:

* Supervising campaigns, events, or activities.
* Supervising the professional and leadership development of staff.
* Building the organization, including tasks such as recruiting new members, accomplishing goals, gaining public legitimacy and support, raising funds, and training volunteers and board members for leadership roles.

In order to facilitate skill development, community organizations also provide orientations for new employees, make arrangements for new hires to be mentored by experienced colleagues, and seek out opportunities for workers to be explicitly trained in skill development and specialized knowledge (such as laws and social policies) through workshops and conferences sponsored by training institutes or advocacy organizations.

The other context in which organizers may work is in political or legislative campaigns. Legislative campaigns are likely to be housed within a coalition or organization and unless the organization structure is very temporary and transitory, supervision is likely to resemble that of a typical community organization with specific expectations and work plans for organizers and documentation of accomplishments. For example, staff hired to obtain signatures on petitions, register voters, or advocacy campaigns will be organized into teams and be required to achieve specific objectives (Kerns, n.d.).

The management structure of political campaigns will differ from other types of community-based or advocacy organizations, characterized by shorter time lines, larger stakes, and situational demands that require flexibility on the part of staff and managers. They are also more likely to have centralized decision-making structures that involve limited direct input into goals or strategies on the part of staff members who are not managers. The reliance on campaign volunteers often requires that a high degree of the staff member's time commitment will involve ensuring that constituents participate in the right activities, at the right time, and the right place. Consequently, these complex types of activities are often difficult to control, manage, or supervise (E-politics, 2009; Stirland, 2008). With innovations in technology, centralized management with uniform procedures and scripts for organizers and volunteers to use when contacting voters is more feasible. However, the use of cell phones and online data banks permit much of the campaign work to be conducted outside the campaign office, making some types of direct oversight of volunteers and staff impossible, but also allowing for micro-targeting of various types of voters and rapid responses to situational demands (Organizing for America, 2008; Schlough, Koster, Barr, & Davis, 2011). However, as with other types of organizing work, paid staff (as well as teams of volunteers) may be asked to comply with specific expectations for task completion (e.g., number of phone calls, number of one-on-one interviews, number of volunteers recruited, or the amount of money raised).

Fulfilling Funder Expectations and Meeting Organizational Demands: Designing Work Plans

Employer expectations are only one set of criteria that are used to develop job descriptions. As noted in Chapter 10, foundations, individual donors, and the government agencies that sometimes fund community projects also want ongoing documentation of what the organization has accomplished in terms of the goals, objectives, activities, and time-lines in funding proposals and the strategy charts used to guide campaigns. In most instances, the organization will need to provide this information at regular intervals during the course of an organizing campaign or project. One way to ensure that this can be accomplished and that individual organizers are held accountable to donors is to provide them with an explicit work plan, derived from the list of objectives and activities submitted to donors, that specifies exactly what they are expected to accomplish (Bobo et al., 2010).

For most organizations, the overall work plan should have its origins in the strategy chart developed by constituency group members. The work plan for an individual staff member should represent a percentage of the overall work to be conducted to reach specific goals and objectives for the organization or in conjunction with a specific campaign. For example, if the organization has indicated that it expects to recruit 100 new members and form 20 block clubs during the next 6 months, then the individual organizer's work plan will specify how much of this plan is to be one's responsibility (see Table 13.1). It is important that these work plan specific time-lines for task accomplishment. It is also critical that work plans take shape in the context of dialogue between the supervisor and the worker and that specific activities can be used to complete each task (Indianapolis Neighborhood Resource Center, n.d.). For example, does the worker have a specific skill that

TABLE 13.1
Sample Work Plan for an Organizing Campaign: Alicia's Work Plan for Environmental Organizing Campaign

Campaign Goals	Campaign Objectives	Alicia's Objectives	Alicia's Activities	Completion Date
Increase public support for antipollution efforts.	Recruit 100 local volunteers for outreach and publicity efforts to raise awareness about the harmful effects of pollution.	Recruit a minimum of 25 local volunteers for an antipollution campaign.	Conduct a minimum of 50 one-on-one interviews with local residentsConduct at least five focus group meetings to determine how local residents perceive the effects of pollution on their livesConduct a minimum of two press conferences to publicize the impact of pollution on the lives of local residents.	June 30, 2013
Reduce local sources of pollution.	Obtain commitments from at least 15 local officials to increase city and state regulation of pollution.	Obtain commitments from at least 8 public officials to work toward increased regulation of pollution.	Coordinate at least 20 lobbying visits to public officials with local volunteersDevelop a policy brief that can be distributed to local officials and other lobbying material.Testify at five public hearings on the negative effects of pollution.	September 30, 2013

can be used to accomplish a task (e.g., knowledge of web page construction or artistic ability) or have pre-existing relationships with constituents or community leaders that can be used for recruiting purposes?

It is also essential for supervisors to follow up on task accomplishment with new hires and provide feedback, support, and skill assessments. While some of the skills used are similar to those used in leadership development with volunteers (such as motivation techniques and praise for work well done), it is important for community organizations to have an explicit system for monitoring work performance (Larson, Day, Springer, Clark, & Vogel, 2003; Perlmutter, Bailey, & Netting, 2001). Specific methods that can be used to structure supervision for organizers include:

* Requiring organizers to report to the supervisor on a regular basis.
* Requiring both individual and written reports.
* Requesting that additional documentation should be provided to illustrate worker activities and skills such as meeting minutes or notes from one-on-one interviews.
* Scheduling staff meetings and retreats that permit analysis of organizing efforts, help motivate staff, and create an atmosphere in which team work is fostered and encouraged.
* Setting clear performance standards for the organizer and periodic, regularly scheduled performance evaluations (Bobo et al., 2010).

Supervision as Praxis

Supervisory sessions in social work internships as well as for employees in community-based organizations also should include ongoing dialogue between the worker and supervisor in terms of how task accomplishment could be improved and what interpersonal skills are necessary to do the job (Burghardt, 2011). As noted in Chapter 9, supervision often requires engagement in reflective practice. The supervisor must assist the staff member in developing appropriate methods for conducting their own analysis of their practice skills, knowledge, and values. Ben Asher (2010) identifies four basic skills that are essential for this process. The supervisor must be able to build a strong relationship with the staff member, provide direct support consisting of both psychological and material resources to aid in task accomplishment, accurately assess the worker's strengths and weaknesses, challenge the worker to take risks, and following up appropriately in response to whether or not the task has been accomplished successfully. This may mean working with the staff member to find ways of improving task accomplishment in the future or to build on successful completion of the task by tackling another challenge. Generally, supervision in this context may bear some passing similarities to social work supervision in that the supervisor poses a series of questions that require the organizer to engage in critical self-reflection and analysis (Tsui, 2005).

In addition to helping staff members engage in reflective practice, the supervisor must also engage in personal self-reflection in order to examine difficulties in motivating staff or managing their work effort. Bobo et al. (2010) identify several questions that supervisors must ask themselves about their performance.

- Do I actually supervise this person (i.e., can I hire, fire, or hold them accountable)? If not, what options do I have in terms of motivating them to do specific tasks?
- Do I assigned tasks in an appropriate manner and provide reasonable deadlines that are enforced?
- Do I communicate how specific tasks fit within long-term campaign or organizational goals?
- Do I encourage staff creativity, strengths, team work and professional development?
- Do I provide clear directions in terms of what decisions can be made at the discretion of the organizer and what decisions must be approved by or made by the organization?
- Do I give staff members praise when it is warranted and criticism when it is deserved?
- Do I treat all workers equally and fairly?
- Do I make decisions or meet with staff in a timely manner?
- Do I refuse to delegate work to staff, delegate too much, or micro manage how the work is completed?

Although it is not included on the Bobo et al. (2010) list, several difficulties that social workers in supervisory positions often face in relation to staff management include completing work assignments by oneself if staff or volunteers cannot be motivated to do so or becoming reluctant to criticize or sanction staff members who fail to perform as expected.

SPECIFIC SUPERVISORY SKILLS FOR COMMUNITY PRACTICE IN SOCIAL WORK

Although there are similarities in the types of interpersonal and analytical skills that community organizers, developers, and planners use, regardless of model of practice, preparing social work students for these types of positions also involves the incorporation of basic social work knowledge, skills, and values into the supervision process (Tsui, 2005). As described in Chapter 1, Hardina and Obel-Jorgensen (2009) have identified a number of interrelated skills areas in which social work instruction and supervision should be provided in both field settings and paid employment that include self-awareness and cultural competency, using verbal and written communication, engagement and dialogue skills, the ability to facilitate constituent self-determination and empowerment, and group methods for problem identification and assessment, helping constituents weigh ethical options for the use of strategies and tactics, planning tactics and taking action, and conducting evaluations.

Supervision for Developing Self-Awareness and Cultural Competency

As noted earlier in this text, self-awareness and cultural competency require that the organizer become familiar with the community, the history and values of community members, understand power relations and how community residents are affected by them, and the power resources and strengths that can be used to address community challenges and concerns. Community practitioners must also become self-aware about how their own histories, social status, and values shape their ability to identify with and establish relationships with community members (Burghardt, 2011). The supervisor also is obligated to assist the new organizer in the development of *cultural humility*, the willingness to abandon self-conceptions about possessing expert knowledge or power over others, learn about the traditions and values of members of other cultures, demographic groups, and communities, understand the sources and impact of institutional oppression, and become an active ally of the community in fighting against oppression and discrimination (Abrams & Moio, 2009; Ross, 2010).

The supervisor's role in this process is to help the new practitioner examine one's experiences and reactions to the community and provide information and referrals that facilitate opportunities to learn from community members (Johnson & Munch, 2009). For example, the supervisor can provide contact information for community leaders and cultural groups including potential gatekeepers and community guides and attend cultural events with the new organizer. Assignments such as ethnographic interviews or observing and eventually providing staff support for meetings, events or activities intended to honor, serve, or address the interests of specific ethnic, demographic, or cultural groups can assist the new social worker in learning cultural competency-related skills. In addition, social work values and ethics can be enhanced through dialogue with the new organizer about the various cultural competency standards used by social workers including both the NASW Code of Ethics (2000) and the NASW (2007) Standards on Cultural Competence, with special emphasis on strategies for meeting these requirements in community settings. Students and new organizers should also be reminded that cultural competence is a lifelong process; no one is completely cultural competent and everyone can and should continue to learn from others (Gutierrez et al., 2005; Johnson & Munch, 2009).

Supervision for Using Verbal and Written Communication

Communication is the key to effective relationship-building and engagement as well as the ability to influence others. These skills include making presentations and public speaking in order to provide information to others, build a case for a particular course of action, or establish collaborative partnerships or coalitions. Communication also includes the ability to create promotional materials (such as flyers and brochures), press releases, and research or policy reports. Increasingly, communication also involves the use of social media to spread the word, frame messages, recruit participants, disseminate information, network with others, and rally people to a cause. As noted earlier in this text, community organizers also must assist constituents in the development of these types of skills (Sen, 2003).

There are a number of supervisory tasks that can be used to facilitate the development of organizers with good communication skills. For example, work assignments can include the expectation that the organizer design flyers or write press releases in preparation for organization sponsored events. Technical skills can be developed or strengthened by asking the organizer to maintain a blog, a Facebook page, or use Twitter in promotional campaigns. The organizer's ability to frame messages and to communicate them to others should be assessed by the supervisor on a regular basis. New organizers should also be assigned to conduct outreach to other constituency groups and organizations and participate in presentations, make speeches, or provide testimony at public hearings (Hoefer, 2006; Richan, 2006). Supervisors should be prepared to assist the new organizer in writing and practicing presentations and assessing their ability to deliver information in public settings.

One area potential area of dialogue between the supervisor and worker may involve examination of the degree to which attempts to use news or social media have been successful (Pyles, 2009a). Did the organizer's communication result in actual press coverage? Was it the type of coverage expected? If not, how could this campaign be strengthened? Did the message reach the right audience? Was there a better way to reach the target group? Once the organizer has acquired basic skills, the next step should be helping or training constituents to work with the media. Participation in such efforts should help the staff member or intern strengthen these communication skills; dialogue can be initiated in terms of best training methods, how to facilitate the development of individual volunteers, and how to motivate constituents to engage in these types of tasks.

Supervision for Engagement and Dialogue Skills

Engagement and dialogue skills include the ability to conduct one-on-one interviews for relationship-building, recruitment, and information gathering purposes as well the ability to facilitate intergroup dialogue and meetings and plan, structure, and carry out larger events, such as community forums, in which community consultation and decision-making can occur. As noted previously in this text, good dialogue skills include the ability to guide the group process, ensure that all participants have a chance to participate, establish common ground across member differences, and manage conflict (VeneKlasen et al., 2007). Effective engagement also requires that organizers gain a particular degree of comfort in talking to strangers and using those conversations to achieve specific types of outcomes that make it possible to hold an event, lobby for a cause, or achieve specific goals related to planning, development, or organizing campaigns. The goal of these engagement opportunities should also be to establish long-term effective relationships with constituents, key informants, and decision-makers that can be used in the future and can help the organization establish strong network linkages to other potential volunteers and influential contacts (Hardcastle et al., 2004).

Supervisory tasks include role plays and exercises to help the organizer use basic social work interviewing and relationship-building skills to reach out to constituents and representatives of partner organizations. Clear expectations should be set for the number and quality of interviews to be conducted and the degree to which documentation is required. Also helpful is dialogue to help the organizer understand that while these skills are intrinsic to good social work practice with other systems, their application in community practice differs substantially from agency practice in that the individual is not a client-seeking service, but a potential partner with skills and strengths that could be of benefit to the organizer or the campaign or project in which the organizer or intern is assigned. Conducting interviews on doorsteps or at community events can also be more challenging in terms of time constraints, unexpected occurrences, and the difficulties inherent in record-keeping. It should also be emphasized that some people simply will not want to participate and that their privacy should be respected.

Role plays and exercises should also focus on the new organizer's ability to facilitate and manage groups, recruiting members, setting agendas, and working with group members to achieve goals (Wint & Sewpaul, 2000). Learning to facilitate often requires a developmental process in which the staff member observes groups, co-facilitates with an experienced organizer, and eventually leads the group. At an advanced level, the organizer should be transmitting some of these skills to constituent leaders, simply providing support to volunteers. In terms of larger events, new organizers should have a variety of opportunities to assist in the setup and coordination of workshops, meetings, and community forums. Supervision can focus on the examination of how effective such events have been in achieving organization goals and the various options that should be explored in planning future events.

Supervision for Facilitating Constituent Self-Determination and Empowerment

Once participants in community practice-related activities have been recruited, organizers need to find ways to ensure their inclusion in decision-making. In some cases, organizations have established decision-making structures and long-standing relationships with community leaders and volunteers. However, real inclusion is often difficult to achieve; new participants may not feel comfortable stating their views, organizational decision-making structures (e.g., board and committee membership and governance rules), organizational ideology, power differentials between leaders and constituents, and the ego or personalities of staff members may limit the degree to which input from other participants is solicited (Hardina et al., 2006; Toomey, 2009). Such impediments can severely restrict the development of true partnerships between community organization staff and constituents.

The supervisor can assist the new organizer or intern by analyzing existing decision-making patterns, suggesting strategies for structuring meetings or supporting leaders, and identifying methods that could be used to help all participants feel included in the decision-making process (Bess et al., 2009; Hunt, 2007). Basic social work methods such as using positive affirmations, identifying individual strengths, and encouraging these individuals to use their expertise to help the organization can be used to encourage participation and identification with the group (Miley et al., 2011). Essentially, empowering practices foster feelings of personal self-efficacy in group members (Itzhaky & York, 2002). Consequently, encouraging group members to volunteer for tasks needed for group maintenance and action, following up when these tasks have been accomplished, and recognizing and praising group members are all essential to the empowerment process; the supervisor should assist the new organizer in the development of these skills (Haski-Leventhal & Cnaan, 2009; Zastrow, 2009). In addition, the new organizers or interns should be encouraged to strengthen their own group work skills, using exercises and posing questions to group members that foster participation (VeneKlasen et al., 2007). Conflict management skills are also important, particularly in situations in which some individuals dominate the discussion or disputes arise among members (Zastrow, 2009).

Supervision for Using Group Methods for Problem Identification and Assessment

Skill development for problem identification and assessment takes place on two levels: the new organizer must develop the capacity to enter a community and learn about issues, problems, and the strengths of community members and use both informal and formal methods to conduct assessments. However, the intern or new organizer must also be prepared to work with constituents, partner organizations, and external consultants to conduct focus groups, use story-telling processes, conduct community forums, and other types of group dialogue sessions to identify problems of concern to constituents and conduct assessments (Pippard, 2004). Interns and new organizers must also have adequate research skills, the ability to recommend and apply research methods that are feasible and realistic (both in terms of time commitment, donor requirements, and constituent interests), and the interpersonal skills necessary to work cooperatively with constituents and partner organizations to develop research plans (Stoecker, 2005). Organizers will also need to work with constituents to identify power resources held by group members, community decision-makers, and opponents (Homan, 2011).

In addition to skills related to engagement with constituents and facilitating self-determination and empowerment, supervisors can help interns and new organizers choose appropriate research techniques, develop group dialogue skills suitable for problem identification and provide information on workshops and training sessions that will assist interns, organizers, and constituent leaders to learn about innovative techniques such asset mapping, social network analysis, Photovoice, the development of neighborhood-specific social indicators, Geographic Information System mapping tools, and power analysis (Johnson et al., 2010; Plitt Donaldson, & Daughtery, 2011). The new organizer may have unrealistic expectations about using these techniques and their appropriateness and accessibility for community members. Consequently, supervision may focus on examining the various options and helping the new organizer make appropriate recommendations to constituent leaders about the use of these methods. In many circumstances, the organizer will be called upon to actually coordinate research studies, follow up with volunteers, negotiate access to research settings, provide training for interviewers or survey administration, maintain data files, and participate in data analysis and report writing. The supervisor will need to provide oversight and help the new organizer design appropriate strategies for making sure that each stage of the process is completed in a timely manner.

Supervision for Group Methods to Assess the Ethical Implications of Strategies and Tactics

Every type of action taken in the context of community practice has ethical implications, ranging from the people who should be included in group decisions, the selection of partner organizations, the choice of assessment and evaluation techniques, and strategic and tactical options available for organizing development, and planning. Social work interns and new organizers must develop the knowledge, skills, and values that allow them to examine both their own ethical options and work with group members to identify ethical issues that may occur during the implementation of community interventions (Hardina, 2004a; Mondros & Wilson, 1994).

While social action or conflict-related tactics may pose some of the most serious challenges for community groups in terms of potential harm to participants or opponents, other types of decisions may have ethical implications as well. Some of the ethical issues that may be encountered in community practice include questions about who should benefit from community development efforts, whether the organization or

coalition should work with people or organizations known to be unethical, or whether funds should be accepted from donors who may impose
restrictions on the organization or alter the course of its advocacy efforts
(Minkler & Pies, 2009; Reisch & Lowe, 2000).

Supervisory tasks to help the social work intern or new organizer
weigh the ethical implications of various options include dialogue
about how social work ethical codes can be applied in community settings and whether other ethical frameworks or the social worker's personal values can be used to examine ethical options (Kirst-Ashman &
Hull, 2009). Although many of these decisions will be made by organization board members, administrators, and constituency group
members, there will be some types of ethical choices that must be
made by the organizer alone. For example, does the organizer have
any conflict of interest or a personal stake in the outcome of any
decision made by the organization or constituency group (Reisch &
Lowe, 2000)? Has the organizer done enough to ensure that constituency group members are fully informed about tactical options and
potential negative effects about any course of action (Kahn, 2010)?

Interns and new organizers will also need to examine the ethical
implications of decisions made by constituency group members and
help them assess the possible consequences of a number of tactical
choices. To some extent, becoming knowledgeable about what can
occur in various situations is a matter of practical experience. However,
the supervisor can help prepare the organizer by assigning reading
material (case studies or narrative accounts of organizing campaigns)
or requiring that the organizer interview experienced community practitioners and community leaders about what they have learned from
prior organizing efforts (Clemens & Minkoff, 2007; Somma, 2006).
The supervisor can also provide assistance by helping the organizer
examine available tactical choices and proposals and giving advice
about how to facilitate consensus-building sessions with constituency
group members and partner organizations to discuss the options
available to them, what is likely to happen under different scenarios,
and engage in contingency planning (Hardina & Obel-Jorgensen,
2011). It is also essential that new organizers develop the ability to
state their own views, particularly in situations that have ethical implications (such as harming individuals or groups), or that can affect the
organization's legitimacy and credibility in the community (Piat,
2000). This is particularly critical for social workers in that members
of the profession are required by the mandates in the NASW Code
of Ethics (2000) and the IFSW Code of Ethics (2012) to engage in
ethical practice.

Supervision for Group Methods for Planning Campaigns and Taking Action

As described in Chapters 7 and 8, planning action campaigns, responding to unexpected occurrences and situational demands, and taking action are the most complex aspects of the organizing process. Successful campaigns require that the organizer have multiple relationships with any number of colleagues, constituents, group leaders, board members, supervisory staff, reporters, external consultants and advisors, partner organizations, elected officials, and other decision-makers (Staples, 2004). New organizers will need to develop skills related to handling requests for assistance and logistical support, following up with volunteers who have task assignments to complete, and filling in any gaps in participation with new recruits or simply handling the task at hand.

New organizers will need assistance from the supervisor in determining what needs to be done, keeping track of the action using appropriate methods of documentation, and responding to situational demands (ben Asher, 2002; Schutz & Sandy, 2011). In addition, group work skills are also essential since not only will the staff member or organization need to change direction, but also constituency group members will need to do so; in most situations they will need to be consulted about or control any response to an unexpected occurrence. The group dialogue process will often involve complex discussions about tactical options and the likely outcome of each (Burghardt, 2011). Such discussions may also involve whether or not negotiations should take place with partner organizations or opponents and what should and should not be offered in the bargaining process.

In this phase of the organizing process, the supervisor should be available for consultation about how to best handle changes in circumstances and negotiations and who should be included in the decision-making process. The supervisor may also be a participant in these decision-making sessions. The organizer or intern may need guidance about the implications of various tactical options and group member experiences with and perceptions about the effectiveness of these methods. The supervisor may be able to suggest alternative plans of action and how group members should be advised about the choices available to them. In such cases, it may be helpful for the supervisor to engage the organizer in some role plays or exercises that illustrate how tactical choices should be made in a group process or how bargaining between two parties can occur (VeneKlasen et al., 2007). The supervisor should also be a good resource for the new organizer or intern in terms of developing appropriate Plan Bs or safety plans in response to situational demands (Timm et al., 2011).

Supervision for Facilitating Participatory Evaluations

As described in Chapter 10, evaluation-related skills are those that pertain to informal assessments of one's own practice, informal consultative group processes in which the implementation of campaigns are examined, and formal evaluations of intervention processes and outcomes. The organizer will also need to apply research skills, values, and knowledge in the evaluation process and, in some situations, provide training in research methodology and data analysis to others Bowers Andrews (2004).

The role of the supervisor in this process has to do with providing assistance on two levels: the application of and strengthening of formal research skills by the new organizer and ensuring that constituents have ample opportunity to participate in, and in many circumstances, control the evaluation process. The new organizer needs to steer a course between relying on personal or other sources of expert knowledge and recognizing that experiential knowledge (and in some cases formal research skills) held by constituents are also essential in ensuring that all voices are heard and that full assessments of what works and what does not work in the organizing process are made (Craig, 2011; Schmuck, 2006). The supervisor should also help the organizer recognize that two other sources of information are often integrated into the evaluation process: practice knowledge held by organizing staff (in terms of organization experience with evaluation methods) and donor requirements for documentations and evaluation of grant- or contract-funded activities.

As noted earlier in this chapter, other supervisory tasks related to evaluation are to assist the organizer in self-evaluation of practice experiences, and to identify any additional skills the organizer needs to ensure that the work is completed as expected and in a timely manner. In most situations, supervisors will likely be active participants in informal group or organization assessments about organizing campaigns and can further discuss the issues raised in these sessions during supervisory meetings with the new organizer. In terms of formal evaluations, the supervisor can help new organizers understand the organization's procedures for evaluation, the relationship between funding and evaluation requirements, and work with the organizer in producing formal research-related documents such as funding proposals, logic models, formal research agreements (with partner organizations or external consultants) evaluation plans, and research reports (Netting, Kettner, & McMurty, 2008). However, it is likely the most important skill the new organizer will need for participatory research are the interpersonal skills necessary to facilitate group evaluations methods (Stringer, 2007). Supervisory strategies can include exercises and role plays related to research options or working through difficult decisions with constituents and critiques about how research studies or reports are progressing (Schmuck, 2006).

PUTTING VALUES IN ACTION: PARALLEL PROCESSES AND ENCOURAGING ORGANIZER AND CONSTITUENT SELF-DETERMINATION AND EMPOWERMENT

Bobo et al. (2010), in describing how supervision should be structured in community organization, caution that despite practice principles that involve fairness and inclusive decision-making styles, someone must be in charge of following up with staff to make sure that work has been accomplished in the manner intended. Consequently, the model they describe entails certain constraints. Organizers must work in a manner consistent with the organization's mission and philosophy, but must be responsive to the needs and preferences of constituents. One dilemma then for community organizations is establishing a hierarchal management structure to facilitate staff training and accountability while encouraging staff member feelings of self-competency and empowerment, creativity, innovation, and independence. This dilemma is not unique to community practice. According to Kadushin (2002), the use of authority in social service provision is problematic because:

> Persistent use of authority increases the social distance between participants in supervisory relationships and results in a greater formality in such relationships. It intensifies a sense of status difference between the supervisor and supervisee and tends to inhibit free communication. (p. 97)

Another consideration on the part of the organization is facilitating the new staff member's or intern's ability to work within the confines of the organization's structure, mission, and rules. Supervisors are often responsible for providing orientation sessions to new hires, informing them of specific policies and rules, advising them about any implicit or unstated expectations about how workers should behave or perform specific tasks, and mentoring them about how to best advocate for change in the organization (Hardina et al., 2006; Kaminski et al., 2000). Supervisors must be prepared to both mentor new staff members and work with them collaboratively colleagues, peers, and team members. In most instances, supervision must be a parallel process in which the supervisor offers general guidance and serves as a role model in the transmission of organization-related goals, skills, knowledge, and values to the new organizer (Hardina et al., 2006). In turn, it is expected that the organizer not only acquire these skills, but transmit some of them to constituent leaders and other volunteers who contribute to the work of the organization (Boehm & Staples, 2002).

One theoretical perspective that can be used to examine how transformation within one system can be used to affect changes in others is empowerment theory. Empowerment theory is especially relevant for organizers because it contains strategies for making changes within organizations and also provides guidance as to how organizations should be structured to enhance the capabilities and feelings of self-competency of staff members as well as the people served by the organization (Gutierrez et al., 1998; Hardina et al., 2006; Wallach & Mueller, 2006). One of the primary assumptions in empowerment theory is that in order to empower others, staff members need to feel empowered themselves (Bartle, Couchonnal, Canda, & Staker, 2002). Therefore, organizations that establish decision-making structures that are explicitly designed to empower the people served by the organization also should engage in activities to empower staff members. In community organizations, constituency group members serve on boards and committees and are encouraged to take leadership positions in the organization and are advocates for changes in organization procedures and policies. In a typical nonprofit organization, staff members do not serve on boards of directors and may have limited input into organization decision-making. Therefore, one of the dilemmas faced by community organizations is how to set up a management structure in which staff are encouraged to provide input into management decisions and advocacy for policy changes and improvements in workplace conditions (Devine, 2010; Turner & Shera, 2005). Particularly for community-based organizations in which mutual learning and partnership among staff and constituents is valued, decision-making structures need to be fluid and flexible, allowing staff some discretion over their work, the ability to bargain for improvements in work conditions, and some degree of participation in campaign and event planning including advocacy for positions and procedures that may be at odds with those of the organization (English, 2005; Wallach & Mueller, 2006). Workers also need to feel supported and nurtured, that they have opportunities for professional development and career advancement, and that decisions about work place conditions and work assignments are made in a fair manner (Bobo et al., 2010; Turner & Shera, 2005).

Another way to view organization leader and supervisor responsibilities for staff member empowerment is as activities undertaken by the organization to enhance feelings of individual self-efficacy, self-perceptions of one's own ability to handle assigned tasks and assume greater responsibility for organization goals (Gutierrez, GlenMaye, & DeLois, 1995). Professional development activities that can be used to empower employees include sending workers to training and workshops, identifying worker strengths, finding opportunities for workers to apply specialized knowledge or skills in challenging work situations, and promoting workers through the ranks (Kaminski et al., 2000; Shera & Page, 1995). In addition, community organizers, given the complexity of organizing in ever-changing circumstances, in a variety of community settings and venues, must have some degree of autonomy in their work, discretion over some types of decisions, the ability to think on their feet, and respond creatively to situational demands. These types of characteristics are often encouraged by empowering organizations (Petter, Byrnes, Choi, Fegan, & Miller, 2002).

Another basic assumption associated with theories about empowerment in organizations is derived in part from feminist theory. Feminists view organizations as hierarchies in which power and control are used in a punitive manner to facilitate work performance (Chernesky & Bombyk, 1995; English, 2005; Morrison & Branigan, 2007). Consequently, in order to alleviate the harmful effects inherent in such organizations, hierarchal structures should be modified or eliminated. Generally, in organizations in which empowerment theory is used to design performance structures and expectations, this means eliminating some supervisory positions and substituting other types of support and accountability structures such as staff support groups, or peer counseling (Gutierrez et al., 1995; Shera & Page, 1995). The rationale for such methods is that they are perceived as providing more personal support and assistance than traditional hierarchal models and are more likely to promote team-building and work sharing among staff. The use of work place teams has also been found to enhance feelings of empowerment among organization staff, requiring that they learn to work together cooperatively and develop a sense of collective identity and solidarity (Brownstein, 2003; Daily & Bishop, 2003; Johnson & Johnson, 2006). Additional benefits associated with workplace teams include reductions in worker turnover and burnout, and increases in job satisfaction, work performance, commitment to the organization, and feelings of personal empowerment and self-competency among staff members (Siebert, Wang, & Courtright, 2011).

Another method often used to facilitate cooperation and sense of community among staff members is group supervision (Kadushin, 2002; Wayne et al., 2010). One of the advantages of this method is that the group facilitation skills employed by the supervisor can serve as a guide to organizing staff who are assigned to facilitate workplace teams, committees, or groups of constituents. Group supervision also serves as a source of peer support and provides an opportunity for staff members to learn from their peers. Another method used to address the harmful effects of organizational hierarchies is to eliminate them entirely. Organizations may be structured as a set of interconnected teams in which a formal structure is established that allows for effective communication among all organization members (Johnson & Johnson, 2006). Small community organizations may also eliminate management hierarchies entirely, using consensus-oriented decision-making models such as worker cooperatives or collectives in which all members have equal status and power to manage the work of the organization (Majee & Hoyt, 2011; Morrison & Branigan, 2007). It should also be noted, however, that in organizations that encourage the development of strong personal bonds among staff people with the intent of minimizing the social distance between administrators and other employees, it may be difficult to implement accountability standards or make decisions about how performance problems should be handled (Morgen, 1994). Also, in larger, more dispersed organizations that operate in a number of locations, such informal or partnership models may not be feasible, requiring that the organization maintain a centralized decision-making structure with designated leaders (Swarts, 2008).

In organizations that establish some type of organizational hierarchy in order to ensure staff accountability, managers and supervisors must have special skills to resolve the dilemma inherent in maintaining an authority and control structure in an organization that is intended to facilitate the empowerment its constituents. Supervisors must be ready to allocate power, encourage the development of staff skills and competencies, and focus on the well-being of staff members and constituents in addition to the maintenance of the organization (Turner & Shera, 2005). They must be able to provide support and inspire staff to do their best, work as members of a team, and use their skills to develop flexibility and creativity in response to situational demands (Hardina et al., 2006; Jaskyte, 2004).

SUMMARY

Becoming a skilled organizer is often a matter of personal experience, values, knowledge, and good interpersonal and analytical skills. Organizers are expected to engage in critical thinking and be flexible, innovative, and creative, provide support and guidance to individuals, groups, and organizations, and interact with partner organizations, elected officials, and powerful decision-makers to influence legislation and policies and change community conditions (Lietz, 2010). However, organizers must also be accountable to the communities they serve, their constituents, and the organizations in which they work. Social workers employed as organizers or completing field internships are also expected to follow social work-related ethical codes. Although some organizers do not receive formal training, social work students and program graduates do have access to training in interpersonal skills and analytical methods that can be applied in community organization settings. Supervisory structures established in community organizations are designed to provide training and support to new organizers and ensure accountability to the organization and its mission. Social work supervisors in community organizations and other macro-related settings (such as government agencies or legislative settings) have a responsibility to help students integrate social work skills and the experiential knowledge necessary to work with constituents and other decision-makers. Supervision should be a parallel process in which students and employees gain the self-confidence and feelings of self-efficacy and personal empowerment necessary to empower others.

EXERCISES AND ASSIGNMENTS

1. Write a two- to five-page analysis of the supervisory structure of your field agency and attach a chart that illustrates how you perceive the organization to be structured in terms of supervision of staff. The paper should examine lines of authority (who is responsible for decision-making and to whom supervisors and administrative staff report), procedures for holding staff accountable, and policies that staff are required to follow. Also describe procedures that a staff member can use for advocating for changes in organization policies and procedures and to what degree such advocacy is encouraged by the organization.
2. What attributes would you associate with good supervision for community practitioners? What types of personality traits and skills should they have? How does this differ from some of the supervisors

that you have had in past employment or internships? What type of supervision complements your personality? What should a supervisor know about you to assist you with completing your work objectives?

3. With a classmate, role play a supervisory session using the following scenario:

A social work intern at a community organization has been asked to conduct at least three one-on-one interviews with community leaders who have cultural backgrounds that are different from that of the organizer, but has not been able to do so. A supervisory meeting has been set up so that the field instructor can explore why the organizer has been unable to meet this objective. In this role play, items to be discussed should include: the organizer's comfort with the assignment, past experience conducting interviews, how one-on-one interviews may be similar to or different from in-agency interviews with clients, and whether the intern has received enough information, guidance, and training from the supervisor or organization in carrying out this assignment. Methods that can be used to obtain entry to culturally different communities should also be discussed.

14

Interpersonal Skills in a Global Context: Advocating for Human Rights

I would again call people to the table and explain to them the amount of time, the number of years that we have been at this. The lives of our children. The integrity of our community .... The civil rights violations. The time was now. That I would have felt that the time [to act] Even if we had to go to the International Court to prove our point ....
We can't keep going like this.
—Interview with an organizer in a faith-based organization, Hardina et al., 2011.

The human rights perspective is often used to examine the process of globalization and its effects on social work constituents. In this chapter, the human rights perspective, introduced in Chapter 1, provides a framework of values for an examination of community organizing and social work practice internationally. One of the rationales for international human rights standards, the process of globalization, and its negative impacts on health, well-being, wage standards, and migration is described. The responsibility of social workers, as identified in the International Federation of Social Workers (2012) Code of Ethics, to advocate on behalf of human rights is also examined. In addition, an overview of the practice of community organizing in the international context is provided with a focus on the practice of social planning, and community development for enhancing social and economic development in developing countries is presented. The use of social action and transformative organizing approaches in the struggle for human rights worldwide is also discussed. In the last section of this chapter, the implications of a global perspective for social work and community practice are examined.

PUTTING VALUES IN ACTION: HUMAN RIGHTS

Philosopher Amartya Sen (2004) asserts that the recognition of human rights implies that individuals, in a position to do so, are ethically obligated to take action to make sure that they are achieved. Often the human rights perspective is equated with social and economic justice. However, Lundy and van Wormer (2007) distinguish between the two terms. The principle of *social justice* pertains to whether people are treated equally, how resources are distributed, and whether people have basic political or civil rights. Groups that experience political, social, or economic marginalization and oppression seldom have access to all the goods and services that they need; consequently they experience economic injustice, unable to maintain a basic standard of living. The term *human rights*, on the other hand, explicitly pertains to universal standards established to measure individual and collective political, social, and economic rights and whether these standards have been met (Healy, 2008).

According to Murdach (2011a), the origin of the human rights perspective occurred in the 18th century in the *United States' Declaration of Independence* and the *Declaration of the Rights of Man and of Citizens during the French Revolution*. However, Wronka (2008) and Ife (2001) place the origins of concept of human rights in the 18th century. Thomas Locke and other philosophers developed the concept of *natural rights*, the belief that all men have natural rights as a consequence of simply being human and consequently should be treated in a manner that is equal to everyone else. Although these philosophical assumptions influenced independence movements in the U.S. and France, the notion of equality was limited to certain segments of the population. Women and people without property were not given the right to vote or serve on juries, slaves and non-White people were not deemed worthy to share these natural rights (Ife, 2001). In addition, Locke, Hume, Rousseau, and Voltaire and other philosophers emphasized property rights and freedom from arbitrary rule or government regulation (Wronka, 2008). Locke's writings also attributed poverty to moral failure on the part of individuals. These ideas are now associated with the contemporary philosophy of individualism, the idea that individuals are solely responsible for their status in society and their ability to acquire the income, goods, and services that they need (Segal & Kilty, 2003).

As noted by Murdach (2011a), individualism and its association with the human rights perspective is actually at odds with other philosophies about how wealth and resources should be distributed such as egalitarianism (equal treatment for everyone) or utilitarianism (the greatest good for the greatest number). Another criticism of this approach is that the concept is Euro-centric and inconsistent with conceptualizations associated with other cultures that focus on group or collective rights and shared responsibility for community well-being (Donnelly, 2007; Ife, 2001). The *UN Universal Declaration of Human Rights* also does not provide an exhaustive list of rights for members of all marginalized groups or for all types of resources, for example, members of the LBGTQ community, people who are disabled, or the rights of all people to have access to clean water or air (Bakker, 2007; Wetzel, 2001).

However, what we currently think of human rights, as described in the *UN Universal Declaration of Human Rights*, has evolved over time and has been strengthened to include additional categories of rights beyond those identified as natural rights by 18th-century thinkers. Ife (2001) identifies three waves or generations of rights:

- *First-generation rights* are those initially identified during the Enlightenment, which have evolved over time. They include political and civil rights such as freedom of speech and assembly, the right to vote, citizenship rights, freedom of religion, and equal treatment under the law. Also included in these categories are rights that have been interpreted as accruing from others such as freedom from discrimination, the right to privacy, and freedom from torture. Most of these rights are specified in legal codes and government constitutions, but of course, vary by country and may not always be enforced.
- *Second-generation rights* include individual and group-related social, political, and cultural rights. They pertain to the right to obtain certain social benefits including jobs, good wages, education, health care, and food. Although recognized in the *UN Declaration of Rights* there is little international consensus that all people are entitled to these benefits or that governments are required to provide them.
- *Third-generation rights* are those that belong to communities, demographic groups, or countries and include the right to benefit from world trade and economic growth, the right to engage in economic development or advancement, the right to live in a stable society, and environmental rights. Environmental rights include the right to clean air and water. This set of rights is a purely 20th century phenomena and is not fully recognized, except in some of the various international conventions and treaties. Obtaining international agreements on these rights is often difficult as such efforts are often viewed as limiting the economic rights of some individuals or restraining economic activity (Bakker, 2007).

The human tights framework has been highly influential in guiding international development efforts and social movements to acquire social, economic, and political rights among members of marginalized groups. Human rights work is most often conducted by the United Nations and regional organizations such as the African Union, the Organization of American States, and the European Union (Healy, 2008; Wronka, 2008). It is also undertaken by numerous international organizations such as Doctors Without Borders, Amnesty International, and Human Rights Watch (Ife, 2001). Although these organizations have name recognition and resources, thousands of national, regional, and local organizations conduct human rights work, or make appeals to the UN or government bodies to address human rights violations. As noted in Chapter 1, human rights have been formally recognized as a component social work practice through the work of the IFSW (Dominelli, 2010; Healy, 2008; Murdach, 2011a). Values associated with the human rights perspective have also been incorporated into criticisms of recent economic trends such as globalization as well as responses to economic hardship by government agencies and nonprofit organizations engaged in community development and social planning or engaging in social action to fight injustice (Midgley, 2007).

THE PROCESS OF GLOBALIZATION: IMPACTING ON HEALTH, WELL-BEING, WAGE RATES, AND MIGRATION

One of the rationales for adopting a standard or universal human rights perspective has to do with the process of globalization and its effects on individual and group well-being, health, and economic status. Globalization is a term given to recent trends related to economic production and consumption (Edwards, 2011). It is premised on the assumption that economic activity and its impact in a variety of contexts (economic behavior, government policies, poverty, personal health, and well-being, and immigration) are interconnected. What happens in individual countries as a result of government action and economic activity has an impact on other nations (Healy, 2008; Lundy, 2004). Technology also plays a role in globalization, creating better opportunities for people to stay interconnected using the Internet, cell phones, and other communication devices (Midgley, 2007).

The process of globalization is also enhanced through decisions made by international organizations such as the World Trade Organization, the World Bank, and the International Monetary Fund that have a role in setting global economic policies and by large transnational corporations that engage in economic activity, sell products, and employ workers in numerous countries (Lundy, 2004). Consequently, economic activities in some nations contribute to reductions in wages, poverty, poor health, pollution, and other social conditions in others (Fox & Meier, 2009; Rispel et al., 2009). Poor living conditions also contribute to the migration of people from one country to the next, seeking better employment and economic opportunities (Xu, 2007). Therefore, globalization does not simply foster economic connections among countries it also has a profound influence on policies, practices, and social systems in most countries and the lives of most individuals and families (Dominelli, 2010).

According to Ife (2001), the basic critique associated with the process of globalization is that rather than improve economic well-being, it creates both "networks of power" and "networks of inequality" that transcend national boundaries. Aided by the Internet and other new communications technology, wealth and power are accumulated by people with assets while others are isolated and excluded. Western industrialized nations tend to benefit from globalization while developing countries, primarily located in the Global South, often experience economic deprivation (Midgley, 2007).

Another consistent critique of the globalization movement is that organizations such as the IMF and the World Bank are responsible for contributing to economic hardship by emphasizing policies characterized as "neo-liberal" and originating in the 1980's in the economic policies of Margaret Thatcher in the United Kingdom and Ronald Regan in the United States. These policies were designed to promote lower taxation and reductions in funding for public programs (Ayers, 2004; Lundy, 2004; Midgley, 2007). Transnational organizations such as the World Bank, the International Monetary Fund, and the World Trade Organizations have a large influence on the economic systems of member nations, especially countries in the Global South that apply for loans or credit from these institutions. Originally established after World War II to fund development projects and controlled by western industrial nations, the IMF in partnership with the World Bank can demand that countries adjust their economies in order to qualify for loans (Prigoff, 2000). The Structural Adjustment Program often requires cuts to public services for the poor, health care, and education funding, the deregulation of public services such as transportation or energy, a switch from subsistence agriculture to crops that are exported resulting in increases in food prices, suppression of unions and wage rates, and the provision of favorable regulations or other benefits to encourage relocation of transnational corporations rather than encouraging local investments (Lundy, 2004). It may also result in the depletion of natural resources (such as rain forests or water) and resources held by indigenous or culturally diverse communities, increasing poverty and further marginalizing members of these communities (Prigoff, 2000; Reed, 2002). Such environmental damage can also contribute to the migration of these populations to other countries.

While such conditions may be necessary to qualify for loans or credits from transnational institutions, often these economic policies have a negative impact on most residents of the countries that adopt them; many of these nations are so impoverished that what they really need to do is spend money on roads, education, and other improvements that will aid economic development (Delonis, 2004; Lundy, 2004; Prigoff, 2000). For example, the country of Haiti has historically suffered from a huge debt crisis that negatively affected its ability to develop a functioning economy or provide for its citizens. The debt originated in part from financial arrangements that secured Haitian independence from France in 1804; in 2010, a devastating earthquake occurred, killing many residents, destroying housing and infrastructure, and placing many people at risk of deadly diseases such as cholera; one relief measure taken by wealthy countries and transnational banking organizations was to "forgive" Haitian debts ("G7 Nations," 2010). As noted by Lundy (2004), countries in the developing world are not the alone in facing economic troubles and cuts in public programs due to the demands of IMF and the World Bank. In 2011, some of the western industrialized nations with large public debts due to heaving borrowing from other nations and the worldwide economic downturn also were required to pare down welfare programs and other public benefits to qualify for credit and loans, leading to public protests in European countries such as Greece and Portugal (Associated Press, 2011; Donadio & Kitsantonis, 2011).

Often, trade agreements such as the North American Free Trade Agreement (NAFTA) permit industrialized countries to operate unregulated (in terms worker safety, and environmental protection) industries in countries such as Mexico (Delgado-Wise & Márquez Covarrubias, 2007). This allows international corporations to pay people less in these countries than they would in western industrialized nations. Consequently, there are fewer jobs for manufacturing and service industry workers in countries such as Australia, Canada, the United States, and the European Union because these jobs have been relocated to Africa, Asian, and Latin American where wage rates are substantially lower (Prigoff, 2000). Advocacy organizations have documented the adverse effects of these arrangements. Transnational corporations often purchase products made in places such as China and El Salvador or operate plants in these countries and then look the other way when workers are mistreated or abused (Kernaghan, 2011).

Large corporations may flood foreign markets with products or agricultural goods that drive prices in those countries down and limit economic opportunities, negatively impacting on income, wage rates, and resident health. However, corporations in industrialized countries hire immigrants to work in jobs that require few skills and pay low wages (Castle, 2004). Therefore, the economy in these countries is often dependent on a supply of labor from this source. Often people migrate from developing countries, in which there are few employment opportunities, to industrialized nations in search of a better life. Some of these immigrants are undocumented, meaning that they were unable to obtain visas or other documents that permit them to live and work legally in their new countries. Undocumented workers often have low levels of education and skills, making it less likely that they can legalize their immigration status, and ensuring that they will be locked into low-paying jobs (Nawyn, 2010).

In addition, industrialized countries differ in terms of policies on legal immigration and access to benefits such as welfare and health care (Xu, 2007). Legal immigrants (such as skilled workers and refugees) are treated differently than people with few job skills or undocumented immigrants. Armed conflict, natural disasters, and climate change increase economic hardship and force many people to flee from their homes for safe havens in other countries (Dominelli, 2010; Frederico et al., 2007). If refugees cannot be fully integrated into the economies of their new countries, they may remain indefinitely in camps until they can be resettled elsewhere or return to their countries of origin (De La Puente, 2011). Often, immigration controls are implemented when people become fearful of others who are different from them or questions are raised about possible competition for low-wage work from refugees, undocumented workers, or other immigrants (Boateng, 2009; Xu, 2007). Another international issue involves human trafficking, with people being moved from their countries of origin against their will and often involving threats of violence for uncompensated labor or the sex trade; in some cases they may be kidnapped and ransomed back to their families when they try to negotiate with traffickers for safe passage into industrialized countries (Androff, 2011; Castle, 2004; Healy, 2008).

Despite these issues, economists often view the impact of globalization positively, citing the growth in transnational business transactions and markets, and the growth of low-wage employment opportunities in many developing countries (Midgley, 2007). Economic processes related to globalization have also promoted increased privatization of previously provided government or nonprofit provided goods and services such as energy, water, and education as well as welfare, child protection, mental health and other services provided by social workers, increasing the profits of the businesses and corporations that provide them (Dominelli, 2010; Lundy, 2004). Some social workers have argued that privatization of social services limits their autonomy over their work and their ability to adequately serve people in need (Healy, 2008; Ife, 2001). Dominelli (2010) summarizes the criticism of the process of globalization from a social work perspective:

> The poorest people on the planet have been adversely affected, through loss of jobs, low-paid work that is insufficient to provide a decent standard of living, health hazards, rising food and energy prices, environmental degradation, arm conflict and resource depletion. (p. 600)

INTERNATIONAL SOCIAL WORK: APPLYING IFSW PRINCIPLES AND TAKING ACTION

Healy (2008) defines international social work as "international professional action and the capacity for international action by the social work profession and its members" (p. 10). She identifies four specific components of international social work practice: everyday practice methods that take place in the social worker's country of origin but that have a relationship to international issues, actual international practice, international professional social work exchanges, and international advocacy and policy development. The IFSW (2005) in partnership with the International Association of Schools of Social Work has developed global standards for social work education that mandate that practice should be guided by the IFSW's (2012) *Code of Ethics* and the *UN Universal Declaration of Human Rights* as well as other U.N charters or covenants of rights (see Chapter 1 for a list of some of these documents). However, it should also be noted that standardization of professional practice methods, including advocacy for a universal set of human rights requires an understanding of cultural and human interaction patterns that may be specific to cultures or societies that are non-western in orientation. In such situations, social workers, especially those working cross-culturally or trans-nationally, must work to adopt social work methods that are appropriate for the political, social, and economic environment and the population served (Jonsson, 2010). Rankopo and Osei-Hwedie (2011) argue that the use of culturally appropriate or indigenous practice methods is critical for effective practice. For example, they cite the reliance in Africa on informal care and social networks for assistance as being culturally distinct from agency-centered practice in the western industrialized nations.

In addition to culturally relevance, human rights advocacy demands practice strategies that are generally outside the scope of traditional practice methods. Although the international origins of many social problems should be obvious to most social work practitioners, not all social workers engage in human rights-related practice nor are they mandated to do so. Lundy and van Wormer (2007) note that in contrast to the social work codes of ethics adopted in many countries and the IFSW (2012) *Code of Ethics* and the NASW (2000) *Code of Ethics* does not include a provision for social workers in the United States to uphold human rights principles. This omission is problematic because:

> Social workers have a responsibility to advocate for human rights and social justice and to question exploitative structures. We can begin by addressing the urgent need for economic security, social equality and better social services and programs. In holding the state accountable for the social protection of the population and the human rights standards, as codified in international law, the effectiveness of the social work mission will be enhanced. (Lundy & van Wormer, 2007, p. 733)

Sen (2004) identifies four types of actions associated with ethical practice from a human rights perspective: securing formal recognition (such as in a charter of rights) that people actually have these rights; organized advocacy to urge governments to comply with these rights, monitoring to make sure that governments actually comply and to pressure them to do so, and legislation to make sure that compliance is required under a country's legal code. In addition, as noted in Chapter 1, advocacy groups may also file formal complaints with various UN bodies and other international organizations (Healy, 2008). While such efforts cannot force compliance, they can draw public, governmental, and media attention to the issue and help pressure authorities to take action. All these activities are consistent with the various codes associated with social work practice worldwide. Ife (2001) explicitly links social work practice on behalf of human rights explicitly to the three generations of rights identified earlier in this chapter:

- First-generation rights. Social workers should advocate for constitutional protections for civil and political rights as well as the enforcement of these rights. While citizens of countries in the developing world do not necessarily have these rights (such as freedom of speech, the right to vote, equal protection of the law, and freedom from arbitrary imprisonment), it is also probable that in some industrialized nations human rights violations can occur. For example, discrimination and high levels of unemployment are issues that occur in every country despite provisions in the UN (1948) *Universal Declaration of Human Rights* related to freedom from discrimination and a right to employment. Same-sex marriage and banning the death penalty are also considered basic human rights in some countries, but not others, providing an opportunity for human rights advocacy on the part of social workers. However, Ife (2001) notes that advocacy should be undertaken by social workers, not on behalf of clients or constituents, but in partnership with them.

- Second-generation rights. Social workers should act to preserve cultural and social rights through direct practice and practice in organizations. Services should be provided in a manner that respects the cultural values of participants and that is adequate to meet the needs of the people served. Social workers can also engage in social action to facilitate policies that reduce poverty and provide access to education and health care.
- Third-generation rights. These rights pertain to collective rights related to economic development, a clean environment, and a stable society. Therefore, the practice methods that should be used are community development and planning as well as social action-oriented community organizing.

The next section of this chapter includes a description of international social work for community development, social planning, and social action organizing.

SOCIAL PLANNING AND COMMUNITY DEVELOPMENT: APPLYING STANDARDS FROM THE *UN UNIVERSAL DECLARATION OF HUMAN RIGHTS*

Often community development and social planning practice are similar in purpose and designed to lift communities and demographic groups out of poverty or increase access to jobs, health care, or education. These activities may be coordinated by government agencies or nonprofit organizations. Often the only distinction between the two processes is that in social planning recommendations are made and decisions are finalized as to how development is to occur. In community and/or economic development public and private agencies establish programs or build roads, factories, or other types of facilities to improve financial or social well-being. International development work is described in the literature as pertaining to one of two types of countries: nations (primarily in the northern portion of the world) that are highly industrialized and countries, many of them former colonies of European countries or the United States, that are not highly industrialized with large numbers of people who live in poverty. Most of these countries are located in the southern hemisphere and have agricultural crops or natural resources such as oil or timber that are sold to or put to use by the industrialized nations (Healy, 2008; Midgley, 2007). Midgley (2005) describes the origin of the term community development in terms of efforts of the colonial powers to modernize or "develop" the Global South. While the stated intent was to improve economic and social conditions for people in many Asian, African, and Latin American countries, often such development efforts actually benefited industrialized nations rather than their citizens (Dominelli, 2005; Fox & Mason Meier, 2009). While economic development efforts have had more success in some countries than others, governments, nonprofit organizations, and citizen advocacy groups have adopted approaches similar to those used in the western industrialized nations to stimulate economic development and improve social conditions for their residents.

Commonalities and Differences in Local Participatory Planning Efforts: Cross-Country Comparisons

Social planning and community development activities often take place in developing countries as a government-mandated effort to increase industrialization, jobs, and access to technology and financial capital for their citizens (Alasah, 2009; Midgley, 2010). Often these programs are funded in part by the World Bank or IMF and focus on building roads and industrial capacity (Oladipo, Fiki, Amuptian, Dabi, & Nyong, 2007). In some situations, these processes are conducted by and coordinated through central governments and rely on rational planning methods (Widianingsih & Morrell, 2007). In some cases, these efforts may be perceived by residents to benefit some population groups, groups, often the political or economic elite, more often than others, creating additional hardships for citizens (Rajgopal, 2002). Often pre-existing ethnic, racial, or class-base disputes (in some cases dating back to colonial governments), actual warfare, or new migration patterns may limit inclusion in financial or political decision-making and acquisition of benefits as a result of economic growth to a handful of demographic groups in diverse societies (Grodofsky, 2007; Ravensbergen & Van der Platt, 2009; Schmid & Salman, 2005).

In part, competing claims and demands from different segments of the population may precede efforts on the part of governments in developing countries to implement policies and procedures designed to increase citizen participation in planning and governance. Sometimes these approaches are used in conjunction with other social capital-related techniques to improve civic engagement, individual capacity, and skill building (Grodofsky, 2007). Gaventa and Valderrama (1999) differentiate between two different types of citizen participation efforts: indirect participation in the political process (that is, electing representatives) and direct participation in local planning efforts. Consequently, participation in government planning efforts serves as a vehicle for building democratic institutions, linking citizens to government agencies ensuring that government services are accountable to the public, and building social integration and solidarity.

In addition, citizen planning councils are prevalent in the western industrialized countries and the developing world in both capitalist and socialist countries. They are typically viewed as a means to reduce the harmful effects of social marginalization and to provide opportunities for low-income and other marginalized communities to have input as to what services they should receive (Bowen, 2007). They also provide an opportunity for people to participate in local decision-making, thus strengthening citizenship rights (Moffat et al., 1999; Schmid & Salman, 2005). According to Lestrelin, Borgoin, Bouahom, and Castella (2011), participatory approaches are believed to lead to better planning processes and outcomes making it more likely that development efforts will be sustainable over time.

Research indicates that there are strengths and limitations of participatory planning approaches. For example, Yen and Luong (2008) describe the adoption of a participatory approach to planning at the village and communal levels in Vietnam. The strengths of this method are that when a variety of groups become involved in the process, both equity and transparency are improved. The limitations of the process include the time and resource commitments required and the lack of skilled facilitators to effectively engage residents in planning.

Effective involvement of citizens in planning also requires sufficient resources, leadership, and people willing to volunteer for participation (Buccus et al., 2008; Moffat et al., 1999). However, many projects are not sufficiently funded and often emphasize expert knowledge rather than provide adequate opportunities for the participation of community residents, especially those people who earn a low income. In addition, decision-making processes are often dominated by local elites and tend to exclude people who traditionally have been marginalized within the culture including women and people in poverty (Hicks, 2011; Ravensbergen & Van der Platt, 2009; Widianingsih & Morrell, 2007).

Gaventa (2004) identifies a number of steps that can and should be taken by government to strengthen citizen involvement in planning:

- Ensuring that participation in planning is one of the legal rights granted to citizens.
- Making a clear delineation of the rights and roles of all participants.
- Providing citizen opportunities for direct representation of individuals and community organizations on government planning councils.
- Providing leadership training and financial incentives to citizens serving on the councils.
- Decentralizing decision-making processes so that opportunities to participate are available on a local level.
- Ensuring "seats at the table" for women, ethnic minorities, low-income people, and members of other politically marginalized groups.
- Providing skilled facilitators and other resources to make sure that effective dialogue and deliberations take place among diverse participants. Skills for facilitators should include conflict resolution, negotiation, and active listening.
- Making sure that participants and other leaders have support from, and are accountable to, strong community organizations.
- Encouraging a culture of information sharing, transparency, and accountability on the part of government participants.

Establishing Economic and Social Development Standards: The Role of Transnational Organizations

Social rights, the right to maintain an adequate standard of living including access to jobs, education, and health care, are among the most controversial in the *UN Universal Declaration of Human Rights* and in subsequent UN covenants and charters. As noted earlier in this chapter, direct provisions of some of these services and resources and, in some instances, even taking action to ensure that people have equal access to jobs, education, and health care are often viewed as at odds with principles related to individualism, the idea that people should be responsible for obtaining their own resources, goods, services, and social status (Segal & Kilty, 2003). According to Mishra (2005), it has been difficult for the UN to enforce these standards for a number of reasons: they require voluntary compliance by countries, the various UN charters and covenants are somewhat vague about how countries are to meet these standards, and some countries simply do not have the economic resources with which to comply especially in the Global South. It is also difficult to monitor the impact of government policies and actions in the attainment of these rights and even to agree how some of the outcomes specified in the standards are to be measured (e.g., poverty or access to health care).

In order to compare the degree to which various countries are "developed" or are able to address the needs of their residents, standardized measures of well-being have been developed by the World Bank, the Organization for Economic Cooperation and Development, and the UN (Healy, 2008). These indicators are intended to measure social progress in both western industrialized and developing counties and make comparisons on a number of factors related to health, income, education levels, gender equity, infant mortality, economic development, and other measures of well-being (Estes, 2005). Although it is tempting to argue that achievement of these standards are based purely on a nation's wealth or individual responsibility for taking care of one's health and well-being (e.g., eating nutritious food, having one's children vaccinated, or seeing a doctor regularly), western industrialized nations sometimes have lower rates of health and well-being than some of the developing countries. Given different measurement tools and standards, rankings may not be consistent among countries. For example, the United States was ranked fourth on the 2010 Human Development Index report issued by the UN after Norway, Australia, and New Zealand. The index includes indicators of life expectancy at birth, average number of years of schooling, the expected number of years of schooling, gross national income (GNI), and the average GNI per person (UN, 2010). In contrast, UNICEF (United Nations Children's Fund) data indicate that between 2003 and 2006, the United States was actually ranked 24th in mortality rates for children under 5, a key human development indicator (Collison, Dey, & Stevenson, 2007). Income distribution or inequities, the provision of public services, the availability of clean water and sanitation, the status of women in terms of educational achievement and reproductive rights, and health care access may have an equal or greater impact than GNI on social indicators such as poverty and infant mortality (Collison et al., 2007; Fox & Mason Meier, 2009).

International Social Development and Aid Organizations

Many of the industrialized nations provide development assistance to nations in the Global South as well as technical assistance and other forms of foreign aid. Some of this assistance is used to attain political and economic goals (such as a strategic ally in a time of war, influence government policies, or access to raw materials) and in some situations it is provided primarily in responses to a natural disaster such as a flood, famine, or displacement due to an armed conflict (Healy, 2008). This type of assistance is usually described as "relief" and typically includes food and health services along with other types of assistance (Keough & Samuels, 2004). These organizations often send staff members, employ local workers, or recruit volunteers with specialized skills (including social workers) to provide assistance (Lough, Moore McBride, Sherraden, & O'Hara, 2011). Development assistance and disaster relief may be delivered by international aid agencies established by the donor countries, or nonprofit organizations (called nongovernment organizations or NGOs in the development literature).

While these organizations provide valuable assistance, particularly material goods and services to people in poverty, especially after disasters, they have been critiqued on a number of levels. Some organizations offer services or development assistance that may be exclusively reflective of North American or Eurocentric values and in the case of faith-based organizations, religious viewpoints (Berger, 2003; Jonsson, 2011). In addition, some of these organizations contract with western governments to distribute foreign aid funds, raising questions about their motives and whether assistance serves some type of political agenda (Edwards, 1999). A related issue is that some development agencies focus only on material assistance such as food and do nothing to change economic, political, or social systems that have contributed to poverty and marginalization may simply sustain existing regimes and perpetuate harmful conditions (Offenheiser & Holcombe, 2003). Other concerns have to do with how assistance is transferred and the likelihood that food and other material goods or funds may actually benefit members of the country's elite residents or corrupt government officials rather than intended beneficiaries (Alasah, 2009; Hicks, 2011).

While nongovernment organizations and donor countries have taken steps to counter such problems, some of these concerns persist. At the beneficiary level, some international organizations have sought to ensure that community planning and implementation have decision-making mechanisms that include local residents (Kang, 2010). Offenheiser and Hocolmbe (2003) describe the human-rights-oriented approach used by one of these organizations, Oxfam, as:

> Assisting poor communities to overcome obstacles rather than about never-ending pursuit of grants for social goods. It assumes that poor people have dignity, aspirations, and ambition and their initiative is being blocked and frustrated

by persistent systemic challenges such as apartheid, biased lending policies, and nonfunctioning state service delivery systems. (p. 271)

Some international agencies focus primarily on economic development work. Such assistance includes environmental protection and types of assistance similar to that provided within the western industrialized countries: human capital development (job training and education) as as well as economic development and finance. Such assistance may also include the provision of technical assistance to upgrade agricultural practices or to improve infrastructure or making basic services (such as water filtration or clean energy) available in remote areas (Oladipo et al., 2007).

According to Healy (2008), while some development agencies see their efforts as quite distinct from temporary provision of food and other direct services, the work of international aid organizations tends to fall on a continuum, with many agencies providing a mixture of programs and services in the regions in which they work that can include material assistance, efforts to engage residents in organizing and development activities, partnering with other agencies to improve service delivery, and policy advocacy. Methods used to facilitate community development efforts that do not simply focus on direct relief resemble aspects of both classic community organizing and social capital approaches including developing individual capacity, leadership skills, and civic engagement, and stimulating the development of citizens' organizations that can interact with and challenge government, at global, national, and local levels.

Strengthening Social Capital in Europe and the Developing World

Social capital development has been used extensively worldwide as a tool for economic and social development. Often approaches to increasing social capital focus on strengthening bonding and bridging capital in communities or linking social capital by forming new associations and community groups that potentially will have the capacity to deliver social services or initiate new businesses and other economic endeavors (Kay, 2006; Lough et al., 2011). As with social capital approaches in the United States, this type of community development effort examines how interpersonal relationships and social networks can be used for economic survival and to improve individual well-being (Boateng, 2009; Oladipo et al., 2007). However, some researchers have noted that approaches designed to promote social capital formation differ by cultural context, gender, and geographic location (De Silva, Harpham, Huttly, Bartolini, & Penny, 2005; Vaiou & Lykogianni, 2006).

The social capital approach has been used extensively for community development purposes in the European Union, Russia and other countries in the former Soviet block, and in the Global South. Social capital efforts within the European Union are oriented toward decreasing "social exclusion." Barata (2000) defines social exclusion as a "progressive process of marginalization leading to economic deprivation and various forms of cultural disadvantage" (p. 4). Individuals and groups can be excluded politically, economically, socially, and culturally; exclusion is associated with limited political power, lack of access to basic services, poverty, and poor health (Rispel et al., 2009). Social exclusion is believed related in part to social isolation and a lack of integration within economic systems; consequently, one of the strategies used to combat social exclusion involves increasing civic engagement and strengthening social networks using bonding and bridging social capital (Daly & Silver, 2008).

The European Union explicitly promotes social capital development as a mechanism that is intended to increase social cohesion and trust in order to produce "enabling institutions and civil society to interact, social capital links organisational structures to the partners capable of translating policy programmes into sustainable forms of development" (Social Capital Research Network, 2009, p. 1). Social capital programs focus on creating cooperative agreements among government agencies to deliver social welfare and employment services, fostering collaborations between government and NGOs in policy development, increasing NGO capacity to participate in policy formulation and economic development, and promoting civic engagement.

Similar efforts to promote social capital formation have been undertaken in Russia and other former Soviet block nations. Prior to the 1980s, before the collapse of Soviet control, most social issues were addressed by communist-controlled central governments rather than through civic engagement (Despotovic, Medic, Shimkus, & Staples, 2007). Efforts initiated in the 1990s to increase social capital were intended to increase local self-help and development efforts (Babajaian, 2008). Projects operated from the "bottom-up" were also designed to stimulate community participation, social integration, feelings of empowerment, and collective action.

In some of the impoverished communities in these counties, social capital approaches to community development are intended to increase economic activity and well-being. In addition, the absence of nonprofit organizations in these nations has been viewed as an impediment to the development of an alternative to government delivery of services, or the establishment of a tradition of civic engagement (Despotovic et al., 2007; Ersing, Loeffler, Tracy, & Onu, 2007; Keough & Samuels, 2004). Consequently, community development efforts have focused on the provision of assistance to set up nonprofit organizations, develop organization and service delivery capacity, and stimulate the growth of civic participation and volunteerism.

In the Global South, much of the theoretical and community development work on social capital has been funded through the World Bank (Woolcock, 1998). Such efforts primarily focus on economic development. Social capital and civic engagement approaches are also used extensively as a response to displacement, economic deprivation, and psychological distress due to armed struggle; these types of interventions are also used to develop solidarity and end divisiveness among members of different ethnic groups, to increase community capacity to develop water and other infrastructure projects, and to help residents obtain jobs, start new businesses, and accumulate land, money, and other assets (Alasah, 2009; Asian, Coalition for Agrarian Reform, and Rural Development, n.d.; De La Puente, 2012; Oladipo et al., 2007). For example, Frederico et al. (2007), describe a project funded by an NGO in the Philippines to assist survivors of an armed conflict. Displaced by warfare, residents were allowed to return to their homes, but had lost housing, employment, farms, sanitation, and education. A social capital-related development project was initiated to assist community members living in refugee camps. In order to build community solidarity and trust, community information centers were established as meeting spaces, training was provided to community members for providing psychological treatment to others for trauma, money was distributed to residents to start cooperative business enterprises, and community leaders were trained to facilitate peace-building and reconciliation efforts to bring people together who had been on different sides of the conflict.

Small-Scale Economic Development: Microcredit Programs, Cooperatives, and Social Enterprise Efforts

Many social capital and economic development projects conducted by developing countries or emerging democracies focus on small-scale financing projects designed to foster individual businesses, social enterprise efforts, and worker cooperatives. Schreiner and Woller (2003) define microcredit or microenterprise programs as "tiny businesses, most have one employee the owner. Microenterprise development programs make loans and/or give classes to poor people to help them start or strengthen their businesses" (p. 1567). The prototype microcredit loan program was developed by and implemented by the Grameen Bank. These loans initially were intended primarily to assist women, both individuals and small groups, in Bangladesh to develop craft, agricultural, and service-related businesses, offering these new business owners the opportunity to improve their economic status, provide adequate food and clothing for their children, and obtain a degree of financial independence from their husbands (Midgley, 2005; Young Laurence, 2008). Recipients are required to repay the loans and also receive technical assistance. These programs are also intended to reduce women's isolation in patriarchal societies, providing them the opportunity to network with other women, and identify other resources that they can use to develop their businesses. The Grameen Bank and similar microcredit programs have been implemented worldwide and are among the economic development projects supported by the World Bank and available to both women and men for small business development.

Microcredit programs have been critiqued on a number of levels. For example, Midgley (2005) argues that such efforts, used in isolation from other strategies, are not effective in reducing poverty. In addition, microcredit and other financial and human capital development approaches may very well put more money in the hands of women, but without changes in a wife's status in her household, these funds may simply be transferred to her husband and out of her control or increase the likelihood that a woman will experience domestic violence (Pardasai, 2005).

Another approach used for strengthening bonding and bridging social capital, making economic improvements, and financing the growth of a social service sector involves the development of a "social economy" or networks nongovernment organizations that produce goods and services (Quarter, Sousa, Richmond, & Carmichael, 2001). These organizations are referred to as social enterprises and are intended to be primarily self-financing. However, they differ from other nonprofit organizations or businesses in that while they are oriented toward making money, all funds benefit the individuals or the community served in a manner that enhances the public good (Kay, 2006). These organizations can be initiated or encouraged by governments or international aid organizations, or developed through the initiative of community residents seeking to improve their communities. Most social enterprises function as cooperatives in which all members have equal status and can participate in organizational decision-making. For example, Ersing et al. (2007) describe a social enterprise in Romania, the Pentru Voi Bakery, which was established by local parents to provide employment opportunities for young adults with intellectual disabilities. Financing for the bakery was obtained through selling products, assistance from the city in which it is located, and international aid organizations.

Another strategy for promoting business formation has been the development of worker cooperatives to support craft work, agricultural endeavors, the fishing industry, or small-scale use of natural resources such as forests (Starr & Adams, 2003). Some of these projects may simply be intended to help people make a living; others also incorporate principles related to sustainability, emphasizing locally grown and environmentally friendly practices. In some cases, international linkages are established for marketing products internationally in order to expand local economies. These projects differ from microcredit programs in that they are collectively owned and operated by participants, often with specific governance structure and well-defined roles for members (Asian, Coalition for Agrarian Reform, and Rural Development, n.d.). While many of these efforts are initiated by local residents, international development organizations may provide technical assistance and start-up capital, or facilitate international marketing campaigns (Debbink & Ornelas, 1997).

SOCIAL ACTION AND TRANSFORMATIVE ORGANIZING: THE ANTIGLOBALIZATION AND ENVIRONMENTAL MOVEMENTS AND THE STRUGGLE FOR DEMOCRACY AND HUMAN RIGHTS IN THE DEVELOPING WORLD

In addition to community development and social planning, regardless of country, community work almost always includes some type of social action organizing to achieve social justice and obtain human rights for people who are marginalized politically, economically, socially, and culturally. Sometimes this organizing takes place on a global basis as people identify common struggles, often those that have their origins in the process of globalization. In many cases, social workers and organizers are involved in assisting local groups to improve their standard of living by contesting the institutional practices that oppress them (Andharia, 2007). Organizing work also takes place in the context of regional and national struggles for political and economic rights and democracy.

The Antiglobalization and Environmental Justice Movements

Globalization has also increased the prevalence and size of social action organizing efforts. Efforts to consolidate power in the hands of international corporations and transnational organizations that regulate economies have engendered protests and civil resistance by international coalitions and social movements. According to Ayers (2004), the coming together of numerous organizations to oppose government policies and economic practices associated with the process of globalization has resulted in a large increase in policy advocacy by nongovernment organizations, unions, and other nonprofit or nongovernment organizations. These international coalitions are made possible by the use of Internet and other technology for communication, information provision, and recruitment purposes.

According to Routledge (2003), these broad-based coalitions create many challenges for member organizations including the lack of actual face-to-face communication among activists, language barriers, and the fact that western activists are more likely that their counterparts in the developing world to have the resources to travel to protests, meetings, and conferences or engage in international exchanges with other groups. These barriers also make it less likely that the organizations involved in antiglobalization work can agree on joint activities or tactics. Consequently, often decision-making processes in these international advocacy networks are characterized by a lack of trust and cultural class, gender, and other issues related to personal and collective identity (Conway, 2007). One of the primary tactical differences among participants in the antiglobalization movement has to do with the use of civil disobedience and tactics such as vandalism and direct confrontation that are often used by members of anarchist groups. This is in contrast to the nonviolent actions of other protestors (Laffey & Weldes, 2010). Although the various protests and street violence have brought attention to the movement (e.g., the Battle for Seattle at the World Trade Organization summit in Seattle in 1999), they have also contributed to police surveillance and suppression of participants (Ayers, 2004; Conway, 2003; DeFilippis, 2001b).

Antiglobalization protests often take place in conjunction with international conferences facilitated by transnational organizations designed to facilitate consensus about economic policies, development aid, the use of natural resources, and the environment. In addition to WTO, IMF, and the World Bank, these organizations include the G-8 Industrial Nations, the Organization for Economic and Co-operative Development (OECD), and regional trade organizations in the developing countries (Prigoff, 2000). One particular target for these protests at international summits are multinational corporations with a worldwide presence such as Starbucks, Kentucky Fried Chicken, and Nike that in addition to symbolizing corporate control are also viewed as interfering with traditional business and cultural practices in some countries (Laffey & Weldes, 2010; Rajgopal, 2002).

Linked to the antiglobalization movement are local and global environmental movements designed to preserve resident control of natural resources and prevent pollution, oil spills and other threats to the health and well-being of local residents. Often, residents taking part in protests or civil disobedience against government or corporate entities are collaborating with global advocacy organizations to fight government or corporate practices and policies that harm the environment and limit their ability to earn income from agriculture, fishing, or other activities that are dependent upon access and control of natural resources (Ayers, 2004; Bakker, 2007; Reed, 2002). Examples of these types of protests activities include efforts to preserve the rainforests in the Amazon jungle in South America and efforts by Indian activists to prevent the flooding of agricultural areas by hydroelectric dam projects designed to promote energy creation and efforts to oppose corporate efforts to replace traditional farming methods with genetically modified seeds (Rajgopal, 2002; Starr & Adams, 2003). Often this work is described in conjunction with international efforts to promote sustainable development and protect environmental resources for future generations. One area of concern involves the right to water. Water supplies have been increasingly brought under the control of corporate owners and rather than being readily accessible or purchased through public agencies, residents may be charged, often high fees for its use, creating economic hardship and displacement of families and small farms (Bakker, 2007; Russell, 2010).

In addition to street protests directed against transnational organizations that engage in economic regulation and corporate control and efforts to stop the privatization or misuse of natural resources, some members of the antiglobalization, environmental protection, or sustainability movements have employed consensus and collaboration tactics to seek better strategies for using the world's resources. This "alter-globalization" movement has focused on setting up decision-making structures, most often referred to as "forums" as a means of countering the WTO and other trade organizations that are viewed as promoting harmful policies (Bakker, 2007). The most visible citizens group is the World Social Forum. Founded in Brazil in 2001 and held yearly, the WSF provides an open space or common ground for social activists worldwide to come together in one place to address common problems associated with the process of globalization. Conway (2007) describes the organization as "a world-wide, movement-based, multi-scale, and multi-sited cultural process . . . a space of spaces, a network of networks" (p. 51).

The WSP provides an opportunity to engage in democratic processes outside established processes in order identify common values and social identifies and develop social movement strategies (della Porta, n.d.). Although organized through an International Council, members do not engage in political advocacy nor does the organization seek to represent the viewpoints of participants (Teivainen, 2003). Policy proposals brought to the Council are debated by members and decisions are made by consensus. In addition to the WSP, a number of regional forums have been initiated and numerous other organizations and decision-making structures have adopted similar approaches such as the World Water Forum and the World March of Women and representatives of many of these smaller gatherings participate in the WSP (Bakker, 2007; Conway, 2007; della Porta, n.d.).

Struggles for Democracy and Human Rights in the Developing World

DeFilippis (2001b) argues that for the antiglobalization movement to be successful it must focus on how globalization affects people at the local level and how local economies impact the international economy. This is particularly important in terms of organizing efforts in the Global South, particularly those that focus on improving the economic, political and social status of low-income populations. Some of this work is facilitated with funding and staff from international development organizations that work from the top down in implementing UN standards while local efforts are locally initiated from the "bottom up" (Pardansani, 2005). According to Ife and Fiske (2006), this approach is preferable because "people are involved in constructing ideas of human rights for themselves and .... human rights emerge from everyday lived experience" (p. 305). Consequently, such efforts are also culturally competent and move away from definitions that may be most relevant in a western context.

Human rights struggles and organizing work often focus on changing traditional attitudes and power relationships. For example, many community organizing efforts in the Global South focus on empowering women (Boateng, 2009; Hicks, 2011; Jonsson, 2010). Pardansani (2005) describes the efforts of women attending a literacy program to develop an antialcohol campaign in a small village in India that focused on the negative impact of drinking on families and in which participants initially put pressure on local shops that sold alcohol to close. The campaign was so successful that it was supported by the mayor and the state government and spread to other small communities. The success of the effort helped the participants obtain a grant from the state government to establish a cooperative credit union that provided funding to women for small business start-ups. De La Puente (2011), in describing efforts to encourage women's leadership in a refugee camp in Dafur, argues that it is essential that international development agencies challenge gender inequities that may not be solely based on cultural patterns, but are encouraged and enforced by relief organizations themselves. Instead, development efforts should provide opportunities for participation in planning as well as leadership roles for women.

In addition to local organizing projects that focus on changing power relationships, organizers and activists in the developing world often risk their physical safety and lives to challenge repressive regimes. As this text was being written in 2011, residents of a number of Middle Eastern countries fought for access to economic resources and democratic governments in countries such as Tunisia, Egypt, Syria, and Yemen. Press reports indicated that high rates of youth unemployment and disparities in wealth among members of different social classes were among the reasons that protests occurred; similar conditions are also prevalent in other developing countries (Githongo, 2011). Some of the positive aspects associated with globalization were viewed by the media as critical to the success of these movements including increased access to information about other countries and how to engage in activism, the use the Internet, Facebook, and Twitter for organizing purposes, and the ability to use cell phones and text messaging to communicate and coordinate protests (Moore, 2011). The Internet was also credited for improving the dissemination of information about the protests to the rest of the world and making it possible for women, who are often isolated, but had access to computers to plan and participate in the protests (Shalhoub-Kervorkian, 2011).

THE IMPLICATIONS OF A GLOBAL PERSPECTIVE FOR SOCIAL WORK AND COMMUNITY PRACTICE

As described in the previous section, much of the literature on international social work and approaches through which social work practitioners should respond to globalization have examined the role of practitioners in international development organizations, social capital development, or economic development. However, here are a number of critiques of traditional international development and social work approaches to work in developing countries that have implications for community practice. For example, Jonsson (2010) argues that, "if empowerment strategies seek to have an emancipatory effect on people who are marginalized and discriminated against, they must go beyond developmental goals, such as higher productivity, higher consumption and higher formal education" (p. 404). Guo and Tsui (2010) have called upon social workers to extend their use of the strengths perspective to move beyond a focus on individual strengths, assets, resilience, and protective versus risk factors to one that recognizes that people are poor or politically marginalized due to social and political structures and their lack of access to political power. This framework suggests that strategies that involve individual or collective rebellion and resistance to oppressive policies or structures are also strengths that should be factored into social work assessments. For example, simple noncompliance with service requirements or agency policies could be viewed as strengths in some situations. However, rebellion and resistance can also be interpreted to include a full range of social action-related activities that include challenges to existing government structures as well as personal transformation and empowerment. Guo and Tsui suggest that the following questions be added to strength-based assessments for international social work and community development:

1. How does the behavior of service users differ from the behavior of the dominant classes?
2. What is the relationship between the behavior or customs of service users and their social positions? Do they have other options available to them?
3. What social capital resources do members of marginalized groups have that will help them improve the quality of their lives?
4. What type of strategies do they typically use to improve their lives and counteract oppression?

Dominelli (2005) also argues that most classic community development models are paternalistic, conducted on behalf of the poor or in a manner that exploits developing communities or their resources. She advocates instead for a "holistic interactional approach" that builds on the transformative model of community organization that emphasizes self-help and capacity building, but also mobilizes people to take action at all systems levels and that incorporates values such as sustainability, interdependence, reciprocity, and mutuality and focuses on strengthening relationships and building solidarity. Consequently, in Dominelli's model, an assessment should include the following systems:

- Individual, family, groups, organization and community.
- The country or countries in which the individual, family, or group resides or has previously resided or in which the organization or community is located.

- The amount of power possessed by the individual, family, group, organization, or group and how they are affected by the power possessed by others.
- The actual physical resources possessed by the individual, family, group, organization, or community.
- The cultural, social, psychological, political, or spiritual/religious resources available to the individual, family, group, organization, or community.
- How the individual, family, group, organization, or the community are affected by social, psychological, political, or spiritual/religious forces operating nationally or transnationally.
- The community's capacity to mobilize to take action to address issues that are negatively impacting its members.

This type of systems analysis can also lead to the identification of specific effects of globalization that have local implication in western industrialized nations and suggest action strategies to address these issues. For example, there may be a link between family hardship and loss of income due to a local garment factory shutting down, government policies that make it economically more feasible for corporations to open plants oversees, and working conditions and wages in factories in Guatemala, operated by the same corporation (Lightman, Mitchell, & Herd, 2005). In addition, social workers and community organizers should possess knowledge about the impact of globalization on new immigrants, the reasons for their relocation, the impact of immigration policies on their entry into a new country, their status under the law and the benefits or sanctions that accrue from this classification, and the hardships and experiences they have before and after entry into the new country (Nawyn, 2010; Xu, 2007). A systems analysis also allows for an examination of how family systems operate within a global context in situations in which family members are located in two or more countries, the effects of relocation, and how they remain connected to loved ones across national boundaries (Healy, 2008).

SUMMARY

The process of globalization affects almost every aspect of modern social life, including health and well-being, the ability to earn an adequate wage, transnational migration, poverty rates, the provision of social welfare services, homelessness, hunger, and maintaining a sustainable environment. As described in the IFSW statement of ethical principles, a response to these issues provides a variety of opportunities for social workers and community organizers to work locally or across borders to address these problems using traditional and innovative methods that can include aspects of social planning, community development social action, and transformative approaches to develop human capacity and attain human rights. However, a response to social exclusion requires not only advocacy and monitoring of social conditions; it also requires recognition of the inherent strength and dignity of all people and explicit efforts on the part of practitioners to partner with local groups and international coalitions in the struggle for social justice.

EXERCISES AND ASSIGNMENTS

1. Review at least one article about international social work or community organizing practice. Possible sources for your article review include the following journals that focus on international issues. *International Social Work*, the *Community Development Journal*, *Social Development Issues*, and *Urban Studies*. U.S.-oriented journals such as the *Journal of Community Practice*, the *Social Service Review*, and the *Journal of Sociology and Social Welfare* also publish articles about international issues. Write a three- to five-page paper that describes the topic of the article and the application of the contents of the article to social work or organizing practice. Compare the article to a similar study or description of practice about social work in the United States or another country in which you are familiar. What aspects of practice seem to be similar in both countries? How do the practice methods described uphold the principles in the IFSW Statement of Principles or *UN Universal Declaration of Human Rights*?

2. Identify a local issue or community problem linked to globalization. Describe the problem, assess the origins of the problem, and describe how the problem is affected by the process of globalization. Identify all the systems (family, community, economic, political, social, international) affected by the problem and in which change can be made to alleviate the impact on the individual and family. You may use an eco-map, social network map, genogram or other type of graphic to analyze and illustrate the issue.

3. Conduct an ethnographic interview with a recent immigrant. Focus on the respondent's immigration experiences, the reason for immigration,

culture, positive aspects of the immigration process or making transitions between different countries, any hardships (if any) experienced in both countries, and the respondent's perceptions of how the two cultures differ in terms of available resources, government policies, and values. Prepare a 10-minute presentation for class. Focus on what you learned from the interview.

15

Future Directions in Community Organizing: Where Do We Go From Here?

> *No movement has been perfect, no organizer has been perfect, and no struggle*
> *or a cause has been perfect. . . . They have improved with time.*
> —Interview with an immigrant rights organizer, Hardina et al., 2011

In this chapter, future directions for community organizing are described. The manner in which technological interventions will continue to affect community practice is examined, including the benefits and limitations of using technology rather than face-to-face interactions that bring people together. Also addressed is the commitment of the social work profession to social justice and to what degree community organizing will be continued to be recognized by social workers as a practice skill. The prevalence of various models of community practice such as community development, social planning, social action, and transformative approaches (including feminist and multicultural organizing) in the future will also be discussed. In the last section of the chapter, the importance of adopting an international or global perspective for social justice and community organizing will be examined.

THE APPLICATION OF TECHNOLOGICAL APPROACHES VERSUS INTERPERSONAL SKILLS FOR RECRUITING PEOPLE AND SUSTAINING INVOLVEMENT IN COMMUNITY PRACTICE

It is likely that technology will play an important role in community practice and social action, using social networking techniques to create social networks and public awareness about issues and personal hardships (Rohlinger & Brown, 2009). One of the major advantages of social media (as noted in Chapter 14) is the potential for reaching people who are fearful or isolated, allowing information to be transmitted among different societal groups and nations, and providing a vehicle for organizing protests and other forms of resistance to oppressive governments. It is likely that such trends will continue and result in new opportunities and freedoms for many people. In addition, the use of social media to facilitate social planning efforts, community development, citizen participation in government decision-making, and less confrontational types of social action such as coordinating rallies, running political campaigns and lobbying for legislation is increasing on almost a daily basis. As the technology evolves, so will the manner in which its use is put into operation for organizing purposes. For example, the idea to engage in activities that evolved into the "Occupy Wall Street" movement in 2011 in the United States, originated on the Internet. Participants effectively used a number of social media techniques to promote their message and illustrate how the protest was undertaken and the often negative responses of city officials and police to the occupations. These techniques included the use of Facebook by local groups, cell phone technology, Twitter, and video streaming (Preston, 2011). The use of social media was particularly critical in the early days of the city by city protests; few mainstream media outlets initially covered these events. While some aspects of the Occupy Movement may be atypical, other organizations with few resources or formal media contacts have also found these technological innovations to be effective for developing political power. Even cell phones or a simple Internet connection can be used as a means of drawing attention to a cause (Rapp, Button, B. Fleury-Steiner, & R. Fleury-Steiner, 2010).

However, despite the potential for social media to inform and bring people together, the Internet also has limitations; conversations may not always be private and some users may volunteer information that put activists at risk. The nature of the Internet and other new technology makes it likely that human rights struggles can be silenced through government control of, and even in some cases, termination of Internet services (New York Times, 2011). For example, in January, 2012, the Iranian government, in an attempt to limit dissent, blocked Internet websites and issued regulations requiring that cyber cafes install surveillance cameras and keep extensive information on computer users (Fassihi, 2012). Another limitation of Internet activism is that although online or "virtual organizations" often can have an impact on public-decision-making, at some point, to make change, people also need to engage in dialogue, rallies, conferences, mass protests, and other activities on a face-to-face basis (Hick & McNutt, 2002). Consequently, the Internet may be most effective when it is used to propose ideas, create opportunities for networking, and rally people to a cause (Theocharis, 2012). Actually getting together and doing something is an essential next step in facilitating social change. As pointed out earlier in this text, organizing is often described as a dance or musical ensemble or band. The interaction among members and their ability to influence group decisions is what makes organizing efforts successful.

Another consideration in terms of the use of technology has to do with the impact it has on the ability to communicate and how it can affect or even limit face-to-face interactions. In some circumstances, the use of cell phones, texting, Twitter, and the Internet may serve as a substitute for face-to-face interaction among friends, family members, business associates, fellow activists, and organization partners—limiting the availability of social support and solidarity. Video conferencing and Skype do allow users to respond to verbal cues and facial expressions, but can also easily be substituted for interpersonal interaction. Increasingly, government, universities, and businesses are using social media resources to conduct meetings, site visits, and events. This type of technology is also used to teach students skills that typically require face-to-face interaction such as the provision of social work services, health care, and psychotherapy, creating situations in which people may have difficulty using these practice skills in everyday life (Smyth, 2011).

In 2000, Reisch and Jarman-Rohde predicted that the Internet, ongoing government funding cuts for higher education, and other emerging types of social media might have implications for how field internships in social work would be offered in the future, allowing field instruction and liaison responsibilities to be conducted at a distance, and reducing the importance of actual interpersonal communication in teaching and practice. The growth in distance education in social work has in fact contributed to an increase in importance of video conferencing and other types of social media for both social work education and practice (Larsen, Visser-Rotgans, & Hole, 2011; Panos, 2005) and challenging social workers to use the new media in a manner that enhances rather than limits interpersonal skill acquisition (B. Moore, 2005).

SOCIAL WORK'S COMMITMENT TO SOCIAL JUSTICE AND COMMUNITY PRACTICE

Although the term *social justice* is often considered as integral to social work practice and is prominently discussed in the NASW Code of Ethics (2000) and the IFSW Statement of Principles (2004), it has sometimes been challenged as a vague, undefined term or as a politically charged concept that has been used to force students and practitioners to engage in advocacy to ensure equal access to goods and services and other social and political rights in a manner that is not consistent with their own religious or ideological beliefs (Galambos, 2008). For example, Hodge (2005, 2007) has argued that social justice education in schools of social work often fails to respect the religious traditions and beliefs of conservative Christians and other more conservative religious groups (such as Muslims or Orthodox Jews). He states that schools of social work discriminate against students with these beliefs by including content on the rights of members of the LGBTQ community in social work courses. Other social work scholars have noted, however, that Hodge's definitions of social justice and oppression ignore the role that social structure and power play in marginalizing some groups and not others, that he often generalizes a certain set of beliefs to all Christians or people of faith, and that he fails to make a case that members of conservative religious groups are actually placed at a disadvantage in terms of social work education or in society in general (Dessel, Bolen, & Shepardson, 2011; Melendez & LaSala, 2006). Also under contention is whether people have a right to refuse to hear viewpoints with which they simply do not agree and whether this right outweighs freedom of expression.

What the dialogue on this issue suggests, is that there appears to be a lack of clarity in definitions used by the profession in teaching from a social justice perspective. For example, Banerjee (2010) argues that social work's use of the term social justice as a justification for redistributing goods and services to assist people who are politically or economically disadvantaged ignores basic assumptions inherent in the theories of John Rawls. These theories describe how goods and services should be distributed and are often cited as inspiring the ethical mandate for social justice advocacy in the NASW Code of Ethics (Larkin, 2004; Reamer, 2006). Rawls (1971, 2001) advocated for the use of a rights-based framework in which resource and benefit allocation is based on the principle of equal and fair treatment for all and did not exclusively focus on the provision of goods and services to members of marginalized groups. Given the lack of actual congruence between Rawls' definition of social justice and social work principles, Banerjee (2011) calls for additional clarification of the concept so that it is consistent with the Code of Ethics. Other social workers have defined social justice as the equal distribution of resources to all members of society (Solas, 2008), achieving the greatest good for the greatest number (Murdach, 2011a; Reamer, 2006), or the process of reducing injustice by addressing both the harmful effects of discrimination and disparities among members of different demographic groups in terms of their access to and receipt of resources such as education, health care, jobs, public and nonprofit services, and political power (Davis & Bent-Goodley, 2004; Reisch, 2011; Rondero Hernandez, Montana, & Clarke, 2010).

Funge (2011) argues that despite the lack of a clear definition of social justice in social work, activities associated with its practice are clearly outlined in curriculum requirements mandated by those organizations that accredit schools of social work. In the United States, the Educational Policy Standards developed by the Council of Social Work Education clearly require that students be taught a variety of strategies that will enable them to advocate for human rights and economic justice. However, Funge's own research indicates that social work educators often are limited in their ability to prepare students for advocacy-related practice. Many of the social work instructors that he interviewed stated that their responsibility for curriculum content was limited to presenting information in the classroom. These respondents identified a number of barriers to teaching advocacy practice including tenure requirements at some universities, the lack of actual program adherence to or enforcement of CSWE's social justice standards, and the instructor's lack of actual advocacy experience or teaching preparation in this area. Research on student perceptions of social work curriculum in Great Britain also indicates that instructors or supervisors may not spend much time discussing power, oppression, social structure, or antidiscriminatory practice (Collins & Wilkie, 2010).

The ability to practice advocacy is often essential for social workers. Recent economic trends and market downturns during the last decade have created a number of challenges for the individuals, families, and groups that typically receive social work services or benefit from the work of community organizations (Reisch & Jarman-Rohde, 2000). Not only is funding for social services limited, more people, especially families and children, are facing economic hardship. At least a quarter of all the wealth in the United States is held disproportionally by only 1% of the population, creating widespread unemployment and poverty among both low-income and formerly middle-income households (Coleman, 2012). Some of the recent developments in terms of how services are funded and delivered have resulted in reducing the ability of social workers to advocate for their clientele or use their discretion in determining what type of services should be offered. In some states, the delivery of public services has been contracted out to private, for-profit firms, reducing the government's responsibility for ensuring that services are delivered in an appropriate and equitable manner (Marx, 2010).

Such trends indicate that well-trained community practitioners are needed more now than ever. However, Fisher and Corciullo (2011) note that despite renewed interest in community organizing following the election of former community organizer, Barack Obama, to the U.S. Presidency, the economic downturn has actually decreased the number of job openings for community workers and made it less likely that the organizers, planners, and developers actually hired will receive appropriate training. They argue that such conditions can be viewed as creating a unique opportunity for schools of social work to strengthen what is an often neglected curriculum area, by creating new courses and actively recruiting community practitioners for enrollment in BSW and MSW programs.

Mott (n.d.) agrees that there are few training opportunities for community organizers. He calls for an increased commitment on the part of university programs, including schools of social work, to prepare students to assume leadership positions in community-based organizations. Mott believes that recruitment efforts should focus on persons of color and other marginalized groups because members of these communities are most likely to feel the negative effects of social stigma and economic hardship. Mott describes why he thinks such preparation should occur in university settings;

> Community change is, in short, a tough and demanding job requiring a broad background, analytic and strategic skills, and practical experience in understanding and motivating people and moving them into action on strategies which will lead to growing success. It is a tremendously challenging—and exciting—responsibility, at least as complex as any other profession. Like other professions, it requires extensive preparation, well beyond what people can learn on a job without a serious educational component, mentoring and guidance. (Mott, n.d., p. 9)

In a follow-up report, Mott (2008) identifies three basic knowledge and competency areas for community organizers:

- Analytical skills including the ability to examine political, economic, and social processes, the ability to conduct research, and the ability to engage in reflective practice and think strategically.
- Interpersonal and organizational skills that can be used for the facilitation of collective action including participatory methods, program development, organization maintenance, and coalition-building.
- Specialized skills related to specific to fields of practice. For example, practitioners may specialize in areas such as environmental justice, poverty alleviation, or housing.

All of these skills are typically offered in social work programs with community practice concentrations. Funding for these expanded and enriched programs will be a challenge for many social work programs. However, community organization-oriented curriculum would also attract while providing an exceptionally experienced and diverse student pool that could benefit from social work knowledge, professional values, and skills training. However, as Hill, Ferguson, and Erickson (2010) note, schools of social work programs face several problems that limit instruction and student interest in community practice including the lack of an explicit macro practice identity and faculty biases that steer interested students away from careers in organizing or policy-making and into clinical practice. Also problematic in terms of attracting students into macro practice are licensing requirements in some states that are often geared primarily to clinical practitioners, but that require that all social workers be licensed in order to be legally eligible for title protection (i.e., the ability to call oneself a social worker). For some types of macro practice activities (such as social action), the ability to maintain flexibility and engage in activities that may challenge political decision-makers or the status quo, may outweigh the benefits of licensure; alternatively, some social work graduates might choose licensure over a career in community organizing to maximize their access to well-paying jobs in clinical practice.

A remaining issue that would need to be addressed if social work commits to preparing the next generation of community practitioners is field practicum. One of the challenges facing field coordinators is the lack of appropriate macro field placements. The Council on Social Work Education requires that field instructors hold MSW degrees. However, in many organizations that engage in organizing and other types of social justice-related advocacy, supervisory staff are not social workers (Wiebe, 2010). Consequently, schools of social work may need to explore alternative field instruction models that can fit with or complement accreditation agency requirements, for example, group supervision models, supervisory partnerships among agency staff and faculty-based field instructors, and additional training in social justice, advocacy, and community practice methods for practitioners interested in supervising macro field experiences. Another potential area for field instructor development involves explicit efforts to recruit recent macro graduates as well as retired micro practitioners with activist backgrounds to supervise community practice-related internships.

FUTURE DIRECTIONS AND MODELS OF COMMUNITY PRACTICE

Macro theorists in social work practice have repeatedly called for a return to community practice methods and an emphasis on community organization and development or the integration of community-based methods with micro or clinically focused practice with individuals (Ager, 2008; Johnson, 1998; Mendes, 2008; Staples, 2009). One of the difficulties in developing competencies and measuring their attainment is facilitating agreement among members of the profession who have different experiences, backgrounds, or practice approaches. As noted in Chapter 13, CSWE (2008) has developed a list of desired competencies for undergraduate social work degree holders and first or foundation year MSW students who are educated in generalist practice across individual, group, family, organization, and community systems. These competencies are fairly generic and do not differentiate between micro and macro practice, especially in terms of the application of interpersonal skills. Micro and/or clinical practice methods are well defined in the literature and are offered in a fairly consistent manner among schools of social work, varying by theoretical focus and practice specializations (Bogo et al., 2011; Cummins et al., 2006; Kramer Tebes et al., 2011). However, there appears to be little agreement among schools of social work about the content of macro courses or concentrations which can differ in terms of practice models or areas of specialization (such as poverty or multicultural practice), the types of internship opportunities offered, or the basic skills that should be developed among macro practitioners in social work (McNutt, 1995; Soska & Butterfield, 2011). Only a few attempts have been made to explicate these skills or develop a generic set of macro competencies that community practitioners should possess (Gamble, 2011; C. Regehr, Bogo, Donavan, Lim, & G. Regehr, 2012; Rothman & Zald, 2008).

The handful of research studies that have been conducted to examine the perceptions of social work graduates about their macro internship experiences indicate that respondents had a mixture of views about the degree to which field education prepared them for future employment. For example, Lane (2011) conducted a survey of over 400 elected officials with social work degrees and found that less than a third had completed internships with political content and only a small minority of respondents felt that they used any social work-related skills other than active listening and communication for campaign work or as elected officials. Holz Deal, Hopkins, Fisher, and Hartin (2007) compared the field experiences of micro and macro social work students and found that although most students were satisfied with their internship experiences, macro students were less likely to be satisfied than students in micro practice settings. The limited time availability of macro field instructors was one of the reasons for student dissatisfaction. In contrast, Mizrahi et al. (2006) surveyed the alumni of Hunter College's MSW program in community organizing between 1995 and 2006. They found that these graduates were very positive about field experiences and the curriculum, but less than 40% initially found employment in community organizing. Many of these graduates were employed as administrators when the study was conducted; only 13% held organizing jobs. An earlier study by Mizrahi and Rosenthal (1998) indicated that many Hunter students, when they did find organizing positions, worked primarily in jobs related to community-building and social planning rather than social action.

Social work education has often focused on noncontroversial types of curriculum that tend to be task focused and that prepare students to be technicians rather than social change agents (Bricout, Pollio, Edmond, & Moore McBride, 2008; Fisher & Corciullo, 2011; Stoecker Loving, Reddy, & Bolling, 2010). What is particularly noticeable is that while both social action and transformative models of practice in both micro and macro settings are idealized, the social work literature on these approach offers limited guidelines for encouraging consumer self-determination, partnerships among social workers and clientele, or engagement in advocacy for economic justice, human rights, or civil rights and liberties (Hardina, 2000; Murdach, 2011b), suggesting that it is social action that is the most endangered of all the various community practice models used by social workers.

The focus on technical knowledge rather than the interpersonal skills required for engagement, relationship-building, and collaboration has also contributed to the gulf between micro and macro practice and limited discussion about how basic social work skills can and should be applied in community practice. An additional concern has to do with the impact of service learning and civic engagement initiatives in inspiring university students to look at community practice and social activism as potential careers. While such activity is a good introduction to the field, it may not actually offer much in the way of formal instruction to these students who often simply serve as volunteers for community groups and write reflective papers about their experiences (Lemieux & Allen, 2007).

Also, when assignments are made in social work and other courses that require service learning or other types of volunteer work, they may not always involve projects that result in free consulting or services to local organizations and groups. They may be part of larger university–community partnerships in which grant money is received to fund university operations and reimburse faculty for research services and other types of consultation. Much of the available funding for community activities is in conjunction with Comprehensive Community

Initiatives that combine social service provision with community and economic development activities. Although such development efforts may bring needed resources to communities, they are often top down or government (and sometimes foundation) initiated and real effort must be made to obtain community support. There are often no sure guarantees that these development efforts will be consistent with the needs of the surrounding communities or will preserve the homes, businesses, or interpersonal networks that create a sense of community among low-income residents (Hawkins & Maurer, 2010; Pyles & Cross, 2008; Silverman, 2009). Such efforts also do not shift control of resources or change power and political dynamics that contribute to perpetuating poverty (van den Berk-Clark & Pyles, 2012). An additional consideration for community practice in social work is that the availability of funding for faculty and students to engage exclusively in community development and social planning efforts may contribute to the continued marginalization of practice methods that focus on increasing the power of historically oppressed communities such as feminist organizing, social action, transformative approaches, and culturally specific methods.

Another way in which preferences for practice models may be distorted involves the Evidence-based Practice movement. As per CSWE guidelines, students receive instruction in EBP and there is explicit advocacy on the part of instructors that practice methods should be chosen only when there is available research evidence (most likely produced through the use of randomized experiments) that the intervention works (Bricout et al., 2008). The dissemination of this type of information may serve to discourage students from pursuing careers in community practice or using intervention models that do not fit this criteria. It also has the effect of denigrating the use of participatory or practice-oriented informed research methods that cannot easily fit into the EBP model and ignoring the value of experiential knowledge held by community members (Epstein, 2011; Freire, 1970; Gaventa & Cornwall, 2002; Newman, 2008).

Also a concern for both practice and social work curriculum, is that sometimes these comprehensive community change initiatives that emphasize large-scale housing and economic redevelopment take the focus away from the type of community development activities described by Biddle and Biddle (1979), the coming together of neighbors and friends to address a common concern, drawing on personal and other local resources, and a shared commitment to making things better. The organizer's role is simply to provide information, support, a safe place where people can meet, and assistance in connecting people with one another in order to strengthen local networks and the capacity for change. It is these basic skills that remain, at the core, what a skilled organizer can do to help improve the quality of life in a community (Delgado, 2000).

It would seem, given social work's historic commitment to social justice, equality, and advocating for cultural diversity and anti-oppressive practices that schools of social work have a duty to give students all the tools they need to engage in social change (Collins & Wilkie, 2010; Reisch, 2011). This should include a variety of strategic and tactical options to use, which transcend preferences for one or two primary practice models. Curriculum content should also include interpersonal skills such as the engagement, interviewing, dialogue, and the group work skills necessary to partner with community groups to identify social problems, issues, and concerns, conduct assessments that address structural conditions that may be holding people and communities back, identify the strengths and skills of community members, develop leaders, create plans for social change, take action, and evaluate what they have accomplished.

These skills should explicitly build upon CSWE's Educational Policy and Accreditation Standards for undergraduate social work and first-year MSW students. Instruction can be integrated into generalist curriculum for undergraduate and graduate students. For example, basic applications of interviewing and engagement skills in community settings could complement instruction that focuses on their use in agency settings. Students could receive instruction in conducting a basic one-on-one interview, facilitating a task group to address a community problem, or participating in a community outreach effort (Timm et al., 2011). In the second or advanced year of MSW programs, students should be required to use engagement, interviewing and dialogue-related skills to recruit participants, work with organization partners, and provide staff support to a group of constituents (either community members or professionals) who are engaging in social change activities: social action, development work, social planning, lobbying, or policy change. Such skills are generic enough that they can be used in most macro concentrations that include content on community practice regardless of how the curriculum is constructed or focused. For example, a second-year concentration involving political practice would probably include a combination of constituency office, legislative, and policy placements. All such internships would require that students develop and apply engagement and interpersonal skills in order to work with constituents, legislators, or organizations to address policy issues that directly affect constituents (see Table 15.1).

TABLE 15.1
Using CSWE Educational Policy and Accreditation Standards (EPAS) to Formulate Advanced Interpersonal Skills for Community Practice

EPAS Competency (Foundation Year)	EPAS Suggested Practice Behavior (Foundation Year)	Advanced Interpersonal Skills
2.1.10(a)–(d)	Engage, assess, intervene, and evaluate with individuals, families, groups, organizations, and communities.	(1) Professional practice involves the dynamic and interactive processes of engagement, assessment, interventions, and evaluation at multiple levels. Social workers have the knowledge and skills to practice with individuals, families, groups, organizations, and communities. Practice knowledge includes identifying, analyzing, and implementing evidence-based interventions designed to achieve client goals; using research and technological advances; evaluating program outcomes and practice effectiveness; developing, analyzing, advocating, and providing leadership for policies and services; and promoting social and economic justice.	(1) Use interpersonal skills and technology to enter communities, engage with, and recruit participants in social change activities that include problem identification, assessment, planning interventions, taking action, and evaluation (2) Develop constituent leaders that can facilitate change in their own communities.

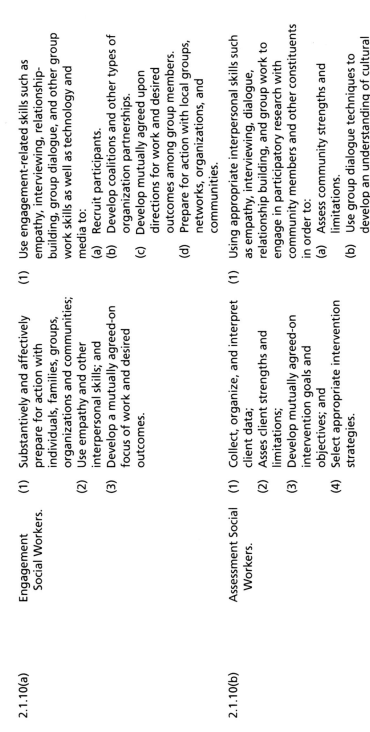

| 2.1.10(a) | Engagement Social Workers. | (1) Substantively and affectively prepare for action with individuals, families, groups, organizations and communities;
(2) Use empathy and other interpersonal skills; and
(3) Develop a mutually agreed-on focus of work and desired outcomes. | (1) Use engagement-related skills such as empathy, interviewing, relationship-building, group dialogue, and other group work skills as well as technology and media to:
(a) Recruit participants.
(b) Develop coalitions and other types of organization partnerships.
(c) Develop mutually agreed upon directions for work and desired outcomes among group members.
(d) Prepare for action with local groups, networks, organizations, and communities. |
| 2.1.10(b) | Assessment Social Workers. | (1) Collect, organize, and interpret client data;
(2) Asses client strengths and limitations;
(3) Develop mutually agreed-on intervention goals and objectives; and
(4) Select appropriate intervention strategies. | (1) Using appropriate interpersonal skills such as empathy, interviewing, dialogue, relationship building, and group work to engage in participatory research with community members and other constituents in order to:
(a) Assess community strengths and limitations.
(b) Use group dialogue techniques to develop an understanding of cultural and social dynamics, community conditions, power relations, and political and economic systems. |

(Continued)

TABLE 15.1

Using CSWE Educational Policy and Accreditation Standards (EPAS) to Formulate Advanced Interpersonal Skills for Community Practice (Continued)

EPAS Competency (Foundation Year)	EPAS Suggested Practice Behavior (Foundation Year)	Advanced Interpersonal Skills
		(c) Develop mutually agreed upon intervention goals and objectives.
		(d) Select appropriate intervention strategies by reviewing options, weighing values and ethical implications, and developing the responsive capacity and flexibility to make decisions based upon situational demands.
2.1.10(c) Intervention Social Workers.	(1) Initiate actions to achieve organizational goals;	(1) Using engagement, empathy, relationship-building, dialogue, and group maintenance skills to:
	(2) Implement prevention interventions that enhance client capacities;	(a) Assist group members in the development of a collective identity.
	(3) Help client resolve problems;	(b) Provide support and assistance to group leaders in facilitating meetings and involving constituency group members in decision-making.
	(4) Negotiate, mediate, and advocate for clients; and	

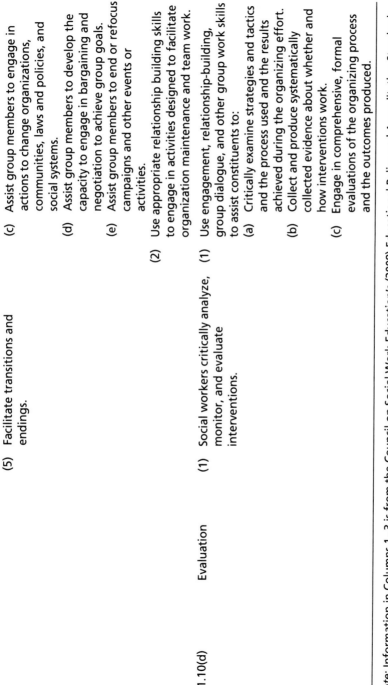

	(5) Facilitate transitions and endings.	(c) Assist group members to engage in actions to change organizations, communities, laws and policies, and social systems.
		(d) Assist group members to develop the capacity to engage in bargaining and negotiation to achieve group goals.
		(e) Assist group members to end or refocus campaigns and other events or activities.
		(2) Use appropriate relationship building skills to engage in activities designed to facilitate organization maintenance and team work.
2.1.10(d)	(1) Social workers critically analyze, monitor, and evaluate interventions.	(1) Use engagement, relationship-building, group dialogue, and other group work skills to assist constituents to:
Evaluation		(a) Critically examine strategies and tactics and the process used and the results achieved during the organizing effort.
		(b) Collect and produce systematically collected evidence about whether and how interventions work.
		(c) Engage in comprehensive, formal evaluations of the organizing process and the outcomes produced.

Note: Information in Columns 1–3 is from the Council on Social Work Education's (2008) Educational Policy and Accreditation Standards.

Given recent trends that seem to have reduced social work's commitment to community practice, a return to our roots, the recognition that interpersonal skills are needed by both micro and macro practitioners would seem to be essential for strengthening the profession and ensuring that macro practice opportunities remain available to our students. All social workers should be able to engage with and build relationships with the individuals we serve and those individuals (such as government officials, agency administrators, business leaders, media representatives, community leaders, and other decision-makers) whose actions are critical for influencing public opinion, changing laws and social policies and making the world a better place.

DEVELOPING AN INTERNATIONAL PERSPECTIVE IN SOCIAL JUSTICE ORGANIZING

As described in the IFSW Statement of Principles (2004), one of the primary responsibilities of social workers is to advocate for human rights. It is likely that as world economies and technology evolve, perceptions about human rights will also evolve. Changes in technology and demands for goods and services may also result in labor abuses or the loss of individual and group access to resources and political rights (Chan & Peng, 2011). To some extent this will be in reaction to globalization, corporate control, and efforts to privatize access to natural resources or public services. However, social values also evolve in response to changes in public perceptions, government or institutional policies, the interconnectedness among individuals, organizations, and population groups, and increased access to information. For example, in the United States, in response to the displacement of residents of New Orleans to Katrina and post-disaster development and the foreclosure crisis in the late 2000s, advocacy groups argued for the recognition of a right to housing that includes the *right of tenancy* or ability to retain one's own home if someone arbitrarily tries to confiscate it (Foscarinis, 2011). In 2011, U.S. Secretary of State Hillary Clinton made headlines with a speech urging the nations of the world to recognize the rights of and provide legal protections for members of the LGBTQ community. In her remarks, Secretary Clinton focused on violence directed at individuals due to their sexual orientation or identity and noted that protection from discrimination and harm is a basic human right for all people. She also described the progress made in protecting human rights since the adoption of the *UN Universal Declaration of Human Rights* in 1948, stating that, "In many places, racist laws have been repealed, legal and social practices that relegated women to second-class status have been abolished, the ability of religious minorities to practice their faith freely has been secured" (Clinton, 2011, para 4). However, she also added the following urgent call for action:

> And to people of all nations, I say supporting human rights is your responsibility too. The lives of gay people are shaped not only by laws, but by the treatment they receive every day from their families, from their neighbors. Eleanor Roosevelt, who did so much to advance human rights worldwide, said that these rights begin in the small places close to home—the streets where people live, the schools they attend, the factories, farms, and offices where they work. These places are your domain. The actions you take, the ideals that you advocate, can determine whether human rights flourish where you are. (Clinton, 2011, para 29)

Although U.S.-centric examples are offered here, we need to be mindful that responses to human rights abuses have their origins in local struggles, occurring in all sections of the global, to retain traditional lands, ensure that all children have access to food, education, and medical care, guarantee that women can vote, run for public office, live independently of husbands and other male family members, and retain ownership of what they have earned, and that people with disabilities have the opportunity to earn a living and engage in all other aspects of daily life. We must also make sure that migrants, refugees, and other stateless people have basic human rights including housing and employment opportunities and are not subject to indefinite detention or separated arbitrarily from children and other family members. In a globalized world, none of these problems occur in isolation and often are the consequence of economic and political decisions made by people or governments far from the people who experience the consequences of these actions.

We need to remember that it is the responsibility of social workers to advocate for human rights, engage in lobbying efforts to make sure nations and local governments actually comply with U.N. standards, and to indentify additional rights that ensure that all people are able to maintain an adequate standard of living and are treated with dignity and respect regardless of their country of origin, citizenship status, social class, disability or mental health status, gender, race, religion, age, or sexual orientation. The interconnections among people and local and global economics make it essential that social workers function as citizens of the world rather than within narrow parameters determined by self-interest, agency affiliations, or field of practice. Scott Harding and Kathryn Libal (2011) in examining the impact on war on refugee families call on social workers to be:

> Obliged to mobilize transnationally to challenge global forms of oppression, and that some practices, such as failing to meet the needs of refugees, require such collaboration beyond borders. As a profession with a clear value base, grounded in opposing war, structural violence and inequality, it is our collective responsibility to offer professional knowledge in a global society and advocate for the realization of human rights. (p. 102)

SUMMARY

Recent economic trends including the concentration of wealth and poverty and the process of globalization make it urgent that social work education recommit to social justice advocacy. One means of doing this is to strengthen community practice curriculum to prepare students for employment in a fast-changing environment in which technology, global interconnections that both facilitate recognition of human rights and make it more difficult to achieve them. Rather than simply experiential education for a few common community organization activities such as needs assessment, program planning, or evaluation, students need education in the use of interpersonal skills such as engagement, interviewing, dialogue, recruitment, group formation and maintenance, framing issues in a manner that has salience to specific groups and the general public, and maintaining group identification and solidarity that require ongoing training, development, and repeated application in a variety of circumstances and settings. Social work programs have been fairly successful in preparing micro and generalist practice students to use interviewing, engagement, and other interpersonal skills in agency settings and consequently, are perfectly situated to instruct students in relationship-building techniques that take them outside organizations and into communities, legislatures, and multicultural gatherings.

EXERCISES AND ASSIGNMENTS

1. Interview an organizer who has been practicing for 10 or more years. Your interview should focus on how practice has evolved over time and how technology has (or has not changed) methods and techniques used to organize, develop, or plan communities.

2. As a class assignment, collaborate with three or more students to create a web or Facebook page that can be used to make people aware of an issue and rally them to a cause. The page should include information about the issue, research data that demonstrate how people will be affected by the issue, reasons why the average person should be concerned about the issue, and action steps that should be taken by the reader to help resolve the problem. Use social media and letter writing or speech preparation tips provided in Chapters 3, 8, and 11 to design your page. Also think about the population group that you wish to reach (in terms of age, language, social class, gender, etc.) when choosing the content of your page and framing the message.

3. How do you define social justice? Can you identify three or four recent examples of how social justice was achieved? How did this occur? Who was responsible for facilitating the change process? How does your definition of social justice differ from your classmates or from the people you interact with in your internship? How you think your definition differs from the way your instructors, university administrators, or elected officials define this concept?

References

Abrams, L., & Moio, J. (2009). Critical race theory and the cultural competence dilemma in social work education. *Journal of Social Work Education, 45*, 245–261.

Affonso, D., Mayberry, L., Shibuya, J., Archambeau, O., Correa, M., Deliramich, A., & Frueh, B. (2010). Cultural context of school communities in rural Hawaii to inform youth violence prevention. *Journal of School Health, 80*(3), 146–152.

Ager, R. (2008). Critical variables for infusing community content into a clinical program: An empirical analysis. *Journal of Community Practice, 13*(3), 91–105.

Aguilar, J., & Sen, S. (2009). Comparing conceptualizations of social capital. *Journal of Community Practice, 17*, 424–443.

Alasah, A. (2009). The impact of government policy on grassroots level community development initiative in the Northwest region of Cameroon. *Community Development Journal, 46*, 196–212.

Alinsky, S. (1971). *Rules for radicals*. New York: Vintage.

Alliance for Justice. (2010). *Core components of community organizing*. Retrieved from http://www.afj.org/for-nonprofits-foundations/reco/core-components. html

Alter, C. (2000). Interorganizational collaboration in the task environment. In R. Patti (Ed.), *The handbook of social welfare management* (pp. 283–302). Thousand Oaks, CA: Sage.

Amidei, N. (2002, December 14). *Working the system: Citizens can exert influence at every step. Seattle PI.* Retrieved from http://www.citizenreviewonline.org/Dec_2002/working.htm

Anderson, A. (n.d.). *The community builder's approach to theory of change: A practical guide to theory development*. Aspen Institute Roundtable on Community Change. Retrieved from http://www.aspeninstitute.org/sites/default/files/content/docs/roundtable%20on%20community%20change/rcccommbuild ersapproach.pdf

Andharia, J. (2007). Reconceptualizing community organization in India: A transdisciplinary perspective. *Journal of Community Practice, 15*(1/2), 91–119.

Andrews, K., Ganz, M., Baggetta, M., Han, H., & Lim, C. (2010). Leadership, membership, and voice: Civic associations that work. *American Journal of Sociology, 115*, 1191–1242.

Androff, D. (2011). The problem of international slavery: An international human rights challenge for social work. *International Social Work, 54*, 209–222.

Annie E. Casey Foundation. (2002). *Team decisionmaking: Involving the family and community in child welfare decisions. Part Two: Building community partnerships in child welfare*. Retrieved from http://www.aecf.org/upload/pdffiles/familytofamily/f2f_tdm_sept_02.pdf

Arizmendi, L., & Ortiz, L. (2004). Neighborhood and community organizing in Colonias: A case study in the development and use of promotoras. *Journal of Community Practice, 12*(1/2), 23–35.

Armstrong, D. (2000). A survey of community gardens in upstate New York: Implications for health promotion and community development. *Health & Place, 6*, 319–327.

Arnstein, S. (1969). A ladder of citizen participation. *Journal of the American Institute of Planners, 35*, 216–224.

Asian NGO Coalition for Agrarian Reform and Rural Development. (n.d.) *10 basic steps in community organizing*. Retrieved from http://www.angoc.org/portal/wp-content/uploads/2010/07/19/ideas-in-action-for-land-rights-advocacy/13-10-Basic-Steps-in-Community-Organizing.pdf

Associated Press. (2010, June 20). *ACLU Arizona travel warning: Civil liberties group urges visitors to avoid state*. Retrieved from Huffington Post website: http://www.huffingtonpost.com/

Associated Press. (2011, March 19). Tens of thousands protest austerity in Portugal. *Bloomberg Businessweek*. Retrieved from http://www.businessweek.com/ap/financialnews/D9M2FLG00.htm

Atkins-Sayre, W. (2010). Articulating identity: People for the ethical treatment of animals and the animal/human divide. *Western Journal of Communication, 74*, 309–328.

Austin, D. (2002). *Human service management: Organizational leadership in social work practice*. New York: Columbia University Press.

Austin, M., Regan, K., Samples, M., Schwartz, S., & Carnochan, S. (2011). Building managerial and organizational capacity in nonprofit human service organizations through a leadership development program. *Administration in Social Work, 35*, 258–281.

Autism Research Institute. (2007). *Advocacy 101: The ins and outs of scheduling and attending a successful Congressional lobbying visit*. Retrieved from http://legacy.autism.com/families/advocacy/advocacy101.htm

Avner, M. (2002). *The lobbying and advocacy handbook for nonprofit organizations: Shaping public policy at the state and local level*. New York: Fieldstone Alliance.

Axner, M. (2010). Building relationships with people from different cultures. *Community Toolbox*. Retrieved from http://ctb.,u.edu/en/tablecontents/sub_section_main_1170

Ayers, J. (2004). Framing collective action against neoliberalism: The case of the anti-globalization movement. *Journal of World System Research, 10*, 11–34.

Ayon, C., & Lee, C. (2009). Building strong communities: An evaluation of a neighborhood leadership program. *Journal of Community Psychology, 37*, 975–986.

Babajaian (2008). Social capital and community participation in post-Soviet Armenia: implications for policy and practice. *Europe-Asia Studies, 60*, 1299–1319.

Baker, D., Melnikow, J., Ly, M. L., Shoultz, J., Niederhauser, V., & Diaz-Escamilla, R. (2010). Translation of health surveys using mixed methods. *Journal of Nursing Scholarship, 42*, 430–438.

Bakker, K. (2007). The "commons" versus the "commodity": Alter-globalization, anti-privatization and the human right to water in the global south. *Antipode, 39*, 430–455.

Balcazar, F., Garcia-Iriarte, E., & Suarez-Balcazar, Y. (2009). Participatory action research with Columbian immigrants. *Hispanic Journal of Behavioral Sciences, 31*, 112–127.

Bandura, A. (1990). Perceived self-efficacy in the exercise of control over AIDS infection. *Evaluation & Program Planning, 13*, 9–17.

Banerjee, M. (2011). Social work scholar's representation of Rawls: A critique. *Journal of Social Work Education, 47*, 189–211.

Bankhead, T., & Erlich, J. (2005). Diverse populations and community practice. In M. Weil, M. Reisch, D. Gamble, L. Gutierrez, E. Mulroy, & R. Cnaan (Eds.), *The handbook of community practice* (pp. 59–83). Thousand Oaks, CA: Sage.

Barata, P. (2000). *Social exclusion in Europe.* Laidlaw Foundation. Retrieved from Web Networks website: http://action.web.ca/home/narcc/attach/Social%20Exclusion%20in%20Europe%20%20a%20literature%20review%20(%202000%20)% 5B1%5D.pdf

Barretti, M. (2009). Organizing for tenants' rights: Insights and approaches from both sides of the fence. *Journal of Progressive Human Services, 20*(1), 8–25.

Bartle, E., Couchonnal, G., Canda, E., & Staker, M. (2002). Empowerment as a dynamically developing concept for practice: Lessons learned from organizational ethnography. *Social Work, 47*, 32–43.

Baum, H. (2001). How should we evaluate community initiatives? *Journal of the American Planning Association, 67*, 147–158.

Baumgartner, F., Berry, J., Hojnacki, M., Kimball, D., & Leech, B. (2009). *Lobbying and policy change. Who wins, who loses, and why.* Chicago, IL: University of Chicago Press.

Bayne-Smith, M., Mizrahi, T., & Garcia, M. (2008). Interdisciplinary community collaboration: Perspectives of community practitioners on successful strategies. *Journal of Community Practice, 16*, 249–269.

Ben-Arieh, A. (2008). The influence of social indicators data on decision making in regard to children's well-being. *Administration in Social Work, 32*, 23–38.

ben Asher, M. (2002). *Writing daily macro practice notes.* Retrieved from Gather the People website: http://www.gatherthepeople.org/Downloads/MACRO_NOTES.pdf

ben Asher, M. (2010). *Staff development and leadership.* Paper Presented on COMM-ORG: The On-line Conference on Community Organizing (Vol. 16). Retrieved from http://comm-org.wisc.edu/papers2010/benasher10.htm

Beck, E., & Eichler, M. (2000). Consensus organizing: A practice model for community building. *Journal of Community Practice, 8*(1), 87–102.

Berg, B. (2009). *Qualitative research methods for the social sciences* (7th ed.). Boston: Allyn & Bacon.

Bergan, D. (2009). Does grassroots lobbying work? A field experiment measuring the effects of an e-mail lobbying campaign on legislative behavior. *American Politics Research, 37*, 327–352.

Berger, J. (2003). Religious non-government organizations: An exploratory analysis. *Voluntas, 14*(1), 15–39.

Bernhardt, R. (n.d.). Section 7, Public participation. *Planners communication guide: Strategies, examples, and tolls for everyday practice.* Retrieved from American Planning Association website: http://www.planning.org/communications guide/pdf/section7.pdf

Berton, J. (2010, May 7). A high-tech hunger strike at UC. *San Francisco Chronicle,* p. C2.

Bess, K., Prillenltensky, I., Perkins, D., & Collins, L. (2009). Participatory organizational change in community-based health and human services: From tokenism to political engagement. *Journal of Community Psychology, 43,* 134–148.

Betigeri, A. (2011, May 11). Japan's Fukushima crisis drives protests over world's largest anti-nuclear plant in India. *Christian Science Monitor.* Retrieved from http://www.csmonitor.com/World/Asia-South-Central/2011/0511/Japan-s-Fukushima-crisis-drives-protests-over-world-s-largest-nuclear-plant-in-India

Biddle, W., & Biddle, L. (1979). Intention and outcome. In F. Cox, J. Erlich, J. Rothman, & J. Tropman (Eds.), *Strategies of community organization* (3rd ed., pp. 365–375), Itasca, IL: Peacock Publishers.

Birkenmaier, J., & Curley, J. (2009). Financial credit: Social work's role in empowering low-income families. *Journal of Community Practice, 17,* 251–268.

Boateng, A. (2009). A mixed methods analysis of social capital of women in Ghana. *Journal of Sociology and Social Work, 36*(3), 59–81.

Bobo, K., Kendall, J., & Max, S. (2010). *Organizing for social change: A manual for activists* (4th ed.). Santa Ana, CA: Forum Press.

Boehm, A., & Staples, L. (2002). The functions of the social worker in empowering. The voices of consumers and professionals. *Social Work, 47,* 337–480.

Boehm, A., & Staples, L. (2006). Grassroots leadership in task-oriented groups: Learning from successful leaders. *Social Work with Groups, 28*(2), 77–96.

Bogo, M., Regehr, C., Logie, C., Katz, E., Mylopoulos, M., & Regehr, G. (2011). Adapting objective structured clinical examinations to assess social work students' performance and reflections. *Journal of Social Work Education, 47,* 5–18.

Boothroyd, R., Fawcett, S., & Foster-Fishman, P. (2006). Community development: Enhancing the knowledge base through participatory action research. In L. Jason, C. Keys, Y. Suarez-Balcazar, R. Taylor, & M. Davis (Eds.), *Participatory community research: Theories and methods in action* (pp. 27–52). Washington, DC: American Psychological Association.

Bourdieu, P. (1986). The forms of capital. In J. Richardson (Ed.), *The handbook of theory and research for the sociology of education* (pp. 241–258). New York: Greenwood Press.

Bowen, G. (2007). An analysis of citizen participation in anti-poverty programs. *Community Development Journal, 43*(1), 65–78.

Bowers Andrews, A. (2004). Start at the end: Empowerment evaluation product planning. *Evaluation and Program Planning, 27,* 275–285.

Bowers Andrews, A., Stone Motes, P., Floyd, A., Crocker Flerx, V., & Lopez-De Fede, A. (2005). Building evaluation capacity in community-based organizations. *Journal of Community Practice, 13*(4), 85–104.

Brager, G., Specht, H., & Torczyner, J. (1987). *Community organizing* (2nd ed.). New York: Columbia University Press.

Briffault, R. (2008). Lobbying and campaign finance: Separate and together. *Stanford Law & Policy Review, 19*(1), 105–129.

Bricout, J., Pollio, D., Edmond, T., & Moore McBride, A. (2008). Macro practice teaching and curriculum development from an evidence-based perspective. *Journal of Evidence-based Social Work, 5,* 597–621.

Briggs, H., & McBeath, B. (2009). Evidence-based management: Origins, challenges, and implications for social service administration. *Administration in Social Work, 33,* 242–261.

Brisson, D., & Roll, S. (2008). An adult education model of resident participation: Building community capacity and strengthening neighborhood-based activities in a comprehensive community initiative. *Advances in Social Work, 9,* 157–175.

Brody, S., Godschalk, D., & Burby, R. (2003). Mandating citizen participation in plan making: Six strategic planning choices. *Journal of the American Planning Association, 69,* 245–264.

Brooks, F. (2005). Resolving the dilemma between organizing and services: Los Angeles ACORN's welfare advocacy. *Social Work, 50,* 262–270.

Brooks, F., Russell, D., & Fisher, R. (2006). ACORN's accelerated income redistribution project: A program evaluation. *Research on Social Work Practice, 16,* 369–387.

Brown, M. (2006). *Building powerful community organizations: A personal guide to creating groups that can solve problems and change the world.* Arlington, MA: Long Haul Press.

Brown, M. (2008). Risk mapping as a tool for CBPR and organizing. In M. Minkler, & N. Wallerstein (Eds.), *Community-based participatory research for health: From processes to outcomes* (pp. 453–457). San Francisco, CA: Jossey-Bass.

Brown, L., & Vega, W. (2008). A protocol for community-based research. In M. Minkler, & N. Wallerstein (Eds.), *Community-based participatory research for health: From processes to outcomes* (pp. 395–397). San Francisco, CA: Jossey-Bass.

Brownstein, L. (2003). A model of interdisciplinary collaboration. *Social Work, 48,* 297–306.

Brumback, K. (2011, June 23). Illegal immigrant youth "come out" in reform push. *Associated Press.* Retrieved from http://www.google.com/hosted news/ap/article/ALeqM5jXF6itgyn8PueQAHV-OeQl6W3j0Q?docId=cc591 090beb741b2a46496c0e7197572

Brunsting, S., & Postmes, T. (2002). Social movement participation in the digital age: Predicting offline and online collective action. *Small Group Research, 33,* 525–554.

Buccus, I., Hemson, D., Hicks, J., & Piper, L. (2008). Community development and engagement with local governance in South Africa. *Community Development Journal, 43,* 297–311.

Burghardt, S. (2011). *Macro practice in social work for the 21st century.* Thousand Oaks, CA: Sage.

Butterfoss, F. (2006). Process evaluation for community participation. *Annual Review of Public Health, 27,* 323–340.

California Attorney General's Office (2003). *The Brown Act. Open meetings for local legislative bodies.* Retrieved from http://ag.ca.gov/publications/2003_Intro_BrownAct.pdf

Caputo, R. (2010). Family characteristics, public program participation, and civic engagement. *Journal of Sociology and Social Welfare, 37*(2), 35–61.

Carlson, E., Engebretson, J., & Chamberlain, R. (2006). Photovoice as a social process of critical consciousness. *Qualitative Health Research, 16,* 836–852.

Carr, A. (2009). *Urban community building through community based organizations in Fresno's areas of concentrated poverty* (Unpublished master's project). Department of Social Work Education, California State University, Fresno.

Carroll, J., & Minkler, M. (2000). Freire's message for social workers: Looking back, looking ahead. *Journal of Community Practice, 8*(1), 21–36.

Castelloe, P., & Prokopy, J. (2001). Recruiting participants for community practice interventions. *Journal of Community Practice, 9*(2), 31–48.

Castelloe, P., Watson, T., & White, C. (2002). Participatory change: An integrative approach to community practice. *Journal of Community Practice, 10*(4), 7–31.

Castle, S. (2004). Why migration policies fail. *Ethnic and Racial Studies, 27,* 205–227.

Castleden, H., Garvin, T. & Huu-ayaht First Nation. (2008). Modifying Photovoice for community-based participatory indigenous research. *Social Science and Medicine, 66,* 1393–1405.

Castro, F., Barrera, M., & Martinez, C. (2004). The cultural adaptation of prevention interventions: Resolving tensions between fidelity and fit. *Prevention Sciences, 5,* 41–45.

Catalani, C., & Minkler, M. (2010). Photovoice: A review of the literature in health and public health. *Health Education & Behavior, 37,* 424–451.

Center for Community Change. (n.d.). *Rules for doing one-on-ones.* Retrieved from http://174.46.184.17:51075/cccdb/www/library/CROSSING-BORDERS-toolkit-07.pdf/?searchterm=None

Center for Progressive Leadership. (n.d.). *Organizing an effective phone bank.* Retrieved from http://www.progressleaders.org

Chambers, E. (2004). *Roots for radicals: Organizing for power, action, and justice.* New York: Continuum.

Chambers, R. (1994). The origins and practice of participatory rural appraisal. *World Development, 22,* 953–969.

Chambers, D., & Wedel, K. (2005). *Social policy and social programs: A method for the practical public policy analyst* (4th ed.). Boston, MA: Allyn & Bacon.

Chambon, A. (1999). Foucault's approach: Making the familiar visible. In
A. Chambon, A. Irving, & L. Epstein (Eds.), *Reading Foucault for social work*
(pp. 51–81). New York: Columbia University Press.

Chan, C. K., & Peng, Z. (2011). From rice bowl to the worlds' biggest sweatshop:
Globalization, institutional constraints, and the rights of Chinese workers.
Social Service Review, 85, 421–445.

Chaskin, R. (2001). Building community capacity: A definitional framework and
case studies from a comprehensive community initiative. *Urban Affairs
Review, 36*, 291–323.

Chaskin, R. (2003). Fostering neighborhood democracy: Legitimacy and
accountability within loosely coupled systems. *Nonprofit and Voluntary
Quarterly, 32*, 161–189.

Chatterton, P., Fuller, D., & Routledge, P. (2007). Relating action to activism:
Theoretical and methodological reflections. In S. Kindon, R. Pain, &
M. Kesby (Eds.), *Participatory research approaches and methods* (pp.
216–222). New York: Routledge.

Chavez, C. (1966). *The organizer's tale*. Retrieved from http://www.hks.harvard.
edu/organizing/tools/toolshome.shtml

Checkoway, B. (2007). Community change for diverse democracy. *Community
Development Journal, 44*, 5–21.

Checkoway, B., & Zimmerman, M. (1992). Correlates of participation in neighborhood organizations. *Administration in Social Work, 16*(3/4), 45–64.

Chernesky, R., & Bombyk, M. (1995). Women's ways and effective management.
In J. Tropman, J. Erlich, & J. Rothman (Eds.), *Tactics and techniques of community intervention* (3rd ed., pp. 232–239). Itasca, IL. Peacock Publishers.

Chernesky, R., & Gutheil, I. (2008). Rethinking needs assessment in planning services for older adults. *Journal of Gerontological Social Work, 51*,
109–125.

Chin, J. (2009). The limits and potential of nonprofit organizations in participatory planning: A case study of the New York HIV Planning Council.
Journal of Urban Affairs, 32, 431–460.

Chino, M., & DeBruyn, L. (2006). Building true capacity: Indigenous models for
indigenous communities. *American Journal of Public Health, 96*(3), 9–11.

Christens, B. (2010). Public relationship building in grassroots community organizing: Relational intervention for individual and systems change. *Journal of
Community Psychology, 38*, 886–900.

Chu, W., Tsui, M., & Yan, M. (2009). Social work as a moral and political practice.
International Social Work, 52, 287–298.

Chutuape, K., Willard, N., Sanchez, K., Straub, D., Ochoa, T., Howell, K. . . . the
Adolescent Medicine Trails Network for HIV/AIDS Interventions. (2010).
Mobilizing communities around HIV prevention for youth: How three
coalitions applied key strategies to bring about structural changes. *AIDS
Education and Prevention, 22*(1), 15–27.

Citizen Works. (2004). *Tools for organizing: Neighborhood organizing*. Retrieved
from http://citizenworks.org/tools/town/tools-town-getting_people.php

Claque, M., Dill, R., Seebaran, R., & Wharf, B. (1984). *Reforming human services.* Vancouver, Canada: University of British Columbia Press.

Clark, J. (n.d.). *Beyond empathy: An ethnographic approach to cross-cultural social work practice.* Retrieved Canadian Association of Schools of Social Work website: from www.mun.ca/cassw-ar/papers2/clark.pdf

Clark, T. (2010). Gaining and maintaining access: Exploring the mechanisms that support and challenge the relationship between gatekeepers and researchers. *Qualitative Social Work, 10,* 485–502.

Clemens, E., & Minkoff, D. (2007). Beyond the iron law: Rethinking the place of organizations in social movement research. In D. Snow, S. Soule, & H. Kriesi (Eds.), *The Blackwell companion to social movements* (pp. 155–170). Malden, MA: Blackwell Publishing.

Cleveland, C. (2010). "We are not criminals": Social work advocacy and unauthorized migrants. *Social Work, 55,* 74–80.

Clifford, C. (2009, April 29). The United States and the rights of the child. *Human Rights Examiner.* Retrieved March 26, 2010, from http://www.examiner.com/

Clinton, H. R., U.S. Secretary of State (2011, December 6). *Transcript: Secretary Clinton—"Free and equal dignity and rights"* (speech delivered at the Palais des Nations, Geneva, Switzerland). Retrieved from Human Rights. Gov website: http://www.humanrights.gov/2011/12/06/remarks-in-recognition-of-international-human-rights-day/

Clover, D. (2011). Successes and challenges of feminist arts-based participatory methodologies with homeless/street-involved women in Victoria. *Action Research, 9,* 12–26.

Cnaan, R. A., Boddie, S. C., & Yancey, G. (2005). Partners rebuilding the cities: Faith-based community organizing. In M. Weil, M. Reisch, D. Gamble, L. Gutierrez, E. Mulroy, & R. Cnaan (Eds.), *The handbook of community practice* (pp. 372–386). Thousand Oaks, CA: Sage.

Cnaan, R., & Rothman, J. (2008). Capacity development and the building of community. Planning and policy practice. In J. Rothman, J. Erlich, & J. Tropman (Eds.), *Strategies of community organization* (7th ed., pp. 243–262). Peosta, IA: Eddie Bowers.

Cohen, D. (2001). Social capital, intervening institutions, and political power. In S. Saegert, S. J. P. Thompson, & M. Warren (Eds.), *Social capital and poor communities* (pp. 267–289). New York: Russell Sage Foundation.

Co-Intelligence Center. (n.d.) *Study circles.* Retrieved from http://www.co-intelligence.org/P-studycircles.html

Coleman, J. (1990). *Foundations of social theory.* Cambridge, MA: Harvard University Press.

Coleman, S. (2012). The decimation of America's middle class and its meaning for social work. *Journal of Progressive Human Services, 23,* 76–93.

Collie, P., Liu, J., Podsiadlowski, A., & Kindon, S. (2010). You can't clap with one hand: Learnings to promote culturally grounded participatory action research with migrant and former refugee communities. *International Journal of Intercultural Relations, 34,* 141–149.

Collins, S., & Wilkie, L. (2010) Anti-oppressive practice and social work students' portfolios in Scotland. *Social Work Education, 29,* 760–777.

Collison, D., Dey, C., & Stevenson, H. (2007). Income inequality and child mortality in wealthy nations. *Journal of Public Health, 29,* 114–117.

Community Mapping Project. (n.d.). *A guide for neighborhood associations and CDCs.* Retrieved from http://www.broadmoorimprovement.com/resources/community_mapping.pdf

Connolly, M. (2006). Fifteen years of family group conferencing: Coordinators talk about their experiences in Aotearoa New Zealand. *British Journal of Social Work, 36,* 523–540.

Conservation Partnership (2002, September). Understanding community power structures. *People, Partnerships, and Communities, 21,* 1–7. Retrieved from http://www.nrcs.usda.gov/Internet/FSE_DOCUMENTS/stelprdb1045565.pdf

Considine, A. (2001, April 1). For activists, tips on safe use of social media. *New York Times.* Retrieved from http://www.nytimes.com/

Conway, J. (2003). Civil resistance and the "diversity of tactics" in the anti-globalization movement: Problems of violence, silence and solidarity in activist politics. *Osgood Hall Law Journal, 41,* 505–529.

Conway, J. (2004). *Identity, place, and knowledge: Social movements contesting globalization.* Halifax, Nova Scotia: Fernwood.

Conway, J. (2007). Transnational feminisms and the World Social Forum: Encounters and transformations in anti-globalization spaces. *Journal of International Women's Studies, 8*(3), 49–70. Retrieved from http://www.bridgew.edu/soas/jiws/april07/Conway.pdf

Coombe, C. M. (2009). Participatory evaluation: Building community while assessing change. In M. Minkler (Ed.), *Community organizing and community building for health* (2nd ed., pp. 368–385). New Brunswick, NJ: Rutgers University Press.

Corrigall-Brown, C., Snow, D., Smith, K., & Quist, T. (2009). Protest among the homeless: Explaining differential participation. *Sociological Perspectives, 52,* 309–336.

Coulton, C. (2005). The place of community in social work practice research: Conceptual and methodological developments. *Social Work Research, 29,* 73–86.

Coulton, C., Chan, T., & Mikelbank, K. (2011). Finding place in community change initiatives: Using GIS to uncover resident perceptions of their neighborhoods. *Journal of Community Practice, 19,* 10–28.

Council on Social Work Education. (2008). *Educational policy and accreditation standards.* Retrieved from http://www.cswe.org/File.aspx?id=13780

Cowell, A. (2011, June 1). Germans' deep suspicions of nuclear power reach a political tipping point. *New York Times.* Retrieved from http://www.nytimes.com/

Craig, S. (2011). Precarious partnerships: Designing a community needs assessment to develop a system of care for gay, lesbian, bisexual, transgender, and questioning (GLBTQ) youths. *Journal of Community Practice, 19,* 274–291.

Cross, T., & Friesen, B. (2005). Community practice in children's mental health: Developing cultural competence and family-centered services in systems of care models. In M. Weil (Ed.), *The handbook of community practice* (pp. 442–459). Thousand Oaks, CA: Sage.

Cummins, L., Sevel, J., & Pedrick, L. (2006). *Social work skills demonstrated*. Boston, MA: Pearson Education.

Daily, B., & Bishop, J. (2003). TQM Workforce factors and employee involvement: The pivotal role of teamwork. *Journal of Management Issues, 15*, 393–412.

Daley, C. (2007). Exploring community connections: Community cohesion and refugee integration at the local level. *Community Development Journal, 44*, 158–171.

Daley, J. (2002). An action guide for nonprofit board diversity. *Journal of Community Practice, 10*(1), 33–54.

Daly, M., & Silver, H. (2008). Social exclusion and social capital: A comparison and critique. *Theoretical Sociology, 37*, 537–566.

Danis, F. (2007). In search of safe campus communities: A campus response against violence to women. *Journal of Community Practice, 14*(3), 29–46.

Davidoff, P. (1973). Advocacy and pluralism in planning. In A. Faludi (Ed.), *A reader in planning theory* (pp. 277–296). New York: Pergamon.

Davis, C. (2007, June 4). Invoking cloture in the Senate. *CRS report for Congress* (Order Code 98–426 GOV). Retrieved from Congressional Research Service website: http://www.senate.gov/reference/resources/pdf/98–425.pdf

Davis, K., & Bent-Goodley, T. (2004). *The color of social policy*. Alexandria, VA: Council on Social Work Education.

Debbink, G., & Ornelas, A. (1997). Cows for campesinos. In S. Smith, D. Willms, & N. Johnson (Eds.), *Nurtured by knowledge: Learning to do participatory action-research* (pp. 13–33). Ottawa, Canada: International Development Research Centre.

DeFilippis, J. (2001a). The myth of social capital in community development. *Housing Policy Debate, 12*, 781–806.

DeFilippis, J. (2001b). *Our resistance must be local as capitalism: Place, scale and the anti-globalization protest movement*. Paper presented on COMM-ORG: The On-Line Conference on Community Organizing and Development (Vol. 7). Retrieved from http://comm.-org.wisc.edu/papers.htm

DeFilippis, J. (2009). Paradoxes of community-building: Community control in a global economy. *International Social Science Journal, 59*, 223–234.

DeFilippis, J., Fisher, R., & Shragge, E. (2010). *Contesting community: The limits and potential of local organizing*. New Brunswick, NJ: Rutgers University Press.

Delgado, C. (2004). Evaluation of needle exchange programs. *Public Health Nursing, 21*, 171–178.

Delgado, G. (1997). *Beyond the politics of place*. Berkeley, CA: Chardon Press.

Delgado, G. (2009). *Does ACORN's work contribute to movement building? The people shall rule* (pp. 251–271). Nashville, TN: Vanderbilt University.

Delgado, M. (1996). Puerto Rican food establishments as social service organizations: Results of an asset assessment. *Journal of Community Practice, 3*(2), 57–77.

Delgado, M. (2000). *Community social work practice in an urban context: The potential of a capacity-enhancement perspective.* New York: Oxford University Press.

Delgado, M., & Staples, L. (2008). *Youth-led organizing: Theory and action.* New York: Oxford University Press.

Delgado-Wise, R., & Márquez Covarrubias, H. (2007). The reshaping of Mexican labor exports under NAFTA: Paradoxes and challenges. *International Migration Review, 41*, 656–679.

della Porta, D. (n.d.). *Making the polis: Social forums and democracy in the global justice movement.* Retrieved from http://unpan1.un.org/intradoc/groups/public/documents/un-dpadm/unpan042190.pdf

della Porta, D., & Diani, M. (2006). *Social movements: An introduction* (2nd ed.). Malden, MA: Blackwell Publishing.

De La Puente, D. (2011). Women's leadership in campus for internally displaced people in Dafur, western Sudan. *Community Development Journal, 46*, 365–377.

Delonis, R. (2004). International financial standards and codes: Mandatory regulation without regulation. *International Law & Politics, 36*, 563–634.

Delp, L., Quan, K., & Haslett, D. (2002). Homecare worker organizing in California: An analysis of a successful strategy. *Labor Studies Journal, 27*, 1–23.

DePoy, E., Hartman, A., & Haslett, D. (1999). Critical action research: A model for social work knowing. *Social Work, 44*, 560–571.

Despotovic, M., Medic, M., Shimkus, D., & Staples, L. (2007). NGO Development in Croatia: De Facto interdisciplinary practice. *Journal of Community Practice, 15*(1/2), 171–191.

Dessel, A., Bolen, R., & Shepardson, C. (2011). Can religious expression and sexual orientation affirmation coexist in social work? A critique of Hodge's theoretical, theological, and conceptual framework. *Journal of Social Work Education, 47*, 213–234.

Dessel, A., Rogge, M., & Garlington, S. (2006). Using intergroup dialogue to promote social justice and change. *Social Work, 51*, 303–339.

De Silva, M., Harpham, T., Huttly, S., Bartolini, R., & Penny, M. (2005). Understanding sources and types of social capital in Peru. *Community Development Journal, 4*, 19–33.

de Tocqueville, A. (1981). *Democracy in America* (abridged translation). New York: Modern Library.

DeVance Taliaferro, J., & Ruggiano, N. (2010). "It's human beings talking to one another": The role of relationship building in nonprofit lobbying. *Prism 7*(2). Retrieved from http://www.prismjournal.org/fileadmin/Praxis/Files/Journal_Files/Taliaferro_Ruggiano.pdf

Devine, M. (2010). Participation in organizational change processes in human service organizations: The experience of one group of frontline social workers. *Administration in Social Work, 34*, 114–134.

Dierwechter, Y., & Coffey, B. (2010). Assessing the effects of neighborhood councils on urban policy and development: The example of Tacoma, Washington. *Social Science Journal, 47,* 471–491.

Dobbie, D., & Richards-Schuster, K. (2008). Building solidarity through difference: A practice model for critical multicultural organizing. *Journal of Community Practice, 16,* 317–337.

Dobelstein, A. (2003). *Social welfare policy and analysis.* Pacific Grove, CA: Thomson/Brooks/Cole.

Domhoff, G. W. (2007). C. Wright Mills. Power structure research, and the failures of mainstream political science. *New Political Science, 29,* 97–114.

Domhoff, G. W. (2009a). The power elite and their challengers: The role of nonprofits in Americans social conflict. *American Behavioral Scientist, 52,* 955–973.

Domhoff, G. W. (2009b). *Who rules America? How to do power structure research.* Retrieved from http://sociology.ucsc.edu/whorulesamerica/methods/how_to_do_power_structure_research.html

Dominelli, L. (2005). Community development across borders: Avoiding dangerous practices in a globalizing world. *International Social Work, 48,* 702–713.

Dominelli, L. (2010). Globalization, contemporary challenges and social work practice. *International Social Work, 53,* 599–612.

Donadio, R., & Kitsantonis, N. (2011, June 21). Greek parliament passes critical confidence vote. *New York Times.* Retrieved from http://www.nytimes.com/

Donnelly, J. (2007). The relative universality of human rights. *Human Rights Quarterly, 29,* 281–306.

Dorius, N. (2009). Understanding change in poor communities: What is it and how will we know when it happens? *Journal of Urban Affairs, 31,* 97–109.

Draper, C., & Freedman, D. (2010). Review and analysis of the benefits, purposes, and motivations associated with community gardening in the United States. *Journal of Community Practice, 18,* 493–512.

Dreier, P. (2008a, September 8). From organizer to elected official. *The Nation.* Retrieved from http://www.thenation.com/article/organizer-elected-official

Dreier, P. (2008b, September 15). Millennials could be key voters in swing states. *The Nation.* Retrieved from http://www.thenation.com/article/millennials-could-be-key-voters-swing-states

Dreier, P. (2009). Community organization, ACORN, and Progressive politics in America. In R. Fisher (Ed.), *The people shall rule: ACORN, community organizing and the struggle for economic justice* (pp. 3–39). Nashville, TN: Vanderbilt University Press.

Driscoll Derickson, K. (2009). Gendered, material, and partial knowledges: A feminist critique of neighborhood-level indicator systems. *Environment and Planning, 41,* 896–910.

Duke, J. (2010). Exploring homeowner opposition to public housing developments. *Journal of Sociology and Social Welfare, 37*(1), 49–74.

Durst, D., MacDonald, J., & Parsons, D. (1999). Finding our way: A community needs assessment on violence in native families in Canada. *Journal of Community Practice, 6*(1), 45–59.

Dutil, P., Howard, C., Langford, J., & Roy, J. (2007). Rethinking government-public relationships in a digital world: Customers, clients, or citizens. *Journal of Information Technology and Politics, 41*(1), 77–90.

Duval-Diop, D., Curtis, A., & Clark, A. (2010). Enhancing equity with public participatory GIS in hurricane rebuilding: Faith based organizations, community mapping, and policy advocacy. *Community Development, 41,* 32–49.

Edwards, B. (2011). Social work education and global issues: Implications for social work practice. *Education, 131,* 580–586.

Edwards, M. (1999). International development NGOs: Agents of foreign aid or vehicles for international cooperation. *Nonprofit and Voluntary Sector Quarterly, 28*(4), 25–37.

Edwards, B., & McCarthy, J. (2007). Resources and social movement mobilization. In D. Snow, S. Soule, & H. Kriesi (Eds.), *The Blackwell companion to social movements* (pp. 116–152). Malden, MA: Blackwell Publishing.

Eichler, M. (1998). Organizing's past, present, and future: Look to the future, learn from the past. *Shelterforce, 101.* Retrieved from http://www.nhi.org/online/issues/101/eichler.html

Eisinger, P. (2002). Organizational capacity and organizational effectiveness among street-level food assistance programs. *Nonprofit and Voluntary Sector Quarterly, 31,* 115–130.

El Teatro Campesino, (2010). *About ETC.* Retrieved from http://www.elteatro-campesino.com/About/missionhistory.html.

Emshoff, J., Darnell, A., Darnell, D., Erickson, S., Schneider, S., & Hudgins, R. (2007). Systems change as an outcome and process in the work of community collaboratives for health. *American Journal of Community Psychology, 39,* 255–267.

English, L. (2005). Narrative research and feminist knowing: A poststructural reading of women's learning in community organizations. *McGill Journal of Education, 40,* 143–155.

Ensalaco, M. (2006). Murder in Ciudad Juárez: A parable of women's struggle for human rights. *Violence against Women, 12,* 417–440.

E-politics: On-line Advocacy Tools & Tactics. (2009, February 24). *Learning from Obama's campaign structure. How to organize for success.* Retrieved from http://www.epolitics.com/2009/02/24/learning-from-obamas-campaign-structure-how-to-organize-for-success/

Epstein, I. (2011). Reconciling evidence-based practice, evidence-informed practice, and practice-based research: The role of clinical data mining. *Social Work, 56,* 284–288.

Esparza, E., Katz, R., & Olmos, E. J. (Producers), & Olmos, E. J. (Director) (2006). *Walkout* [Motion Picture]. United States: Home Box Office.

Ersing, R., Loeffler, D., Tracy, M., & Onu, L. (2007). Pentru Voi Fundatia: Interdisciplinary community development using social enterprise in Romania. *Journal of Community Practice, 15*(1/2), 193–215.

Estes, R. (2005). Global change and indicators of social development. In M. Weil, M. Reisch, D. Gamble, L. Gutierrez, E. Mulroy, & R. Cnaan

(Eds.), *The handbook of community practice* (pp. 508–528). Thousand Oaks, CA: Sage.

Evans, M., & Shirley, D. (2008). The development of collective moral leadership among parents through education organizing. *New Directions for Youth Development, 117,* 77–91.

Evenson, K., Sotres-Alvarez, D., Herring, A., Messer, L., Laraia, B., & Rodriguez, D. (2009). Assessing urban and rural neighborhood characteristics using audit and GIS data; Derivation and reliability of constructs. *International Journal of Behavioral Nutrition and Physical Activity, 6,* 44–61. Retrieved from http://www.ijbnpa.org/contents/6/1/44

Everyday Democracy. (1997) *Toward a more perfect union in the age of diversity: A guide for building stronger communities through public dialogue.* Retrieved from http://www.everyday-democracy.org/en/Resource.12.aspx

Exley, Z. (2008). *The new organizers, what's really behind Obama's ground game?* Retrieved from Huffington Post website: http://www.huffingtonpost.com/

Ezell, M., Chernesky, R., & Healy, L. (2004). The learning climate for administration students. *Administration in Social Work, 28*(1), 57–76.

Fals Borda, O. (2002). Participatory action research in social theory: Origins and challenges. In P. Reason, & H. Bradbury (Eds.), *The handbook of action research: Participative inquiry and practice* (pp. 27–37). Thousand Oaks, CA: Sage.

Family and Community Services, New Zealand Ministry of Social Development (2011). *Record keeping. Community Resource Kit* (Version 1). Retrieved from http://www.community.net.nz/NR/rdonlyres/D322AC87–1901–423A-B2C6–3FC965096887/76094/DIA_CRK_Section_8.pdf

Family Health International. (n.d.). *Qualitative research methods: A data collector's field guide* (Module 2—Participant observation). Retrieved from http://www.fhi.org/NR/rdonlyres/ed2ruznpftevg34lxuftzjiho65asz7betpqigbbyorggs6tetjic367v44baysyomnbdjkdtbsium/participantobservation1.pdf

Farrell, W., Johnson, J., Sapp, M., Pumphrey, R., & Freeman, S. (1995). Redirecting the lives of urban black males: An assessment of Milwaukee's midnight basketball league. *Journal of Community Practice, 2*(4), 91–107.

Fassihi, F. (2012, January 6). Iran mounts new web crackdown. *Wall Street Journal* Retrieved from http://online.wsu.com/

Fenge, L. (2010). Striving towards inclusive research: An example of participatory action research with older lesbians and gay men. *British Journal of Social Work, 40,* 878–894.

Fertig, A., & Reingold, D. (2008). Homelessness among at-risk families with children in twenty American cities. *Social Service Review, 82,* 485–510.

Fetterman, D. (2001). *Foundations of empowerment evaluation.* Thousand Oaks, CA: Sage.

Fetterman, D., Kaftarian, S., & Wandersman, A. (Eds.). (1996). *Empowerment evaluation: Knowledge and tools for self-assessment and accountability.* Thousand Oaks, CA: Sage.

Fetterman, D., & Wandersman, A. (2007). Empowerment evaluation: Yesterday, today, and tomorrow. *American Journal of Evaluation, 28,* 179–198.

Figueira-McDonough, J. (1991). Community structure and delinquency: A typology. *Social Service Review, 65*, 68–91.

Flicker, S., Maley, O., Ridgley, A., Biscope, S., Lombardo, C., & Skinner, H. (2008). e-PAR: Using technology and participatory action research to engage youth in health promotion. *Action Research, 6*, 285–303.

Fisher, R., Brooks, F., & Russell, D. (2009). ACORN, Protest tactics, and organizational scale. In R. Fisher (Ed.), *The people shall rule: ACORN, community organizing and the struggle for economic justice* (pp. 206–234). Nashville, TN: Vanderbilt University Press.

Fisher, R., & Corciullo, D. (2011). Rebuilding community organizing education in social work. *Journal of Community Practice, 19*, 355–358.

Foley, E. (2011, June 22). *Comprehensive immigration reform relaunched in Senate.* Retrieved from Huffington Post website: http://www.huffingtonpost.com/

Fook, J. (2003). Critical social work: The current issues. *Qualitative Social Work, 2*, 123–130.

Forcarinis, M. (2011, December 14). The human right to housing: Housing and homelessness are human rights issues- and that can be an organizing strength. *Shelterforce.* Retrieved from http://www.shelterforce.org/article/print/2485/

Forester, J. (1989). *Planning in the face of power.* Berkeley, CA: University of California Press.

Forester, J. (1999). *The deliberative practitioner: Encouraging participatory planning processes.* Cambridge: Massachusetts Institute of Technology.

Foster, C., & Louie, J. (2010, March). *Grassroots action and learning for social change: Evaluating community organization.* Center for Evaluation Innovation. Retrieved from http://www.innonet.org/client_docs/File/center_pubs/evaluating_community_organizing.pdf

Foster-Fishman, P., Berkowitz, S., Lounsbury, D., Jacobson, S., & Allen, N. (2001). Building collaborative capacity in community coalitions: A review and integrative framework. *American Journal of Community Psychology, 29*, 241–261.

Foster-Fishman, P., Fitzgerald, K., Brandell, C., Nowell, B., Chavis, D., & Van Egeren, L. (2006). Mobilizing residents for action: The role of small wins and strategic supports. *American Journal of Community Psychology, 38*, 143–152.

Foster-Fishman, P., Nowell, B., Deacon, Z., Nievar, M. A., & McCann, P. (2005). Using methods that matter: The impact of reflection, dialogue and voice. *American Journal of Community Psychology, 36*(3/4), 275–291.

Foster-Fishman, P., Pierce, S., & Van Egeren, L. (2009). Who participates and why: Building a process model of citizen participation. *Health Education Behavior, 36*, 550–569.

Fox, A., & Mason Meier, B. (2009). Health as freedom: Addressing social determinants of global health inequities through the human right to development. *Bioethics, 23*(2), 112–122.

Fraser, E., Dougill, A., Mabee, W., Reed, M., & McAlpine, P. (2006). Bottom up and top down: Analysis of participatory processes for sustainability indicator identification as a pathway to community empowerment and sustainable environmental management. *Journal of Environmental Management*, *78*, 114–127.

Fraser, J., & Kick, E. (2005). Understanding community building in urban America. *Journal of Poverty*, *9*(1), 23–43.

Frederico, M., Pincton, C., Muncy, S., Ongsiapco, L., Santos, C., & Hernandez, C. (2007). Building community following displacement due to armed conflict: A case study. *International Social Work*, *50*, 171–184.

Freire, P. (1970). *Pedagogy of the oppressed*. New York: Continuum.

Freire, P. (1997). Forward. *Nurtured by knowledge: Learning to do participatory action-research* (pp. xi–xii). In S. Smith, D. Willms, & N. Johnson (Eds.). Ottawa, Canada: International Development Research Centre.

Friedmann, J. (1987). *Planning in the public domain: From knowledge to action*. Princeton, NJ: Princeton University Press.

Frisch, M., & Servon, L. (2006). CDCs and the changing context for urban community development: A review of the field and the environment. *Community Development*, *37*(4), 88–108.

Funge, S. (2011). Promoting the social justice orientation of students: The role of the educator. *Journal of Social Work Education*, *47*, 73–90.

G7 nations pledge debt relief for quake-hit Haiti. (2010, February 7). *BBC News*. http://news.bbc.co.uk/2/hi/8502567.stm

Galambos, C. (2008). A dialogue on social justice [Editorial]. *Journal of Social Work Education*, *44*, 1–5.

Galster, G., Hayes, C., & Johnson, J. (2005). Identifying robust, parsimonious neighborhood indicators. *Journal of Planning Education and Research*, *24*, 265–280.

Gamble, D. (2011). Advanced concentration macro competencies for social work practitioners: Identifying knowledge, values, judgment and skills to promote human well-being. *Journal of Community Practice*, *19*, 369–402.

Gamble, D., & Weil, M. (1995). Citizen participation. In R. L. Edwards (Ed.), *Encyclopedia of social work* (19th ed., pp. 483–494). Washington, DC: National Association of Social Workers.

Gamble, D., Shaffer, G., & Weil, M. (1994). Assessing the integrity of community organization and administration content in field practice. *Journal of Community Practice*, *1*(3), 73–92.

Gamble, D., & Weil, M. (2010). *Community practice skills: Local to global perspectives*. New York: Columbia University Press.

Gambrill, E. (2007). Views of evidence-based practice: Social workers' Code of Ethics and Accreditation standards as guides for choice. *Journal of Social Work Education*, *43*, 447–462.

Gant, L., Shimshock, K., Allen-Meares, P., Smith, L., Miller, P., ... Shanks, T. (2009). Effects of Photovoice: Civic engagement among older youth in urban communities. *Journal of Community Practice*, *17*, 358–376.

Ganz, M. (2001). *The power of story in social movements*. Retrieved from Kennedy School of Government, Harvard University website: http://ksghome.

harvard.edu/~MGanz/Current%20Publications/MG%20POWER%20OF%20STORY.pdf

Ganz, M. (2007, March 29). *Staying connected to our moral sources.* Retrieved from Talking Points Memo website: http://tpmcafe.talkingpointsmemo.com/2007/03/29/staying_connected_to_our_moral/

Ganz, M. (2008, June 6). *Leading change: Leadership, organization, and social movements.* Paper presented at the Advancing Leadership Conference, Harvard Business School, Boston, MA. Retrieved from http://mitsloan.mit.edu/iwer/pdf/0809-ganz.pdf

Ganz, M. (2009). *Why David sometimes wins: Leadership, organization and strategy in the California farm worker movement.* New York: Oxford University Press.

Gardner, F. (2003). Critical reflection in community-based evaluation. *Qualitative Social Work, 2,* 197–212.

Garkovich, L. (2011). A historical view of community development. In J. Robinson, & P. Green (Eds.), *Introduction to community development: Theory, practice, and service learning* (pp. 11–34). Thousand Oaks, CA: Sage.

Gaventa, J. (2004). Strengthening participatory approaches to local governance: learning the lessons from abroad. *National Civic Review, 93*(4), 16–27.

Gaventa, J., & Cornwall, A. (2002). Power and knowledge. Participatory action research in social theory: Origins and challenges. In P. Reason, & H. Bradbury (Eds.), *The handbook of action research: Participative inquiry and practice* (pp. 70–80). Thousand Oaks, CA: Sage.

Gaventa, J., & Valderrama, C. (1999). *Participation, citizenship, and local governance.* Retrieved from University of Valencia website: http://www.uv.es/~fernandm/Gaventa,%20Valderrama.pdf

Gazley, B. (2010). Linking collaborative capacity to performance measurement in government-nonprofit partnerships. *Nonprofit and Voluntary Sector Quarterly, 39,* 653–673.

Gelack, D. (2008). *Lobbying and advocacy.* Alexandria, VA: TheCapitolNet

Giguere, B., & Lalande, R. (2010). Why do students strike? Direct and indirect determinants of collective action participation. *Political Psychology, 31,* 227–358.

Gil, D. (1998). *Confronting injustice and oppression.* New York: Columbia University Press.

Gil de Gigaja, M. (2001). An exploratory study of administrative practices in collaboratives. *Administration in Social Work, 25*(2), 39–58.

Gilbert, N., & Terrell, P. (2009). *Dimensions of social welfare policy* (6th ed.). Boston: Allyn and Bacon.

Gilchrist, A. (2009). *The well-connected community. A networking approach to community development* (2nd ed.). Bristol, UK: University of Bristol.

Gillian, K. (2008). Understanding meaning in movements: A hermeneutic approach to frames and ideologies. *Social Movement Studies, 7,* 247–263.

Ginsberg, L. (2001). *Social work evaluation: Principles and methods.* Boston, MA: Allyn & Bacon.

Githongo, J. (2011, July 23). When wealth breeds rage. *New York Times*. Retrieved from http://www.nytimes.com/

Gittell, R., & Thompson, J. (2001). Making social capital work: Social capital and community economic development. In S. Saegert, S. J. P. Thompson, & M. Warren (Eds.), *Social capital and poor communities* (pp. 115–135). New York: Russell Sage Foundation.

Gittell, R., & Vidal, A. (1998). *Community organizing: Building social capital as a development strategy*. Thousand Oaks, CA: Sage.

Gjecovi, S., James, E., & Chenweth, J. (2006). *Immigrant-led organizers in their own voices: Local realities and shared visions*. Retrieved from Catholic Legal Immigration Network, Inc. (Clinic) website: http://www.racialequitytools.org/resourcefiles/gjecovi.pdf

Glover Blackwell, A., Minkler, M., & Thompson, M. (2009). Using community organizing and community building to influence policy. In M. Minkler (Ed.), *Community organizing and community building for health* (2nd ed., pp. 405–418). New Brunswick, NJ: Rutgers University Press.

Goode, L. (2009). Social news, citizen journalism and democracy. *New Media & Society, 11*(8), 1287–1305.

Goodkind, J. (2006). Promoting Hmong refugees' well-being through mutual learning: Valuing knowledge, culture, and experience. *American Journal of Community Psychology, 37*(1/2), 77–93.

Good Neighborhoods Initiative. (2007, April). *Lessons learned from comprehensive community initiatives*. Retrieved from http://www.ssw.umich.edu/public/currentProjects/goodNeighborhoods/CCI_lessons_learned.pdf

Goodwin, J., Jasper, J., & Polletta, F. (2007). The emotional dimensions of social movements. In D. Snow, S. Soule, & H. Kriesi (Eds.), *The Blackwell companion to social movements* (pp. 413–432). Malden, MA: Blackwell Publishing.

Goto, K., Pelto, G., Pelletier, D., & Tiffany, J. (2010). "It really opened my eyes:" The effects on youth peer educators of participating in an action research project. *Human Organization, 69*, 192–199.

Graddy, E., & Chen, B. (2006). *The consequences of partner selection in service delivery collaborations*. Los Angeles, CA: Bedrosian Center on Governance and the Public Enterprise, University of Southern California, Collaborative Governance, WP-October 2006–1. Retrieved from http://www.usc.edu/schools/sppd/bedrosian/private/docs/graddypaper.pdf

Green, J. (1999). *Cultural awareness in the human services: A multi-ethnic approach*. Boston: Allyn & Bacon.

Green, S. (2005). Including young mothers: Community-based participation and the continuum of active citizenship. *Community Development Journal, 42*(2), 167–180.

Green, P. (2011). The self-help approach to community development. In J. Robinson, & P. Green (Eds.), *Introduction to community development: Theory, practice, and service learning* (pp. 71–83). Thousand Oaks, CA: Sage.

Green, J., & Haines, A. (2002). *Asset building and community development*. Thousand Oaks, CA: Sage.

Green, J., & Kleiner, A. (2011). Action research and evaluation in community development. In J. Robinson, & P. Green (Eds.), *Introduction to community development: Theory, practice, and service learning* (pp. 119–139). Thousand Oaks, CA: Sage.

Greene, A., & Latting, J. (2004). Whistle-blowing as a form of advocacy: Guidelines for practitioners and organizations. *Social Work, 27*, 219–229.

Gremier, D. (2004). The critical incident technique in service research. *Journal of Service Research, 7*(1), 65–89.

Grodofsky, M. (2007). The contribution of law and social work to interdisciplinary community development and peace building in the Middle East. *Journal of Community Practice, 15*(1/2), 45–65.

Grigg-Saito, D., Och, S., Liang, S., Toof, R., & Silka, L. (2008). Building on the strengths of a Cambodian refugee community through community-based outreach. *Health Promotion Practice, 9*, 415–425.

Grinstein-Weiss, M., Curley, J., & Charles, P. (2007). Asset-building in rural communities. The experience of individual development accounts. *Rural Sociology, 72*, 25–46.

Grodach, C. (2009). Art spaces, public space and the link to community economic development. *Community Development Journal, 45*, 474–493.

Guba, E., & Lincoln, Y. (1989). *Fourth generation evaluation*. Newbury Park, CA: Sage.

Guba, E., & Lincoln, Y. (2001). *Guidelines and checklist for constructivist* (a.k.a. Fourth Generation) evaluation. Retrieved from http://www.wmich.edu/evalctr/archive_checklists/constructivisteval.pdf

Guo, W., & Tsui, M. (2010). From resilience to resistance: A reconstruction of the strengths perspective in social work practice: *International Social Work, 53*, 233–245.

Gutierrez, L., & Alvarez, A. (2000). Educating students for multicultural community practice. *Journal of Community Practice, 7*, 39–56.

Gutierrez, L., GlenMaye, L., & DeLois, K. (1995). The organizational context of empowerment practice: Implications for social work administration. *Social Work, 40*, 249–258.

Gutierrez, L., & Lewis, E. (1999). *Empowering women of color*. New York: Columbia University Press.

Gutierrez, L., Lewis, E., Nagda, B., Wernick, L., & Shore, N. (2005). Multicultural community practice strategies and intergroup empowerment. In M. Weil, M. Reisch, D. Gamble, L. Gutierrez, E. Mulroy, & R. Cnaan (Eds.), *The handbook of community practice* (pp. 341–359). Thousand Oaks, CA: Sage.

Gutierrez, L., Parsons, R., & Cox, E. (1998). *Empowerment in social work practice: A sourcebook*. Pacific Grove, CA: Brooks/Cole.

Halseth, G., & Ryser, L. (2007). The deployment of partnerships by the voluntary sector to address service needs in rural and small town Canada. *Voluntas, 18*, 241–265.

Hancock, T., & Minkler, M. (2009). Community health assessment or healthy community assessment: Whose community? Whose health? In M. Minkler

(Ed.), *Community organizing and community building for health* (2nd ed., pp. 138–157). New Brunswick, NJ: Rutgers University Press.

Handy, F., & Greenspan, I. (2008). Immigrant volunteering: A stepping stone to integration? *Nonprofit and Voluntary Sector Quarterly, 38,* 956–982.

Hardcastle, D., Powers, P., & Wenocur, S. (2004). *Community practice: Theories and skills for social worker* (2nd ed.). New York: Oxford University Press.

Hardina, D. (2000). Models and tactics taught in community organization courses: Findings from a survey of practice instructors. *Journal of Community Practice, 7*(1), 5–18.

Hardina, D. (2002). *Analytical skills for community organization practice.* New York: Columbia University Press.

Hardina, D. (2003). Linking citizen participation to empowerment practice: A historical overview. *Journal of Community Practice, 11,* 11–38.

Hardina, D. (2004a). Guidelines for ethical practice in community organization. *Social Work, 49,* 595–604.

Hardina, D. (2004b). What social workers need to know about the right to vote. *Social Policy Journal, 2*(4), 53–70.

Hardina, D. (2005). Using the web to teach power analysis: Identifying campaign donors and elites. *Social Policy Journal, 4*(2), 51–68.

Hardina, D., Jendian, M., & Garoupa-White, C. (2009, November 7). *The ethics of social action organizing: Organizers describe tactical decision-making.* Paper presented at the 2009 Annual Program Meeting of the Council on Social Work Education, San Antonio, Texas.

Hardina, D., Jendian, M., Garoupa-White, C., & Cerda, H. (2011). [Community organizer interviews about tactics and ethical decision-making]. Unpublished raw data.

Harding, S., & Libal, K. (2012). Iraqi refugees and the humanitarian costs of the Iraq war: What role for social work? *International Journal of Social Welfare, 21,* 94–104.

Hardina, D., & Malott, O. W. (1996). Strategies for the empowerment of low income consumers on community-based planning boards. *Journal of Progressive Human Services, 7*(2), 43–61.

Hardina, D., Middleton, J., Simpson, R., & Montana, S. (2006). *An empowering approach for managing social service organizations.* New York: Springer.

Hardina, D., & Obel-Jorgensen, R. (2009). Increasing social action competency: A framework for supervision. *Journal of Policy Practice, 8*(2), 89–109.

Hardina, D., & Obel-Jorgensen, R. (2011). Organizing on campus for civil liberties and social justice. In J. Birkenmaier, A. Cruce, E. Burkemper, J. Curley, R. J. Wilson, & J. J. Stretch (Eds.), *Educating for social justice: Transformative experiential learning* (pp. 286–305). Chicago: Lyceum Books.

Hardina, D., Yamaguchi, J., Moua, X., Yang, M., & Moua, P. (2008). Competition and cooperation among organizations serving an ethnic community. In L. Ginsberg (Ed.), *Management and leadership in social work education and practice* (pp. 90–103). Alexandria, VA: Council on Social Work Education.

Harkavy, I., & Puckett, J. (1994). Lessons from Hull House for the contemporary urban university. *Social Service Review, 68*, 299–321.

Harrell, S., & Bond, M. (2006). Listening to diversity stories: Principles for practice in community research and action. *American Journal of Community Psychology, 37*, 365–376.

Harris, A. (2010). Panic at the church: The use of frames, social problems, and moral panics in the formation of an AIDS social movement organization. *Western Journal of Black Studies, 34*, 337–346.

Harvard Family Research Project. (2003, December). *Transforming schools through community organizing: A research review.* Retrieved from http://www. hfrp.org/publications-resources/browse-our-publications/transforming-schoolsthrough-community-organizing-a-research-review

Haski-Leventhal, D., & Cnaan, R. A. (2009). Group processes and volunteering: Enhancing recruitment and retention. *Administration in Social Work, 33*, 1–20.

Hawkins, R., & Maurer, K. (2010). Bonding, bridging, and linking: How social capital operated in New Orleans following Hurricane Katrina. *British Journal of Social Work, 40*, 1777–1793.

Haynes, K., & Mickelson, J. (2003). *Affecting change: Social workers in the political arena* (5h ed.). Boston, MA: Allyn & Bacon.

Healy, L. (2008). *International social work: Professional action in an interdependent world.* New York: Oxford University Press.

Hein, J. (2000). Interpersonal discrimination against Hmong Americans. *Sociological Quarterly, 41*, 413–429.

Heierbacher, S. (n.d.). *NCDD's engagement stream framework.* Retrieved from http://ncdd.org/rc/wp-content/uploads/2010/08/full-streams-hi-res.pdf

Heidemann, G., Fertig, R., Jansson, B., & Kim, H. (2011). Practicing policy, pursing change, and promoting social justice: A policy instructional approach. *Journal of Social Work Education, 47*, 37–52.

Hembd, J., & Silberstein, J. (2011). In J. Robinson, & P. Green (Eds.), *Introduction to community development: Theory, practice, service learning* (pp. 261–277). Thousand Oaks, CA: Sage.

Heywood, P. (2011). *Community planning: Integrating social and physical environments.* Chichester, UK: Blackwell/Wiley.

Hick, S., & McNutt, J. (2002). *Advocacy, activism, and the Internet: Community organization and social policy.* Chicago: Lyceum Books.

Hicks, J. (2011). Bringing women into local governance: A review of enabling mechanisms in South Africa. *Community Development Journal, 46*, 351–365.

Hill, K., Ferguson, S., & Erickson, C. (2010). Sustaining and strengthening a macro identity: The Association of Macro Practice Social Work. *Journal of Community Practice, 18*, 513–527.

Hillier, A., Wernecke, M., & McKelvey, H. (2005). Removing barriers to the use of community information systems. *Journal of Community Practice, 13*(1), 121–139.

Hodge, D. (2005). Spiritual life maps: A client-centered pictorial instrument for spiritual assessment, planning, and intervention. *Social Work, 50,* 77–87.

Hodge, D. (2007). Learning to hear each other's voice: A response to Melendez and LaSala. *Social Work, 52,* 365–374.

Hoefer, R. (2001). Highly effective human services interest groups: Seven key practices. *Journal of Community Practice, 9*(2), 1–14.

Hoefer, R. (2006). *Advocacy practice for social justice.* Chicago, IL: Lyceum.

Hofmann-Pinilla, A., Olvarria, M., & Ospina, S. (2005). *Collective narrative, identity, and leadership: A comparative analysis of immigrant worker, environmental and indigenous grassroots group (draft).* Paper presented at the Annual Conference of the Association for Research on Nonprofit Organizations and Voluntary Action, Washington, DC.

Hoggard, C. (2010, November 19). *Fresno State ASI President leads cry for immigration reform. ABC 30.* Retrieved from http://abclocal.go.com/kfsn/story?section=news/local&id=7799839

Hogarth, P. (2010, May 12). "Caught in a bad hotel" = The future of protest? *Huffington Post.* Retrieved from http://www.huffingtonpost.com/paul-hogarth/caught-in-a-bad-hotel-the_b_573407.html

Holland, L. (2004). Diversity and connections in community gardens: A contribution to local sustainability. *Local Environment, 9,* 285–305.

Holz Deal, K., Hopkins, K., Fisher, L., & Hartin, J. (2007). Field practicum experiences of macro-oriented graduate students: Are we doing them justice. *Administration in Social Work, 31,* 41–58.

Homan, M. (2011). *Promoting community change: Making it happen in the real world.* Belmont, CA: Brooks/Cole.

Hooker, S., Cirill, L., & Gerahty, A. (2008). Evaluation of the walkable neighborhoods for seniors project in Sacramento County. *Health Promotion Practice, 10,* 402–410.

Hoover, D. (2010, April 12). What fundraising and recruiting have in common. *Chronicle of Higher Education.* Retrieved from http://chronicle.com/blogPost/What-Fund-Raising-and/22461/

Horton, M., Kohl, J., & Kohl, H. (1998). *The long haul: An autobiography.* New York: Teachers College Press.

Hrebenar, R. (1997). *Interest group politics in America.* Armonk, NY: M.E. Sharpe.

Hughey, J., Peterson, N., Lowe, J., & Oprescu, F. (2008). Empowerment and sense of community: Clarifying their relationship in community organizations. *Health Education Behavior, 35,* 651–663.

Hume-Cook, G., Curtis, T., Woods, K., Potaka, J., Wagner, A., & Kindon, S. (2010). Uniting people with place using participatory video in Aoteroa/New Zealand: A Ngati Hauiti journey. In S. Kindon, R. Pain, & M. Kesby (Eds.), *Participatory research approaches and methods* (pp. 160–169). New York: Routledge.

Hunt, V. (2007). Community development corporations and public participation: Lessons from a case study in the Arkansas Delta. *Journal of Sociology and Social Welfare, 34*(3), 9–35.

Hunt, S., & Benford, R. (2007). Collective identity, solidarity, and commitment. In D. Snow, S. Soule, & H. Kriesi (Eds.), *The Blackwell companion to social movements* (pp. 433–457). Malden, MA: Blackwell Publishing.

Hyde, C. (2005). Feminist community practice. In M. Weil, M. Reisch, D. Gamble, L. Gutierrez, E. Mulroy, & R. Cnaan (Eds.), *The handbook of community practice* (pp. 360–371). Thousand Oaks, CA: Sage.

Ibanez-Carrasco, F., & Riano-Acala, P. (2009). Organizing community-based research knowledge between universities and communities: Lessons learned. *Community Development Journal, 46,* 72–88.

Ife, J. (2001). *Human rights and social work.* Cambridge, UK: Cambridge University Press.

Ife, J., & Fiske, L. (2006). Human rights and community work: Complementary theories and practices. *International Social Work, 49,* 297–308.

Iglehart, A., & Becerra, R. (2011). *Social services and the ethnic community: History and analysis* (2nd ed.). Long Grove, IL: Waveland Press.

Incite: Women of Color Against Violence. (n.d.). *Participatory action research.* Retrieved from http://www.incite-national.org/index.php?s=129

Indianapolis Neighborhood Resource Center. (n.d.). *Organizer's workbook.* Retrieved from http://www.inrc.org/Assets/docs/workbook/3_workplan.pdf

International Federation of Social Workers. (2005). *Global standards for social work education and training.* Retrieved from http://www.ifsw.org/p38000868.html

International Federation of Social Workers. (2012). *Code of ethics,* Retrieved from http://ifsw.org/policies/code-of-ethics/

Internal Revenue Service. (2007). *Election year activities and the prohibition on political campaign intervention for section 501 (c)(3) organizations.* Retrieved from http://www.irs.gov/newsroom/article/0,,id=154712,00.html

Internal Revenue Service. (2010). *Measuring lobbying activity: Expenditure test.* Retrieved from http://www.irs.gov/charities/article/0,,id=163394,00.html

Israel, B., Schultz, A., Parker, E., Becker, A., Allen, A., & Guzman, R. (2008). Critical issues in developing and following CBPR principles. In M. Minkler, & N. Wallerstein (Eds.), *Community-based participatory research for health: From processes to outcomes* (pp. 47–62). San Francisco, CA: Jossey-Bass.

Itzhaky, H., & York, A. (2002). Showing results in community organization. *Social Work, 47*(2), 125–131.

Ivery, J. (2008). Policy mandated collaboration. *Journal of Sociology and Social Welfare, 35*(4), 53–70.

Jackson-Elmore, C. (2005). Informing state policymakers: Opportunities for social workers. *Social Work, 50,* 251–261.

James, S., Schultz, A., & van Olpen, J. (2001). Social capital, poverty, and community health: An exploration of the linkages. In S. Saegert, J. P. Thompson, & M. Warren (Eds.), *Social capital and poor communities* (pp. 165–188). New York: Russell Sage Foundation.

446 *References*

Jansson, B. (2008). *Becoming an effective policy advocate: From policy practice to social justice* (5th ed.). Belmont, CA: Thomson Brooks/Cole.
Jaskyte, K. (2004). Transformational leadership, organization culture, and innovativeness in nonprofit organizations. *Nonprofit Leadership and Management, 15,* 153–168.
Jennings, L., Parra-Medina, D., Hilfinger-Messias, D., & McLoughlin, K. (2006). Toward a critical social theory of youth empowerment. *Journal of Community Practice, 14*(1/2), 31–55.
Johnson, A. (1998). The revitalization of community practice: Characteristics, competencies, and curricula for community-based services. *Journal of Community Practice, 5,* 37–62.
Johnson, A. (2000). The community practice pilot project: Integrating methods, field, community assessment, and experiential learning. *Journal of Community Practice, 8*(4), 5–25.
Johnson, D., & Johnson, F. (2006). *Joining together: Group theory and group skills* (9th ed.). Boston, MA: Allyn & Bacon.
Johnson, J., Honnald, J., & Stevens, F. P. (2010). Using social network analysis to enhance nonprofit organizational research. *Journal of Community Practice, 18,* 493–512.
Johnson, Y., & Munch, S. (2009). Fundamental contradictions in cultural competence. *Social Work, 54,* 220–231.
Jonsson, J. (2010). Beyond empowerment: Changing local communities. *International Social Work, 53,* 393–406.
Kadushin, A. (2002). *Supervision in social work* (4th ed.). New York: Columbia University Press.
Kahn, S. (1991). *Organizing: A guide for grass-roots leaders.* Washington, DC: National Association for Social Workers.
Kahn, S. (2010). *Creative community organizing.* San Francisco: Berrett-Koehler.
Kaminski, M., Kaufman, J., Graubarth, R., & Robins, T. (2000). How do people become empowered? A case study of union activism. *Human Relations, 53,* 53–63.
Kang, J. (2010). Understanding non-governmental organizations in community development: Strengths, limitations and suggestions. *International Social Work, 54,* 223–237.
Kay, A. (2006). Social capital, the social economy, and community development. *Community Development Journal, 4,* 160–173.
Kennedy, M. (2009). *Transformative planning for community development.* IRLE Working Papers (WP 2009–18) Institute for Research on Labor and Employment, University of California Los Angles. Retrieved from http://escholarship.org/uc/item/14r1s460;jsessionid=4E36FC43007CEA88CB3AB B3492642E7A
Keough, M. E., & Samuels, M. (2004). The Kosovo family support project: Offering psychosocial support for families with missing persons. *Social Work, 49,* 587–594.

Kerlin, J., & Reid, E. (2010). The financing and programming of advocacy in complex nonprofit structures. *Nonprofit and Voluntary Sector Quarterly, 39,* 802–824.

Kernaghan, C. (2011, June 24). *Hanes and Target linked to sexual abuse: Classic factory in Jordon.* Institute for Global Labor and Human Rights. Retrieved from http://www.globallabourrights.org/reports?id=0634

Kerns, M. (n.d). *Net-centric advocacy campaigns.* Green Media Toolshed. Retrieved from http://netcentriccampaigns.com/files/NetworkCentricAdvocacyPAper.pdf

Kerr Chandler, S. (2009). Working hard, living poor: Social work and the movement for livable wages. *Journal of Community Practice, 17,* 170–183.

King, C., Feltey, K., & Susel, B. (1998). The question of participation: Toward authentic public participation in public administration. *Public Administration Review, 58*(4), 317–327.

Kingdon, J. (2003). *Agendas, alternatives, and public policies* (2nd ed.). New York: Addison Wesley.

Kirschenbaum, J., & Russ, L. (2009). In M. Minkler (Ed.), Community mapping, geographic information systems. *Community organizing, community building for health* (2nd ed., pp. 450–454). New Brunswick, NJ: Rutgers University Press.

Kirst-Ashman, K., & Hull, G. (2009). *Generalist practice with organizations and communities* (4th ed.). Belmont, CA: Brooks/Cole.

Kirk, P., & Shuttee, A. (2004). Community leadership development. *Community Development Journal, 39,* 234–251.

Kirk, R., & Schill, D. (2011). A digital agora: Citizen participation in the 2008 Presidential debates. *American Behavioral Scientists, 55,* 325–347.

Kirst-Ashman, K., & Hull, G. (2008). *Understanding generalist practice* (5th ed.). Belmont, CA: Brooks/Cole.

Kissane, R., & Gingerich, J. (2004). Do you see what I see? Nonprofit and resident perceptions of their neighborhoods. *Nonprofit and Voluntary Sector Quarterly, 33,* 311–333.

Klandermans, B. (2007). The demand and supply of participation: Social-psychological correlates of participation in social movements. (2009). In D. Snow, S. Soule, & H. Kriesi (Eds.), *The Blackwell companion to social movements* (pp. 360–379). Malden, MA: Blackwell Publishing.

Knapp, J., & Diehm, J. (2009). *The Hatch Act: It's not just for Federal employees anymore.* Retrieved from http://apps.americanbar.org/buslaw/commit tees/CL121000pub/newsletter/200911/knapp.pdf

Korazim-Korosy, Y., Mizrahi, T., Katz, C., Karmon, A., Garcia, M., & Bayne-Smith, M. (2007). Toward interdisciplinary community collaboration and development: Knowledge and experience from Israel and the USA. *Journal of Community Practice, 15*(1/2), 13–44.

Kraft, M., & Furlong, S. (2007). *Public policy: Politics, analysis, and alternatives* (2nd ed.). Washington, DC: CQ Press.

Kramer Tebes, J., Matlin, S., Migdole, S., Farkas, M., Money, R., . . . Hoge, M. (2011). Providing competency training to clinical supervisors through an interactional supervision approach. *Research on Social Work Practice, 2*, 190–199.

Kretzmann, J., & McKnight, J. (1993). *Building communities from the inside out.* Chicago: ATCA.

Kretzmann, J., & McKnight, J. (1996). *Mapping community capacity* (revised). Retrieved from Asset-based Community Development Institute, Institute for Policy Research, Northwestern University website: http://www.north western.edu/ipr/publications/papers/mcc.pdf

Krishna, A., & Shrader, E. (1999). *Social capital assessment tool.* Retrieved from http://siteresources.worldbank.org/INTSOCIALCAPITAL/Resources/Social-Capital-Assessment-Tool--SOCAT-/sciwp22.pdf

Krumholz, N., Keating, D., Star, P., & Chupp, M. (2006). The long-term impact of CDCs on urban neighborhoods: Case studies of Cleveland's Broadway-Slavic Village and Tremont neighborhoods. *Community Development, 37*(4), 33–52.

Kryda, A., & Compton, M. (2009). Mistrust of outreach workers and lack of confidence in available services among individuals who are chronically street homeless. *Community Mental Health Journal, 45*, 144–150.

Kubisch, A., Auspos, P., Brown, P., Chaskin, R., Fulbright-Anderson, K., & Hamilton, R. (2002). *Voices from the field II: Reflections on comprehensive community change.* Retrieved from Aspen Institute website: http://www.aspen institute.org/sites/default/files/content/docs/roundtable%20on%20comm unity%20change/voicesIIbook.pdf

Kubisch, A., Auspos, P., Brown, P., & Dewar, T. (2010). *Voices from the field III: Lessons and challenges from two decades of community change efforts.* Retrieved from Aspen Institute website: http://www.aspeninstitute.org/sites/ default/files/content/docs/pubs/VoicesIII_FINAL_0.pdf

Labonte, R. (2009). Community, community development, and the forming of authentic partnerships: Some critical reflections. In M. Minkler, & N. Wallerstein (Eds.), *Community-based participatory research for health: From processes to outcomes* (pp. 82–96). San Francisco, CA: Jossey-Bass.

Lafferty, C., & Mahoney, C. (2003). A framework for evaluating comprehensive community initiatives. *Health Promotion Practice, 4*, 31–44.

Laffey, M., & Weldes, J. (2010). *"Antiglobalization" protests and the future of democracy.* Retrieved from Asrudian Center website: http://asrudiancenter. wordpress.com/2010/11/03/%E2%80%9Cantiglobalization%E2%80%9D-protests-and-the-future-of-democracy/

Lambright, K., Mischen, P., & Laramee, C. (2010). Building trust in public and nonprofit networks: Personal, dyadic, and third-party influences. *American Review of Public Administration, 40*, 64–82.

Lane, S. (2011). Political content in social work education as reported by elected social workers. *Journal of Social Work Education, 47*, 53–72.

Larkin, H. (2004). Justice implications of a proposed Medicare prescription drug policy. *Social Work, 49*(3), 406–414.

Larsen, A., Visser-Rotgans, R., & Hole, G. (2011). Teaching and learning community work online: Can E-learning promote competences for future practice? *Journal of Technology in Human Services, 29*(1), 13–32.

Larson, L., Day, S., Springer, S., Clark, M., & Vogel, D. (2003). Developing a supervisor feedback rating scale: A brief report. *Measurement and Evaluation in Counseling and Development, 35,* 230–238.

Lasker, R., & Weiss, E. (2003). Broadening participation in community problem solving: A multidisciplinary model to support collaborative practice and research. *Journal of Urban Health, 80*(1), 14–60.

Laurian, L., & Shaw, M. (2009). Evaluation of public participation: The practices of certified planners. *Journal of Planning Education and Research, 28,* 293–309.

Lee, J. (2001). *The empowerment approach to social work practice: Building the beloved community* (2nd ed.). New York: Columbia University Press.

Lemieux, C., & Allen, P. (2007). Service learning in social work education: The state of knowledge, pedagogical practicalities, and practice conundrums. *Journal of Social Work Education, 43,* 309–325.

Lennie, J. (2006). Increasing the rigour and trustworthiness of participatory evaluations: Learning from the field. *Evaluation Journal of Australasia, 6,* 27–35.

Leung, A., Lam, C. W., Yao, T. Y., & Chu, W. (2010). Re-empowering social workers through the online community: The experience of SWForum in Hong Kong. *Critical Social Policy, 30*(1), 48–73.

Lestrelin, G., Borgoin, J., Bouahom, B., & Castella, J. (2011). Measuring participation: Case studies on village land use planning in northern Laos PDR. *Applied Geography, 31,* 950–958.

Lewin, K. (1951). *Field theory in social science: Selected theoretical papers.* New York: Harper & Row.

Lewis, H. (2002). Participatory research and education for social change: Highlander Research and Education Center. In P. Reason, & H. Bradbury (Eds.), *The handbook of action research: Participative inquiry and practice* (pp. 356–362). Thousand Oaks, CA: Sage.

Lietz, C. (2010). Critical thinking in child welfare supervision. *Administration in Social Work, 34,* 68–78.

Light, I. (2004). Social capital for what? In R. Silverman (Ed.), *Community-based organizations: The intersection of social capital and local context in contemporary urban society* (pp. 19–33). Detroit, MI: Wayne State University Press.

Lightman, E., Mitchell, A., & Herd, D. (2005). One year on: Tracking the experiences of current and former welfare recipients in Toronto. *Journal of Poverty, 9*(4), 5–21.

Lim, C. (2010). Mobilizing on the margin. How does interpersonal recruitment affect citizen participation in politics? *Social Science Research, 39,* 341–355.

Lincoln, Y. (2002). Engaging sympathies: Relationships between action research and social constructivism. In P. Reason, & H. Bradbury (Eds.), *The handbook of action research* (pp. 124–132). Thousand Oaks, CA: Sage.

Lindblom, C. (1959). The science of muddling through. *Public Administration Review, 19,* 79–88.

Linhorst, D. (2002). A review of the use and potential of focus groups in social work research. *Qualitative Social Work, 1,* 208–228.

Linhorst, D., Ekert, A., & Hamilton, G. (2005). Promoting participation in organizational decision making by clients with severe mental illness. *Social Work, 50,* 21–30.

Li Puma, G., & Koelble, T. (2009). Social capital in emerging democracies. *Voluntas, 20, 1–14,*

Little, D. (2010). Identity, efficacy, and disability rights movement recruitment. *Disability Studies Journal, 30*(1), 2–14.

Little, R., & Froggett, L. (2009). Making meaning in muddy waters: Representing complexity through community based story-telling. *Community Development Journal, 45*(4), 458–473.

Littrell, J., & Brooks, F. (2010). In defense of the community reinvestment act. *Journal of Community Practice, 17,* 417–439.

Lohmann, R., & Lohmann, N. (2002). *Social administration.* New York: Columbia University Press.

Longres, J. (2008). Diversity in community life. In J. Rothman, J. Erlich, & J. Tropman (Eds.), *Strategies of community intervention* (7th ed., pp. 171–186). Peosta, IA: Eddie Bowers Publishing.

Lopez, M. L., & Stack, C. (2001). Social capital and the culture of power: Lessons from the field. In S. Saegert, J. P. Thompson, & M. Warren (Eds.), *Social capital and poor communities* (pp. 31–59). New York: Russell Sage Foundation.

Lough, B., Moore McBride, A., Sherraden, M., & O'Hara, K. (2011). Capacity building contributions of short-term international volunteers. *Journal of Community Practice, 19,* 120–137.

Lowenberg, F., & Dolgoff, R. (1996). *Ethical decisions for social work practice* (5th ed.). Itasca, Il: F.E.Peacock.

Lukas, C., & Hoskins, L. (2003). *Conducting community forums: Engaging citizens and mobilizing communities.* St. Paul, MN: Wilder Publishing Center.

Lum, D. (2007). *Culturally competent practice: A framework for understanding diverse groups and justice issues* (3rd ed.). New York: Wadsworth.

Lundy, C. (2004). *Social work and social justice: A structural approach to practice.* Orchard Park, NY: Broadview Press.

Lundy, C., & van Wormer, K. (2007). Social and economic justice, human rights, and peace: The challenge for social work in Canada and the USA. *International Social Work, 50,* 727–739.

McDonald, M., Sarche, J., & Wang, C. (2009). Using the arts in community organizing and community building. In M. Minkler (Ed.), *Community organizing and community building for health* (2nd ed., pp. 346–364). New Brunswick, NJ: Rutgers University Press.

Mackelprang, R., & Salsgiver, R. (2009). *Disability: A diversity model approach in human service practice.* Chicago, IL: Lyceum Books.

Maiter, S., Simich, L., Jacobson, N., & Wise, J. (2008). Reciprocity: An ethic for community-based participatory action research. *Action Research, 6,* 305–325.

Majee, W., & Hoyt, A. (2009). Building community trust through cooperatives: A case study of a worker-owned home care co-operative. *Journal of Community Practice, 17,* 444–463.

Maloney, W., Smith, G., & Stoker, G. (2000). Social capital and urban governance: Adding a more contextualized "top down" perspective. *Political Studies, 48,* 802–820.

Maman, S., Lane, T., Ntogwisangu, J., Modiba, P., Vanrooyen, H., Timbe, A., ... Fritz, K. (2009). Using participatory mapping to inform a community-randomized trial of HIV counseling and testing. *Field Methods, 21,* 368–386.

Marcum, D. (2006, February 10). Agency may have violated civil rights. *Fresno Bee,* pp. A1–A5.

Marcum, D. (2010, November 28). Students want the Dream Act to become reality. *Los Angeles Times.* Retrieved from http://articles.latimes.com/2010/nov/28/local/la-me-dream-act-20101128

Marlantes, L., Bradley, T., & Burns, Q. (2006, September 20). Another day, another star on Capitol Hill. *ABC News.* Retrieved from http://abcnews.go.com/

Marois, S. (2006). *Beyond polarities: Collaboration and conflict in community health partnerships.* Paper presented on COMM-ORG: The On-Line Conference on Community Organizing and Development (Vol. 12). Retrieved from http://comm-org.wisc.edu/pipermail/colist/2006-January/004148.html

Marris, P., & Rein, M. (1982). *Dilemmas of social reform.* Chicago: University of Chicago Press.

Marshall, C., & Rossman, G. (2006). *Designing qualitative research* (4th ed.). Thousand Oaks, CA: Sage.

Marti-Costa, S., & Serrano-Garcia, I. (1995). Needs assessment and community development: An ideological perspective. In J. Rothman, J. Erlich, & J. Tropman (Eds.), *Strategies of community intervention* (5th ed., pp. 257–267) Itasca, IL: Peacock.

Martinez, L. (2008). "Flowers from the same soil." Latino solidarity in the wake of the 2006 immigrant mobilizations. *American Behavioral Scientist, 52,* 557–579.

Marx, J. (2010). Deregulating social welfare. *Social Work, 55,* 371–372.

Mathie, A., & Cunningham, G. (2003). From clients to citizens: Asset-based community development as a strategy for community-driven development. *Development in Practice, 13,* 474–486.

Maxwell, J. (n.d.). *Demonstrations 101.* Retrieved from Syracuse Peace Council website: http://www.peacecouncil.net/pnl/03/720/720_demonstrations_101.htm

Maxwell, J. A. (2004). Reemergent scientism, postmodernism, and dialogue across differences. *Qualitative Inquiry, 10,* 35–41.

McAdam, D., & Tarrow, S. (2000). Nonviolence as contentious interaction. *Political Science & Politics, 33,* 149–154.

McBeath, B., & Briggs, H. (2008). Designing client-centered, performance-based human service programs. In L. Ginsberg (Ed.), *Management and leadership in social work education and practice* (pp. 126–142). Alexandria, VA: Council on Social Work Education.

McCoy, M., & Scully, P. (2002). Deliberative dialogue to expand civic engagement: What kind of talk does democracy need? *National Civic Review, 91*(2), 117–134.

McCreary, L., Lorenz, R., Neufeld, M. (Producers), & Eastwood, C., (Director). (2009). *Invictus [Motion picture].* United States: Warner Brothers.

McGrath, C. (2007). Framing lobbying messages: defining and communicating political issues persuasively. *Journal of Public Affairs, 7,* 269–280.

McKnight, J. (1995). *The careless society: Community and its counterfeits.* New York: Basic books.

McKnight, J., & Block, P. (2010). *The abundant community: Awakening the power of families and neighborhoods.* San Francisco, CA: Berrett-Koehler.

McKnight, J., & Kretzmann, J. (2009). Mapping community capacity. In M. Minkler (Ed.), *Community organizing and community building for health* (2nd ed., pp. 158–172). New Brunswick, NJ: Rutgers University Press.

McNutt, J. (2011). Is social work advocacy worth the cost? Issues and barriers to an economic analysis of social work political practices. *Research on Social Work Practice, 21,* 397–403.

McNutt, J. (1995). The macro practice curriculum in graduate social work education: Results of a national study. *Administration in Social Work, 19,* 59074.

McTighe, J. (2011). Teaching the use of self through the process of clinical supervision. *Clinical Social Work, 39,* 301–307.

Melendez, M., & LaSala, M. (2006). Who's oppressing whom?: Homosexuality, Christianity, and social work. *Social Work, 51,* 355–364.

Mendes, P. (2008). Teaching community development to social work students: A critical reflection. *Community Development Journal, 44,* 248–262.

Meenaghan, T., Kilty, K., & McNutt, J. (2004). *Social policy analysis and practice.* Chicago, IL: Lyceum.

Meenaghan, T., Washington, R., & Ryan, R. (1982). *Macro practice in the human services.* New York: Free Press.

Messinger, L. (2004). Comprehensive community initiatives: A rural perspective. *Social Work, 49,* 535–546.

Methiratta, K., & Smith, C. (2001, August). *Advancing community organizing practice: Lessons from grassroots organizations in India.* Paper presented on COMM-ORG: The On-Line Conference on Community Organizing and Development (Vol. 7). Retrieved from http://comm-org.wisc.edu/papers2001/mediratta/title.htm

Midgley, J. (2005). Development theory and community practice. In M. Weil, M. Reisch, D. Gamble, L. Gutierrez, E. Mulroy, & R. Cnaan (Eds.), *The handbook of community practice* (pp. 153–168). Thousand Oaks, CA: Sage.

Midgley, J. (2007). Perspectives on globalization, social justice, and welfare. *Journal of Sociology and Social Welfare, 34*(2), 17–34.

Midgley, J. (2008). Microenterprise, global poverty and social development. *International Social Work, 51,* 467–479.

Midgley, J. (2010). Community practice and developmental social work. In J. Midgley (Ed.), *Social work and social development* (pp. 167–189). New York: Oxford University Press.

Mika, M. (2006). Framing the issue: Religion, secular ethics and the case of animal rights mobilization. *Social Forces, 85,* 915–941.

Milam Handley, D., & Howell-Moroney, M. (2010). Ordering stakeholder relationships and citizen participation: Evidence from the Community Development Block Grant Program. *Public Administration Review,* (July/August), 601–609.

Miley, K., O'Melia, M., & Dubois, B. (2011). *Generalist social work practice: An empowering approach* (6th ed.). Boston: Pearson Education.

Miller, R., & Cambell, R. (2006). Taking stock of empowerment evaluation: An empirical review. *American Journal of Evaluation, 27,* 296–319.

Minkler, M. (2000). Using participatory action research to build healthy communities. *Public Health Reports, 115,* 191–197.

Minkler, M., Breckwich Vasquez, V. B., Tajik, M., & Petersen, D. (2008). Promoting environmental justice through community-based participatory research: The role of community and partnership capacity. *Health Education & Behavior, 35,* 119–137.

Minkler, M., & Coombe, C. (2009). Using force field and SWOT analysis as strategic tools in community organizing. In M. Minkler (Ed.), *Community organizing and community building for health* (2nd ed., pp. 444–447). New Brunswick, NJ: Rutgers University Press.

Minkler, M., & Pies, C. (2009). Ethical issues and practical dilemmas in community organization and community participation. In M. Minkler (Ed.), *Community organizing and community building for health* (2nd ed., pp. 116–113). New Brunswick, NJ: Rutgers University Press.

Mishra, R. (2005). Social rights as human rights: Globalizing social protection. *International Social Work, 48,* 9–20.

Mizrahi, T. (n.d.). *Community organizers: For a change.* Retrieved from the Silberman School of Social Work, Hunter College website: http://www.hunter.cuny.edu/socwork/ecco/cocareer.htm

Mizrahi, T. (2007). Women's ways of organizing. *Affilia, 22*(1), 39–55.

Mizrahi, T., Bayne-Smith, M., & Garcia, M. L. (2009). Comparative perspectives on interdisciplinary community collaboration between academics and community practitioners. *Community Development, 39*(3), 1–15.

Mizrahi, T. & CO faculty. (2006). *Where have all the organizers gone? A study of Hunter CO alumna from 1996–2006: Perspectives on the competencies and values in the curriculum looking back and career tracks moving forward.* Retrieved from the Silberman School of Social Work, Hunter College website: http://www.hunter.cuny.edu/socwork/programs/community_organization/COPD_Alumni_Study-1995–2006.pdf

Mizrahi, T., Lopez Humphreys, M., & Torres, D. (2009). The social construction of client participation: The evolution and transformation of the role of service recipients in child welfare and mental disabilities. *Journal of Sociology and Social Welfare, 36*(2), 35–61.

Mizrahi, T., & Rosenthal, B. (1998). "A whole lot of organizing going on": The status and needs of organizers in community-based organizations. *Journal of Community Practice, 5*(4), 1–24.

Mizrahi, T., & Rosenthal, B. (2001). Complexities of coalition building: Leaders' successes, strategies, struggles, and solutions. *Social Work, 46*(1), 64–78.

Moffat, K., George, U., Lee, B., & McGrath, S. (1999). Advancing citizenship: A study of social planning. *Community Development Journal, 34*, 308–317.

Moore, B. (2005). Faculty perceptions of the effectiveness of web-based instruction in social work education: A national study. *Journal of Technology in Human Services, 23*(1/2), 53–66.

Moore, J. (2011, June 30). Did Twitter, Facebook really build a revolution? *Christian Science Monitor*. Retrieved from MSNBC News website: http://today.msnbc.msn.com/

Moore, K. (2005). What's class got to do with it? Community development and racial identity. *Journal of Urban Affairs, 27*, 437–451.

Mondros, J. (2005). Political, social, and legislative action. In M. Weil, M. Reisch, D. Gamble, L. Gutierrez, E. Mulroy, & R. Cnaan (Eds.), *The handbook of community practice* (pp. 276–286). Thousand Oaks, CA: Sage.

Mondros, J., & Wilson, S. (1994). *Organizing for power and empowerment.* New York: Columbia University Press.

Montana, S., Rondero Hernandez, V., Siegel, D., & Jackson, M. (2010). *Cultural brokers research project: An approach to community engagement with African American families in child welfare.* Fresno, CA: Social Welfare Evaluation Research and Training Center, Department of Social Work Education, California State University, Fresno.

Morgen, S. (1994). Personalizing personnel decisions in feminist organizational theory and practice. *Human Relations, 47*, 665–684.

Morrison, J., & Branigan, E. (2007). Working collectively in competitive times: Case studies from New Zealand and Australia. *Community Development Journal, 44*, 68–79.

Mosley, J. (2010). Organizational resources and environmental incentives: Understanding the policy advocacy involvement of human service nonprofits. *Social Service Review, 84*, 57–76.

Mott, A. (n.d.). *University education for community change*: A vital strategy for progress on poverty, race, and community-building. Retrieved from Coimmunity-Wealth.org website: http://www.community-wealth.org/_pdfs/articles-publications/universities/report-mott.pdf

Mott, A. (2003). *Strengthening social change through organizational learning and evaluation.* Paper presented on COMM-ORG: The On-Line Conference on Community Organizing and Development (Vol. 9). Retrieved from http://comm-org.wisc.edu/papers2005/mott.htm

Mott, A. (2008). *University education for community change: A vital strategy for progress on poverty, race, and community-building* (2nd ed.). Retrieved from Community

Learning Partnership website: http://www.communitylearningpartnership. org/docs/ue4change.pdf

Moua, X. (2001). *Hmong clan leaders' roles and responsibilities.* (Unpublished master's thesis). Department of Social Work Education, California State University, Fresno.

Mowbray, C., Holter, M., Teague, G., & Bybee, D. (2003). Fidelity criteria: Development, measurement, and validation. *American Journal of Evaluation, 24,* 315–349.

Moynihan, D. (1969). *Maximum feasible misunderstanding.* New York: Free Press.

Mulroy, E. (2008). University community partnerships that promote evidence-based practice. *Journal of Evidence-based Social Work, 5,* 497–517.

Mulroy, E., & Lauber, H. (2002). Community building in hard times: A post-welfare view from the streets. *Journal of Community Practice, 10,* 1–16.

Mulroy, E., & Lauber, H. (2004). A user-friendly approach to program evaluation and effective community interventions for families at risk of homelessness. *Social Work, 49,* 573–586.

Mulroy, E., Nelson, K., & Gour, D. (2005). Community building and family-centered service collaboratives. In M. Weil, M. Reisch, D. Gamble, L. Gutierrez, E. Mulroy, & R. Cnaan (Eds.), *The handbook of community practice* (pp. 460–474) Thousand Oaks, CA: Sage.

Murdach, A. (2011a). Is social work a human rights profession? *Social Work, 56,* 281–283.

Murdach, A. (2011b). What happened to self-determination? *Social Work, 56,* 371–373.

Nadler, J., & Schulman, S. (2006). *Open meetings, open records, and transparency in government.* Retrieved from Markkula Center for Applied Ethics, Santa Clara University website: http://www.scu.edu/ethics/practicing/focus areas/government_ethics/introduction/open-meetings.html

Nagda, B., & Zuniga, X. (2003). Fostering meaningful racial engagement through intergroup dialogues. *Group Processes Intergroup Relations, 6,* 111–128.

National Association of Social Workers. (n.d.). *PACE: Building political power for social workers.* Retrieved from http://www.socialworkers.org/pace/default. asp

National Association of Social Workers. (2000). *Code of ethics of the National Association of Social Workers.* Washington, D.C.: Author.

National Association of Social Workers. (2007). *Indicators for the achievement of the NASW standards for cultural competence in social work practice.* Retrieved from http://www.socialworkers.org/practice/standards/NASWCulturalStan dardsIndicators2006.pdf

National Association of Social Workers. (2011). *Social workers in Congress (112th Congress).* Retrieved from http://www.socialworkers.org/pace/ swCongress/SW_InCongress.pdf

National Center for Dialogue and Deliberation. (n.d.). *What are dialogue and deliberation?* Retrieved from http://ncdd.org/rc/what-are-dd

National Council on Crime and Deliquency. (2009). *Developing a successful street outreach program: Recommendations and lessons learned.* Retrieved from http://www.ccgpn.org/Publications/Street%20Outreach%20Final%2010.20.09.pdf

National Economic & Social Rights Initiative (Executive Producer) & Stephenson, M. (Director). (2010). *Coming home: The dry storm [DVD].* Available from: http://www.esri.org

National Legal Council on Alcohol and Tobacco Prevention. (n.d.). *Take action, create change: A community organization toolkit.* Retrieved from http://www.ccgpn.org/Publications/Street%20Outreach%20Final%2010.20.09.pdf

National Neighborhood Indicators Partnership. (n.d). *NNIP concept.* Retrieved from http://www.neighborhoodindicators.org/about-nnip/nnip-concept

National Public Radio. (2010, March 22). *ACORN's Board approves group's shutdown.* Retrieved from http://www.npr.org/blogs/thetwo-way/2010/03/acorn_board_approves_groups_sh.html

Nawyn, S. (2010). Institutional structures of opportunity in refugee resettlement: Gender, race/ethnicity, and refugee NGOs. *Journal of Sociology and Social Welfare, 37,* 149–167.

Neighborhood Funders Group. (2011). *Measuring results: How to evaluate CO initiatives.* Retrieved from http://www.nfg.org/index.php?ht=display/ContentDetails/i/3167

Neighborhood Works America. (2011). *Professional certificates and graduate credits.* Retrieved from http://www.nw.org/network/training/programs/cb.asp

Netting, F. E., & O'Connor, M. K. (2003). *Organization practice: A social worker's guide to understanding human services.* Boston: Allyn & Bacon.

Netting, F. E., O'Connor, M. K., & Fauri, D. (2008). *Comparative approaches for program planning.* Hoboken: John Wiley and Sons.

Netting, F. E., Kettner, P., & McMurty, S. (2008). *Social work macro practice* (4th ed.). Boston, MA: Pearson.

Neuman, L. (2003). *Social research methods: Qualitative and quantitative approaches.* Boston, MA: Allyn & Bacon.

Newman, K. (2008). Whose view matters? Using participatory processes to evaluate Reflect in Nigeria. *Community Development Journal, 22,* 382–394.

New York Times. (2011, July 3). Free speech and the Internet (Editorial). Retrieved from http://www.nytimes.com/

Nowell, B. (2009). Profiling capacity for coordination and systems change. The relative contribution of stakeholder relationships in interorganizational collaboratives. *American Journal of Community Psychology, 44,* 196–212.

Nowell, B., & Boyd, N. (2010). Viewing community as a responsibility as well as a resource: Deconstructing the theoretical roots of psychological sense of community. *Journal of Community Psychology, 38,* 828–841.

Nowell, B., & Foster-Fishman, P. (2010). Examining multi-sector community collaboratives as vehicles for building organizational capacity. *American Journal of Community Psychology, 48,* 193–207.

Noy, D. (2008). Power mapping: Enhancing sociological knowledge by developing generalizeable analytical public tools. *American Sociologist, 39*, 3–18.

Nygreen, K., Kwon, S. A., & Sanchez, P. (2006). Urban youth building community: Social change and participatory research in schools, homes, and community-based organizations. *Journal of Community Practice, 14*(1/2), 107–123.

Oden, K., Hernandez, B., & Hidalgo, M. (2010). Payoffs of participatory action research: Racial and ethnic minorities with disabilities reflect on their research experiences. *Community Development, 41*, 21–31.

Offenheiser, R., & Holcombe, S. (2003). Challenges and opportunities in implementing a rights-based approach to development: An Oxfam America perspective. *Nonprofit and Voluntary Sector Quarterly, 32*, 268–306.

Ohmer, M. (2008). The relationship between citizen participation and organizational processes and outcomes and the benefits of citizen participation in neighborhood organizations. *Journal of Social Service Research, 34*(4), 41–60.

Ohmer, M. (2010). How theory and research inform citizen participation in poor communities: The ecological perspective and theories on self- and collective efficacy and sense of community. *Journal of Human Behavior in the Social Environment, 20*, 1–19.

Ohmer, M., & Beck, E. (2006). Citizen participation in neighborhood organizations in poor communities and its relationship to neighborhood and organizational collective efficacy. *Journal of Sociology and Social Welfare, 33*(1), 179–202.

Ohmer, M., & DeMasi, K. (2009). *Consensus organizing: A community development workbook.* Los Angeles, CA: Sage.

Ohmer, M., & Korr, W. (2006). The effectiveness of community practice interventions: A review of the literature. *Research in Social Work Practice, 16*, 132–145.

Ohmer, M., Meadowcraft, P., Freed, K., & Lewis, E. (2009). Community gardening and community development: Individual, social, and community benefits of a community conservation program. *Journal of Community Practice, 17*, 377–399.

Oladipo Fiki, C., Amuptian, J., Dabi, D., & Nyong, A. (2007). From disciplinary to interdisciplinary community development: The Jos-McMaster drought and rural water use project in Nigeria. *Journal of Community Practice, 15*(1/2), 147–170.

Oliver, M. (2001). Preface. In S. Saegert, J. P. Thompson, & M. Warren (Eds.), *Social capital and poor communities* (pp. xi–xiv). New York: Russell Sage Foundation.

O'Neill, K., Williams, K., & Reznick, V. (2008). Engaging Latino residents to build a healthier community in Mid-City San Diego. *American Journal of Preventive Medicine, 34*(3sS), S36–41.

Organizing for America. (2008). *Guide to running your own phone bank.* Retrieved from http://my.barackobama.com/page/content/phonebankguide

Ortiz, L., Wirz, C. Semion K., & Rodriguez, C. (2004). Legislative casework: Where policy and practice interest. *Journal of Sociology and Social Welfare, 31*(2), 49–68.

Paarlberg, L., & Varda, D. (2009). Community carrying capacity: A network perspective. *Nonprofit and Voluntary Sector Quarterly, 38*, 597–613.

Padgett, D. (2008). *Qualitative methods in social work research* (2nd ed.). Thousand Oaks, CA: Sage.

Panos, P. (2005). A model for using videoconferencing technology to support international social work field practicum students. *International Social Work, 48*, 834–841.

Pardasani, M. (2005). A context-specific community practice model of women's empowerment: Lessons learned in rural India. *Journal of Community Practice, 13*(1), 87–103.

Parker, L., & Betz, D. (1996). *Diverse partners in planning and decision making. Partnerships in education and research.* Retrieved from Washington State University Extension website: http://cru.cahe.wsu.edu/CEPublications/wrep0133/wrep0133.html

Parks, V., & Warren, D. (2009). The politics and practice of economic justice: Community benefits agreements as tactic of the new accountable development movement. *Journal of Community Practice, 17*, 88–106.

Patton, M. (2008). *Utilization-focused evaluation* (4th ed.). Thousand Oaks, CA: Brooks/Cole.

Payne, M. (2005). *Modern social work theory* (3rd ed.). Chicago, IL: Lyceum Books.

Pecukonis, E., & Wenocur, W. (1994). Perceptions of self and collective efficacy in community organization theory and practice. *Journal of Community Practice 1*(2), 5–21.

Pennell, J. (n.d.). *Mainstreaming Family Group Conferencing: Building and sustaining partnerships.* Retrieved from http://www.iirp.org/library/vt/vt_pennell.html

Perlmutter, S., Bailey, D., & Netting, F. E. (2001). *Managing human resources in the human services.* Silver Springs, MD: National Association of Social Workers.

Petersen, D. (2002). The potential of social capital measures in the evaluation of comprehensive community-based health initiatives. *American Journal of Evaluation, 23*, 53–64.

Peterson, N., Speer, P., Hughey, J., Armstead, T., Schneider, J., & Sheffer, M. (2008). Community organizations and sense of community: Further development in theory and measurement. *Journal of Community Psychology, 36*, 798–813.

Petter, J., Byrnes, P., Choi, D., Fegan, F., & Miller, R. (2002). Dimensions and patterns in employee empowerment: Assessing what matters to street-level bureaucrats. *Journal of Public Administration Research and Theory, 12*, 377–401.

Pewewardy, N. (2004). The political is personal: The essential obligation of white feminist family therapists to deconstruct white privilege. *Journal of Feminist Family Therapy, 16*, 53–67.

Phillips, R. (2003). *Community indicators.* American Planning Association, Planning Advisory Service (Report Number 517). Retrieved from http://www.planning.org/pas/reports/subscribers/pdf/PAS517.pdf

Piat, M. (2000). The NIMBY phenomenon: community residents' concerns about housing for deinstitutionalized people ... not in my back yard. *Health and Social Work 25*, 127–138.

PICO National Network. (n.d.). *Organizing tools: PICO training 1–1.* Retrieved from http://www.piconetwork.org/organizing/tools?id=0002

PICO National Network. (2010). *Issues and results.* Retrieved from http://www.piconetwork.org/issues/

PICO National Network. (2011). *About PICO.* Retrieved from http://www.piconetwork.org/about

Pilisuk, M., McAllister, J., Rothman, J., & Larin, L. (2009). New contexts of organizing: Functions, challenges, and solutions. *Community organizing and community building for health* (2nd ed., pp. 97–115). New Brunswick, NJ: Rutgers University Press.

Pippard, J. (2004). Identifying essential techniques for social work community practice. *Journal of Community Practice, 11*(4), 101–116.

Piven, F. F., & Cloward, R. (2000). *Why Americans still don't vote.* Boston: Beacon.

Plitt Donaldson, L. (2004). Toward validating the therapeutic benefits of empowerment-oriented social action groups. *Social Work with Groups, 27*(2/3), 159–175.

Plitt Donaldson, L., & Daughtery, L. (2011). Introducing asset-based models of social justice into service learning: A social work approach. *Journal of Community Practice, 19*, 80–99.

PolicyLink., (n.d.). *Community mapping.* Equitable development toolkit. Retrieved from http://www.policylink.org/site/c.lkIXLbMNJrE/b.5136917/k.AB67/Community_Mapping.htm

Polletta, F. (2002). *Freedom is an endless meeting: Democracy in American social movements.* Chicago, IL: University of Chicago Press.

Polletta, F. (2006). *It was like a fever: Storytelling in protest and politics.* Chicago, IL: University of Chicago Press.

Polletta, F., & Jasper, J. (2001). Collective identity and social movements. *Annual Review of Sociology, 27*, 283–305.

Portney, K. (2005). Civic engagement and sustainable cities in the United States. *Public Administration Review, 65*, 579–591.

Posadas, J. (2008). Community organizing as congregational practice: Social-scientific and theological perspectives. *International Journal of Practical Theology, 12*, 274–294.

Potter, D. (2010). "Wrong parents" and "right parents": Shared perspectives about citizen participation in policy implementation. *Social Science & Medicine, 70*, 1705–1713.

Poulin, J. (2010). *Strengths-based generalist practice: A collaborative approach* (3rd ed.). Belmont, CA: Wadsworth/Cengage Learning.

Preston, J. (2011, November 24). Protesters look for ways to feed the web. *New York Times.* Retrieved from http://www.nytimes.com/

Prigoff, A. (2000). *Economics for social workers: Social outcomes of economic globalization with strategies for community action.* Belmont, CA: Brooks/Cole.

Provan, K., & Milward, H. B. (2001). Do networks really work? A framework for evaluating public-sector organizational networks. *Public Administration Review, 61*(4), 414–423.

Putnam, R. (2000). *Bowling alone: The collapse and revival of American community.* New York: Simon & Schuster.

Pyles, L. (2009a). *Progressive community organizing. A critical approach for a globalizing world.* New York: Routledge.

Pyles, L. (2009b). Where's the freedom in free trade? Framing practices and global economic justice. *Journal of Community Practice, 17*, 73–87.

Pyles, L., & Cross, T. (2008). Community revitalization in post-Katrina New Orleans: A critical analysis of social capital in an African American community. *Journal of Community Practice, 16*, 383–401.

Quaghebeur, K., Masschelein, J., & Nguyen, H. (2004). Paradox of participation: Giving or taking part. *Journal of Community and Applied Social Psychology, 14*, 154–165.

Quarter, J., Sousa, J., Richmond, B., & Carmichael, I. (2001). Comparing member-based organizations within a social economy framework. *Nonprofit and Voluntary Sector Quarterly, 30*, 351–375.

Rajgopal, S. (2002). Reclaiming democracy? The anti-globalization movement in South Asia. *Feminist Review, 70*, 134–137.

Ramirez-Valles, J. (2001). "I was not invited to be a {CHW]...I asked to be one": Motives for community mobilization among women community health workers in Mexico. *Health Education Behavior, 28*, 150–165.

Ramirez-Valles, J., Fergus, S., Reisen, C., Poppen, P., & Zea, M. (2005). Confronting stigma: Community involvement and psychological well-being among HIV-positive Latino gay men. *Hispanic Journal of Behavioral Sciences, 27*, 101–119.

Rankopo, M., & Osei-Hwedie, K. (2011). Globalization and culturally relevant social work: African perspectives on indigenization. *International Social Work, 54*, 137–147.

Rapp, L., Button, D., Fleury-Steiner, B., & Fleury-Steiner, R. (2010). The Internet as a tool for black feminist activism: Lessons from an online protest. *Feminist Criminology, 5*, 244–262.

Rappaport, J. (1995). Empowerment meets narrative: Listening to stories and creating settings. *American Journal of Community Psychology, 23*, 795–807.

Ravensbergen, F., & Van der Platt, M. (2009). Barriers to citizen participation: The missing voices of people living with low income. *Community Development Journal, 45*, 389–403.

Rawls, J. (1971). *A theory of justice.* Cambridge, MA: Harvard University Press.

Rawls, J. (2001). *Justice as fairness*: A restatement: Cambridge, MA: Belknap Press.

Reamer, F. (2003). Boundary issues in social work: Managing dual relationships. *Social Work, 48*, 121–133.

Reamer, F. (2006). *Social work values and ethics.* New York: Columbia University Press.

Reason, P., & Bradbury, H. (2002). *The handbook of action research. Participative inquiry and practice.* Thousand Oaks, CA: Sage.

Reed, D. (2002). Poverty and the environment: Can sustainable development survive globalization? *Natural Resources Forum, 26,* 176–184.

Reed, J., & Cook, G. (2007). Older people involved in policy and planning: Factors that support engagement. *Journal of Aging Studies, 22,* 273–281.

Reed-Danahay, D. (2005). *Locating Bourdieu.* Bloomington, IN: University of Indiana Press.

Regehr, C., Bogo, M., Donovan, K., Lim, A., & Reghr, G. (2012). Evaluating a scale to measure student competencies in macro social work practice. *Journal of Social Service Research, 38,* 100–109.

Reisch, M. (2011). Defining social justice in a socially unjust world. In J. M. Birkenmaier, A. Cruce, E. Burkemper, J. Curley, R. J. Wilson, & J. J. Stretch (Eds.), *Educating for social justice: Transformative experiential learning* (pp. 1–28). Chicago: Lyceum Books.

Reisch, M., & Jarman-Rohde, L. (2000). The future of social work in the United States: Implications for field education. *Journal of Social Work Education, 36,* 201–214.

Reisch, M., & Lowe, J. I. (2000). "Of means and ends" revisited: Teaching ethical community organizing in an unethical society. *Journal of Community Practice, 7*(1), 19–38.

Reinelt, C., Foster, P., & Sullivan, S. (2003). *Evaluating outcomes and impacts: A scan of 55 leadership development programs.* Retrieved from Kellogg Foundation website: http://www.afj.org/for-nonprofits-foundations/reco/resources/kellogg.html

Results. (2005). *Toolkit: Organizing a community forum.* Retrieved from http://www.results.techriver.net/website/navdispatch.asp?id=1676

Richan, W. (2006). *Lobbying for social change* (3th ed). New York: Hayward Press.

Richards, L., & Dalbey, M. (2006). Creating great places: The role of citizen participation. *Journal of the Community Development Society, 37*(4), 18–32.

Risher, M., Schlosser, A., & Swain, R. (2010). *Know your rights: Free speech, protests and demonstrations in California.* Retrieved from American Civil Liberties Union of Northern California website: http://www.aclunc.org/issues/freedom_of_press_and_speech/asset_upload_file749_8880.pdf

Rispel, L., de Sousa, C., & Molomo, B. (2009). Can social inclusion policies reduce health inequalities in sub-Saharan Africa?- A rapid policy appraisal. *Journal of Health, Population, and Nutrition, 27*(4), 492–504.

Ritas, C., Minkler, M., Ni, A., & Halpin, A. (2008). Using CBPR to promote policy change. In M. Minkler, & N. Wallerstein (Eds.), *Community-based participatory research for health: From processes to outcomes* (pp. 459–463). San Francisco, CA: Jossey-Bass.

Robert, H., Corbin Robert, C., Robert, H. M., Evans, W., Honemann, D., Balch,T., ... Gerber, S. (2011). *Robert's rules of order: Newly revised* (11th ed.). Philadelphia, PA: Da Capa Press.

Roberts-DeGennaro, M. (2011). Application of principles for evidence-based practice in organizations and communities. In M. DeGennaro, & S. Fogel

(Eds.), *Using evidence to inform practice for community and organizational change* (pp. 1–14). Chicago: Lyceum Books.

Roberts-DeGennaro, M., & Mizrahi, T. (2005). Coalitions as change agents. In M. Weil, M. Reisch, D. Gamble, L. Gutierrez, E. Mulroy, & R. Cnaan (Eds.), *The handbook of community practice* (pp. 305–318). Thousand Oaks, CA: Sage.

Rocha, C., Poe, B., & Thomas, V. (2010). Political activities of social workers: Addressing perceived barriers to political participation. *Social Work, 55*(4), 317–325.

Rock the Vote. (2008, June). *Winning young voters: New media tactics*. Retrieved from http://www.rockthevote.com/assets/publications/research/rtv_new_media_tactics-june-2008.pdf

Roe, K. M., Roe, K., Goette Carpenter, C., & Berenstein Sibley, C. (2009). Community building through empowering evaluation: A case study of community planning for HIV Prevention. In M. Minkler (Ed.), *Community organizing and community building for health* (2nd ed., pp. 386–404). New Brunswick, NJ: Rutgers University Press.

Rogge, M., & Rocha, C. (2004). University-community partnership centers: An important link for social work education. *Journal of Community Practice, 12*, 103–121.

Rohlinger, D. A., & Brown, J. (2009). Democracy, action, and the Internet after 9/11. *American Behavioral Scientist, 53*(1), 133–150.

Rondero Hernandez, V., Montana, S., & Clarke, K. (2010). Child health inequality: Framing a social work response. *Health and Social Work, 35*, 291–301.

Rose, S. (1972). *The betrayal of the poor*. Cambridge, MA: Schenkman.

Rose, S. (2000). Reflections on empowerment-based practice. *Social Work, 45*(5), 403–420.

Rosenthal, B., & Mizrahi, T. (2004). Coalitions: Essential tools for organizing. In L. Staples (Ed.). *Roots to power: A manual for grassroots organizing* (pp. 316–330). Westport, CT: Praeger.

Rosing, H., & Hofman, N. (2010). Service leaning and the development of multidisciplinary community-based research initiatives. *Journal of Community Practice, 18*, 213–232.

Ross, L. (2010). Notes from the field: Learning cultural humility through critical incidents and central challenges in community-based participatory research. *Journal of Community Practice, 18*, 315–335.

Rothman, J. (1997). *Successful community leadership*. Washington, D.C.: NASW Press.

Rothman, J. (1979). Three models of community organization practice, their mixing and phasing. In F. Cox, J. Erlich, J. Rothman, & J. Tropman (Eds.), *Strategies of community organization* (3rd ed. pp. 25–45). Itasca, IL: F.E. Peacock Publishers.

Rothman, J. (1996). The interweaving of community intervention approaches. *Journal of Community Practice, 3*(3/4): 69–99.

Rothman, J. (2008). Multi modes of community intervention. In J. Rothman, J. Erlich, & J. Tropman (Eds.), *Strategies of community organization* (7th ed., pp. 141–170). Peosta, IA: Eddie Bowers.

Rothman, J., & Zald, M. (2008). Planning and policy practice. In J. Rothman, J. Erlich, & J. Tropman (Eds.), *Strategies of community organization* (7th ed., pp. 171–185). Peosta, IA: Eddie Bowers.

Routledge, P. (2003). Convergence space: Process geographies of grassroots globalization networks, *Transactions of the British Institute of Geographers, 28*, 333–349.

Royse, D., & Dignan, M. (2008). The Appalachia community cancer network: Issues and challenges in evaluation. *Research on Social Work Practice, 18*, 507–513.

Royse, D., Thyer, B., & Padgett, D. (2010). *Program evaluation: An introduction* (5th ed.). Belmont, CA: Thomson: Brooks/Cole.

Rubin, A., & Babbie, E. (2010). *Research methods for social work* (7th ed.). Belmont, CA: Brooks/Cole, Cengage Learning.

Rubin, A., & Parrish, D. (2007). Challenges to the future of evidence-based practice in social work education. *Journal of Social Work Education, 43*, 405–428.

Rubin, H. (2000). *Renewing hope within neighborhoods of despair: The community-based development model.* Albany, NY: State University of New York Press.

Rubin, H., & Rubin, I. (2005). *Qualitative interviewing: The art of hearing data,* (2nd ed.). Thousand Oaks, CA: Sage.

Rubin, H., & Rubin, I. (2008). *Community organizing and development* (4th ed.). Boston: Pearson Education.

Rudig, W. (2010). Assessing nonresponse bias in activist surveys. *Quality and Quantity, 44*(1), 173–180.

Russell, A. (2010). International organizations and human rights: Realizing, resisting or repackaging the right to water? *Journal of Human Rights, 9*, 1–23.

Saegert, S. (2006). Building civic capacity in urban neighborhoods: An empirically grounded anatomy. *Journal of Urban Affairs, 28*, 275–294.

Saegert, S., Thompson, J., & Warren, M. (2005). *Social capital and poor communities.* New York: Russell Sage.

Saewyc, E., Solsvig, W., & Edinburgh, L. (2007). The Hmong Youth Task Force: Evaluation of a coalition to address the sexual exploitation of young runaways. *Public Health Nursing, 25*(1), 69–76.

Sager, J. S. (2008). Planning democracy on the ground. In J. Rothman, J. Erlich, & J. Tropman (Eds.), *Strategies of community organization* (7th ed., pp. 205–216). Peosta, IA: Eddie Bowers.

Salahu-Din, S. (2003). *Social work research: An applied approach.* Boston, MA: Allyn & Bacon.

Salcido, R., Ornelas, V., & Lee, N. (2002). Cross cultural field assignments in an undergraduate community practice course: Integrating multimedia documentation. *Journal of Community Practice, 10*(4), 49–65.

Saldivar-Tanaka, L., & Krasny, M. (2004). Culturing community development, neighborhood open space, and civic agriculture: The case of Latino community gardens in New York City. *Agriculture and Human Values, 21*, 399–412.

Saleeby, D. (2008). *The strengths perspective in social work practice* (5th ed.). Boston: Allyn & Bacon.

Sampson, R., Morenoff, J., & Gannon-Rowley, T. (2002). Assessing "neighborhood effects": Social processes and new directions in research. *Annual Review of Sociology, 28*, 443–478.

Sanders, J. (2011, May 13). California Latinos hope Gov. Brown will sign farm, immigration bills. *Sacramento Bee*. Retrieved from http://www.sacbee.com/

Santos, C., Ferguson, N., & Trippel, A. (2010). Engaging urban youth through technology. *Journal of Planning Education and Research, 20*, 1–14.

Satterwhite, F., & Teng, S. (2007). *Culturally-based capacity building: An approach to working in communities of color for social change*. Oakland, CA: National Community Development Institute. Retrieved from http://www.ncdinet.org

Savage, D. (2011, June 13). Supreme Court upholds ethics laws. *Los Angeles Times*. Retrieved from http://www.latimes.com/

Savaya, R., & Waysman, M. (2005). The logic model: A tool for incorporating theory in development and evaluation of programs. *Administration in Social Work, 29*, 85–103.

Schatz, M., Furman, R., & Jenkins, L. (2003). Space to grow: Using dialogue techniques for multinational, multicultural learning. *International Social Work, 46*, 481–494.

Schlough, J. D., Koster, J., Barr, A., & Davis, T. (2011). Persuasion points online - Helping Harry Reid, one click at a time. *Campaigns & Elections*. Retrieved from http://www.campaignsandelections.com/case-studies/176152/persuasion-points-online-helping-harry-reid-one-click-at-a-time.thtml

Schmid, H., & Salman, H. (2005). Citizen perceptions of the neighborhood council: The case of Arab neighborhoods in East Jerusalem. *Journal of Community Practice, 13*(2), 61–75.

Schmuck, R. (2006). *Practical action research for change*. Arlington Heights, IL: SkyLight Professional Development.

Schneider, J. (2007). Connections and disconnections between civic engagement and social capital in community-based nonprofits. *Nonprofit and Voluntary Sector Quarterly, 36*, 572–597.

Schon, D. (1983). *The reflective practitioner: How professionals think in action*. New York: Basic Books.

Schorr, L. (1997). *Common purpose: Strengthening families and neighborhoods to rebuild America*. New York: Anchor Books.

Schreiner, M., & Woller, G. (2003). Microenterprise development programs in the United States and in the developing world. *World Development, 31*, 1567–1580.

Schukoske, J. (2000). Community development through gardening: State and local policies transforming urban open space. *Legislation and Public Policy, 3*, 351–392.

Schultz, J. (2003). *The democracy owner's manual: A practical guide to changing the world*. New Brunswick, NJ: Rutgers University Press.

Schutz, A. (n.d.). *One-on-ones*. Retrieved from Education Action website: http://www.educationaction.org/uploads/1/0/4/. . ./171–one_on_ones- f.doc

Schutz, A., & Sandy, M. (2011). *Collective action for social change: An introduction to community organizing.* New York: Palgrave Macmillan.

Segal, E. (2007). Social empathy: A new paradigm to address poverty. *Journal of Poverty, 11 (3),* 65–81.

Segal, E., & Kilty, K. (2003). Political promises for welfare reform. *Journal of Poverty,* 7(1/2), 51–57.

Sen, A. (2004). Elements of a theory of human rights. *Philosophy & Public Affairs, 32,* 315–356.

Sen, R. (2003). *Stir it up: Lessons in community organizing and advocacy.* San Francisco, CA: Jossey-Bass.

Sellsky, J. (1998). Developmental dynamics in nonprofit-sector federations. *Voluntas, 9,* 283–303.

Shah, S., & Mediratta, K. (2008). Negotiating reform: Young people's leadership in the educational area. *New Directions for Youth Development, 117,* 43–59.

Shalhoub-Kervorkian, N. (2011). E-resistance among Palestinian women: Coping in conflict-ridden areas. *Social Service Review, 85,* 180–204.

Shaw, R. (2001). *The activist's handbook: A primer.* Berkeley: University of California Press.

Shaw, R. (2008). *Beyond the fields: Cesar Chavez, the UFW, and the struggle for justice in the 21st century.* Berkeley, CA: University of California Press.

Shera, W., & Page, J. (1995). Creating more effective human service organizations through strategies of empowerment. *Administration in Social Work, 19*(4), 1–15.

Sherraden, M., Schreiner, M., & Beverly, S. (n.d.) *Income, institutions and saving performance in Individual Development Accounts.* Retrieved from http://microfinance.com/English/Papers/IDAs_Income.pdf

Shobe, M. A., & Boyd, A. S. (2005). Relationships between assets and perceived economic strain: Findings from an anti-poverty policy demonstration. *Journal of Community Practice, 13*(2), 21–44.

Siegel, J. (2011). Felon disenfranchisement and the fight for universal suffrage. *Social Work, 16,* 89–91.

Siebert, S., Wang, G., & Courtright, S. (2011). Antecedents and consequences of psychological and team empowerment in organizations: A meta-analytic review. *Journal of Applied Psychology, 96,* 981–1003.

Silverman, R. (2003). Citizens' district councils in Detroit: The promise and limits of using planning advisory boards to promote citizen participation. *National Civic Review, 92*(4), 3–13.

Silverman, R. (2004). Introduction: Social capital and community development. In R. Silverman (Ed.), *Community-based organizations: The intersection of social capital and local context in contemporary urban society* (pp. 1–15). Detroit, MI: Wayne State University Press.

Silverman, R. (2009). Sandwiched between patronage and bureaucracy: The plight of citizen participation in community-based housing organizations in the US. *Urban Studies, 46,* 3–25.

Silvestre, A., Faber, J., Shankle, M., & Kopelman, J. (2002). A model for involving youth in health planning: HIV prevention in Pennsylvania. *Perspectives on Sexual and Reproductive Health, 34*(2), 91–98.

Silvestre, A., Hylton, J., Johnson, L., Houston, C., Witt, M., & Jacobson, L. (2006). Recruiting minority men who have sex with men for HIV research: Results from a 4-city campaign. *American Journal of Public Health, 96,* 1020–1027.

Silvestre, A., Quinn, S., & Rinaldo, Ch. (2010). A 22-year old community advisory board: health research as an opportunity for social change. *Journal of Community Practice, 18*(1), 58–75.

Singh, S. (2003). *Neighborhood strengthening through community building.* Paper presented on COMM-ORG: The On-Line Conference on Community Organizing and Development (Vol. 9). Retrieved from http://comm-org.wisc.edu/papers2003/singh.htm

Sitt-Gohdes, W., Lambrecht, J., & Redman, D. (2000). The critical-incident technique in job behavior research. *Journal of Vocational Educational Research, 25*(1), 63–89.

Skocpol, T. (2004, March). APSA Presidential Address: Voice and inequality: The transformation of American civic democracy. *Perspectives on Politics, 2*(1), 3–20.

Small, M. (2007). Racial differences in networks: Do neighborhood conditions matter. *Social Science Quarterly, 88,* 320–343.

Small, M. L., & Newman, K. (2001). Urban poverty after the truly disadvantaged: The rediscovery of the family, the neighborhood, and culture. *American Review of Sociology, 27,* 23–45.

Smith, S. R. (2010). Nonprofits and public administration: Reconciling performance management and citizen engagement. *American Review of Public Administration, 20,* 129–152.

Smock, K. (2004). *Democracy in action: Community organizing and urban change.* New York: Columbia University Press.

Smyth, R. (2011). Enhancing learner–learner interaction using video communications in higher education: Implications from theorising about a new model. *British Journal of Educational Technology, 42,* 113–127.

Snow, D. (2001). *Collective identity and expressive forms.* Retrieved from http://escholarship.org/uc/item/2zn1t7bj#page-1

Snow, D. (2007). Framing process, ideology, and discursive fields. In D. Snow, S. Soule, & H. Kriesi (Eds.), *The Blackwell companion to social movements* (pp. 380–412). Malden, MA: Blackwell Publishing.

Snow, D., Soule, S., & Kriesi, H. (2007). Mapping the terrain. In D. Snow, S. Soule, & H. Kriesi (Eds.), *The Blackwell companion to social movements* (pp. 3–16). Malden, MA: Blackwell Publishing.

Sobeck, J. (2008). How cost effective is capacity building in grassroots organizations? *Administration in Social Work, 32*(2), 49–68.

Social Capital Research Network. (2007). *Social capital and cohesion: Toward a common good*. Retrieved from http://ec.europa.eu/research/social-sciences/pdf/policy-briefs-soccoh-sobczak_en.pdf

Sohng, S. (1995). *Participatory action research and community organizing*. Retrieved from http://www.cdra.org.za

Solas, J. (2008). What kind of social justice does social work seek? *International Social Work, 51*, 813–822.

Somma, M. (2006). Revolutionary environmentalism: An introduction. In S. Best, & A. Nocella (Eds.), *Igniting a revolution: Voices in defense of the earth* (pp. 37–46). Oakland, CA: AK Press.

Somma, N. (2009). How strong are strong ties? The conditional effectiveness of strong ties in protest recruitment attempts. *Sociological Perspectives, 52*, 289–308.

Soska, T., & Butterfield, A. (2011). Community organizing and practice coming of age: Are we sitting on the sidelines. *Journal of Community Practice, 19*, 345–354.

Spatig, L., Swedberg, An., Legrow, T., & Flaherty, P. (2010). The power of process: A story of collaboration and community change. *Community Development, 41*, 3–20.

Speer, P., & Zippay, A. (2005). Participatory decision-making among community coalitions: An analysis of task group meetings. *Administration in Social Work, 29*(3), 61–77.

Speer, P., Peterson, N. A., Zippay, A., & Christens, B. (2011). Participation in congregation-based organizing: A mixed method study of civic engagement. In M. Roberts-DeGennaro & S. Fogel (Eds.). *Using evidence to inform practice for community and organizational change* (pp. 200-217). Chicago: Lyceum Books.

Stack, C. (1974). *All our kin: Strategies for survival in a Black community*. New York: Basic Books.

Staples, L. (2004). *Roots to power: A manual for grassroots organizing* (2nd ed.). Westport, CT: Praeger.

Staples, L. (2009). In praise of community organizers. *Social Work with Groups, 32*(4), 270–273.

Starr, A., & Adams, J. (2003). Anti-globalization: The global fight for local autonomy. *New Political Science, 25*(1), 19–42.

Stein, D. (n.d.). *The ethics of NIMBYism*. Retrieved from http://www.vcn.bc.ca/citizens-handbook/gcastrategies/article_co_2.html

Stirland, S. L. (2008, October 29). *Obama's secret weapons: Internet, databases and psychology*. Retrieved from http://www.wired.com/threatlevel/2008/10/obamas-secret-w/

Stoecker, R. (2002). Cyberspace vs. face-to-face: Community organizing in the new millennium. *Perspectives on Global Development and Technology, 1*, 143–164.

Stoecker, R. (2004). The mystery of the missing capital and the ghost of social structure: Why community development can't win. In R. Silverman (Ed.), *Community-based organizations: The intersection of social capital and local context in contemporary urban society* (pp. 53–66). Detroit, MI: Wayne State University Press.

Stoecker, R. (2005). *Research methods for community change: A project-based approach.* Thousand Oaks, CA: Sage.

Stoecker, R. (2006). Neighborhood data systems: A best practice analysis. *Community Development, 37*(4), 109–122.

Stoecker, R. (2008). Are academics irrelevant?: Approaches and roles for scholars in CBPR. In M. Minkler, & N. Wallerstein (Eds.), *Community-based participatory research for health: From processes to outcomes* (pp. 107–120). San Francisco, CA: Jossey-Bass.

Stoecker, R., Loving, K., Reddy, M., & Bolling, N. (2010). Can community-based research guide service learning? *Journal of Community Practice, 18,* 280–295.

Stone, D. (2002). *Policy paradox: The art of political decision making* (revised edition). New York: W.W. Norton & Company.

Stovall, D. (2005). A challenge to traditional theory: Critical race theory, African American community organizers and education. *Discourse: Studies in the Cultural Politics of Education, 26*(1), 95–108.

Stringer, E. (2007). *Action research* (3rd ed.). Thousand Oaks, CA: Sage.

Su, C. (2007). Cracking silent codes: Critical race theory and education organizing. *Discourse: Studies in the Cultural Politics of Education, 28,* 531–548.

Su, C. (2009). We call ourselves by many names: Storytelling and inter-minority coalition-building. *Community Development Journal, 45,* 439–457.

Subban, J. (2007). Adult literacy education and community development. *Journal of Community Practice, 15*(1/2), 69–90.

Suarez-Balcazar, Y., Hellwig, M., Kouba, J., Redmond, L., Martinez, L., Block, D., ... Peterman, W. (2006). The making of an interdisciplinary partnership: The case of the Chicago Food system collaborative. *American Journal of Psychology, 38,* 113–123.

Swarts, H. (2008). *Organizing urban America: Secular and faith-based social movements.* Minneapolis: University of Minnesota Press.

Swarts, H. (2010, February 12). Organizing nationally to win locally: Faith-based community organizing's new frontier. *Shelterforce.* Retrieved from http://www.shelterforce.org/article/1868/organizing_nationally_to_win_locally_faith-based_community_organizings_new_/

Szakos, J. (2005). *A collective recruitment plan is needed for community organizers.* Paper presented on COMM-ORG: The On-Line Conference on Community Organizing and Development (Vol. 11). Retrieved from http://comm-org.wisc.edu/papers.htm

Szakos, K., & Szakos, J. (2007). *We make change: Community organizers talk about what they do—and why.* Nashville, TN: Vanderbilt University Press.

Taylor, V., Kimport, K., Van Dyke, N., & Anderson, E. (2009). Gay activism, culture and mobilization: Tactical repertoires, same-sex weddings, and the impact on gay activism. *American Sociological Review, 74,* 865–890.

Taylor, V., & Van Dyke, N. (2007). Tactical repertoires of social movements. In D. Snow, S. Soule, & H. Kriesi (Eds.), *The Blackwell companion to social movements* (pp. 262–392). Malden, MA: Blackwell Publishing.

Teivainen, T. (2003, March 28). *World social forum: Arena or actor?* Paper presented at the Latin American Studies Association (LASA) meeting. Retrieved from http://lasa.international.pitt.edu/members/congresspapers/lasa2003/files/TeivainenTeivo.pdf

Theall, K., Scribner, R., Cohen, D., Bluthenthal, R., Schonlau, M., & Farley, T. (2009). Social capital and the neighborhood alcohol environment. *Health & Place, 15*(1), 323–332.

Theocharis, Y. (2012). Cuts, tweets, solidarity and mobilization: How the Internet shaped the student occupations. *Parliamentary Affairs, 65,* 162–194.

Thurston, W., & Potvin, L. (2003). Evaluability assessment: A tool for incorporating evaluation in social change programmes. *Evaluation, 9,* 453–469.

Timm, T., Birkenmaier, J., & Tebb, S. (2011). The experiential community assessment project: Integrating social work practice skills. *Journal of Community Practice, 19,* 175–188.

Toomey, A. (2009). Empowerment and disempowerment in community development practice: Eight roles practitioners play. *Community Development Journal, 46,* 181–195.

Toseland, R., & Rivas, R. (2008). Task groups: Specialized methods. In J. Rothman, J. Erlich, & J. Tropman (Eds.), *Strategies of community organization* (7th ed., pp. 27–60). Peosta, IA: Eddie Bowers.

Traynor, B. (2002). *Reflections on community organizing and resident engagement in the rebuilding communities initiative.* Retrieved from Annie E. Casey Foundation website: http://ourblocks.net/reflections-on-community-organizing-and-resident-engagement-in-the-rebuilding-communities-initiative/

Treleaven, L. (2001). The turn to action and the linguistic turn: Toward an integrated methodology. In P. Reason, & H. Bradbury (Eds.), *The handbook of action research: Participative inquiry and practice* (pp. 261–272). Thousand Oaks, CA: Sage

Tsui, M. (2005). *Social work supervision: Contexts and concepts.* Thousand Oaks, CA: Sage.

Turner, L., & Shera, W. (2005). Empowerment of human service workers: Beyond intra-organizational strategies. *Administration in Social Work, 29*(3), 79–94.

Twain, N., Stone, S. (Producers), & Johnson, C. (Director). (2001). *Boycott.* [Motion picture]. United States: Home Box Office.

Twiss, J., Duma, S., Kleinman, T., Paulsen, H., & Rivera, L. (2003). Community gardens: Lessons learned from California Healthy Cities and Communities. *American Journal of Public Health, 93,* 1435–1438.

Ungar, M., Manuel, S., Mealy, S., Thomas, G., & Campbell, C. (2004). A study of community guides: Lessons for professionals practicing with and in communities. *Social Work, 49,* 550–561.

United Nations. (1948). *The universal declaration of human rights.* Retrieved from http://www.un.org/en/documents/udhr/

United Nations. (1979). *Convention on the elimination of all forms of discrimination against women.* Retrieved from http://www.un.org/womenwatch/daw/cedaw/

United Nations. (2010). *Table 1: Human development index and its components.* Retrieved from http://hdr.undp.org/en/media/HDR_2010_EN_Table1_reprint.pdf

United States Environmental Protection Agency. (n.d.). *Children's environmental health disparities: Black and African American children and asthma.* Retrieved from http://yosemite.epa.gov/ochp/ochpweb.nsf/content/HD_AA_Asthma.htm/$File/HD_AA_Asthma.pdf

United States Office of Special Council. (2011). *Political activity (Hatch Act).* Retrieved from http://www.osc.gov/hatchact.htm

United States Student Association. (2009). *Pass the federal Dream Act Now: Federal Dream Act organizing kit.* Retrieved from http://www.nw.org/network/training/programs/cb.asp

Upper Arlington Progressive Action. (n.d.). *House meeting FAQ.* Retrieved from http://uaprogressiveaction.com/node/350

Vaiou, D., & Lykogianni, R. (2006). Women, neighbourhoods and everyday life. *Urban Studies, 43,* 731–743.

Van Den Bergh, N., & Cooper, L. (1995). Introduction to feminist visions for social work. In J. Tropman, J. Erlich, & J. Rothman, *Tactics and techniques of community intervention* (3rd ed., pp. 74–93).

van den Berk-Clark, C., & Pyles, L. (2012). Deconstructing neoliberal community development approaches and a case for the solidarity economy. *Journal of Progressive Human Services, 23,* 1–17.

Vanderkooy, P., & Nawyn, S. (2011). Identifying the battle-lines: Local-national tensions in organizing for comprehensive immigration reform. *American Behavioral Scientist, 55,* 1267–1286.

Van Dyke, N., & Cress, R. (2006). Political opportunities and collective identity in Ohio's gay and lesbian movement, 1970–2000. *Sociological Perspectives, 49,* 503–526.

Van Dyke, N., & McCammon, H. (2010). Introduction: Social movement coalition formation. In N. Van Dyke, & H. McCammon (Eds.), *Strategic alliances: Coalition building and social movements.* Minneapolis: University of Minnesota Press.

Vangen, S., & Huxham, C. (2003). Nurturing collaborative relations: Building trust in interorganizational collaboration. *Journal of Applied Behavioral Science, 32*(1), 5–31.

Van Voorhis, R., & Hostetter, C. (2006). The impact of MSW education on social worker empowerment and commitment to client empowerment through social justice advocacy. *Journal of Social Work Education, 42*(1), 105–121.

VeneKlasen, L., Miller, V., Budlender, D., & Clark, C. (2007). *A new weave of power, people, and politics.* Warwickshire, U.K. Practical Action Publishing.

Venkatesh, S. (2008). *Gang leader for a day: A rogue sociologist takes to the streets.* New York: Penguin Books.

Verba, S., Schlozman, K., & Brady, H. (1995). *Voice and equality: Civic voluntarism in American politics*. Cambridge, MA: Harvard University Press.

Vidal, A., & Keating, W. D. (2004). Community development: Current issues and emerging challenges: *Journal of Urban Affairs, 26*, 125–137.

Virginia Organizing Project. (n.d.). *Holding house meetings*. Retrieved from http://archive.virginia-organizing.org/articles/house_meetings.php

Viswanathan, M., Ammerman, A., Eng, E., Gartlehner, G., Lohr, K., Griffith, D., ... Whitener, L. (2004). Community-based participatory research: Assessing the evidence. *Evidence/Technology Report* (No. 99). Rockville, MD: Agency for Healthcare Research and Quality, U.S. Department of Health and Human Services. Retrieved from http://www.mycbpr.org/CBPR-project/articles/AHRQ-cbpr-assessing-evidence.pdf

Wallace, S. (2004). Social capital and African American church leadership. In R. Silverman (Ed.), *Community-based organizations: The intersection of social capital and local context in contemporary urban society* (pp. 147–170). Detroit, MI: Wayne State University Press.

Walker, J., Briggs, H., Koroloff, N., & Friesen, B. (2007). Implementing and sustaining evidence-based practice in social work. *Journal of Social Work Education, 43*, 361–375.

Walker, E., & McCarthy, J. (2010). Legitimacy, strategy, and resources in the survival of community-based organizations. *Social Problems, 57*, 315–340.

Wallach, V., & Mueller, C. (2006). Job characteristics and organizational predictors of psychological empowerment among paraprofessionals within human service organizations: An exploratory study. *Administration in Social Work, 30*(1), 95–115.

Wallerstein, N. (2009). Criteria for creating triggers or codes. *Community organizing and community building for health* (2nd ed., pp. 455–456). New Brunswick, NJ: Rutgers University Press.

Wallerstein, N., & Duran, B. (2008). The theoretical, historical, and practice roots of CBPR. In M. Minkler, & N. Wallerstein (Eds.), *Community-based participatory research for health: From processes to outcomes* (pp. 25–46). San Francisco, CA: Jossey-Bass.

Walter, C. (2009). Community building practice: A conceptual framework. In M. Minkler, & N. Wallerstein (Eds.), *Community-based participatory research for health: From processes to outcomes* (pp. 66–78). San Francisco, CA: Jossey-Bass.

Wang, C. (2006). Youth participation in Photovoice as a strategy for community change. *Journal of Community Practice, 14*(1/2), 147–161.

Wang, C., & Pies, C. (2008). A protocol for community-based research. In M. Minkler, & N. Wallerstein (Eds.), *Community-based participatory research for health: From processes to outcomes* (pp. 183–197). San Francisco, CA: Jossey-Bass.

Wang, C., Yi, W. K., Tao, Z. W., & Carovano, K. (1998). Photovoice as a participatory health promotion strategy. *Health Promotion International, 13*, 75–86.

Wayne, J., Bogo, M., & Raskin, M. (2010). Field evaluation as the signature pedagogy of social work education. *Journal of Social Work Education, 46,* 327–339.

Warren, M. (2001, January/February). Building democracy: Faith-based community organizing today. *Shelterforce On-line.* Retrieved from http://www.nhi.org/online/issues/115/Warren.html

Warren, M., Thompson, J. P., & Saegert, S. (2001). The role of social capital in combating poverty. In S. Saegert, J. P. Thompson, & M. Warren (Eds.), *Social capital and poor communities* (pp. 1–28). New York: Russell Sage Foundation.

Washington, R. (1995). Alternative frameworks for program evaluation. In J. Tropman, J. Erlich, & J. Rothman, *Tactics and techniques of community intervention* (3rd ed., pp. 296–307). Itasca, IL: Peacock Publishers.

Wayne, E. K. (2008). Is it just talk? Understanding and evaluating intergroup dialogue. *Conflict Resolution Quarterly, 25,* 451–478.

Weaver, K. (2010, February). But will it work? Implementation analysis to improve government performance. *Issues in governance studies* (No. 32). Retrieved from http://www.brookings.edu/~/media/Files/rc/papers/2010/02_implementation_analysis_weaver/02_implementation_analysis_weaver.pdf

Webb, S. (2001). Some considerations on the validity of evidence-based practice in social work. *British Journal of Social Work, 31,* 57–79.

Wiebe, M. (2010). Pushing the boundaries of the social work practicum: Rethinking sites and supervision toward radical practice. *Journal of Progressive Human Services, 21,* 66–82.

Wells, R., Ward, A., Feinberg, M., & Alexander, J. (2008). What motivates people to participate more in community-based coalitions? *American Journal of Community Psychology, 42,* 94–104.

Wellstone, P. (2001). *The conscience of a liberal: Reclaiming the compassionate agenda.* Minneapolis: University of Minnesota Press.

Wetzel, J. (2001). Human rights in the 20th century: Weren't gays and lesbians human? *Journal of Gay & Lesbian Social Services, 13*(1/2), 15–31.

Whitcher, J., Coyne, F., McCauley, S., & Rauenhorst, S. (2009–10). *Community organizing handbook.* Retrieved from Center for Community Engagement and Service-Learning, University of Denver website: http://www.du.edu/ccesl/docs/CO_Handbook_2009_Pri.pdf

Widianingsih, I., & Morrell, E. (2007). Participatory planning in Indonesia: Seeking a path to democracy. *Policy Studies, 28*(1), 1–15.

Williams, T., Boddie, S., & Rice, S. (2003). Family-centered, community-based asset building: A strategic use of individual development accounts. *Journal of Community Practice, 18*(1), 94–117.

Williams, L., Labonte, R., & O'Brien, M. (2003). Empowering social action through narratives of identity and culture. *Health Promotion International, 18,* 33–40.

Wilson, W. (1996). *When work disappears.* New York: Vintage.

Wilson, J. (2011). Approaches to measuring transformative education experiences. In J. Birkenmaier, A. Cruce, E. Burkemper, J. Curley, R. J. Wilson, & J. J. Stretch (Eds.), *Educating for social justice: Transformative experiential learning* (pp. 309–327). Chicago: Lyceum Books.

Wilson, J., Abram, F., & Anderson, J. (2010). Exploring a feminist-based empowerment model of community building. *Qualitative Social Work, 9,* 519–535.

Wint, E., & Sewpaul, V. (2000). Product and process dialectic: Developing an indigenous approach to community development training. *Journal of Community Practice, 7*(1), 57–70.

Wise, K. (2007). Lobbying and relationship management: The K Street connection. *Journal of Public Relations Research, 19*(4), 357–376.

Wolf, J. (2007). Sociological theories of poverty in urban America. *Journal of Human Behavior in the Social Environment, 16*(1), 41–56.

Wollebaek, D., & Selle, P. (2002). Does participation in voluntary associations contribute to social capital? The impact of intensity, scope, and type. *Nonprofit and Voluntary Sector Quarterly, 31,* 32–61.

Wood, R. (2007). Higher power: Strategic capacity for state and national organizing. In M. Orr (Ed.), *Community organizing and political change in the city* (pp. 162–192). Lawrence, KS: University of Kansas Press.

Woolcock, M. (1998). *Social capital and economic development: Toward a theoretical synthesis and policy framework.* Retrieved from http://social.cs.uiuc.edu/class/cs598kgk/papers/SocialCapital.pdf

Work Group for Community Health and Development. (2010). *Community Toolbox.* Retrieved from http://ctb.ku.edu/en/

Wronka, J. (2008). *Human rights and social justice: Social action and service for the helping and health professions.* Los Angeles, CA: Sage.

Wu, E., & Martinez, M. (2006, October). *Taking cultural competency from theory to action.* California Pan–Ethnic Health Network. Retrieved from Commonwealth Fund website: http://www.commonwealthfund.org/Content/Publications/Fund-Reports/2006/Oct/Taking-Cultural-Competency-from-Theory-to-Action.asp

Wyly, E., & Hammel, D. (2004). Gentrification, segregation, and discrimination in the American urban system. *Environment and Planning, 36,* 1215–1241.

Xu, Q. (2007). Globalization, immigration, and the welfare state: A cross-national comparison. *Journal of Sociology & Social Welfare, 34,* 87–106.

Yalom, I., & Leszcz, M. (2005). *Theory and practice of group psychotherapy* (5th ed.). New York: Basic Books.

Yen, N., & Van Luong, P. (2008). Participatory village and community development planning (VDP/CDP) and its contribution to local community development in Vietnam. *Community Development Journal, 43,* 329–340.

Yoshihama, M., & Carr, E. (2002). Community participation reconsidered: Feminist participatory action research with Hmong women. *Journal of Community Practice, 10*(4), 85–103.

Young Laing, B. (2009). A critique of Rothman's and other standard community organizing models: Toward developing a culturally proficient community organizing framework. *Community Development, 40*, 20–36.

Young Laurence, L. (2008). Fostering social capital through NGO design: Grameen Bank membership in Bangladesh. *International Social Work, 44*, 7–17.

Zachary, E. (2000). Grassroots leadership training. *Journal of Community Practice, 7*(1), 71–93.

Zastrow, C. (2009). *Social work with groups. A comprehensive workbook* (7th ed.). Belmont, CA: Brooks/Cole.

Zimmerman, M., & Rappaport, J. (1988). Citizen participation, perceived control, and psychological empowerment. *American Journal of Community Psychology, 16*(5), 725–750.

Zimmerman, M., Stewart, S., Morrel-Samuels, S., Franzen, S., & Reischel, T. (2011). Youth empowerment solutions for peaceful communities: Combining theory and practice in a community-level violence prevention curriculum. *Health Promotion Practice, 12*, 425–439.

Index

cultural brokers, 43
cultural community, 40–41
  anthropological research, 40
  ethnographic interviews, 40–41
  guidelines for organizers, 41
  hiring members, 42–43
  skills for empowering, 43–44
cultural competency, 39, 191
  conveying respect, 41, 42
  cross-cultural organizing, 44, 46
  cultural community, 40–41
  development in supervision,
      360, 361
  gaining trust, 41, 42
  hiring community members, 42–43
  inclusion, 46
  partnership, 46
  self-awareness, 39–40
  skills for community empowerment,
      43–44
  transparency, 46
cultural humility, 232, 361

decision making process, 100. *See also*
      public decision making
  citizen participation, 167–168
  citizens role, 163
  civic engagement, 164–167
  community participation, 339–340
  empowerment, 7–8
  grassroots, 173
  hierarchal, 192
  interpersonal skills, 176
  leadership development, 168–171
  public, 207–208
dialogue-related skills, 19
disengagement phase, 18
Dream Act campaign, 313

EBP. *See* evidence-based practice
Educational Policy and Accreditation
      Standards (EPAS), 414
egalitarianism, 377
electronic communications, 300, 301
elitist communities, 150

empowerment, 7–8, 190, 191. *See also*
      self-determination
  evaluation, 272–273
  supervision for, 363–364
empowerment theory, 370
  organizational hierarchy
      establishment, 372
  staff member, 370–371
  supervision for, 364
engagement phase, 18
  community assessments, 125
  interpersonal skill types, 20–21
environmental justice movements, 396
EPAS. *See* Educational Policy and
      Accreditation Standards
ethnographic interviews, 40–41
evaluability assessment, 257
evaluation in community practice, 250,
      255. *See also* participatory
      evaluation in community
      practice
  case studies, 267, 268
  challenges in conducting, 252–253
  community member goals, 255
  community-based research,
      256–259
  critical incident analysis, 267, 268
  data collection, 259–260
  EBP, 253–255
  engagement activities, 256
  goal attainment, 251, 260–261
  implementation analysis, 266–267
  limitations, 253
  process analysis, 265–266
  purpose and politics, 250–251, 252
  qualitative approaches, 268–269
  quantitative research, 262–265
  social indicator analysis, 261–262
  survey data, 261
  university–community partnerships,
      255–256
evidence-based practice (EBP), 253. *See
      also* community-based research
  difficulties, 255
  interpretations and applications, 254